Mig rrior

A MIGRAINE TRACKER

WELLNESS WARRIOR PRESS

ISBN: 978-1-990271-47-2

This journal belongs to...

____

DOCTOR / SPECIALIST INFORMATION

Name	Address	Contact

DAILY MEDICATION / SUPPLEMENTS

Medication / Supplement	Dosage

APPOINTMENTS / SURGERIES

Details	Time / Location	Notes

Summary

For each journal entry, return to this summary page and rate your overall pain / discomfort level
(1 being no pain and 10 being unbearable)

(1 No fatigue and 10 being wiped out for 3 days)

	Entry #	Rating	Entry #	Rating	Entry #	Rating
14 dys	1 29/8/23	2 6	31		61	
2 wks	2 11/9	2 5	32		62	
5 dys	3 16/9	1.5 5	33		63	
1 dy	4 17/9	1 3	34		64	
2 days	5 19/9	1 5	35		65	
5 days	6 24/9	1 2	36		66	
19 days	7 13/10		37		67	
7 days	8 20/10		38		68	
15 days	9 3/11		39		69	
16 days	10 19/11	2 5	40		70	
12 wks	11 10/2/24	2 6	41		71	
1day (9)	12 11/2/24	3 4	42		72	
5 wks	13 21/3/24	2 3	43		73	
2d	14 23/3/24	1 3	44		74	
1d	15 24/3	1 3	45		75	
2 wks	16 6/4		46		76	
	17		47		77	
	18		48		78	
	19		49		79	
	20		50		80	
	21		51		81	
	22		52		82	
	23		53		83	
	24		54		84	
	25		55		85	
	26		56		86	
	27		57		87	
	28		58		88	
	29		59		89	
	30		60		90	

Summary

For each journal entry, return to this summary page and rate your overall pain / discomfort level (1 being no pain and 10 being unbearable)

Entry #	Rating	Entry #	Rating	Entry #	Rating
91		121		151	
92		122		152	
93		123		153	
94		124		154	
95		125		155	
96		126		156	
97		127		157	
98		128		158	
99		129		159	
100		130		160	
101		131		161	
102		132		162	
103		133		163	
104		134		164	
105		135		165	
106		136		166	
107		137		167	
108		138		168	
109		139		169	
110		140		170	
111		141		171	
112		142		172	
113		143		173	
114		144		174	
115		145		175	
116		146		176	
117		147		177	
118		148		178	
119		149		179	
120		150		180	

My Calendar

	January	February	March	April	May	June	July	August	September	October	November	December
1												
2												
3												
4												
5												
6												
7												
8												
9												
10												
11												
12												
13												
14												
15												
16												
17												
18												
19												
20												
21												
22												
23												
24												
25												
26												
27												
28												
29												
30												
31												

Calendar Legend

Create your own legend using colors or codes.

- MIGRAINE
- GOOD MOOD
- WELL-RESTED
- STRESSED
- LACK OF SLEEP

Additional Notes

AURA END; 10:30 (fatigue)

START: 09:00 **END:** **DURATION:** 2 DAYS **DATE** 29/8/28 *Entry #1*

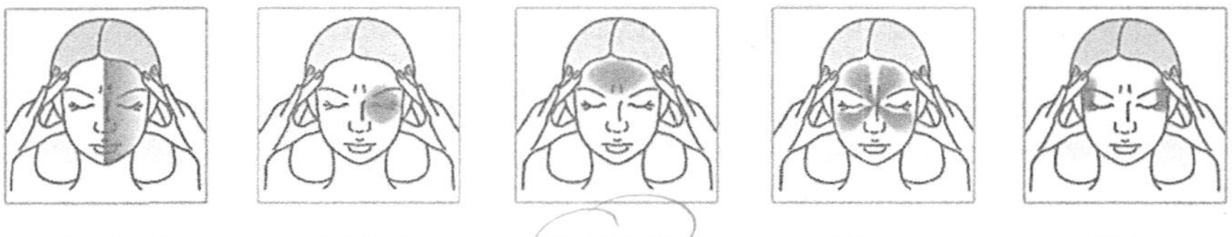

MIGRAINE | CLUSTER | TENSION (circled) | SINUS | TMJ

HOW WOULD YOU RATE...?

Mood	1 2 3 4 (marked) 5
Energy	1 2 3 (marked) 4 5
Mental clarity	1 2 3 (marked) 4 5

PAIN LEVEL

1	2	3	4	5	6	7	8	9	10

(2 circled)

Not too bad. *Well, I'm not enjoying this.* *Make it stop!*

ONSET

☐ Slow ☑ Average
☐ Rapid ☐ Sudden

DETAILED DESCRIPTION

☐ Constant ☐ Squeezing ☑ Throbbing ☐ Pounding ☐ Dull aching ☐ Burning
☐ Sharp ☐ Debilitating ☐ Other: But mild

WHERE DOES IT HURT, EXACTLY?

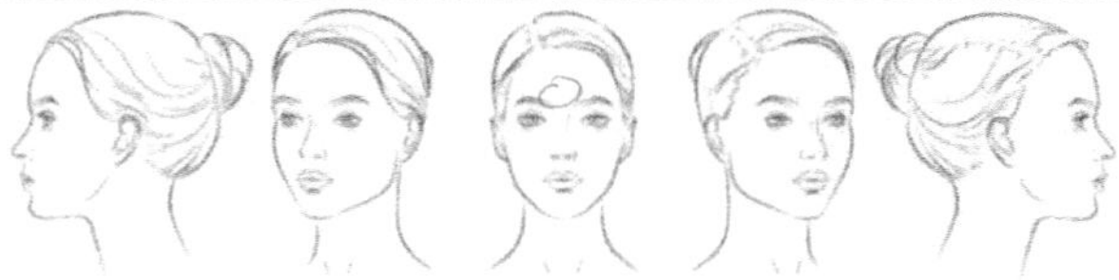

OTHER SYMPTOMS

☐ Lightheaded ☐ Dizziness
☑ Light sensitivity ☐ Sound sensitivity
☐ Confusion ☑ Auras
☐ Muscle stiffness ☐ Muscle aches

FEELING SICK?

☐ Nausea ☐ Diarrhea ☐ Vomiting ☐ Sore throat ☐ Congestion ☐ Coughing
☐ Chills ☐ Fever ☐ Other: ____________

SLEEP

hours 8 *quality* 1 2 3 4 (circled) 5

WEATHER

☐ Cold ☐ Mild ☐ Hot Allergen levels: ________
☐ Dry ☐ Humid ☐ Wet BM Pressure: ________

STRESS LEVELS

None	Low (circled)	Medium	High	Max	@$#%!

item / meal	*time*	*meds / supplements*	*dose*	*time*	*drinks*
					water 1 2 3 4 5 6 7 8 9 10
					caffeine 1 2 3 4 5 6 7 8 9 10
					alcohol 1 2 3 4 5 6 7 8 9 10

HORMONES

☐ Menstruating ☐ Menopause
☑ PMS ☐ N/A | other

COMPUTER / MOBILE DEVICE / TV

☐ None ☑ Some ☐ A lot Total Time: ______
☐ Sitting ☐ Standing ☐ Mixture Breaks every: ______

PHYSICAL ACTIVITY

☑ None ☐ Minimal ☐ Some ☐ Sweatin' ☐ I'm beat DETAILS: ____________

RELIEF MEASURES

☑ Medication ☐ Massage ☑ Sleep ☐ Exercise ☐ Water ☐ Cold/Ice
☐ Heat/Bath ☐ Other: ____________
Did it work? ☐ Nope ☐ A bit ☑ Mostly ☐ 100%

Notes

☐ *See back notes*

START: 11:00	END:	DURATION:	DATE 11 / 9 / 23	*Entry #2*

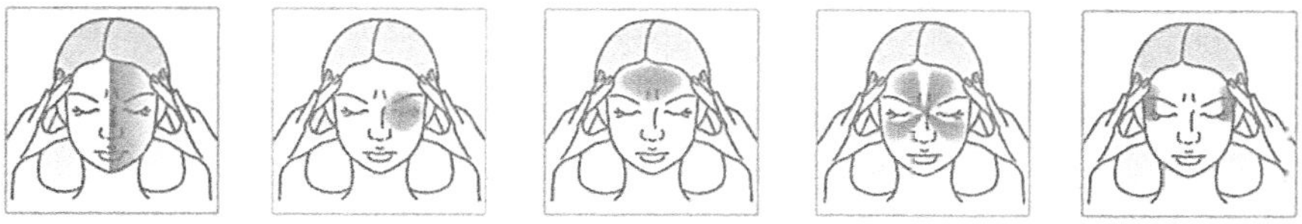

MIGRAINE | CLUSTER | TENSION | SINUS | TMJ

HOW WOULD YOU RATE...?

Mood	1	2	3	(4) circled	5
Energy	1	2	3	(4) circled	5
Mental clarity	1	2	3	(4) circled	5

PAIN LEVEL

1	2	3	4	5	6	7	8	9	10

Not too bad. *Well, I'm not enjoying this.* *Make it stop!*

ONSET

☐ Slow ☑ Average
☐ Rapid ☐ Sudden

DETAILED DESCRIPTION

☐ Constant ☐ Squeezing ☑ Throbbing ☐ Pounding ☐ Dull aching ☐ Burning
☑ Sharp ☐ Debilitating ☐ Other: ____________________

WHERE DOES IT HURT, EXACTLY?

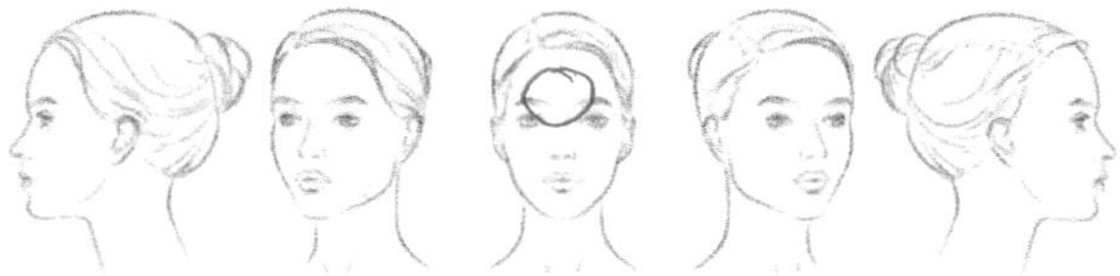

OTHER SYMPTOMS

☐ Lightheaded ☐ Dizziness
☑ Light sensitivity ☐ Sound sensitivity
☐ Confusion ☑ Auras
☐ Muscle stiffness ☐ Muscle aches

FEELING SICK?

☐ Nausea ☐ Diarrhea ☐ Vomiting ☐ Sore throat ☐ Congestion ☐ Coughing
☐ Chills ☐ Fever ☐ Other: ____________________

SLEEP

hours 8
quality 1 2 (3) circled 4 5

WEATHER

☐ Cold ☐ Mild ☑ Hot Allergen levels: __________
☐ Dry ☐ Humid ☐ Wet BM Pressure: __________

STRESS LEVELS

None (circled)	Low	Medium	High	Max	@$#%!

item / meal	*time*	*meds / supplements*	*dose*	*time*
Decaf coffee	08:00			
Musli - fruits + nuts	08:30			
- migraine -				
Garlic + tom pasta	12:30			

drinks

water	1	2	3	4	5	6	7	8	9	10
caffeine	1	2	3	4	5	6	7	8	9	10
alcohol	1	2	3	4	5	6	7	8	9	10

HORMONES

☐ Menstruating ☐ Menopause
☐ PMS ☐ N/A | other

COMPUTER / MOBILE DEVICE / TV

☐ None ☐ Some ☐ A lot Total Time: ______
☐ Sitting ☐ Standing ☐ Mixture Breaks every: ______

PHYSICAL ACTIVITY

☐ None ☐ Minimal ☐ Some ☐ Sweatin' ☐ I'm beat DETAILS: ____________

RELIEF MEASURES

☐ Medication ☐ Massage ☐ Sleep ☐ Exercise ☐ Water ☐ Cold/Ice
☐ Heat/Bath ☐ Other: ____________________
Did it work? ☐ Nope ☐ A bit ☐ Mostly ☐ 100%

Notes ☐ *See back notes*

START:	END:	DURATION:	DATE 10/9/23	*Entry #3*

MIGRAINE | CLUSTER | TENSION | SINUS | TMJ

HOW WOULD YOU RATE...?

Mood	1	2	(3)	(4)	5
Energy	1	(2)	3	4	5
Mental clarity	1	2	3	(4)	5

PAIN LEVEL

1	(2)	3	4	5	6	7	8	9	10

Not too bad. *Well, I'm not enjoying this.* *Make it stop!*

ONSET

- [ ] Slow
- [x] Average
- [ ] Rapid
- [ ] Sudden

DETAILED DESCRIPTION

- [ ] Constant
- [ ] Squeezing
- [ ] Throbbing
- [ ] Pounding
- [x] Dull aching
- [ ] Burning
- [ ] Sharp
- [ ] Debilitating
- [ ] Other: mild

WHERE DOES IT HURT, EXACTLY?

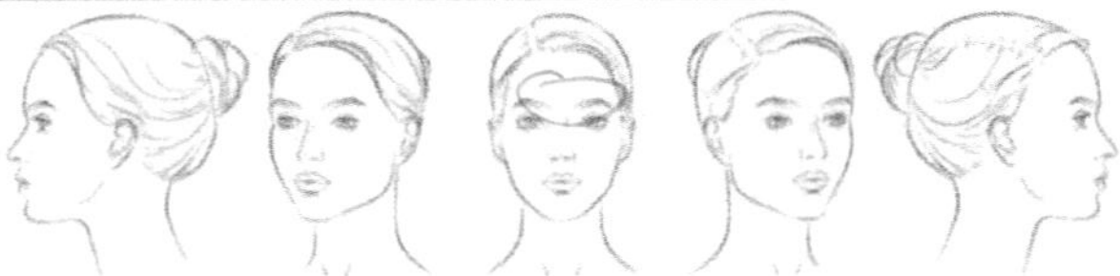

OTHER SYMPTOMS

- [ ] Lightheaded
- [ ] Dizziness
- [x] Light sensitivity
- [x] Sound sensitivity
- [ ] Confusion
- [x] Auras
- [ ] Muscle stiffness
- [ ] Muscle aches

FEELING SICK?

- [ ] Nausea
- [ ] Diarrhea
- [ ] Vomiting
- [ ] Sore throat
- [ ] Congestion
- [ ] Coughing
- [ ] Chills
- [ ] Fever
- [ ] Other: ______

SLEEP

hours ______ *quality* 1 2 3 4 5

WEATHER

- [ ] Cold
- [ ] Mild
- [ ] Hot
- [ ] Dry
- [ ] Humid
- [ ] Wet

Allergen levels: ______

BM Pressure: ______

STRESS LEVELS

None	Low	Medium	High	Max	@$#%!

item / meal	*time*	*meds / supplements*	*dose*	*time*	*drinks*
					water: 1 2 3 4 5 6 7 8 9 10
					caffeine: 1 2 3 4 5 6 7 8 9 10
					alcohol: 1 2 3 4 5 6 7 8 9 10

HORMONES

- [ ] Menstruating
- [ ] Menopause
- [ ] PMS
- [ ] N/A | other

COMPUTER / MOBILE DEVICE / TV

- [ ] None
- [ ] Some
- [ ] A lot
- [ ] Sitting
- [ ] Standing
- [ ] Mixture

Total Time: ______

Breaks every: ______

PHYSICAL ACTIVITY

- [ ] None
- [ ] Minimal
- [ ] Some
- [ ] Sweatin'
- [ ] I'm beat

DETAILS: ______

RELIEF MEASURES

- [ ] Medication
- [ ] Massage
- [ ] Sleep
- [ ] Exercise
- [ ] Water
- [ ] Cold/Ice
- [ ] Heat/Bath
- [ ] Other: ______

Did it work? [ ] Nope [ ] A bit [ ] Mostly [ ] 100%

Notes

[ ] *See back notes*

START:		END:		DURATION:		DATE	16/9/23	*Entry #4*

HOW WOULD YOU RATE...?

Mood	1	2	3	4	5
Energy	1	2	3	4	5
Mental clarity	1	2	3	4	5

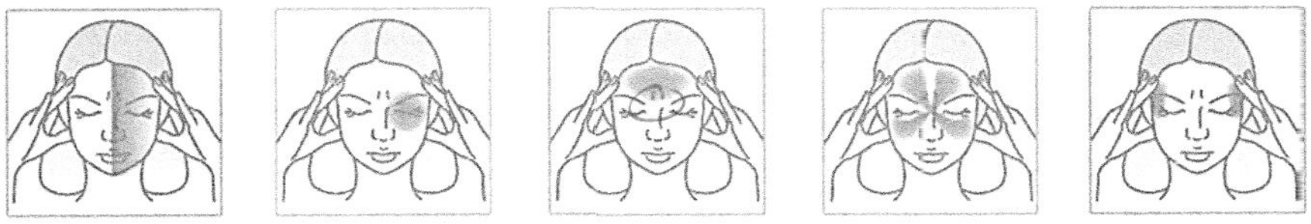

MIGRAINE CLUSTER TENSION SINUS TMJ

PAIN LEVEL

(1)	2	3	4	5	6	7	8	9	10

Not too bad. *Well, I'm not enjoying this.* *Make it stop!*

ONSET

☐ Slow ☐ Average
☐ Rapid ☐ Sudden

DETAILED DESCRIPTION

☐ Constant ☐ Squeezing ☐ Throbbing ☐ Pounding ☐ Dull aching ☐ Burning
☐ Sharp ☐ Debilitating ☐ Other: slept through

WHERE DOES IT HURT, EXACTLY?

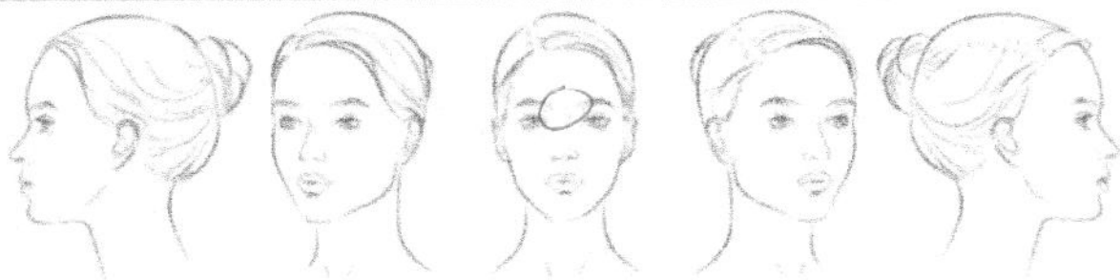

OTHER SYMPTOMS

☐ Lightheaded ☐ Dizziness
☐ Light sensitivity ☐ Sound sensitivity
☐ Confusion ☑ Auras - only
☐ Muscle stiffness ☐ Muscle aches

FEELING SICK?

☐ Nausea ☐ Diarrhea ☐ Vomiting ☐ Sore throat ☐ Congestion ☐ Coughing
☐ Chills ☐ Fever ☐ Other: ____________

SLEEP

hours ________ *quality* 1 2 3 4 5

WEATHER

☐ Cold ☐ Mild ☐ Hot Allergen levels: ________
☐ Dry ☐ Humid ☐ Wet BM Pressure: ________

STRESS LEVELS

None	Low	Medium	High	Max	@$#%!

item / meal	*time*	*meds / supplements*	*dose*	*time*	*drinks*
					water 1 2 3 4 5 6 7 8 9 10
					caffeine 1 2 3 4 5 6 7 8 9 10
					alcohol 1 2 3 4 5 6 7 8 9 10

HORMONES

☐ Menstruating ☐ Menopause
☐ PMS ☐ N/A | other

COMPUTER / MOBILE DEVICE / TV

☐ None ☐ Some ☐ A lot Total Time: ______
☐ Sitting ☐ Standing ☐ Mixture Breaks every: ______

PHYSICAL ACTIVITY

☐ None ☐ Minimal ☐ Some ☐ Sweatin' ☐ I'm beat DETAILS: ____________

RELIEF MEASURES

☐ Medication ☐ Massage ☐ Sleep ☐ Exercise ☐ Water ☐ Cold/Ice
☐ Heat/Bath ☐ Other: ____________
Did it work? ☐ Nope ☐ A bit ☐ Mostly ☐ 100%

Notes ☐ *See back notes*

START: 17.30 END: 18.15 DURATION: DATE 19/9/23 *Entry #5*

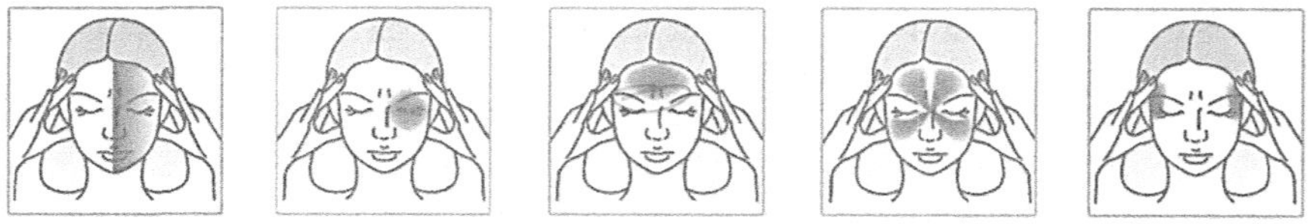

MIGRAINE CLUSTER TENSION SINUS TMJ

HOW WOULD YOU RATE...?

Mood	1 2 3 (4) 5
Energy	1 2 (3) 4 5
Mental clarity	1 2 (3) 4 5

PAIN LEVEL

(1)	2	3	4	5	6	7	8	9	10

Not too bad. *Well, I'm not enjoying this.* *Make it stop!*

ONSET

☐ Slow ☑ Average
☐ Rapid ☐ Sudden

DETAILED DESCRIPTION

☐ Constant ☐ Squeezing ☐ Throbbing ☐ Pounding ☑ Dull aching ☐ Burning
☐ Sharp ☐ Debilitating ☐ Other: ____________

WHERE DOES IT HURT, EXACTLY?

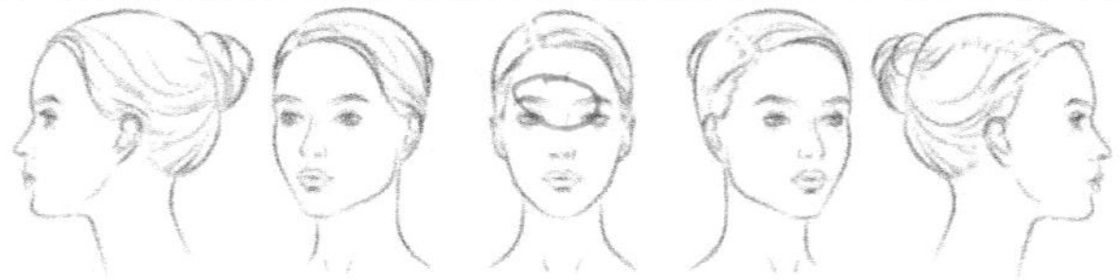

OTHER SYMPTOMS

☐ Lightheaded ☑ Dizziness
☐ Light sensitivity ☐ Sound sensitivity
☐ Confusion ☑ Auras
☐ Muscle stiffness ☐ Muscle aches

FEELING SICK?

☐ Nausea ☐ Diarrhea ☐ Vomiting ☐ Sore throat ☐ Congestion ☐ Coughing
☐ Chills ☐ Fever ☐ Other: ____________

SLEEP

hours 8 *quality* 1 2 3 4 (5)

WEATHER

☐ Cold ☑ Mild ☐ Hot Allergen levels: ________
☐ Dry ☐ Humid ☐ Wet BM Pressure: ________

STRESS LEVELS

(None)	Low	Medium	High	Max	@$#%!

item / meal	*time*	*meds / supplements*	*dose*	*time*	*drinks*
					water: 1 2 3 4 5 6 7 8 9 10
					caffeine: 1 2 3 4 5 6 7 8 9 10
					alcohol: 1 2 3 4 5 6 7 8 9 10

HORMONES

☐ Menstruating ☐ Menopause
☐ PMS ☐ N/A | other

COMPUTER / MOBILE DEVICE / TV

☐ None ☐ Some ☐ A lot Total Time: ______
☐ Sitting ☐ Standing ☐ Mixture Breaks every: ______

PHYSICAL ACTIVITY

☐ None ☐ Minimal ☐ Some ☐ Sweatin' ☐ I'm beat DETAILS: ____________

RELIEF MEASURES

☑ Medication ☐ Massage ☐ Sleep ☐ Exercise ☐ Water ☐ Cold/Ice
☐ Heat/Bath ☐ Other: ____________
Did it work? ☐ Nope ☐ A bit ☐ Mostly ☐ 100%

Notes

☐ *See back notes*

25min - Aura

START: 12:40 END: 13:05 DURATION: DATE 6/14/24 *Entry #6*

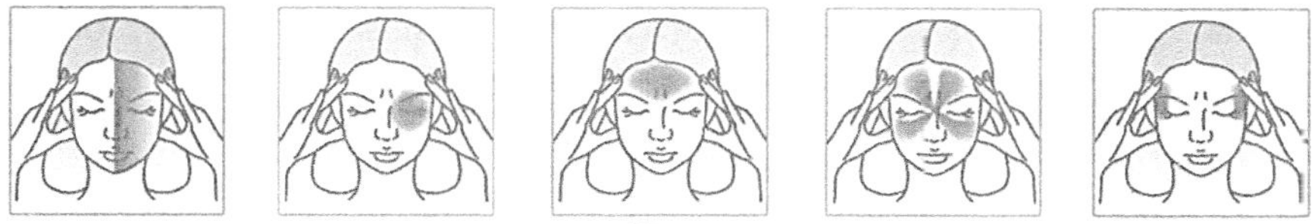

HOW WOULD YOU RATE...?

Mood	1	2	3	4	5
Energy	1	2	3	4	5
Mental clarity	1	2	3	4	5

PAIN LEVEL

1	2	3	4	5	6	7	8	9	10

Not too bad. *Well, I'm not enjoying this.* *Make it stop!*

ONSET

☐ Slow ☐ Average
☐ Rapid ☐ Sudden

DETAILED DESCRIPTION

☐ Constant ☐ Squeezing ☐ Throbbing ☐ Pounding ☑ Dull aching ☐ Burning
☐ Sharp ☐ Debilitating ☐ Other: ______

WHERE DOES IT HURT, EXACTLY?

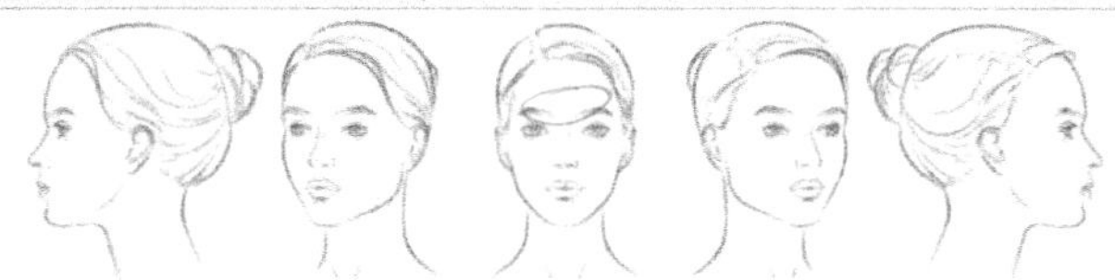

OTHER SYMPTOMS

☐ Lightheaded ☑ Dizziness
☑ Light sensitivity ☐ Sound sensitivity
☐ Confusion ☑ Auras
☐ Muscle stiffness ☑ Muscle aches

FEELING SICK?

☐ Nausea ☐ Diarrhea ☐ Vomiting ☐ Sore throat ☐ Congestion ☐ Coughing
☐ Chills ☐ Fever ☐ Other: ______

SLEEP

hours 10 *quality* 1 2 3 4 5

WEATHER

☐ Cold ☐ Mild ☐ Hot Allergen levels: ______
☐ Dry ☐ Humid ☐ Wet BM Pressure: WINDY

STRESS LEVELS

None	Low	Medium	High	Max	@$#%!

item / meal	*time*	*meds / supplements*	*dose*	*time*
DECAF / REGULAR COFFEE		RIZOTRIPTAN	1	12:40
CEREAL				
YOGHURT				
WATER				

drinks

water 1 2 3 4 5 6 7 8 9 10
caffeine 1 2 3 4 5 6 7 8 9 10
alcohol 1 2 3 4 5 6 7 8 9 10

HORMONES

☑ Menstruating ☐ Menopause
☐ PMS ☐ N/A | other

COMPUTER / MOBILE DEVICE / TV

☐ None ☐ Some ☑ A lot Total Time: ______
☐ Sitting ☐ Standing ☐ Mixture Breaks every: ______

PHYSICAL ACTIVITY

☐ None ☐ Minimal ☐ Some ☑ Sweatin' ☐ I'm beat DETAILS: 10 MIN JOG

RELIEF MEASURES

☑ Medication ☐ Massage ☐ Sleep ☐ Exercise ☐ Water ☐ Cold/Ice
☐ Heat/Bath ☐ Other: ______
Did it work? ☐ Nope ☐ A bit ☐ Mostly ☐ 100%

Notes ☐ *See back notes*

START:		END:		DURATION:		DATE		*Entry #7*

MIGRAINE | CLUSTER | TENSION | SINUS | TMJ

HOW WOULD YOU RATE...?

Mood	1	2	3	4	5
Energy	1	2	3	4	5
Mental clarity	1	2	3	4	5

PAIN LEVEL

1	2	3	4	5	6	7	8	9	10

Not too bad. *Well, I'm not enjoying this.* *Make it stop!*

ONSET

☐ Slow ☐ Average
☐ Rapid ☐ Sudden

DETAILED DESCRIPTION

☐ Constant ☐ Squeezing ☐ Throbbing ☐ Pounding ☐ Dull aching ☐ Burning
☐ Sharp ☐ Debilitating ☐ Other: ____________________

WHERE DOES IT HURT, EXACTLY?

OTHER SYMPTOMS

☐ Lightheaded ☐ Dizziness
☐ Light sensitivity ☐ Sound sensitivity
☐ Confusion ☐ Auras
☐ Muscle stiffness ☐ Muscle aches

FEELING SICK?

☐ Nausea ☐ Diarrhea ☐ Vomiting ☐ Sore throat ☐ Congestion ☐ Coughing
☐ Chills ☐ Fever ☐ Other: ____________________

SLEEP

hours ________ *quality* 1 2 3 4 5

WEATHER

☐ Cold ☐ Mild ☐ Hot Allergen levels: __________
☐ Dry ☐ Humid ☐ Wet BM Pressure: __________

STRESS LEVELS

None	Low	Medium	High	Max	@$#%!

item / meal	*time*	*meds / supplements*	*dose*	*time*	*drinks*
					water 1 2 3 4 5 6 7 8 9 10
					caffeine 1 2 3 4 5 6 7 8 9 10
					alcohol 1 2 3 4 5 6 7 8 9 10

HORMONES

☐ Menstruating ☐ Menopause
☐ PMS ☐ N/A | other

COMPUTER / MOBILE DEVICE / TV

☐ None ☐ Some ☐ A lot Total Time: ______
☐ Sitting ☐ Standing ☐ Mixture Breaks every: ______

PHYSICAL ACTIVITY

☐ None ☐ Minimal ☐ Some ☐ Sweatin' ☐ I'm beat DETAILS: ____________

RELIEF MEASURES

☐ Medication ☐ Massage ☐ Sleep ☐ Exercise ☐ Water ☐ Cold/Ice
☐ Heat/Bath ☐ Other: ____________________
Did it work? ☐ Nope ☐ A bit ☐ Mostly ☐ 100%

Notes ☐ *See back notes*

START: 17:00 **END:** Nextdy **DURATION:** ____ **DATE** 10/2/24 *Entry #8*

[MIGRAINE circled]

HOW WOULD YOU RATE...?

Mood	1	2	3	4	5
Energy	1	2	3	4	5
Mental clarity	1	2	3	4	5

PAIN LEVEL

1	2	3	4	5	6	7	8	9	10

Not too bad. *Well, I'm not enjoying this.* *Make it stop!*

[2 circled]

ONSET

☐ Slow ☑ Average
☐ Rapid ☐ Sudden

DETAILED DESCRIPTION

☐ Constant ☐ Squeezing ☑ Throbbing ☐ Pounding ☐ Dull aching ☐ Burning
☐ Sharp ☐ Debilitating ☐ Other: ____

WHERE DOES IT HURT, EXACTLY?

OTHER SYMPTOMS

☐ Lightheaded ☐ Dizziness
☐ Light sensitivity ☐ Sound sensitivity
☐ Confusion ☑ Auras
☐ Muscle stiffness ☐ Muscle aches

FEELING SICK?

☐ Nausea ☐ Diarrhea ☐ Vomiting ☐ Sore throat ☐ Congestion ☐ Coughing
☐ Chills ☐ Fever ☐ Other: ____

SLEEP (after)

hours 10 *quality* 1 2 3 4 5 [4 circled]

WEATHER

☐ Cold ☐ Mild ☐ Hot Allergen levels: ____
☐ Dry ☐ Humid ☐ Wet BM Pressure: ____

STRESS LEVELS

None	Low	Medium	High	Max	@$#%!

item / meal	*time*	*meds / supplements*	*dose*	*time*	*drinks*
					water: 1 2 3 4 5 6 7 8 9 10
					caffeine: 1 2 3 4 5 6 7 8 9 10
					alcohol: 1 2 3 4 5 6 7 8 9 10

HORMONES

☐ Menstruating ☐ Menopause
☐ PMS ☐ N/A | other

COMPUTER / MOBILE DEVICE / TV

☐ None ☐ Some ☐ A lot Total Time: ____
☐ Sitting ☐ Standing ☐ Mixture Breaks every: ____

PHYSICAL ACTIVITY

☐ None ☐ Minimal ☐ Some ☐ Sweatin' ☐ I'm beat DETAILS: ____

RELIEF MEASURES

☐ Medication ☐ Massage ☐ Sleep ☐ Exercise ☐ Water ☐ Cold/Ice
☐ Heat/Bath ☐ Other: ____
Did it work? ☐ Nope ☐ A bit ☐ Mostly ☐ 100%

Notes ☐ *See back notes*

HEADACHES

8:55 AURA: 9:15

START: ~~8:55~~ 9:00	END:	DURATION: 20 mins	DATE 14/2/24	*Entry #9*

MIGRAINE | CLUSTER | TENSION | SINUS | TMJ

HOW WOULD YOU RATE...?

Mood	①	②	③	④	⑤ ✓
Energy	①	②	③	④	⑤ ✓
Mental clarity	①	②	③	④	⑤ ✓

PAIN LEVEL

1	2	~~3~~	(4)	5	6	7	8	9	10

Not too bad. *Well, I'm not enjoying this.* *Make it stop!*

ONSET

☐ Slow ☐ Average
☑ Rapid ☐ Sudden

DETAILED DESCRIPTION

☐ Constant ☐ Squeezing ☑ Throbbing ☐ Pounding ☑ Dull aching ☐ Burning
☐ Sharp ☐ Debilitating ☐ Other: __________

WHERE DOES IT HURT, EXACTLY?

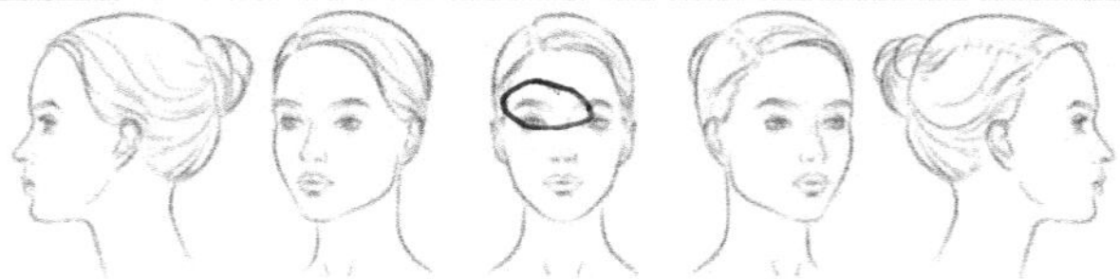

OTHER SYMPTOMS

☐ Lightheaded ☐ Dizziness
☐ Light sensitivity ☐ Sound sensitivity
☐ Confusion ☑ Auras
☐ Muscle stiffness ☐ Muscle aches

FEELING SICK?

☐ Nausea ☐ Diarrhea ☐ Vomiting ☐ Sore throat ☐ Congestion ☐ Coughing
☐ Chills ☐ Fever ☐ Other: __________

SLEEP

hours 8 *quality* ① ② ③ (④) ⑤

WEATHER

☑ Cold ☑ Mild ☐ Hot Allergen levels: ______
☐ Dry ☐ Humid ☑ Wet BM Pressure: ______

STRESS LEVELS

(None)	Low	Medium	High	Max	@$#%!

item / meal	*time*	*meds / supplements*	*dose*	*time*
BFAST BLUEBERRY SOFT BAKE	07:35	NUROFEN	2x	9:00

drinks

water: (①) ② ③ ④ ⑤ ⑥ ⑦ ⑧ ⑨ ⑩

caffeine: / ① ② ③ ④ ⑤ ⑥ ⑦ ⑧ ⑨ ⑩

alcohol: / ① ② ③ ④ ⑤ ⑥ ⑦ ⑧ ⑨ ⑩

HORMONES

☐ Menstruating ☐ Menopause
☐ PMS ☑ N/A | other

COMPUTER / MOBILE DEVICE / TV

☑ None ☐ Some ☐ A lot Total Time: ____
☐ Sitting ☐ Standing ☐ Mixture Breaks every: ____

PHYSICAL ACTIVITY

☐ None ☐ Minimal ☑ Some ☐ Sweatin' ☐ I'm beat DETAILS: 30min weight

RELIEF MEASURES

☑ Medication ☐ Massage ☐ Sleep ☐ Exercise ☐ Water ☐ Cold/Ice
☐ Heat/Bath ☐ Other: __________

Did it work? ☐ Nope ☐ A bit ☐ Mostly ☐ 100%

Notes ☐ *See back notes*

START: 07:05 | END: 08:00 | DURATION: 1 hr | DATE 21/3/24 | *Entry #10*

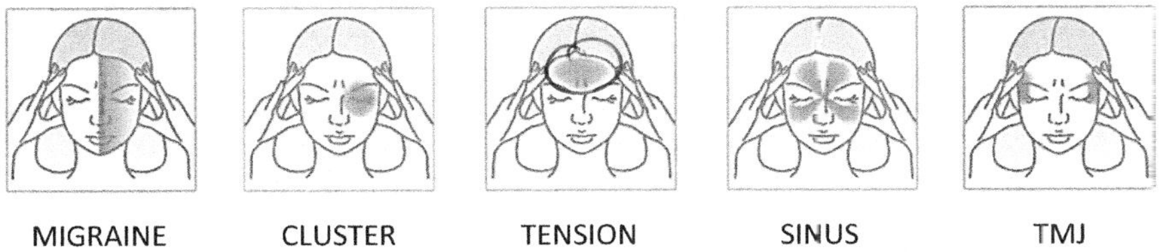

HOW WOULD YOU RATE...?

Mood	① ② ③ ④ ⑤ (5 circled)
Energy	① ② ③ ④ ⑤ (5 circled)
Mental clarity	① ② ③ ④ ⑤ (4 circled)

PAIN LEVEL 0

1	2	3	4	5	6	7	8	9	10

Not too bad. *Well, I'm not enjoying this.* *Make it stop!*

ONSET

☐ Slow ☑ Average
☐ Rapid ☐ Sudden

DETAILED DESCRIPTION

☐ Constant ☐ Squeezing ☐ Throbbing ☐ Pounding ☐ Dull aching ☐ Burning
☐ Sharp ☐ Debilitating ☐ Other: SUBTLE

WHERE DOES IT HURT, EXACTLY?

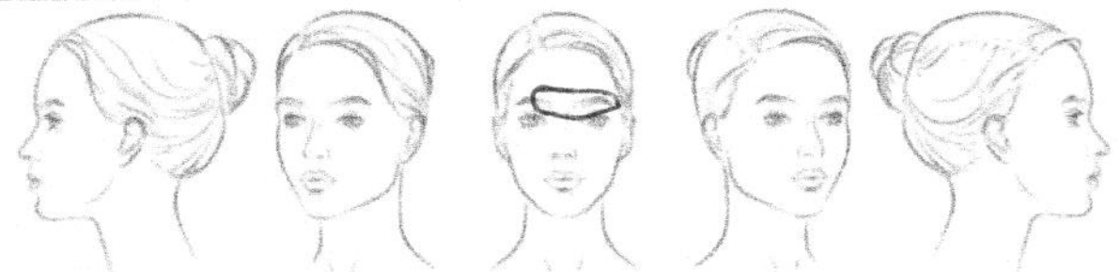

OTHER SYMPTOMS

☐ Lightheaded ☐ Dizziness
☑ Light sensitivity ☑ Sound sensitivity
☐ Confusion ☑ Auras
☐ Muscle stiffness ☐ Muscle aches

FEELING SICK?

☐ Nausea ☐ Diarrhea ☐ Vomiting ☐ Sore throat ☐ Congestion ☐ Coughing
☐ Chills ☐ Fever ☐ Other: —

SLEEP

hours: 9 quality: ① ② ③ ④ ⑤ (4 circled)

WEATHER

☑ Cold ☐ Mild ☐ Hot Allergen levels: ______
☐ Dry ☐ Humid ☐ Wet BM Pressure: ______

STRESS LEVELS (day before)

None	Low	Medium	High	Max	@$#%!

(circled between Low and Medium)

item / meal	*time*	*meds / supplements*	*dose*	*time*
Cereal	7:30			
Fish mac + cheese	12:00			
veg, fish cake	19:00			
dark choc	19:30			
hot cross bun	20:30			

drinks

water: ① ② ③ ④ ⑤ ⑥ ⑦ ⑧ ⑨ ⑩ (3 circled)
caffeine: ① ② ③ ④ ⑤ ⑥ ⑦ ⑧ ⑨ ⑩ (1 circled)
alcohol: 0 ① ② ③ ④ ⑤ ⑥ ⑦ ⑧ ⑨ ⑩

HORMONES

☐ Menstruating ☐ Menopause
☐ PMS ☐ N/A | other

COMPUTER / MOBILE DEVICE / TV

☐ None ☐ Some ☑ A lot Total Time: 8.5
☐ Sitting ☐ Standing ☐ Mixture Breaks every: —

PHYSICAL ACTIVITY

☐ None ☑ Minimal ☐ Some ☐ Sweatin' ☐ I'm beat DETAILS: WALK TO STATION

RELIEF MEASURES

☑ Medication ☐ Massage ☐ Sleep ☐ Exercise ☐ Water ☐ Cold/Ice
☐ Heat/Bath ☐ Other: ______

Did it work? ☐ Nope ☐ A bit ☑ Mostly ☐ 100%

Notes Tired + wanted to sleep but had work + meetings. Fatigue but don't feel as bad as usual. Doc appt at 11. Need repeat n20 prescription or something new.

☐ See back notes

START: 20:00 END: 20:30 DURATION: ______ DATE 23/3/24 *Entry #11*

MIGRAINE CLUSTER TENSION SINUS TMJ

HOW WOULD YOU RATE...?

Mood ① ② ③ ④ ⑤
Energy ① ② ③ ④ ⑤
Mental clarity ① ② ③ ④ ⑤

PAIN LEVEL

(1)	2	3	4	5	6	7	8	9	10

Not too bad. *Well, I'm not enjoying this.* *Make it stop!*

ONSET

☐ Slow ☐ Average
☐ Rapid ☐ Sudden

DETAILED DESCRIPTION

☐ Constant ☐ Squeezing ☑ Throbbing ☐ Pounding ☐ Dull aching ☐ Burning
☐ Sharp ☐ Debilitating ☐ Other: ______

WHERE DOES IT HURT, EXACTLY?

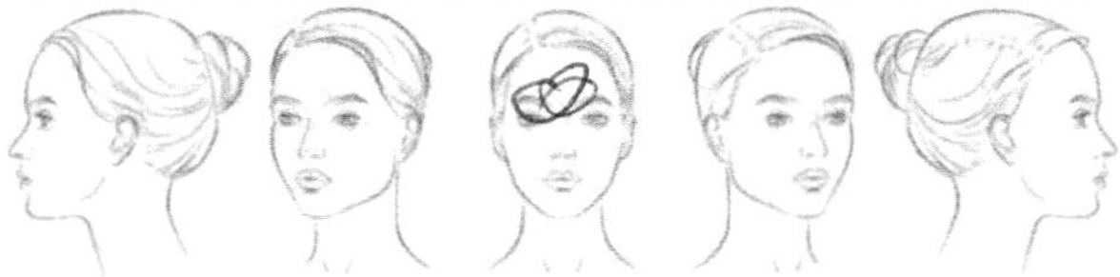

OTHER SYMPTOMS

☐ Lightheaded ☐ Dizziness
☐ Light sensitivity ☐ Sound sensitivity
☐ Confusion ☐ Auras
☐ Muscle stiffness ☐ Muscle aches

FEELING SICK?

☐ Nausea ☐ Diarrhea ☐ Vomiting ☐ Sore throat ☐ Congestion ☐ Coughing
☐ Chills ☐ Fever ☐ Other: ______

SLEEP

hours 5 *quality* ① ② (3) ④ ⑤

WEATHER

☐ Cold ☐ Mild ☐ Hot Allergen levels: ______
☐ Dry ☐ Humid ☐ Wet BM Pressure: ______

STRESS LEVELS

(None)	Low	Medium	High	Max	@$#%!

item / meal	*time*	*meds / supplements*	*dose*	*time*	*drinks*
NOT MUCH		TRIPTAN		20:00	water ① ② ③ ④ ⑤ ⑥ ⑦ ⑧ ⑨ ⑩
					caffeine ① ② ③ ④ ⑤ ⑥ ⑦ ⑧ ⑨ ⑩
					alcohol ① ② ③ ④ ⑤ ⑥ ⑦ ⑧ ⑨ ⑩

HORMONES

☐ Menstruating ☐ Menopause
☐ PMS ☐ N/A | other

COMPUTER / MOBILE DEVICE / TV

☐ None ☐ Some ☐ A lot Total Time: ______
☐ Sitting ☐ Standing ☐ Mixture Breaks every: ______

PHYSICAL ACTIVITY

☐ None ☐ Minimal ☐ Some ☐ Sweatin' ☐ I'm beat DETAILS: ______

RELIEF MEASURES

☐ Medication ☐ Massage ☐ Sleep ☐ Exercise ☐ Water ☐ Cold/Ice
☐ Heat/Bath ☐ Other: ______
Did it work? ☐ Nope ☐ A bit ☐ Mostly ☐ 100%

Notes ☐ *See back notes*

START: NIGHT TIME END: DURATION: DATE 24/3/24 *Entry #12*

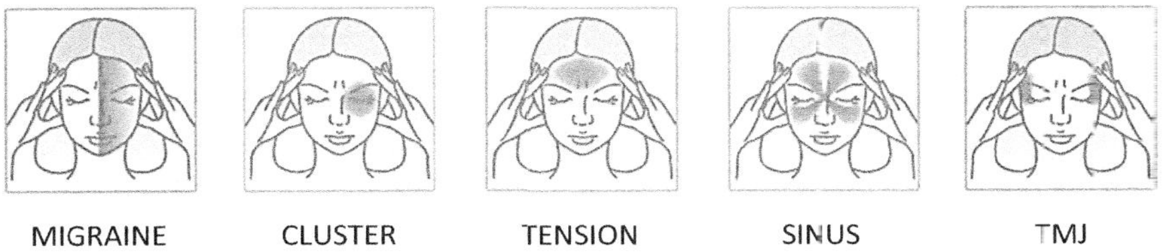

HOW WOULD YOU RATE...?

Mood	① ② ③ ④ ⑤
Energy	① ② ③ ④ ⑤
Mental clarity	① ② ③ ④ ⑤

PAIN LEVEL

1	2	3	4	5	6	7	8	9	10

Not too bad. *Well, I'm not enjoying this.* *Make it stop!*

ONSET

☐ Slow ☐ Average
☐ Rapid ☐ Sudden

DETAILED DESCRIPTION

☐ Constant ☐ Squeezing ☐ Throbbing ☐ Pounding ☐ Dull aching ☐ Burning
☐ Sharp ☐ Debilitating ☐ Other: ______

WHERE DOES IT HURT, EXACTLY?

OTHER SYMPTOMS

☐ Lightheaded ☐ Dizziness
☐ Light sensitivity ☐ Sound sensitivity
☐ Confusion ☐ Auras
☐ Muscle stiffness ☐ Muscle aches

FEELING SICK?

☐ Nausea ☐ Diarrhea ☐ Vomiting ☐ Sore throat ☐ Congestion ☐ Coughing
☐ Chills ☐ Fever ☐ Other: ______

SLEEP

hours ______ *quality* ① ② ③ ④ ⑤

WEATHER

☐ Cold ☐ Mild ☐ Hot Allergen levels: ______
☐ Dry ☐ Humid ☐ Wet BM Pressure: ______

STRESS LEVELS

None	Low	Medium	High	Max	@$#%!

item / meal	*time*	*meds / supplements*	*dose*	*time*	*drinks*
					water ① ② ③ ④ ⑤ ⑥ ⑦ ⑧ ⑨ ⑩
					caffeine ① ② ③ ④ ⑤ ⑥ ⑦ ⑧ ⑨ ⑩
					alcohol ① ② ③ ④ ⑤ ⑥ ⑦ ⑧ ⑨ ⑩

HORMONES

☐ Menstruating ☐ Menopause
☐ PMS ☐ N/A | other

COMPUTER / MOBILE DEVICE / TV

☐ None ☐ Some ☐ A lot Total Time: ______
☐ Sitting ☐ Standing ☐ Mixture Breaks every: ______

PHYSICAL ACTIVITY

☐ None ☐ Minimal ☐ Some ☐ Sweatin' ☐ I'm beat DETAILS: ______

RELIEF MEASURES

☐ Medication ☐ Massage ☐ Sleep ☐ Exercise ☐ Water ☐ Cold/Ice
☐ Heat/Bath ☐ Other: ______
Did it work? ☐ Nope ☐ A bit ☐ Mostly ☐ 100%

Notes ☐ *See back notes*

START: | END: | DURATION: | DATE | *Entry #13*

MIGRAINE | CLUSTER | TENSION | SINUS | TMJ

HOW WOULD YOU RATE...?

Mood	① ② ③ ④ ⑤
Energy	① ② ③ ④ ⑤
Mental clarity	① ② ③ ④ ⑤

PAIN LEVEL

1	2	3	4	5	6	7	8	9	10

Not too bad. *Well, I'm not enjoying this.* *Make it stop!*

ONSET

☐ Slow ☐ Average
☐ Rapid ☐ Sudden

DETAILED DESCRIPTION

☐ Constant ☐ Squeezing ☐ Throbbing ☐ Pounding ☐ Dull aching ☐ Burning
☐ Sharp ☐ Debilitating ☐ Other: ______

WHERE DOES IT HURT, EXACTLY?

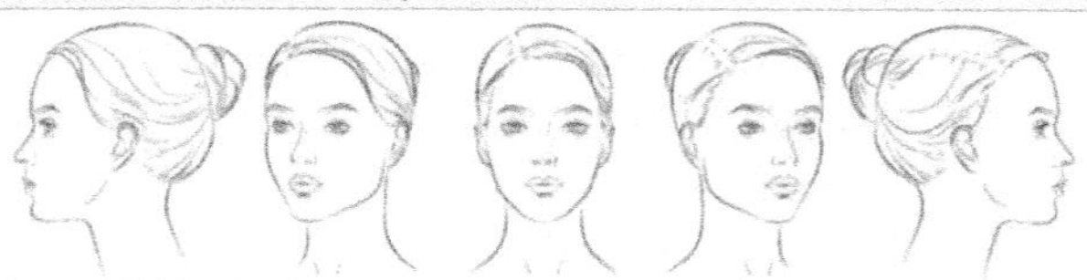

OTHER SYMPTOMS

☐ Lightheaded ☐ Dizziness
☐ Light sensitivity ☐ Sound sensitivity
☐ Confusion ☐ Auras
☐ Muscle stiffness ☐ Muscle aches

FEELING SICK?

☐ Nausea ☐ Diarrhea ☐ Vomiting ☐ Sore throat ☐ Congestion ☐ Coughing
☐ Chills ☐ Fever ☐ Other: ______

SLEEP

hours ______ *quality* ① ② ③ ④ ⑤

WEATHER

☐ Cold ☐ Mild ☐ Hot Allergen levels: ______
☐ Dry ☐ Humid ☐ Wet BM Pressure: ______

STRESS LEVELS

None	Low	Medium	High	Max	@$#%!

item / meal	*time*	*meds / supplements*	*dose*	*time*	*drinks*
					water: ① ② ③ ④ ⑤ ⑥ ⑦ ⑧ ⑨ ⑩
					caffeine: ① ② ③ ④ ⑤ ⑥ ⑦ ⑧ ⑨ ⑩
					alcohol: ① ② ③ ④ ⑤ ⑥ ⑦ ⑧ ⑨ ⑩

HORMONES

☐ Menstruating ☐ Menopause
☐ PMS ☐ N/A | other

COMPUTER / MOBILE DEVICE / TV

☐ None ☐ Some ☐ A lot Total Time: ______
☐ Sitting ☐ Standing ☐ Mixture Breaks every: ______

PHYSICAL ACTIVITY

☐ None ☐ Minimal ☐ Some ☐ Sweatin' ☐ I'm beat DETAILS: ______

RELIEF MEASURES

☐ Medication ☐ Massage ☐ Sleep ☐ Exercise ☐ Water ☐ Cold/Ice
☐ Heat/Bath ☐ Other: ______
Did it work? ☐ Nope ☐ A bit ☐ Mostly ☐ 100%

Notes

☐ *See back notes*

START: ______ END: ______ DURATION: ______ DATE ______ *Entry #14*

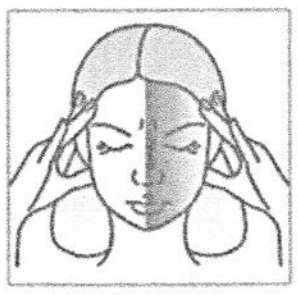
MIGRAINE

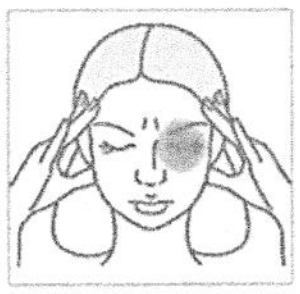
CLUSTER

TENSION

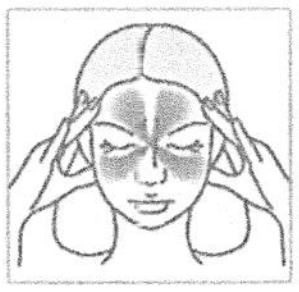
SINUS

TMJ

HOW WOULD YOU RATE...?

Mood	① ② ③ ④ ⑤
Energy	① ② ③ ④ ⑤
Mental clarity	① ② ③ ④ ⑤

PAIN LEVEL

1	2	3	4	5	6	7	8	9	10

Not too bad. *Well, I'm not enjoying this.* *Make it stop!*

ONSET

☐ Slow ☐ Average
☐ Rapid ☐ Sudden

DETAILED DESCRIPTION

☐ Constant ☐ Squeezing ☐ Throbbing ☐ Pounding ☐ Dull aching ☐ Burning
☐ Sharp ☐ Debilitating ☐ Other: ____________________

WHERE DOES IT HURT, EXACTLY?

OTHER SYMPTOMS

☐ Lightheaded ☐ Dizziness
☐ Light sensitivity ☐ Sound sensitivity
☐ Confusion ☐ Auras
☐ Muscle stiffness ☐ Muscle aches

FEELING SICK?

☐ Nausea ☐ Diarrhea ☐ Vomiting ☐ Sore throat ☐ Congestion ☐ Coughing
☐ Chills ☐ Fever ☐ Other: ____________________

SLEEP

hours ______ *quality* ① ② ③ ④ ⑤

WEATHER

☐ Cold ☐ Mild ☐ Hot Allergen levels: ______
☐ Dry ☐ Humid ☐ Wet BM Pressure: ______

STRESS LEVELS

None	Low	Medium	High	Max	@$#%!

item / meal	*time*	*meds / supplements*	*dose*	*time*	*drinks*
					water ① ② ③ ④ ⑤ ⑥ ⑦ ⑧ ⑨ ⑩
					caffeine ① ② ③ ④ ⑤ ⑥ ⑦ ⑧ ⑨ ⑩
					alcohol ① ② ③ ④ ⑤ ⑥ ⑦ ⑧ ⑨ ⑩

HORMONES

☐ Menstruating ☐ Menopause
☐ PMS ☐ N/A | other

COMPUTER / MOBILE DEVICE / TV

☐ None ☐ Some ☐ A lot Total Time: ______
☐ Sitting ☐ Standing ☐ Mixture Breaks every: ______

PHYSICAL ACTIVITY

☐ None ☐ Minimal ☐ Some ☐ Sweatin' ☐ I'm beat DETAILS: ____________________

RELIEF MEASURES

☐ Medication ☐ Massage ☐ Sleep ☐ Exercise ☐ Water ☐ Cold/Ice
☐ Heat/Bath ☐ Other: ____________________
Did it work? ☐ Nope ☐ A bit ☐ Mostly ☐ 100%

Notes ☐ *See back notes*

START: 19:00	END: 19:34	DURATION: 35-40	DATE 12/8/24	*Entry #15*

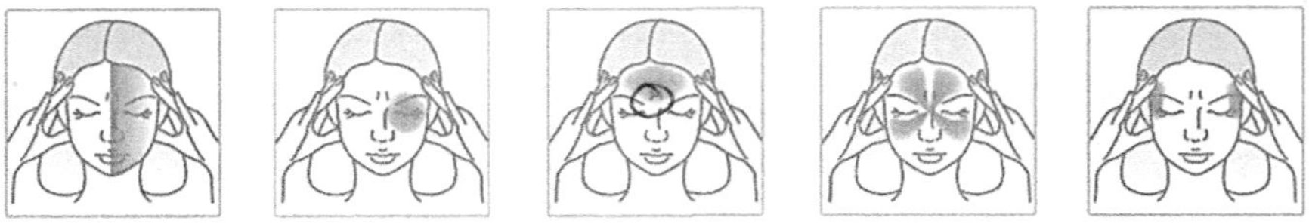

HOW WOULD YOU RATE...?

Mood	1	2	3	(4) circled	5
Energy	1	2	3	(4) circled	5
Mental clarity	1	2	3	(4) circled	5

PAIN LEVEL

(1) circled	2	3	4	5	6	7	8	9	10

Not too bad. *Well, I'm not enjoying this.* *Make it stop!*

ONSET

- ☐ Slow ☐ Average
- ☐ Rapid ☐ Sudden

DETAILED DESCRIPTION

☐ Constant ☐ Squeezing ☐ Throbbing ☐ Pounding ☑ Dull aching ☐ Burning
☐ Sharp ☐ Debilitating ☐ Other: ____

WHERE DOES IT HURT, EXACTLY?

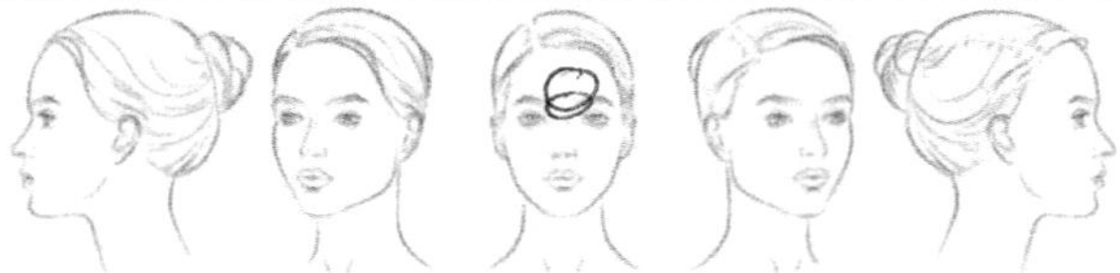

OTHER SYMPTOMS

☐ Lightheaded ☐ Dizziness
☐ Light sensitivity ☐ Sound sensitivity
☐ Confusion ☑ Auras
☐ Muscle stiffness ☐ Muscle aches

FEELING SICK?

☐ Nausea ☐ Diarrhea ☐ Vomiting ☐ Sore throat ☐ Congestion ☐ Coughing
☐ Chills ☐ Fever ☐ Other: /

SLEEP

hours: 8 quality: 1 2 3 (4) circled 5

WEATHER

☐ Cold ☑ Mild ☐ Hot Allergen levels: ____
☐ Dry ☐ Humid ☐ Wet BM Pressure: ____

STRESS LEVELS

None	(Low) circled	Medium	High	Max	@$#%!

item / meal	*time*	*meds / supplements*	*dose*	*time*
CEREAL	07:00			
SUBWAY - TUNA	13:00			
SWEETCORN	18:30			
PASTA SPINACH + CHEESE	19.00			
ICE CREAM				

drinks

- water: 1 (2) circled 3 4 5 6 7 8 9 10
- caffeine: (1) circled 2 3 4 5 6 7 8 9 10
- alcohol: 1 2 (struck through) 3 4 5 6 7 8 9 10

HORMONES

☑ Menstruating ☐ Menopause
☐ PMS ☐ N/A | other

COMPUTER / MOBILE DEVICE / TV

☐ None ☐ Some ☑ A lot Total Time: 8
☐ Sitting ☐ Standing ☐ Mixture Breaks every: ____

PHYSICAL ACTIVITY

☐ None ☐ Minimal ☑ Some ☐ Sweatin' ☐ I'm beat DETAILS: Cycle work

RELIEF MEASURES

☑ Medication ☐ Massage ☐ Sleep ☐ Exercise ☐ Water ☐ Cold/Ice
☐ Heat/Bath ☐ Other: IBUPROFEN
Did it work? ☐ Nope ☑ A bit ☐ Mostly ☐ 100%

Notes ☐ *See back notes*

START: ______ END: ______ DURATION: ______ DATE ______ *Entry #16*

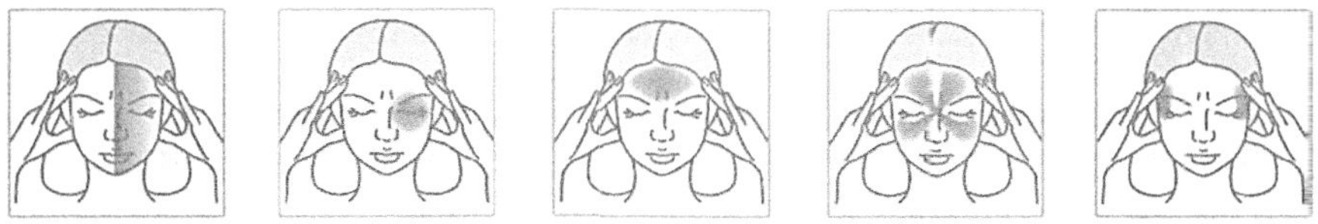

MIGRAINE | CLUSTER | TENSION | SINUS | TMJ

HOW WOULD YOU RATE...?

Mood	① ② ③ ④ ⑤
Energy	① ② ③ ④ ⑤
Mental clarity	① ② ③ ④ ⑤

PAIN LEVEL

1	2	3	4	5	6	7	8	9	10

Not too bad. *Well, I'm not enjoying this.* *Make it stop!*

ONSET

☐ Slow ☐ Average
☐ Rapid ☐ Sudden

DETAILED DESCRIPTION

☐ Constant ☐ Squeezing ☐ Throbbing ☐ Pounding ☐ Dull aching ☐ Burning
☐ Sharp ☐ Debilitating ☐ Other: ______________________

WHERE DOES IT HURT, EXACTLY?

OTHER SYMPTOMS

☐ Lightheaded ☐ Dizziness
☐ Light sensitivity ☐ Sound sensitivity
☐ Confusion ☐ Auras
☐ Muscle stiffness ☐ Muscle aches

FEELING SICK?

☐ Nausea ☐ Diarrhea ☐ Vomiting ☐ Sore throat ☐ Congestion ☐ Coughing
☐ Chills ☐ Fever ☐ Other: ______________________

SLEEP

hours ______ *quality* ① ② ③ ④ ⑤

WEATHER

☐ Cold ☐ Mild ☐ Hot Allergen levels: ____________
☐ Dry ☐ Humid ☐ Wet BM Pressure: ____________

STRESS LEVELS

None	Low	Medium	High	Max	@$#%!

item / meal	*time*	*meds / supplements*	*dose*	*time*	*drinks*
					water
					① ② ③ ④ ⑤ ⑥ ⑦ ⑧ ⑨ ⑩
					caffeine
					① ② ③ ④ ⑤ ⑥ ⑦ ⑧ ⑨ ⑩
					alcohol
					① ② ③ ④ ⑤ ⑥ ⑦ ⑧ ⑨ ⑩

HORMONES

☐ Menstruating ☐ Menopause
☐ PMS ☐ N/A | other

COMPUTER / MOBILE DEVICE / TV

☐ None ☐ Some ☐ A lot Total Time: ______
☐ Sitting ☐ Standing ☐ Mixture Breaks every: ______

PHYSICAL ACTIVITY

☐ None ☐ Minimal ☐ Some ☐ Sweatin' ☐ I'm beat DETAILS: ______________

RELIEF MEASURES

☐ Medication ☐ Massage ☐ Sleep ☐ Exercise ☐ Water ☐ Cold/Ice
☐ Heat/Bath ☐ Other: ______________________
Did it work? ☐ Nope ☐ A bit ☐ Mostly ☐ 100%

Notes ☐ *See back notes*

START:		END:		DURATION:		DATE		*Entry #17*

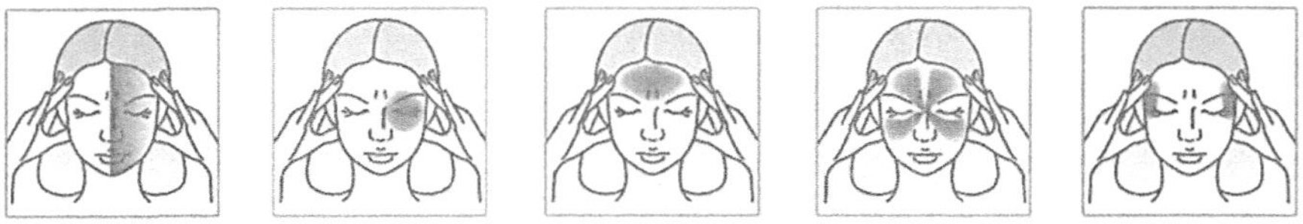

MIGRAINE CLUSTER TENSION SINUS TMJ

HOW WOULD YOU RATE...?

Mood	① ② ③ ④ ⑤
Energy	① ② ③ ④ ⑤
Mental clarity	① ② ③ ④ ⑤

PAIN LEVEL

1	2	3	4	5	6	7	8	9	10

Not too bad. *Well, I'm not enjoying this.* *Make it stop!*

ONSET

☐ Slow ☐ Average
☐ Rapid ☐ Sudden

DETAILED DESCRIPTION

☐ Constant ☐ Squeezing ☐ Throbbing ☐ Pounding ☐ Dull aching ☐ Burning
☐ Sharp ☐ Debilitating ☐ Other: ____________________

WHERE DOES IT HURT, EXACTLY?

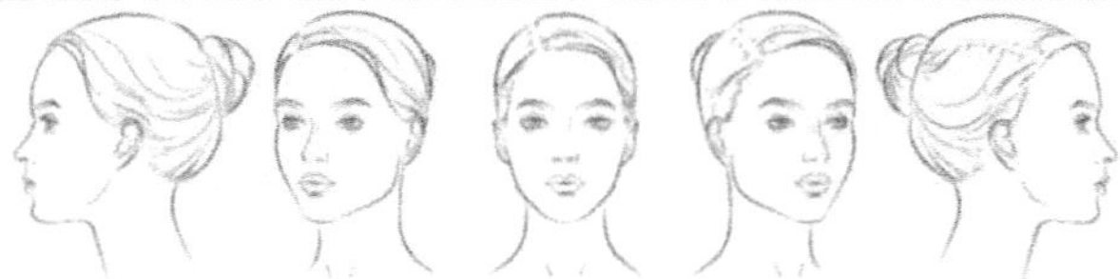

OTHER SYMPTOMS

☐ Lightheaded ☐ Dizziness
☐ Light sensitivity ☐ Sound sensitivity
☐ Confusion ☐ Auras
☐ Muscle stiffness ☐ Muscle aches

FEELING SICK?

☐ Nausea ☐ Diarrhea ☐ Vomiting ☐ Sore throat ☐ Congestion ☐ Coughing
☐ Chills ☐ Fever ☐ Other: ____________________

SLEEP

hours *quality*
________ ① ② ③ ④ ⑤

WEATHER

☐ Cold ☐ Mild ☐ Hot Allergen levels: ____________
☐ Dry ☐ Humid ☐ Wet BM Pressure: ____________

STRESS LEVELS

None	Low	Medium	High	Max	@$#%!

item / meal	*time*	*meds / supplements*	*dose*	*time*	*drinks*
					water
					① ② ③ ④ ⑤ ⑥ ⑦ ⑧ ⑨ ⑩
					caffeine
					① ② ③ ④ ⑤ ⑥ ⑦ ⑧ ⑨ ⑩
					alcohol
					① ② ③ ④ ⑤ ⑥ ⑦ ⑧ ⑨ ⑩

HORMONES

☐ Menstruating ☐ Menopause
☐ PMS ☐ N/A | other

COMPUTER / MOBILE DEVICE / TV

☐ None ☐ Some ☐ A lot Total Time: ______
☐ Sitting ☐ Standing ☐ Mixture Breaks every: ______

PHYSICAL ACTIVITY

☐ None ☐ Minimal ☐ Some ☐ Sweatin' ☐ I'm beat DETAILS: ____________

RELIEF MEASURES

☐ Medication ☐ Massage ☐ Sleep ☐ Exercise ☐ Water ☐ Cold/Ice
☐ Heat/Bath ☐ Other: ____________________
Did it work? ☐ Nope ☐ A bit ☐ Mostly ☐ 100%

Notes

☐ *See back notes*

START:		END:		DURATION:		DATE		*Entry #18*

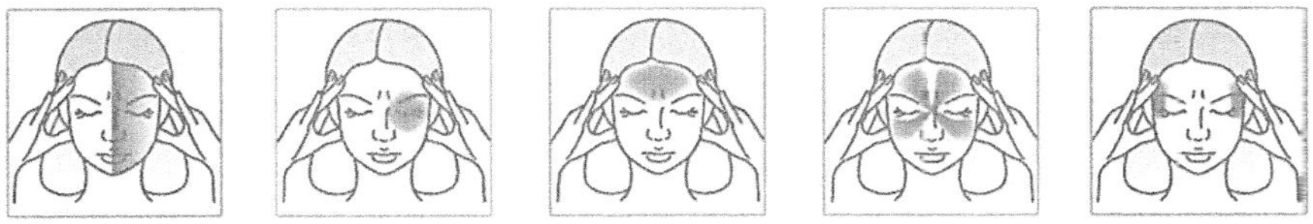

MIGRAINE CLUSTER TENSION SINUS TMJ

HOW WOULD YOU RATE...?					
Mood	1	2	3	4	5
Energy	1	2	3	4	5
Mental clarity	1	2	3	4	5

PAIN LEVEL

1	2	3	4	5	6	7	8	9	10

Not too bad. *Well, I'm not enjoying this.* *Make it stop!*

ONSET

☐ Slow ☐ Average
☐ Rapid ☐ Sudden

DETAILED DESCRIPTION

☐ Constant ☐ Squeezing ☐ Throbbing ☐ Pounding ☐ Dull aching ☐ Burning
☐ Sharp ☐ Debilitating ☐ Other: ______

WHERE DOES IT HURT, EXACTLY?

OTHER SYMPTOMS

☐ Lightheaded ☐ Dizziness
☐ Light sensitivity ☐ Sound sensitivity
☐ Confusion ☐ Auras
☐ Muscle stiffness ☐ Muscle aches

FEELING SICK?

☐ Nausea ☐ Diarrhea ☐ Vomiting ☐ Sore throat ☐ Congestion ☐ Coughing
☐ Chills ☐ Fever ☐ Other: ______

SLEEP

hours ______ *quality* 1 2 3 4 5

WEATHER

☐ Cold ☐ Mild ☐ Hot Allergen levels: ______
☐ Dry ☐ Humid ☐ Wet BM Pressure: ______

STRESS LEVELS

None	Low	Medium	High	Max	@$#%!

item / meal	*time*	*meds / supplements*	*dose*	*time*	*drinks*
					water: 1 2 3 4 5 6 7 8 9 10
					caffeine: 1 2 3 4 5 6 7 8 9 10
					alcohol: 1 2 3 4 5 6 7 8 9 10

HORMONES

☐ Menstruating ☐ Menopause
☐ PMS ☐ N/A | other

COMPUTER / MOBILE DEVICE / TV

☐ None ☐ Some ☐ A lot Total Time: ______
☐ Sitting ☐ Standing ☐ Mixture Breaks every: ______

PHYSICAL ACTIVITY

☐ None ☐ Minimal ☐ Some ☐ Sweatin' ☐ I'm beat DETAILS: ______

RELIEF MEASURES

☐ Medication ☐ Massage ☐ Sleep ☐ Exercise ☐ Water ☐ Cold/Ice
☐ Heat/Bath ☐ Other: ______
Did it work? ☐ Nope ☐ A bit ☐ Mostly ☐ 100%

Notes ☐ *See back notes*

START:		END:		DURATION:		DATE		*Entry #19*

MIGRAINE

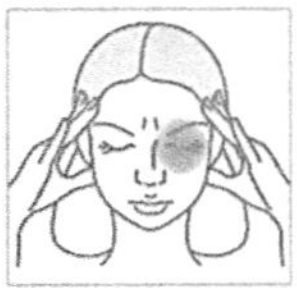

CLUSTER

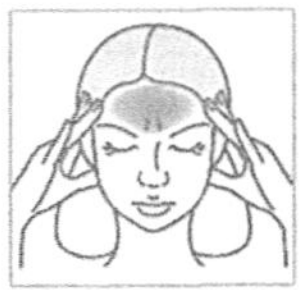

TENSION

SINUS

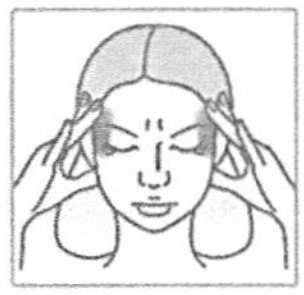

TMJ

HOW WOULD YOU RATE...?

Mood	① ② ③ ④ ⑤
Energy	① ② ③ ④ ⑤
Mental clarity	① ② ③ ④ ⑤

PAIN LEVEL

1	2	3	4	5	6	7	8	9	10

Not too bad. *Well, I'm not enjoying this.* *Make it stop!*

ONSET

☐ Slow ☐ Average
☐ Rapid ☐ Sudden

DETAILED DESCRIPTION

☐ Constant ☐ Squeezing ☐ Throbbing ☐ Pounding ☐ Dull aching ☐ Burning
☐ Sharp ☐ Debilitating ☐ Other: ______________________________

WHERE DOES IT HURT, EXACTLY?

OTHER SYMPTOMS

☐ Lightheaded ☐ Dizziness
☐ Light sensitivity ☐ Sound sensitivity
☐ Confusion ☐ Auras
☐ Muscle stiffness ☐ Muscle aches

FEELING SICK?

☐ Nausea ☐ Diarrhea ☐ Vomiting ☐ Sore throat ☐ Congestion ☐ Coughing
☐ Chills ☐ Fever ☐ Other: ______________________________

SLEEP

hours ________ *quality* ① ② ③ ④ ⑤

WEATHER

☐ Cold ☐ Mild ☐ Hot Allergen levels: ____________
☐ Dry ☐ Humid ☐ Wet BM Pressure: ____________

STRESS LEVELS

None	Low	Medium	High	Max	@$#%!

item / meal	*time*	*meds / supplements*	*dose*	*time*	*drinks*
					water
					① ② ③ ④ ⑤ ⑥ ⑦ ⑧ ⑨ ⑩
					caffeine
					① ② ③ ④ ⑤ ⑥ ⑦ ⑧ ⑨ ⑩
					alcohol
					① ② ③ ④ ⑤ ⑥ ⑦ ⑧ ⑨ ⑩

HORMONES

☐ Menstruating ☐ Menopause
☐ PMS ☐ N/A | other

COMPUTER / MOBILE DEVICE / TV

☐ None ☐ Some ☐ A lot Total Time: ______
☐ Sitting ☐ Standing ☐ Mixture Breaks every: ______

PHYSICAL ACTIVITY

☐ None ☐ Minimal ☐ Some ☐ Sweatin' ☐ I'm beat DETAILS: ____________________

RELIEF MEASURES

☐ Medication ☐ Massage ☐ Sleep ☐ Exercise ☐ Water ☐ Cold/Ice
☐ Heat/Bath ☐ Other: ______________________________
Did it work? ☐ Nope ☐ A bit ☐ Mostly ☐ 100%

Notes ☐ *See back notes*

START: ____ END: ____ DURATION: ____ DATE ____ *Entry #20*

MIGRAINE | CLUSTER | TENSION | SINUS | TMJ

HOW WOULD YOU RATE...?

Mood	① ② ③ ④ ⑤
Energy	① ② ③ ④ ⑤
Mental clarity	① ② ③ ④ ⑤

PAIN LEVEL

1	2	3	4	5	6	7	8	9	10

Not too bad. *Well, I'm not enjoying this.* *Make it stop!*

ONSET

☐ Slow ☐ Average
☐ Rapid ☐ Sudden

DETAILED DESCRIPTION

☐ Constant ☐ Squeezing ☐ Throbbing ☐ Pounding ☐ Dull aching ☐ Burning
☐ Sharp ☐ Debilitating ☐ Other: ____

WHERE DOES IT HURT, EXACTLY?

OTHER SYMPTOMS

☐ Lightheaded ☐ Dizziness
☐ Light sensitivity ☐ Sound sensitivity
☐ Confusion ☐ Auras
☐ Muscle stiffness ☐ Muscle aches

FEELING SICK?

☐ Nausea ☐ Diarrhea ☐ Vomiting ☐ Sore throat ☐ Congestion ☐ Coughing
☐ Chills ☐ Fever ☐ Other: ____

SLEEP

hours ____ *quality* ① ② ③ ④ ⑤

WEATHER

☐ Cold ☐ Mild ☐ Hot Allergen levels: ____
☐ Dry ☐ Humid ☐ Wet BM Pressure: ____

STRESS LEVELS

None	Low	Medium	High	Max	@$#%!

item / meal	*time*	*meds / supplements*	*dose*	*time*	*drinks*
					water ① ② ③ ④ ⑤ ⑥ ⑦ ⑧ ⑨ ⑩
					caffeine ① ② ③ ④ ⑤ ⑥ ⑦ ⑧ ⑨ ⑩
					alcohol ① ② ③ ④ ⑤ ⑥ ⑦ ⑧ ⑨ ⑩

HORMONES

☐ Menstruating ☐ Menopause
☐ PMS ☐ N/A | other

COMPUTER / MOBILE DEVICE / TV

☐ None ☐ Some ☐ A lot Total Time: ____
☐ Sitting ☐ Standing ☐ Mixture Breaks every: ____

PHYSICAL ACTIVITY

☐ None ☐ Minimal ☐ Some ☐ Sweatin' ☐ I'm beat DETAILS: ____

RELIEF MEASURES

☐ Medication ☐ Massage ☐ Sleep ☐ Exercise ☐ Water ☐ Cold/Ice
☐ Heat/Bath ☐ Other: ____
Did it work? ☐ Nope ☐ A bit ☐ Mostly ☐ 100%

Notes ☐ *See back notes*

START: ______ END: ______ DURATION: ______ DATE ______ *Entry #21*

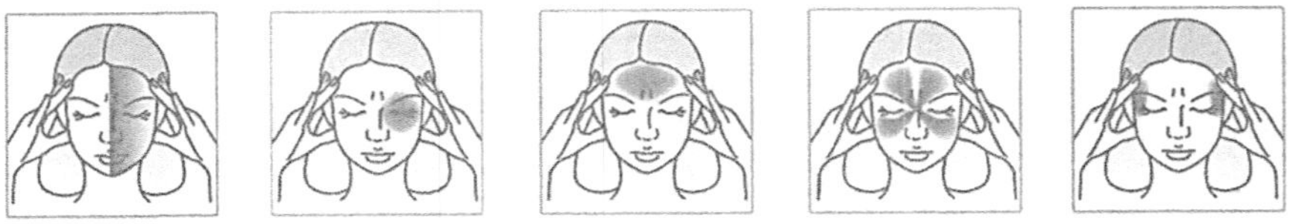

MIGRAINE CLUSTER TENSION SINUS TMJ

HOW WOULD YOU RATE...?

Mood	1	2	3	4	5
Energy	1	2	3	4	5
Mental clarity	1	2	3	4	5

PAIN LEVEL

1	2	3	4	5	6	7	8	9	10

Not too bad. *Well, I'm not enjoying this.* *Make it stop!*

ONSET

☐ Slow ☐ Average
☐ Rapid ☐ Sudden

DETAILED DESCRIPTION

☐ Constant ☐ Squeezing ☐ Throbbing ☐ Pounding ☐ Dull aching ☐ Burning
☐ Sharp ☐ Debilitating ☐ Other: ______

WHERE DOES IT HURT, EXACTLY?

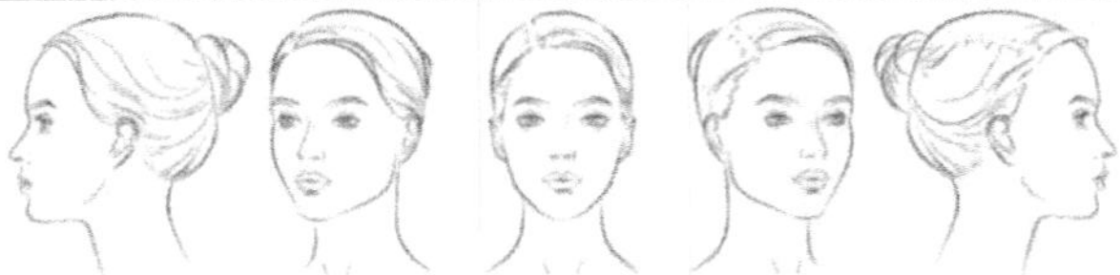

OTHER SYMPTOMS

☐ Lightheaded ☐ Dizziness
☐ Light sensitivity ☐ Sound sensitivity
☐ Confusion ☐ Auras
☐ Muscle stiffness ☐ Muscle aches

FEELING SICK?

☐ Nausea ☐ Diarrhea ☐ Vomiting ☐ Sore throat ☐ Congestion ☐ Coughing
☐ Chills ☐ Fever ☐ Other: ______

SLEEP

hours ______ *quality* 1 2 3 4 5

WEATHER

☐ Cold ☐ Mild ☐ Hot Allergen levels: ______
☐ Dry ☐ Humid ☐ Wet BM Pressure: ______

STRESS LEVELS

None	Low	Medium	High	Max	@$#%!

item / meal	*time*	*meds / supplements*	*dose*	*time*	*drinks*
					water
					1 2 3 4 5 6 7 8 9 10
					caffeine
					1 2 3 4 5 6 7 8 9 10
					alcohol
					1 2 3 4 5 6 7 8 9 10

HORMONES

☐ Menstruating ☐ Menopause
☐ PMS ☐ N/A | other

COMPUTER / MOBILE DEVICE / TV

☐ None ☐ Some ☐ A lot Total Time: ______
☐ Sitting ☐ Standing ☐ Mixture Breaks every: ______

PHYSICAL ACTIVITY

☐ None ☐ Minimal ☐ Some ☐ Sweatin' ☐ I'm beat DETAILS: ______

RELIEF MEASURES

☐ Medication ☐ Massage ☐ Sleep ☐ Exercise ☐ Water ☐ Cold/Ice
☐ Heat/Bath ☐ Other: ______
Did it work? ☐ Nope ☐ A bit ☐ Mostly ☐ 100%

Notes ☐ *See back notes*

START:		END:		DURATION:		DATE		Entry #22

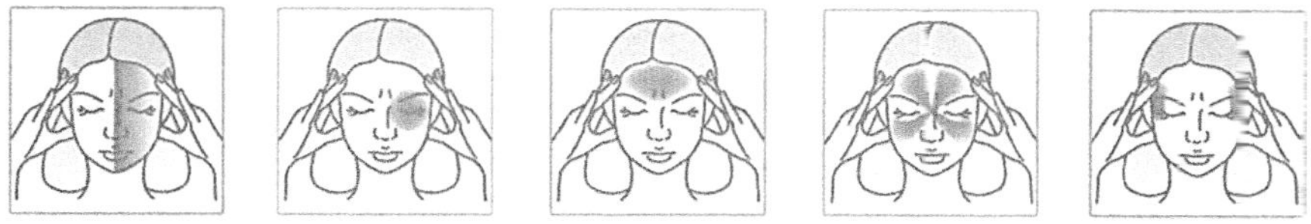

MIGRAINE CLUSTER TENSION SINUS TMJ

HOW WOULD YOU RATE...?

Mood	1	2	3	4	5
Energy	1	2	3	4	5
Mental clarity	1	2	3	4	5

PAIN LEVEL

1	2	3	4	5	6	7	8	9	10

Not too bad. *Well, I'm not enjoying this.* *Make it stop!*

ONSET

☐ Slow ☐ Average
☐ Rapid ☐ Sudden

DETAILED DESCRIPTION

☐ Constant ☐ Squeezing ☐ Throbbing ☐ Pounding ☐ Dull aching ☐ Burning
☐ Sharp ☐ Debilitating ☐ Other: ____________________

WHERE DOES IT HURT, EXACTLY?

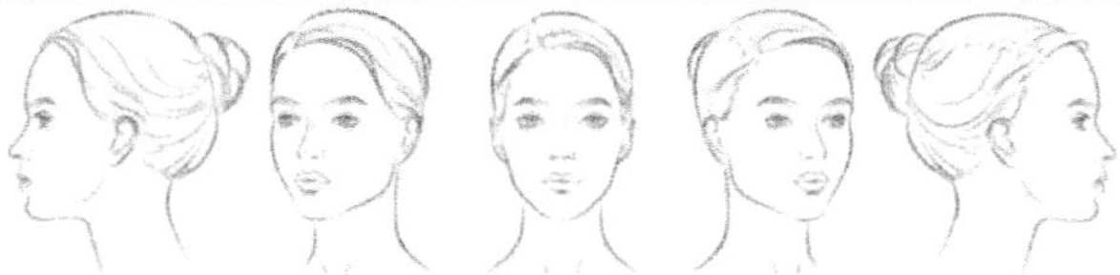

OTHER SYMPTOMS

☐ Lightheaded ☐ Dizziness
☐ Light sensitivity ☐ Sound sensitivity
☐ Confusion ☐ Auras
☐ Muscle stiffness ☐ Muscle aches

FEELING SICK?

☐ Nausea ☐ Diarrhea ☐ Vomiting ☐ Sore throat ☐ Congestion ☐ Coughing
☐ Chills ☐ Fever ☐ Other: ____________________

SLEEP

hours ________ *quality* 1 2 3 4 5

WEATHER

☐ Cold ☐ Mild ☐ Hot Allergen levels: __________
☐ Dry ☐ Humid ☐ Wet BM Pressure: __________

STRESS LEVELS

None	Low	Medium	High	Max	@$#%!

item / meal	*time*	*meds / supplements*	*dose*	*time*	*drinks*
					water: 1 2 3 4 5 6 7 8 9 10
					caffeine: 1 2 3 4 5 6 7 8 9 10
					alcohol: 1 2 3 4 5 6 7 8 9 10

HORMONES

☐ Menstruating ☐ Menopause
☐ PMS ☐ N/A | other

COMPUTER / MOBILE DEVICE / TV

☐ None ☐ Some ☐ A lot Total Time: ______
☐ Sitting ☐ Standing ☐ Mixture Breaks every: ______

PHYSICAL ACTIVITY

☐ None ☐ Minimal ☐ Some ☐ Sweatin' ☐ I'm beat DETAILS: ____________________

RELIEF MEASURES

☐ Medication ☐ Massage ☐ Sleep ☐ Exercise ☐ Water ☐ Cold/Ice
☐ Heat/Bath ☐ Other: ____________________
Did it work? ☐ Nope ☐ A bit ☐ Mostly ☐ 100%

Notes ☐ *See back notes*

START: ______ END: ______ DURATION: ______ DATE ______ *Entry #23*

MIGRAINE

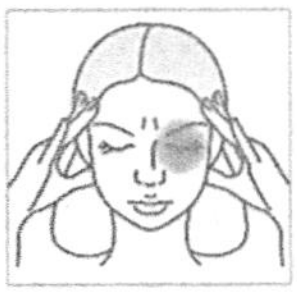
CLUSTER

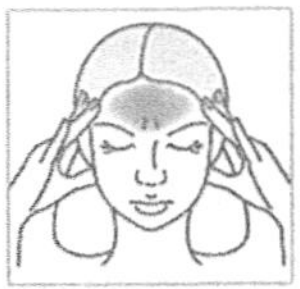
TENSION

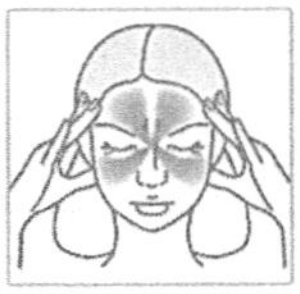
SINUS

TMJ

HOW WOULD YOU RATE...?

Mood	① ② ③ ④ ⑤
Energy	① ② ③ ④ ⑤
Mental clarity	① ② ③ ④ ⑤

PAIN LEVEL

1	2	3	4	5	6	7	8	9	10

Not too bad. *Well, I'm not enjoying this.* *Make it stop!*

ONSET

☐ Slow ☐ Average
☐ Rapid ☐ Sudden

DETAILED DESCRIPTION

☐ Constant ☐ Squeezing ☐ Throbbing ☐ Pounding ☐ Dull aching ☐ Burning
☐ Sharp ☐ Debilitating ☐ Other: ____________________

WHERE DOES IT HURT, EXACTLY?

OTHER SYMPTOMS

☐ Lightheaded ☐ Dizziness
☐ Light sensitivity ☐ Sound sensitivity
☐ Confusion ☐ Auras
☐ Muscle stiffness ☐ Muscle aches

FEELING SICK?

☐ Nausea ☐ Diarrhea ☐ Vomiting ☐ Sore throat ☐ Congestion ☐ Coughing
☐ Chills ☐ Fever ☐ Other: ____________________

SLEEP

hours ______ *quality* ① ② ③ ④ ⑤

WEATHER

☐ Cold ☐ Mild ☐ Hot Allergen levels: __________
☐ Dry ☐ Humid ☐ Wet BM Pressure: __________

STRESS LEVELS

None	Low	Medium	High	Max	@$#%!

item / meal	*time*	*meds / supplements*	*dose*	*time*	*drinks*
					water: ① ② ③ ④ ⑤ ⑥ ⑦ ⑧ ⑨ ⑩
					caffeine: ① ② ③ ④ ⑤ ⑥ ⑦ ⑧ ⑨ ⑩
					alcohol: ① ② ③ ④ ⑤ ⑥ ⑦ ⑧ ⑨ ⑩

HORMONES

☐ Menstruating ☐ Menopause
☐ PMS ☐ N/A | other

COMPUTER / MOBILE DEVICE / TV

☐ None ☐ Some ☐ A lot Total Time: ______
☐ Sitting ☐ Standing ☐ Mixture Breaks every: ______

PHYSICAL ACTIVITY

☐ None ☐ Minimal ☐ Some ☐ Sweatin' ☐ I'm beat DETAILS: ____________

RELIEF MEASURES

☐ Medication ☐ Massage ☐ Sleep ☐ Exercise ☐ Water ☐ Cold/Ice
☐ Heat/Bath ☐ Other: ____________________
Did it work? ☐ Nope ☐ A bit ☐ Mostly ☐ 100%

Notes ☐ *See back notes*

START:		END:		DURATION:		DATE		*Entry #24*

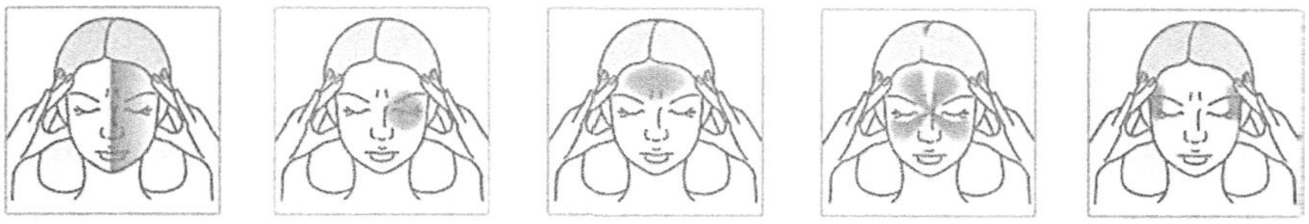

MIGRAINE CLUSTER TENSION SINUS TMJ

HOW WOULD YOU RATE...?

Mood	1	2	3	4	5
Energy	1	2	3	4	5
Mental clarity	1	2	3	4	5

PAIN LEVEL

1	2	3	4	5	6	7	8	9	10

Not too bad. *Well, I'm not enjoying this.* *Make it stop!*

ONSET

☐ Slow ☐ Average
☐ Rapid ☐ Sudden

DETAILED DESCRIPTION

☐ Constant ☐ Squeezing ☐ Throbbing ☐ Pounding ☐ Dull aching ☐ Burning
☐ Sharp ☐ Debilitating ☐ Other: ______________________________

WHERE DOES IT HURT, EXACTLY?

OTHER SYMPTOMS

☐ Lightheaded ☐ Dizziness
☐ Light sensitivity ☐ Sound sensitivity
☐ Confusion ☐ Auras
☐ Muscle stiffness ☐ Muscle aches

FEELING SICK?

☐ Nausea ☐ Diarrhea ☐ Vomiting ☐ Sore throat ☐ Congestion ☐ Coughing
☐ Chills ☐ Fever ☐ Other: ______________________________

SLEEP

hours ________ *quality* 1 2 3 4 5

WEATHER

☐ Cold ☐ Mild ☐ Hot Allergen levels: ____________
☐ Dry ☐ Humid ☐ Wet BM Pressure: ____________

STRESS LEVELS

None	Low	Medium	High	Max	@$#%!

item / meal	*time*	*meds / supplements*	*dose*	*time*	*drinks*
					water
					1 2 3 4 5 6 7 8 9 10
					caffeine
					1 2 3 4 5 6 7 8 9 10
					alcohol
					1 2 3 4 5 6 7 8 9 10

HORMONES

☐ Menstruating ☐ Menopause
☐ PMS ☐ N/A | other

COMPUTER / MOBILE DEVICE / TV

☐ None ☐ Some ☐ A lot Total Time: _____
☐ Sitting ☐ Standing ☐ Mixture Breaks every: _____

PHYSICAL ACTIVITY

☐ None ☐ Minimal ☐ Some ☐ Sweatin' ☐ I'm beat DETAILS: ______________

RELIEF MEASURES

☐ Medication ☐ Massage ☐ Sleep ☐ Exercise ☐ Water ☐ Cold/Ice
☐ Heat/Bath ☐ Other: ______________________________

Did it work? ☐ Nope ☐ A bit ☐ Mostly ☐ 100%

Notes ☐ *See back notes*

START:		END:		DURATION:		DATE		*Entry #25*

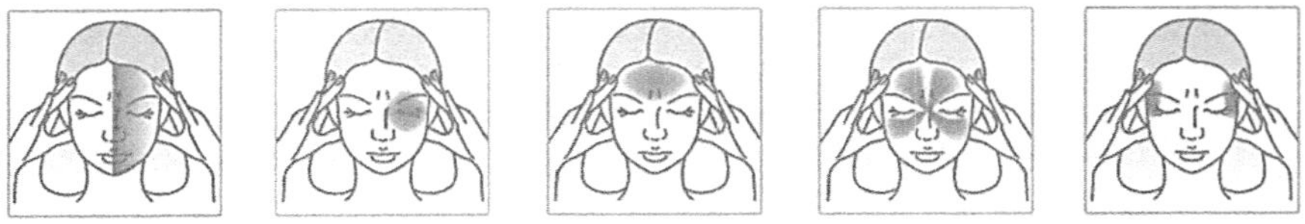

MIGRAINE CLUSTER TENSION SINUS TMJ

HOW WOULD YOU RATE...?

Mood ① ② ③ ④ ⑤

Energy ① ② ③ ④ ⑤

Mental clarity ① ② ③ ④ ⑤

PAIN LEVEL

1	2	3	4	5	6	7	8	9	10

Not too bad. *Well, I'm not enjoying this.* *Make it stop!*

ONSET

☐ Slow ☐ Average
☐ Rapid ☐ Sudden

DETAILED DESCRIPTION

☐ Constant ☐ Squeezing ☐ Throbbing ☐ Pounding ☐ Dull aching ☐ Burning
☐ Sharp ☐ Debilitating ☐ Other: ______________________________

WHERE DOES IT HURT, EXACTLY?

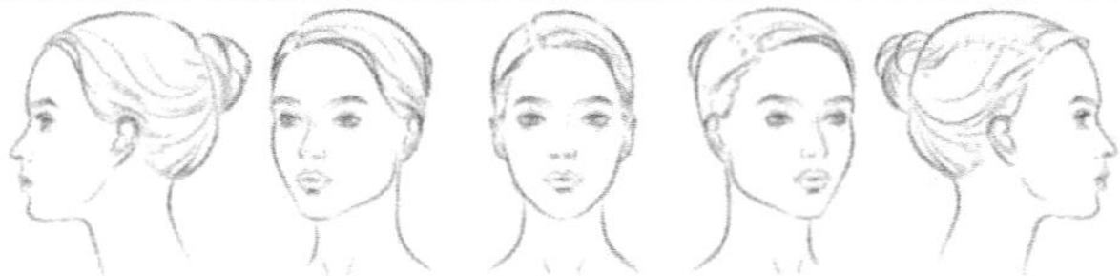

OTHER SYMPTOMS

☐ Lightheaded ☐ Dizziness
☐ Light sensitivity ☐ Sound sensitivity
☐ Confusion ☐ Auras
☐ Muscle stiffness ☐ Muscle aches

FEELING SICK?

☐ Nausea ☐ Diarrhea ☐ Vomiting ☐ Sore throat ☐ Congestion ☐ Coughing
☐ Chills ☐ Fever ☐ Other: ______________________________

SLEEP

hours ________ *quality* ① ② ③ ④ ⑤

WEATHER

☐ Cold ☐ Mild ☐ Hot Allergen levels: __________
☐ Dry ☐ Humid ☐ Wet BM Pressure: __________

STRESS LEVELS

None	Low	Medium	High	Max	@$#%!

item / meal	*time*	*meds / supplements*	*dose*	*time*	*drinks*
					water ① ② ③ ④ ⑤ ⑥ ⑦ ⑧ ⑨ ⑩
					caffeine ① ② ③ ④ ⑤ ⑥ ⑦ ⑧ ⑨ ⑩
					alcohol ① ② ③ ④ ⑤ ⑥ ⑦ ⑧ ⑨ ⑩

HORMONES

☐ Menstruating ☐ Menopause
☐ PMS ☐ N/A | other

COMPUTER / MOBILE DEVICE / TV

☐ None ☐ Some ☐ A lot Total Time: ______
☐ Sitting ☐ Standing ☐ Mixture Breaks every: ______

PHYSICAL ACTIVITY

☐ None ☐ Minimal ☐ Some ☐ Sweatin' ☐ I'm beat DETAILS: __________

RELIEF MEASURES

☐ Medication ☐ Massage ☐ Sleep ☐ Exercise ☐ Water ☐ Cold/Ice
☐ Heat/Bath ☐ Other: ______________________________
Did it work? ☐ Nope ☐ A bit ☐ Mostly ☐ 100%

Notes ☐ *See back notes*

START:		END:		DURATION:		DATE		*Entry #26*

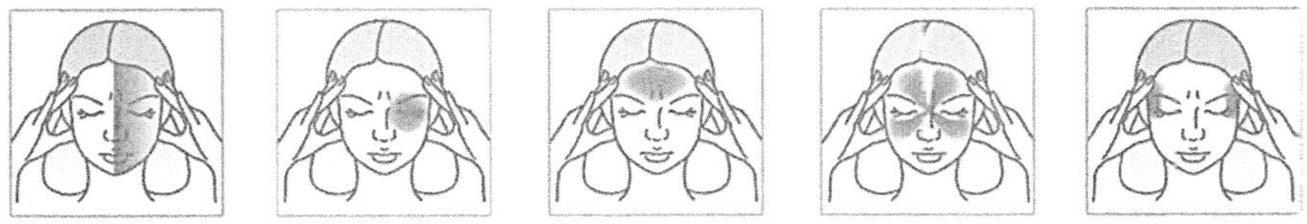

MIGRAINE | CLUSTER | TENSION | SINUS | TMJ

HOW WOULD YOU RATE...?

Mood	1	2	3	4	5
Energy	1	2	3	4	5
Mental clarity	1	2	3	4	5

PAIN LEVEL

1	2	3	4	5	6	7	8	9	10

Not too bad. *Well, I'm not enjoying this.* *Make it stop!*

ONSET

☐ Slow ☐ Average
☐ Rapid ☐ Sudden

DETAILED DESCRIPTION

☐ Constant ☐ Squeezing ☐ Throbbing ☐ Pounding ☐ Dull aching ☐ Burning
☐ Sharp ☐ Debilitating ☐ Other: ____________________

WHERE DOES IT HURT, EXACTLY?

OTHER SYMPTOMS

☐ Lightheaded ☐ Dizziness
☐ Light sensitivity ☐ Sound sensitivity
☐ Confusion ☐ Auras
☐ Muscle stiffness ☐ Muscle aches

FEELING SICK?

☐ Nausea ☐ Diarrhea ☐ Vomiting ☐ Sore throat ☐ Congestion ☐ Coughing
☐ Chills ☐ Fever ☐ Other: ____________________

SLEEP

hours ________ *quality* 1 2 3 4 5

WEATHER

☐ Cold ☐ Mild ☐ Hot Allergen levels: ____________
☐ Dry ☐ Humid ☐ Wet BM Pressure: ____________

STRESS LEVELS

None	Low	Medium	High	Max	@$#%!

item / meal	*time*	*meds / supplements*	*dose*	*time*	*drinks*
					water
					1 2 3 4 5 6 7 8 9 10
					caffeine
					1 2 3 4 5 6 7 8 9 10
					alcohol
					1 2 3 4 5 6 7 8 9 10

HORMONES

☐ Menstruating ☐ Menopause
☐ PMS ☐ N/A | other

COMPUTER / MOBILE DEVICE / TV

☐ None ☐ Some ☐ A lot Total Time: ______
☐ Sitting ☐ Standing ☐ Mixture Breaks every: ______

PHYSICAL ACTIVITY

☐ None ☐ Minimal ☐ Some ☐ Sweatin' ☐ I'm beat DETAILS: ____________________

RELIEF MEASURES

☐ Medication ☐ Massage ☐ Sleep ☐ Exercise ☐ Water ☐ Cold/Ice
☐ Heat/Bath ☐ Other: ____________________
Did it work? ☐ Nope ☐ A bit ☐ Mostly ☐ 100%

Notes ☐ *See back notes*

START:		END:		DURATION:		DATE		*Entry #27*

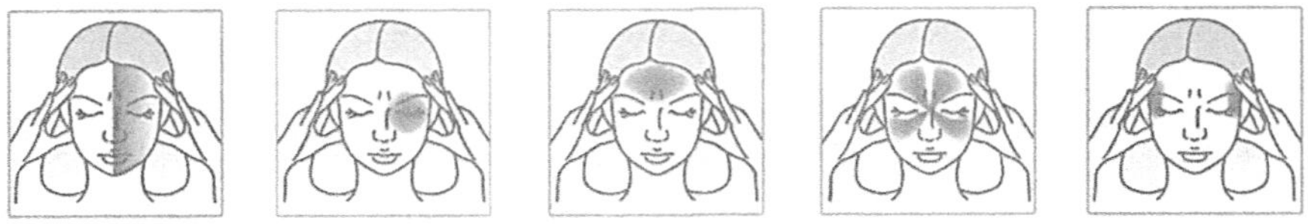

MIGRAINE   CLUSTER   TENSION   SINUS   TMJ

HOW WOULD YOU RATE...?

Mood	① ② ③ ④ ⑤
Energy	① ② ③ ④ ⑤
Mental clarity	① ② ③ ④ ⑤

PAIN LEVEL

1	2	3	4	5	6	7	8	9	10

Not too bad.   *Well, I'm not enjoying this.*   *Make it stop!*

ONSET

☐ Slow   ☐ Average
☐ Rapid   ☐ Sudden

DETAILED DESCRIPTION

☐ Constant   ☐ Squeezing   ☐ Throbbing   ☐ Pounding   ☐ Dull aching   ☐ Burning
☐ Sharp   ☐ Debilitating   ☐ Other: ____________________

WHERE DOES IT HURT, EXACTLY?

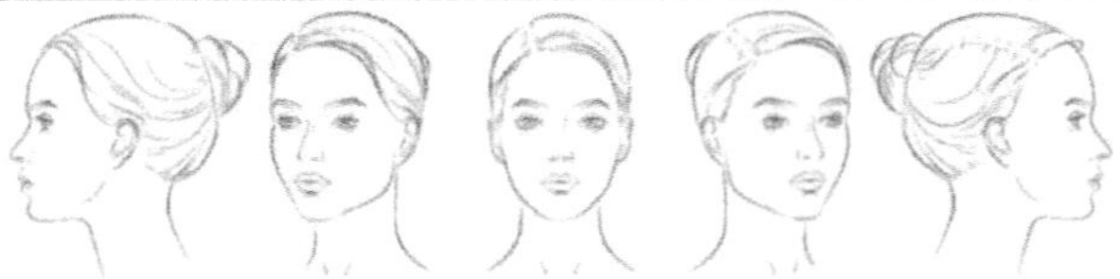

OTHER SYMPTOMS

☐ Lightheaded   ☐ Dizziness
☐ Light sensitivity   ☐ Sound sensitivity
☐ Confusion   ☐ Auras
☐ Muscle stiffness   ☐ Muscle aches

FEELING SICK?

☐ Nausea   ☐ Diarrhea   ☐ Vomiting   ☐ Sore throat   ☐ Congestion   ☐ Coughing
☐ Chills   ☐ Fever   ☐ Other: ____________________

SLEEP

hours ________   *quality* ① ② ③ ④ ⑤

WEATHER

☐ Cold   ☐ Mild   ☐ Hot   Allergen levels: ____________
☐ Dry   ☐ Humid   ☐ Wet   BM Pressure: ____________

STRESS LEVELS

None	Low	Medium	High	Max	@$#%!

item / meal	*time*	*meds / supplements*	*dose*	*time*	*drinks*
					water: ① ② ③ ④ ⑤ ⑥ ⑦ ⑧ ⑨ ⑩
					caffeine: ① ② ③ ④ ⑤ ⑥ ⑦ ⑧ ⑨ ⑩
					alcohol: ① ② ③ ④ ⑤ ⑥ ⑦ ⑧ ⑨ ⑩

HORMONES

☐ Menstruating   ☐ Menopause
☐ PMS   ☐ N/A | other

COMPUTER / MOBILE DEVICE / TV

☐ None   ☐ Some   ☐ A lot   Total Time: ______
☐ Sitting   ☐ Standing   ☐ Mixture   Breaks every: ______

PHYSICAL ACTIVITY

☐ None   ☐ Minimal   ☐ Some   ☐ Sweatin'   ☐ I'm beat   DETAILS: ____________

RELIEF MEASURES

☐ Medication   ☐ Massage   ☐ Sleep   ☐ Exercise   ☐ Water   ☐ Cold/Ice
☐ Heat/Bath   ☐ Other: ____________________

Did it work?   ☐ Nope   ☐ A bit   ☐ Mostly   ☐ 100%

Notes   ☐ *See back notes*

START:		END:		DURATION:		DATE		*Entry #28*

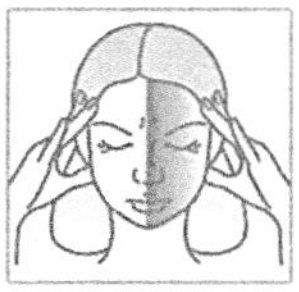
MIGRAINE
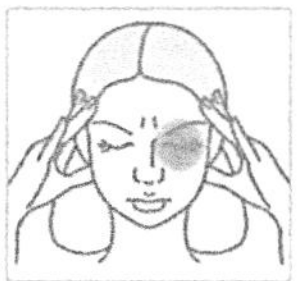
CLUSTER
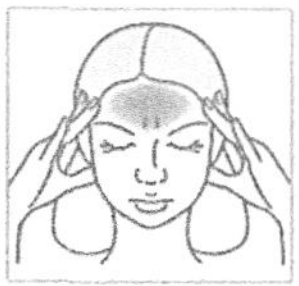
TENSION

SINUS

TMJ

HOW WOULD YOU RATE...?

Mood	1	2	3	4	5
Energy	1	2	3	4	5
Mental clarity	1	2	3	4	5

PAIN LEVEL

1	2	3	4	5	6	7	8	9	10

Not too bad. *Well, I'm not enjoying this.* *Make it stop!*

ONSET

☐ Slow ☐ Average
☐ Rapid ☐ Sudden

DETAILED DESCRIPTION

☐ Constant ☐ Squeezing ☐ Throbbing ☐ Pounding ☐ Dull aching ☐ Burning
☐ Sharp ☐ Debilitating ☐ Other: ______

WHERE DOES IT HURT, EXACTLY?

OTHER SYMPTOMS

☐ Lightheaded ☐ Dizziness
☐ Light sensitivity ☐ Sound sensitivity
☐ Confusion ☐ Auras
☐ Muscle stiffness ☐ Muscle aches

FEELING SICK?

☐ Nausea ☐ Diarrhea ☐ Vomiting ☐ Sore throat ☐ Congestion ☐ Coughing
☐ Chills ☐ Fever ☐ Other: ______

SLEEP

hours ______
quality 1 2 3 4 5

WEATHER

☐ Cold ☐ Mild ☐ Hot Allergen levels: ______
☐ Dry ☐ Humid ☐ Wet BM Pressure: ______

STRESS LEVELS

None	Low	Medium	High	Max	@$#%!

item / meal	*time*	*meds / supplements*	*dose*	*time*	*drinks*
					water
					1 2 3 4 5 6 7 8 9 10
					caffeine
					1 2 3 4 5 6 7 8 9 10
					alcohol
					1 2 3 4 5 6 7 8 9 10

HORMONES

☐ Menstruating ☐ Menopause
☐ PMS ☐ N/A | other

COMPUTER / MOBILE DEVICE / TV

☐ None ☐ Some ☐ A lot Total Time: ______
☐ Sitting ☐ Standing ☐ Mixture Breaks every: ______

PHYSICAL ACTIVITY

☐ None ☐ Minimal ☐ Some ☐ Sweatin' ☐ I'm beat DETAILS: ______

RELIEF MEASURES

☐ Medication ☐ Massage ☐ Sleep ☐ Exercise ☐ Water ☐ Cold/Ice
☐ Heat/Bath ☐ Other: ______
Did it work? ☐ Nope ☐ A bit ☐ Mostly ☐ 100%

Notes ☐ *See back notes*

START:		END:		DURATION:		DATE		*Entry #29*

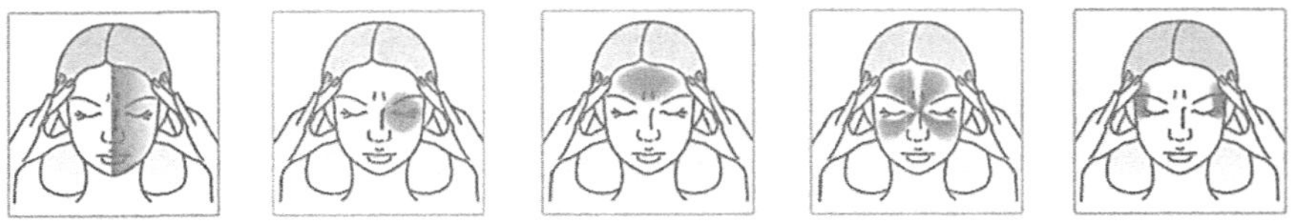

MIGRAINE CLUSTER TENSION SINUS TMJ

HOW WOULD YOU RATE...?

Mood	① ② ③ ④ ⑤
Energy	① ② ③ ④ ⑤
Mental clarity	① ② ③ ④ ⑤

PAIN LEVEL

1	2	3	4	5	6	7	8	9	10

Not too bad. *Well, I'm not enjoying this.* *Make it stop!*

ONSET

☐ Slow ☐ Average
☐ Rapid ☐ Sudden

DETAILED DESCRIPTION

☐ Constant ☐ Squeezing ☐ Throbbing ☐ Pounding ☐ Dull aching ☐ Burning
☐ Sharp ☐ Debilitating ☐ Other: ____________________

WHERE DOES IT HURT, EXACTLY?

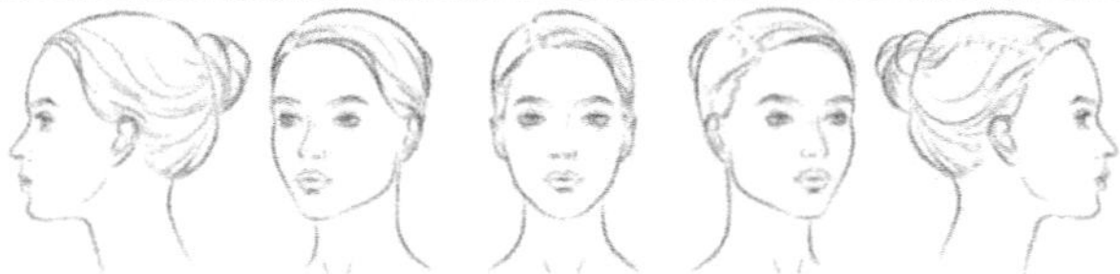

OTHER SYMPTOMS

☐ Lightheaded ☐ Dizziness
☐ Light sensitivity ☐ Sound sensitivity
☐ Confusion ☐ Auras
☐ Muscle stiffness ☐ Muscle aches

FEELING SICK?

☐ Nausea ☐ Diarrhea ☐ Vomiting ☐ Sore throat ☐ Congestion ☐ Coughing
☐ Chills ☐ Fever ☐ Other: ____________________

SLEEP

hours ________ *quality* ① ② ③ ④ ⑤

WEATHER

☐ Cold ☐ Mild ☐ Hot Allergen levels: ____________
☐ Dry ☐ Humid ☐ Wet BM Pressure: ____________

STRESS LEVELS

None	Low	Medium	High	Max	@$#%!

item / meal	*time*	*meds / supplements*	*dose*	*time*	*drinks*
					water
					① ② ③ ④ ⑤ ⑥ ⑦ ⑧ ⑨ ⑩
					caffeine
					① ② ③ ④ ⑤ ⑥ ⑦ ⑧ ⑨ ⑩
					alcohol
					① ② ③ ④ ⑤ ⑥ ⑦ ⑧ ⑨ ⑩

HORMONES

☐ Menstruating ☐ Menopause
☐ PMS ☐ N/A | other

COMPUTER / MOBILE DEVICE / TV

☐ None ☐ Some ☐ A lot Total Time: ______
☐ Sitting ☐ Standing ☐ Mixture Breaks every: ______

PHYSICAL ACTIVITY

☐ None ☐ Minimal ☐ Some ☐ Sweatin' ☐ I'm beat DETAILS: ____________

RELIEF MEASURES

☐ Medication ☐ Massage ☐ Sleep ☐ Exercise ☐ Water ☐ Cold/Ice
☐ Heat/Bath ☐ Other: ____________________
Did it work? ☐ Nope ☐ A bit ☐ Mostly ☐ 100%

Notes ☐ *See back notes*

START:		END:		DURATION:		DATE		*Entry #30*

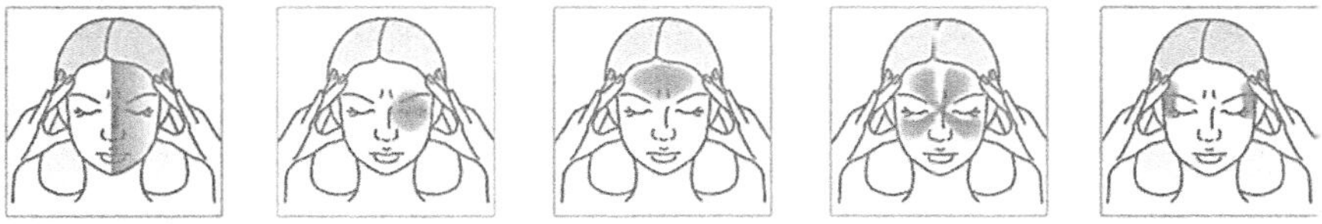

HOW WOULD YOU RATE...?

Mood	①	②	③	④	⑤
Energy	①	②	③	④	⑤
Mental clarity	①	②	③	④	⑤

PAIN LEVEL

1	2	3	4	5	6	7	8	9	10

Not too bad. *Well, I'm not enjoying this.* *Make it stop!*

ONSET

☐ Slow ☐ Average
☐ Rapid ☐ Sudden

DETAILED DESCRIPTION

☐ Constant ☐ Squeezing ☐ Throbbing ☐ Pounding ☐ Dull aching ☐ Burning
☐ Sharp ☐ Debilitating ☐ Other: ____________________

WHERE DOES IT HURT, EXACTLY?

OTHER SYMPTOMS

☐ Lightheaded ☐ Dizziness
☐ Light sensitivity ☐ Sound sensitivity
☐ Confusion ☐ Auras
☐ Muscle stiffness ☐ Muscle aches

FEELING SICK?

☐ Nausea ☐ Diarrhea ☐ Vomiting ☐ Sore throat ☐ Congestion ☐ Coughing
☐ Chills ☐ Fever ☐ Other: ____________________

SLEEP

hours ________ *quality* ① ② ③ ④ ⑤

WEATHER

☐ Cold ☐ Mild ☐ Hot Allergen levels: __________
☐ Dry ☐ Humid ☐ Wet BM Pressure: __________

STRESS LEVELS

None	Low	Medium	High	Max	@$#%!

item / meal	*time*	*meds / supplements*	*dose*	*time*	*drinks*
					water: ① ② ③ ④ ⑤ ⑥ ⑦ ⑧ ⑨ ⑩
					caffeine: ① ② ③ ④ ⑤ ⑥ ⑦ ⑧ ⑨ ⑩
					alcohol: ① ② ③ ④ ⑤ ⑥ ⑦ ⑧ ⑨ ⑩

HORMONES

☐ Menstruating ☐ Menopause
☐ PMS ☐ N/A | other

COMPUTER / MOBILE DEVICE / TV

☐ None ☐ Some ☐ A lot Total Time: ______
☐ Sitting ☐ Standing ☐ Mixture Breaks every: ______

PHYSICAL ACTIVITY

☐ None ☐ Minimal ☐ Some ☐ Sweatin' ☐ I'm beat DETAILS: ____________________

RELIEF MEASURES

☐ Medication ☐ Massage ☐ Sleep ☐ Exercise ☐ Water ☐ Cold/Ice
☐ Heat/Bath ☐ Other: ____________________
Did it work? ☐ Nope ☐ A bit ☐ Mostly ☐ 100%

Notes ☐ *See back notes*

START: ______ END: ______ DURATION: ______ DATE ______ *Entry #31*

MIGRAINE | CLUSTER | TENSION | SINUS | TMJ

HOW WOULD YOU RATE...?

Mood	1	2	3	4	5
Energy	1	2	3	4	5
Mental clarity	1	2	3	4	5

PAIN LEVEL

1	2	3	4	5	6	7	8	9	10

Not too bad. *Well, I'm not enjoying this.* *Make it stop!*

ONSET

☐ Slow ☐ Average
☐ Rapid ☐ Sudden

DETAILED DESCRIPTION

☐ Constant ☐ Squeezing ☐ Throbbing ☐ Pounding ☐ Dull aching ☐ Burning
☐ Sharp ☐ Debilitating ☐ Other: ____________

WHERE DOES IT HURT, EXACTLY?

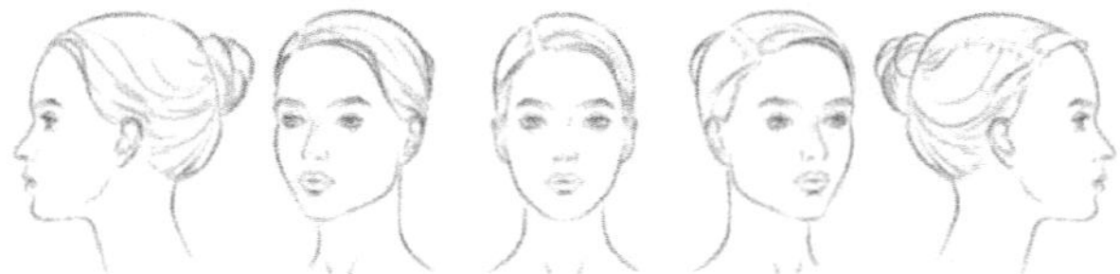

OTHER SYMPTOMS

☐ Lightheaded ☐ Dizziness
☐ Light sensitivity ☐ Sound sensitivity
☐ Confusion ☐ Auras
☐ Muscle stiffness ☐ Muscle aches

FEELING SICK?

☐ Nausea ☐ Diarrhea ☐ Vomiting ☐ Sore throat ☐ Congestion ☐ Coughing
☐ Chills ☐ Fever ☐ Other: ____________

SLEEP

hours ______ *quality* 1 2 3 4 5

WEATHER

☐ Cold ☐ Mild ☐ Hot Allergen levels: ______
☐ Dry ☐ Humid ☐ Wet BM Pressure: ______

STRESS LEVELS

None	Low	Medium	High	Max	@$#%!

item / meal	*time*	*meds / supplements*	*dose*	*time*	*drinks*
					water: 1 2 3 4 5 6 7 8 9 10
					caffeine: 1 2 3 4 5 6 7 8 9 10
					alcohol: 1 2 3 4 5 6 7 8 9 10

HORMONES

☐ Menstruating ☐ Menopause
☐ PMS ☐ N/A | other

COMPUTER / MOBILE DEVICE / TV

☐ None ☐ Some ☐ A lot Total Time: ______
☐ Sitting ☐ Standing ☐ Mixture Breaks every: ______

PHYSICAL ACTIVITY

☐ None ☐ Minimal ☐ Some ☐ Sweatin' ☐ I'm beat DETAILS: ____________

RELIEF MEASURES

☐ Medication ☐ Massage ☐ Sleep ☐ Exercise ☐ Water ☐ Cold/Ice
☐ Heat/Bath ☐ Other: ____________
Did it work? ☐ Nope ☐ A bit ☐ Mostly ☐ 100%

Notes

☐ *See back notes*

START:		END:		DURATION:		DATE		*Entry #32*

MIGRAINE CLUSTER TENSION SINUS TMJ

HOW WOULD YOU RATE...?

Mood	1	2	3	4	5
Energy	1	2	3	4	5
Mental clarity	1	2	3	4	5

PAIN LEVEL

1	2	3	4	5	6	7	8	9	10

Not too bad. *Well, I'm not enjoying this.* *Make it stop!*

ONSET

☐ Slow ☐ Average
☐ Rapid ☐ Sudden

DETAILED DESCRIPTION

☐ Constant ☐ Squeezing ☐ Throbbing ☐ Pounding ☐ Dull aching ☐ Burning
☐ Sharp ☐ Debilitating ☐ Other: ______

WHERE DOES IT HURT, EXACTLY?

OTHER SYMPTOMS

☐ Lightheaded ☐ Dizziness
☐ Light sensitivity ☐ Sound sensitivity
☐ Confusion ☐ Auras
☐ Muscle stiffness ☐ Muscle aches

FEELING SICK?

☐ Nausea ☐ Diarrhea ☐ Vomiting ☐ Sore throat ☐ Congestion ☐ Coughing
☐ Chills ☐ Fever ☐ Other: ______

SLEEP

hours ______ *quality* 1 2 3 4 5

WEATHER

☐ Cold ☐ Mild ☐ Hot Allergen levels: ______
☐ Dry ☐ Humid ☐ Wet BM Pressure: ______

STRESS LEVELS

None	Low	Medium	High	Max	@$#%!

item / meal	*time*	*meds / supplements*	*dose*	*time*	*drinks*
					water: 1 2 3 4 5 6 7 8 9 10
					caffeine: 1 2 3 4 5 6 7 8 9 10
					alcohol: 1 2 3 4 5 6 7 8 9 10

HORMONES

☐ Menstruating ☐ Menopause
☐ PMS ☐ N/A | other

COMPUTER / MOBILE DEVICE / TV

☐ None ☐ Some ☐ A lot Total Time: ______
☐ Sitting ☐ Standing ☐ Mixture Breaks every: ______

PHYSICAL ACTIVITY

☐ None ☐ Minimal ☐ Some ☐ Sweatin' ☐ I'm beat DETAILS: ______

RELIEF MEASURES

☐ Medication ☐ Massage ☐ Sleep ☐ Exercise ☐ Water ☐ Cold/Ice
☐ Heat/Bath ☐ Other: ______
Did it work? ☐ Nope ☐ A bit ☐ Mostly ☐ 100%

Notes ☐ *See back notes*

START:		END:		DURATION:		DATE		*Entry #33*

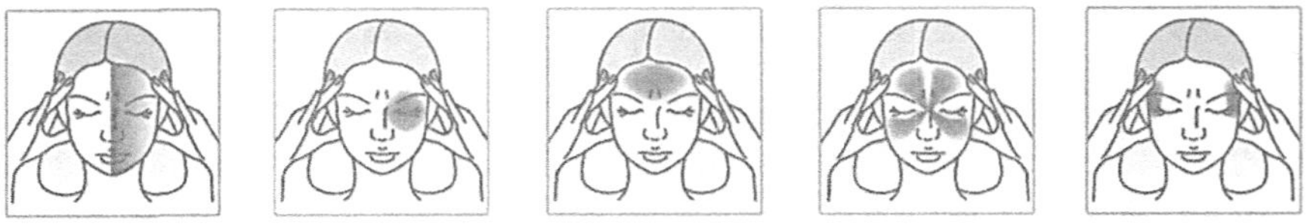

MIGRAINE CLUSTER TENSION SINUS TMJ

HOW WOULD YOU RATE...?

Mood	①	②	③	④	⑤
Energy	①	②	③	④	⑤
Mental clarity	①	②	③	④	⑤

PAIN LEVEL

1	2	3	4	5	6	7	8	9	10

Not too bad. *Well, I'm not enjoying this.* *Make it stop!*

ONSET

☐ Slow ☐ Average
☐ Rapid ☐ Sudden

DETAILED DESCRIPTION

☐ Constant ☐ Squeezing ☐ Throbbing ☐ Pounding ☐ Dull aching ☐ Burning
☐ Sharp ☐ Debilitating ☐ Other: ____________________

WHERE DOES IT HURT, EXACTLY?

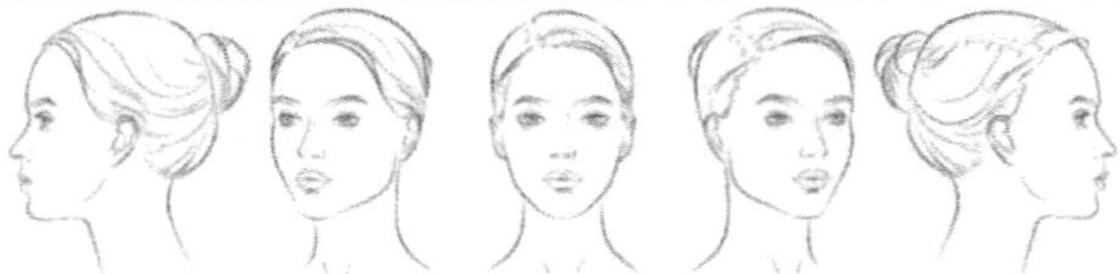

OTHER SYMPTOMS

☐ Lightheaded ☐ Dizziness
☐ Light sensitivity ☐ Sound sensitivity
☐ Confusion ☐ Auras
☐ Muscle stiffness ☐ Muscle aches

FEELING SICK?

☐ Nausea ☐ Diarrhea ☐ Vomiting ☐ Sore throat ☐ Congestion ☐ Coughing
☐ Chills ☐ Fever ☐ Other: ____________________

SLEEP

hours ________ *quality* ① ② ③ ④ ⑤

WEATHER

☐ Cold ☐ Mild ☐ Hot Allergen levels: ____________
☐ Dry ☐ Humid ☐ Wet BM Pressure: ____________

STRESS LEVELS

None	Low	Medium	High	Max	@$#%!

item / meal	*time*	*meds / supplements*	*dose*	*time*	*drinks*
					water
					① ② ③ ④ ⑤ ⑥ ⑦ ⑧ ⑨ ⑩
					caffeine
					① ② ③ ④ ⑤ ⑥ ⑦ ⑧ ⑨ ⑩
					alcohol
					① ② ③ ④ ⑤ ⑥ ⑦ ⑧ ⑨ ⑩

HORMONES

☐ Menstruating ☐ Menopause
☐ PMS ☐ N/A | other

COMPUTER / MOBILE DEVICE / TV

☐ None ☐ Some ☐ A lot Total Time: _____
☐ Sitting ☐ Standing ☐ Mixture Breaks every: _____

PHYSICAL ACTIVITY

☐ None ☐ Minimal ☐ Some ☐ Sweatin' ☐ I'm beat DETAILS: ____________

RELIEF MEASURES

☐ Medication ☐ Massage ☐ Sleep ☐ Exercise ☐ Water ☐ Cold/Ice
☐ Heat/Bath ☐ Other: ____________________
Did it work? ☐ Nope ☐ A bit ☐ Mostly ☐ 100%

Notes ☐ *See back notes*

START:		END:		DURATION:		DATE		*Entry #34*

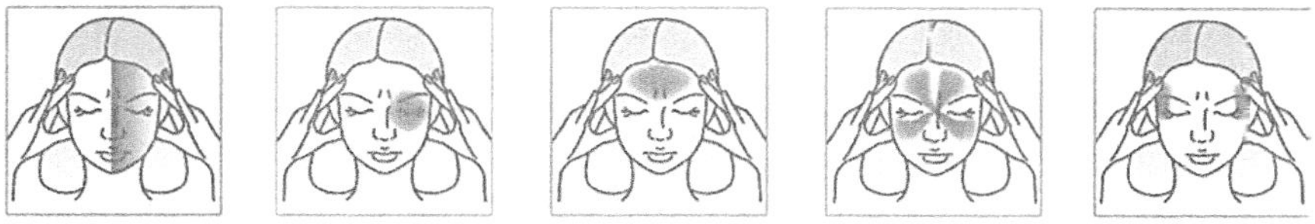

MIGRAINE CLUSTER TENSION SINUS TMJ

HOW WOULD YOU RATE...?

Mood	1	2	3	4	5
Energy	1	2	3	4	5
Mental clarity	1	2	3	4	5

PAIN LEVEL

1	2	3	4	5	6	7	8	9	10

Not too bad. *Well, I'm not enjoying this.* *Make it stop!*

ONSET

☐ Slow ☐ Average
☐ Rapid ☐ Sudden

DETAILED DESCRIPTION

☐ Constant ☐ Squeezing ☐ Throbbing ☐ Pounding ☐ Dull aching ☐ Burning
☐ Sharp ☐ Debilitating ☐ Other: ____________________

WHERE DOES IT HURT, EXACTLY?

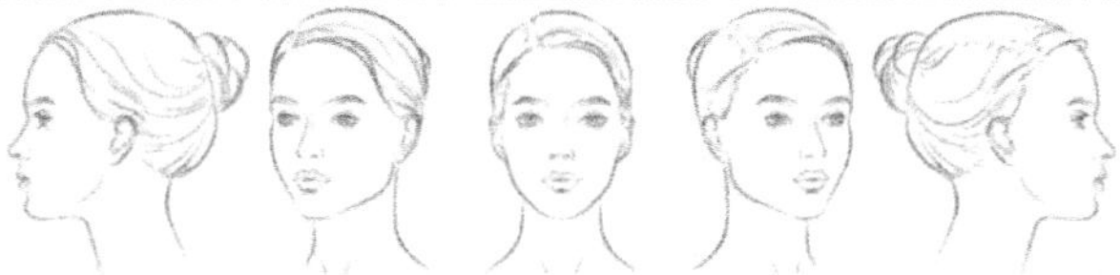

OTHER SYMPTOMS

☐ Lightheaded ☐ Dizziness
☐ Light sensitivity ☐ Sound sensitivity
☐ Confusion ☐ Auras
☐ Muscle stiffness ☐ Muscle aches

FEELING SICK?

☐ Nausea ☐ Diarrhea ☐ Vomiting ☐ Sore throat ☐ Congestion ☐ Coughing
☐ Chills ☐ Fever ☐ Other: ____________________

SLEEP

hours ________ *quality* 1 2 3 4 5

WEATHER

☐ Cold ☐ Mild ☐ Hot Allergen levels: ____________
☐ Dry ☐ Humid ☐ Wet BM Pressure: ____________

STRESS LEVELS

None	Low	Medium	High	Max	@$#%!

item / meal	*time*	*meds / supplements*	*dose*	*time*	*drinks*
					water
					1 2 3 4 5 6 7 8 9 10
					caffeine
					1 2 3 4 5 6 7 8 9 10
					alcohol
					1 2 3 4 5 6 7 8 9 10

HORMONES

☐ Menstruating ☐ Menopause
☐ PMS ☐ N/A | other

COMPUTER / MOBILE DEVICE / TV

☐ None ☐ Some ☐ A lot Total Time: ______
☐ Sitting ☐ Standing ☐ Mixture Breaks every: ______

PHYSICAL ACTIVITY

☐ None ☐ Minimal ☐ Some ☐ Sweatin' ☐ I'm beat DETAILS: ____________________

RELIEF MEASURES

☐ Medication ☐ Massage ☐ Sleep ☐ Exercise ☐ Water ☐ Cold/Ice
☐ Heat/Bath ☐ Other: ____________________

Did it work? ☐ Nope ☐ A bit ☐ Mostly ☐ 100%

Notes ☐ *See back notes*

START: | END: | DURATION: | DATE | *Entry #35*

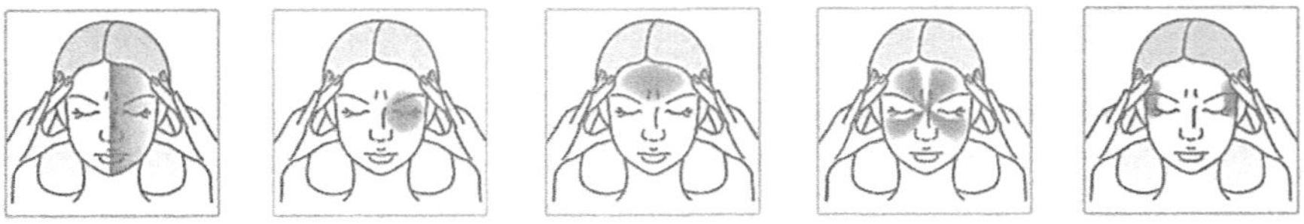

MIGRAINE | CLUSTER | TENSION | SINUS | TMJ

HOW WOULD YOU RATE...?

Mood	① ② ③ ④ ⑤
Energy	① ② ③ ④ ⑤
Mental clarity	① ② ③ ④ ⑤

PAIN LEVEL

1	2	3	4	5	6	7	8	9	10

Not too bad. *Well, I'm not enjoying this.* *Make it stop!*

ONSET

☐ Slow ☐ Average
☐ Rapid ☐ Sudden

DETAILED DESCRIPTION

☐ Constant ☐ Squeezing ☐ Throbbing ☐ Pounding ☐ Dull aching ☐ Burning
☐ Sharp ☐ Debilitating ☐ Other: ____________

WHERE DOES IT HURT, EXACTLY?

OTHER SYMPTOMS

☐ Lightheaded ☐ Dizziness
☐ Light sensitivity ☐ Sound sensitivity
☐ Confusion ☐ Auras
☐ Muscle stiffness ☐ Muscle aches

FEELING SICK?

☐ Nausea ☐ Diarrhea ☐ Vomiting ☐ Sore throat ☐ Congestion ☐ Coughing
☐ Chills ☐ Fever ☐ Other: ____________

SLEEP

hours ______ *quality* ① ② ③ ④ ⑤

WEATHER

☐ Cold ☐ Mild ☐ Hot Allergen levels: ______
☐ Dry ☐ Humid ☐ Wet BM Pressure: ______

STRESS LEVELS

None	Low	Medium	High	Max	@$#%!

item / meal	*time*	*meds / supplements*	*dose*	*time*	*drinks*
					water
					① ② ③ ④ ⑤ ⑥ ⑦ ⑧ ⑨ ⑩
					caffeine
					① ② ③ ④ ⑤ ⑥ ⑦ ⑧ ⑨ ⑩
					alcohol
					① ② ③ ④ ⑤ ⑥ ⑦ ⑧ ⑨ ⑩

HORMONES

☐ Menstruating ☐ Menopause
☐ PMS ☐ N/A | other

COMPUTER / MOBILE DEVICE / TV

☐ None ☐ Some ☐ A lot Total Time: ______
☐ Sitting ☐ Standing ☐ Mixture Breaks every: ______

PHYSICAL ACTIVITY

☐ None ☐ Minimal ☐ Some ☐ Sweatin' ☐ I'm beat DETAILS: ____________

RELIEF MEASURES

☐ Medication ☐ Massage ☐ Sleep ☐ Exercise ☐ Water ☐ Cold/Ice
☐ Heat/Bath ☐ Other: ____________
Did it work? ☐ Nope ☐ A bit ☐ Mostly ☐ 100%

Notes ☐ *See back notes*

START:		END:		DURATION:		DATE		*Entry #36*

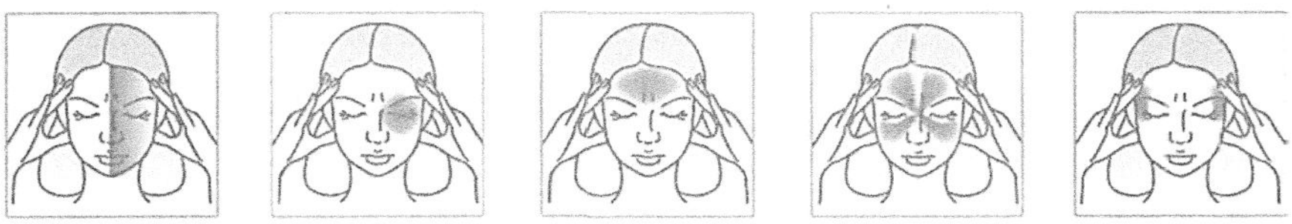

MIGRAINE CLUSTER TENSION SINUS TMJ

HOW WOULD YOU RATE...?

- Mood ① ② ③ ④ ⑤
- Energy ① ② ③ ④ ⑤
- Mental clarity ① ② ③ ④ ⑤

PAIN LEVEL

1	2	3	4	5	6	7	8	9	10

Not too bad. *Wel, I'm not enjoying this.* *Make it stop.*

ONSET

☐ Slow ☐ Average
☐ Rapid ☐ Sudden

DETAILED DESCRIPTION

☐ Constant ☐ Squeezing ☐ Throbbing ☐ Pounding ☐ Dull aching ☐ Burning
☐ Sharp ☐ Debilitating ☐ Other: ____________________

WHERE DOES IT HURT, EXACTLY?

OTHER SYMPTOMS

☐ Lightheaded ☐ Dizziness
☐ Light sensitivity ☐ Sound sensitivity
☐ Confusion ☐ Auras
☐ Muscle stiffness ☐ Muscle aches

FEELING SICK?

☐ Nausea ☐ Diarrhea ☐ Vomiting ☐ Sore throat ☐ Congestion ☐ Coughing
☐ Chills ☐ Fever ☐ Other: ____________________

SLEEP

hours ________ *quality* ① ② ③ ④ ⑤

WEATHER

☐ Cold ☐ Mild ☐ Hot Allergen levels: ____________
☐ Dry ☐ Humid ☐ Wet BM Pressure: ____________

STRESS LEVELS

None	Low	Medium	High	Max	@$#%!

item / meal	*time*	*meds / supplements*	*dose*	*time*	*drinks*
					water
					① ② ③ ④ ⑤ ⑥ ⑦ ⑧ ⑨ ⑩
					caffeine
					① ② ③ ④ ⑤ ⑥ ⑦ ⑧ ⑨ ⑩
					alcohol
					① ② ③ ④ ⑤ ⑥ ⑦ ⑧ ⑨ ⑩

HORMONES

☐ Menstruating ☐ Menopause
☐ PMS ☐ N/A | other

COMPUTER / MOBILE DEVICE / TV

☐ None ☐ Some ☐ A lot Total Time: ______
☐ Sitting ☐ Standing ☐ Mixture Breaks every: ______

PHYSICAL ACTIVITY

☐ None ☐ Minimal ☐ Some ☐ Sweatin' ☐ I'm beat DETAILS: ____________

RELIEF MEASURES

☐ Medication ☐ Massage ☐ Sleep ☐ Exercise ☐ Water ☐ Cold/Ice
☐ Heat/Bath ☐ Other: ____________________
Did it work? ☐ Nope ☐ A bit ☐ Mostly ☐ 100%

Notes ☐ *See back notes*

START:	END:	DURATION:	DATE	*Entry #37*

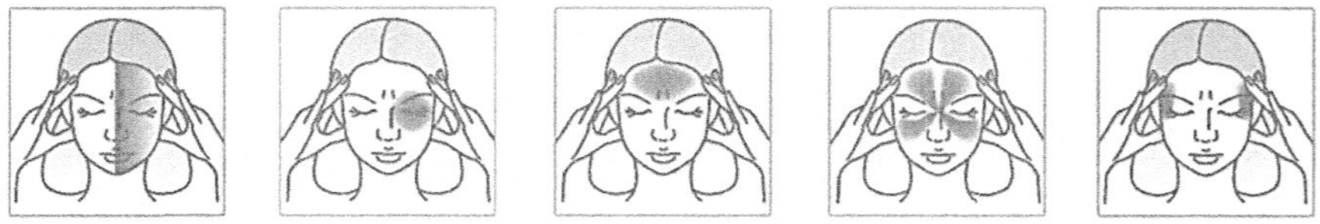

MIGRAINE | CLUSTER | TENSION | SINUS | TMJ

HOW WOULD YOU RATE...?	
Mood	① ② ③ ④ ⑤
Energy	① ② ③ ④ ⑤
Mental clarity	① ② ③ ④ ⑤

PAIN LEVEL

1	2	3	4	5	6	7	8	9	10

Not too bad. *Well, I'm not enjoying this.* *Make it stop!*

ONSET

☐ Slow ☐ Average
☐ Rapid ☐ Sudden

DETAILED DESCRIPTION

☐ Constant ☐ Squeezing ☐ Throbbing ☐ Pounding ☐ Dull aching ☐ Burning
☐ Sharp ☐ Debilitating ☐ Other: ______

WHERE DOES IT HURT, EXACTLY?

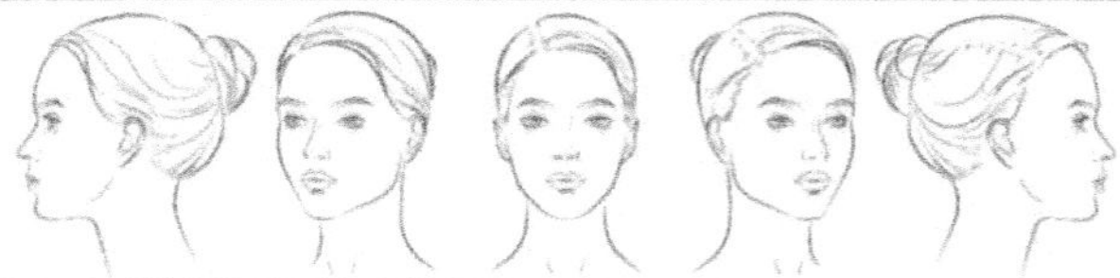

OTHER SYMPTOMS

☐ Lightheaded ☐ Dizziness
☐ Light sensitivity ☐ Sound sensitivity
☐ Confusion ☐ Auras
☐ Muscle stiffness ☐ Muscle aches

FEELING SICK?

☐ Nausea ☐ Diarrhea ☐ Vomiting ☐ Sore throat ☐ Congestion ☐ Coughing
☐ Chills ☐ Fever ☐ Other: ______

SLEEP

hours ______ *quality* ① ② ③ ④ ⑤

WEATHER

☐ Cold ☐ Mild ☐ Hot Allergen levels: ______
☐ Dry ☐ Humid ☐ Wet BM Pressure: ______

STRESS LEVELS

None	Low	Medium	High	Max	@$#%!

item / meal	*time*	*meds / supplements*	*dose*	*time*	*drinks*
					water
					① ② ③ ④ ⑤ ⑥ ⑦ ⑧ ⑨ ⑩
					caffeine
					① ② ③ ④ ⑤ ⑥ ⑦ ⑧ ⑨ ⑩
					alcohol
					① ② ③ ④ ⑤ ⑥ ⑦ ⑧ ⑨ ⑩

HORMONES

☐ Menstruating ☐ Menopause
☐ PMS ☐ N/A | other

COMPUTER / MOBILE DEVICE / TV

☐ None ☐ Some ☐ A lot Total Time: ______
☐ Sitting ☐ Standing ☐ Mixture Breaks every: ______

PHYSICAL ACTIVITY

☐ None ☐ Minimal ☐ Some ☐ Sweatin' ☐ I'm beat DETAILS: ______

RELIEF MEASURES

☐ Medication ☐ Massage ☐ Sleep ☐ Exercise ☐ Water ☐ Cold/Ice
☐ Heat/Bath ☐ Other: ______
Did it work? ☐ Nope ☐ A bit ☐ Mostly ☐ 100%

Notes

☐ *See back notes*

START: ______ END: ______ DURATION: ______ DATE ______ *Entry #38*

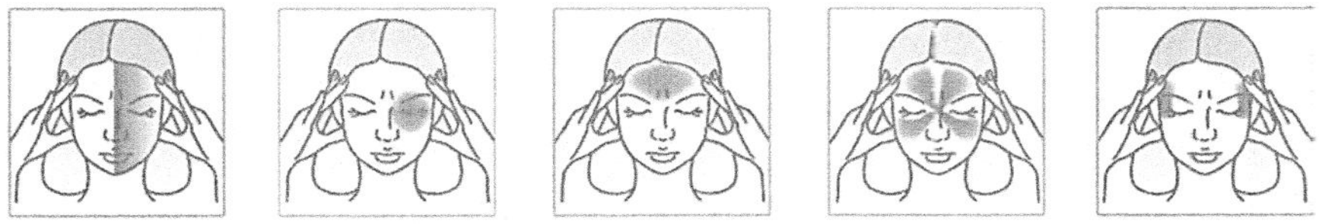

MIGRAINE | CLUSTER | TENSION | SINUS | TMJ

HOW WOULD YOU RATE...?

Mood	① ② ③ ④ ⑤
Energy	① ② ③ ④ ⑤
Mental clarity	① ② ③ ④ ⑤

PAIN LEVEL

1	2	3	4	5	6	7	8	9	10

Not too bad. *We'l, I'm not enjoying this.* *Make it stop.*

ONSET

☐ Slow ☐ Average
☐ Rapid ☐ Sudden

DETAILED DESCRIPTION

☐ Constant ☐ Squeezing ☐ Throbbing ☐ Pounding ☐ Dull aching ☐ Burning
☐ Sharp ☐ Debilitating ☐ Other: ______________________________

WHERE DOES IT HURT, EXACTLY?

OTHER SYMPTOMS

☐ Lightheaded ☐ Dizziness
☐ Light sensitivity ☐ Sound sensitivity
☐ Confusion ☐ Auras
☐ Muscle stiffness ☐ Muscle aches

FEELING SICK?

☐ Nausea ☐ Diarrhea ☐ Vomiting ☐ Sore throat ☐ Congestion ☐ Coughing
☐ Chills ☐ Fever ☐ Other: ______________________________

SLEEP

hours ________ *quality* ① ② ③ ④ ⑤

WEATHER

☐ Cold ☐ Mild ☐ Hot Allergen levels: ____________
☐ Dry ☐ Humid ☐ Wet BM Pressure: ____________

STRESS LEVELS

None	Low	Medium	High	Max	@$#%!

item / meal	*time*	*meds / supplements*	*dose*	*time*	*drinks*
					water ① ② ③ ④ ⑤ ⑥ ⑦ ⑧ ⑨ ⑩
					caffeine ① ② ③ ④ ⑤ ⑥ ⑦ ⑧ ⑨ ⑩
					alcohol ① ② ③ ④ ⑤ ⑥ ⑦ ⑧ ⑨ ⑩

HORMONES

☐ Menstruating ☐ Menopause
☐ PMS ☐ N/A | other

COMPUTER / MOBILE DEVICE / TV

☐ None ☐ Some ☐ A lot Total Time: ______
☐ Sitting ☐ Standing ☐ Mixture Breaks every: ______

PHYSICAL ACTIVITY

☐ None ☐ Minimal ☐ Some ☐ Sweatin' ☐ I'm beat DETAILS: ______________

RELIEF MEASURES

☐ Medication ☐ Massage ☐ Sleep ☐ Exercise ☐ Water ☐ Cold/Ice
☐ Heat/Bath ☐ Other: ______________________________
Did it work? ☐ Nope ☐ A bit ☐ Mostly ☐ 100%

Notes ☐ *See back notes*

START:		END:		DURATION:		DATE		*Entry #39*

MIGRAINE

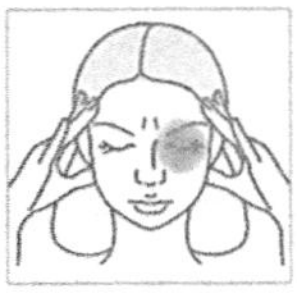
CLUSTER

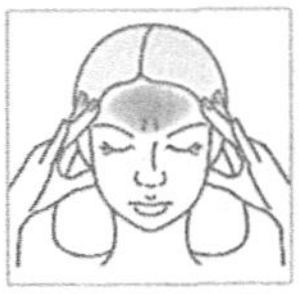
TENSION

SINUS

TMJ

HOW WOULD YOU RATE...?					
Mood	1	2	3	4	5
Energy	1	2	3	4	5
Mental clarity	1	2	3	4	5

PAIN LEVEL

1	2	3	4	5	6	7	8	9	10

Not too bad. *Well, I'm not enjoying this.* *Make it stop!*

ONSET

☐ Slow ☐ Average
☐ Rapid ☐ Sudden

DETAILED DESCRIPTION

☐ Constant ☐ Squeezing ☐ Throbbing ☐ Pounding ☐ Dull aching ☐ Burning
☐ Sharp ☐ Debilitating ☐ Other: ____________________

WHERE DOES IT HURT, EXACTLY?

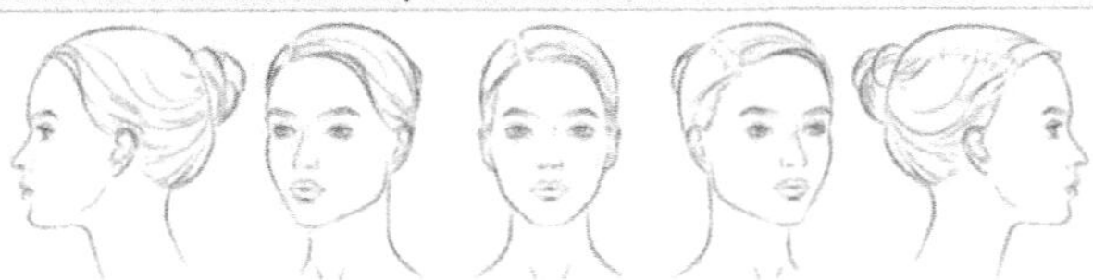

OTHER SYMPTOMS

☐ Lightheaded ☐ Dizziness
☐ Light sensitivity ☐ Sound sensitivity
☐ Confusion ☐ Auras
☐ Muscle stiffness ☐ Muscle aches

FEELING SICK?

☐ Nausea ☐ Diarrhea ☐ Vomiting ☐ Sore throat ☐ Congestion ☐ Coughing
☐ Chills ☐ Fever ☐ Other: ____________________

SLEEP

hours ________ *quality* 1 2 3 4 5

WEATHER

☐ Cold ☐ Mild ☐ Hot Allergen levels: ____________
☐ Dry ☐ Humid ☐ Wet BM Pressure: ____________

STRESS LEVELS

None	Low	Medium	High	Max	@$#%!

item / meal	*time*	*meds / supplements*	*dose*	*time*	*drinks*
					water
					1 2 3 4 5 6 7 8 9 10
					caffeine
					1 2 3 4 5 6 7 8 9 10
					alcohol
					1 2 3 4 5 6 7 8 9 10

HORMONES

☐ Menstruating ☐ Menopause
☐ PMS ☐ N/A | other

COMPUTER / MOBILE DEVICE / TV

☐ None ☐ Some ☐ A lot Total Time: ______
☐ Sitting ☐ Standing ☐ Mixture Breaks every: ______

PHYSICAL ACTIVITY

☐ None ☐ Minimal ☐ Some ☐ Sweatin' ☐ I'm beat DETAILS: ____________

RELIEF MEASURES

☐ Medication ☐ Massage ☐ Sleep ☐ Exercise ☐ Water ☐ Cold/Ice
☐ Heat/Bath ☐ Other: ____________________
Did it work? ☐ Nope ☐ A bit ☐ Mostly ☐ 100%

Notes ☐ *See back notes*

START:	END:	DURATION:	DATE	*Entry #40*

MIGRAINE CLUSTER TENSION SINUS TMJ

HOW WOULD YOU RATE...?	
Mood	① ② ③ ④ ⑤
Energy	① ② ③ ④ ⑤
Mental clarity	① ② ③ ④ ⑤

PAIN LEVEL

1	2	3	4	5	6	7	8	9	10

Not too bad. *Well, I'm not enjoying this.* *Make it stop!*

ONSET

☐ Slow ☐ Average
☐ Rapid ☐ Sudden

DETAILED DESCRIPTION

☐ Constant ☐ Squeezing ☐ Throbbing ☐ Pounding ☐ Dull aching ☐ Burning
☐ Sharp ☐ Debilitating ☐ Other: ____________________

WHERE DOES IT HURT, EXACTLY?

OTHER SYMPTOMS

☐ Lightheaded ☐ Dizziness
☐ Light sensitivity ☐ Sound sensitivity
☐ Confusion ☐ Auras
☐ Muscle stiffness ☐ Muscle aches

FEELING SICK?

☐ Nausea ☐ Diarrhea ☐ Vomiting ☐ Sore throat ☐ Congestion ☐ Coughing
☐ Chills ☐ Fever ☐ Other: ____________________

SLEEP

hours ________ *quality* ① ② ③ ④ ⑤

WEATHER

☐ Cold ☐ Mild ☐ Hot Allergen levels: __________
☐ Dry ☐ Humid ☐ Wet BM Pressure: __________

STRESS LEVELS

None	Low	Medium	High	Max	@$#%!

item / meal	*time*	*meds / supplements*	*dose*	*time*	*drinks*
					water
					① ② ③ ④ ⑤ ⑥ ⑦ ⑧ ⑨ ⑩
					caffeine
					① ② ③ ④ ⑤ ⑥ ⑦ ⑧ ⑨ ⑩
					alcohol
					① ② ③ ④ ⑤ ⑥ ⑦ ⑧ ⑨ ⑩

HORMONES

☐ Menstruating ☐ Menopause
☐ PMS ☐ N/A | other

COMPUTER / MOBILE DEVICE / TV

☐ None ☐ Some ☐ A lot Total Time: ______
☐ Sitting ☐ Standing ☐ Mixture Breaks every: ______

PHYSICAL ACTIVITY

☐ None ☐ Minimal ☐ Some ☐ Sweatin' ☐ I'm beat DETAILS: ____________________

RELIEF MEASURES

☐ Medication ☐ Massage ☐ Sleep ☐ Exercise ☐ Water ☐ Cold/Ice
☐ Heat/Bath ☐ Other: ____________________
Did it work? ☐ Nope ☐ A bit ☐ Mostly ☐ 100%

Notes ☐ *See back notes*

START:		END:		DURATION:		DATE		*Entry #41*

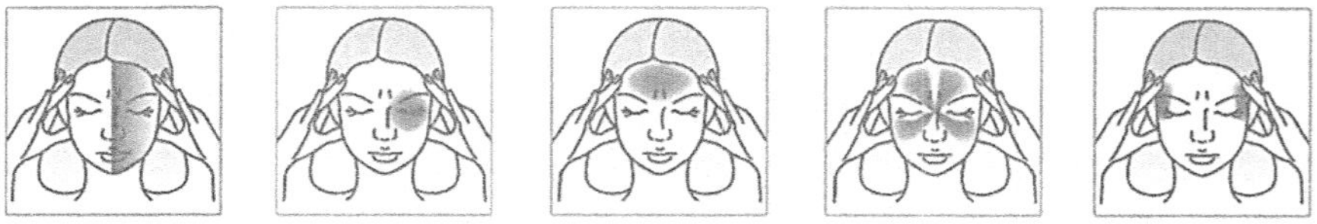

MIGRAINE CLUSTER TENSION SINUS TMJ

HOW WOULD YOU RATE...?

Mood	① ② ③ ④ ⑤
Energy	① ② ③ ④ ⑤
Mental clarity	① ② ③ ④ ⑤

PAIN LEVEL

1	2	3	4	5	6	7	8	9	10

Not too bad. *Well, I'm not enjoying this.* *Make it stop!*

ONSET

☐ Slow ☐ Average
☐ Rapid ☐ Sudden

DETAILED DESCRIPTION

☐ Constant ☐ Squeezing ☐ Throbbing ☐ Pounding ☐ Dull aching ☐ Burning
☐ Sharp ☐ Debilitating ☐ Other: ______

WHERE DOES IT HURT, EXACTLY?

OTHER SYMPTOMS

☐ Lightheaded ☐ Dizziness
☐ Light sensitivity ☐ Sound sensitivity
☐ Confusion ☐ Auras
☐ Muscle stiffness ☐ Muscle aches

FEELING SICK?

☐ Nausea ☐ Diarrhea ☐ Vomiting ☐ Sore throat ☐ Congestion ☐ Coughing
☐ Chills ☐ Fever ☐ Other: ______

SLEEP

hours ______ *quality* ① ② ③ ④ ⑤

WEATHER

☐ Cold ☐ Mild ☐ Hot Allergen levels: ______
☐ Dry ☐ Humid ☐ Wet BM Pressure: ______

STRESS LEVELS

None	Low	Medium	High	Max	@$#%!

item / meal	*time*	*meds / supplements*	*dose*	*time*	*drinks*
					water
					① ② ③ ④ ⑤ ⑥ ⑦ ⑧ ⑨ ⑩
					caffeine
					① ② ③ ④ ⑤ ⑥ ⑦ ⑧ ⑨ ⑩
					alcohol
					① ② ③ ④ ⑤ ⑥ ⑦ ⑧ ⑨ ⑩

HORMONES

☐ Menstruating ☐ Menopause
☐ PMS ☐ N/A | other

COMPUTER / MOBILE DEVICE / TV

☐ None ☐ Some ☐ A lot Total Time: ______
☐ Sitting ☐ Standing ☐ Mixture Breaks every: ______

PHYSICAL ACTIVITY

☐ None ☐ Minimal ☐ Some ☐ Sweatin' ☐ I'm beat DETAILS: ______

RELIEF MEASURES

☐ Medication ☐ Massage ☐ Sleep ☐ Exercise ☐ Water ☐ Cold/Ice
☐ Heat/Bath ☐ Other: ______
Did it work? ☐ Nope ☐ A bit ☐ Mostly ☐ 100%

Notes ☐ *See back notes*

START: ______ END: ______ DURATION: ______ DATE ______ *Entry #42*

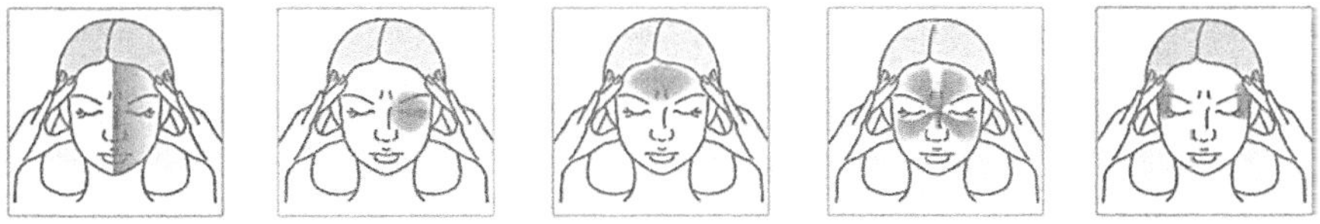

MIGRAINE | CLUSTER | TENSION | SINUS | TMJ

HOW WOULD YOU RATE...?					
Mood	1	2	3	4	5
Energy	1	2	3	4	5
Mental clarity	1	2	3	4	5

PAIN LEVEL

1	2	3	4	5	6	7	8	9	10

Not too bad. *Well, I'm not enjoying this.* *Make it stop!*

ONSET

☐ Slow ☐ Average
☐ Rapid ☐ Sudden

DETAILED DESCRIPTION

☐ Constant ☐ Squeezing ☐ Throbbing ☐ Pounding ☐ Dull aching ☐ Burning
☐ Sharp ☐ Debilitating ☐ Other: ______

WHERE DOES IT HURT, EXACTLY?

OTHER SYMPTOMS

☐ Lightheaded ☐ Dizziness
☐ Light sensitivity ☐ Sound sensitivity
☐ Confusion ☐ Auras
☐ Muscle stiffness ☐ Muscle aches

FEELING SICK?

☐ Nausea ☐ Diarrhea ☐ Vomiting ☐ Sore throat ☐ Congestion ☐ Coughing
☐ Chills ☐ Fever ☐ Other: ______

SLEEP

hours ______ *quality* 1 2 3 4 5

WEATHER

☐ Cold ☐ Mild ☐ Hot Allergen levels: ______
☐ Dry ☐ Humid ☐ Wet BM Pressure: ______

STRESS LEVELS

None	Low	Medium	High	Max	@$#%!

item / meal	*time*	*meds / supplements*	*dose*	*time*	*drinks*
					water: 1 2 3 4 5 6 7 8 9 10
					caffeine: 1 2 3 4 5 6 7 8 9 10
					alcohol: 1 2 3 4 5 6 7 8 9 10

HORMONES

☐ Menstruating ☐ Menopause
☐ PMS ☐ N/A | other

COMPUTER / MOBILE DEVICE / TV

☐ None ☐ Some ☐ A lot Total Time: ______
☐ Sitting ☐ Standing ☐ Mixture Breaks every: ______

PHYSICAL ACTIVITY

☐ None ☐ Minimal ☐ Some ☐ Sweatin' ☐ I'm beat DETAILS: ______

RELIEF MEASURES

☐ Medication ☐ Massage ☐ Sleep ☐ Exercise ☐ Water ☐ Cold/Ice
☐ Heat/Bath ☐ Other: ______
Did it work? ☐ Nope ☐ A bit ☐ Mostly ☐ 100%

Notes ☐ *See back notes*

START:		END:		DURATION:		DATE		*Entry #43*

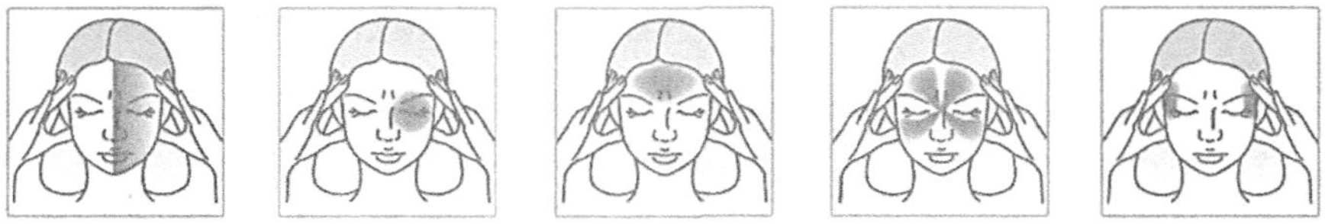

MIGRAINE CLUSTER TENSION SINUS TMJ

HOW WOULD YOU RATE...?

Mood	① ② ③ ④ ⑤
Energy	① ② ③ ④ ⑤
Mental clarity	① ② ③ ④ ⑤

PAIN LEVEL

1	2	3	4	5	6	7	8	9	10

Not too bad. *Well, I'm not enjoying this.* *Make it stop!*

ONSET

☐ Slow ☐ Average
☐ Rapid ☐ Sudden

DETAILED DESCRIPTION

☐ Constant ☐ Squeezing ☐ Throbbing ☐ Pounding ☐ Dull aching ☐ Burning
☐ Sharp ☐ Debilitating ☐ Other: ______________________________

WHERE DOES IT HURT, EXACTLY?

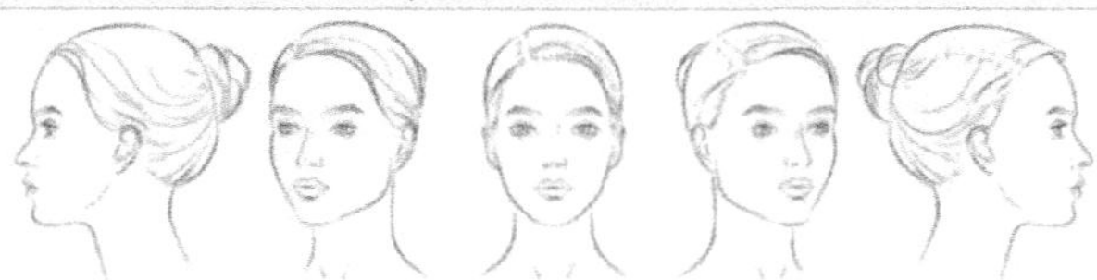

OTHER SYMPTOMS

☐ Lightheaded ☐ Dizziness
☐ Light sensitivity ☐ Sound sensitivity
☐ Confusion ☐ Auras
☐ Muscle stiffness ☐ Muscle aches

FEELING SICK?

☐ Nausea ☐ Diarrhea ☐ Vomiting ☐ Sore throat ☐ Congestion ☐ Coughing
☐ Chills ☐ Fever ☐ Other: ______________________________

SLEEP

hours ________ *quality* ① ② ③ ④ ⑤

WEATHER

☐ Cold ☐ Mild ☐ Hot Allergen levels: ____________
☐ Dry ☐ Humid ☐ Wet BM Pressure: ____________

STRESS LEVELS

None	Low	Medium	High	Max	@$#%!

item / meal	*time*	*meds / supplements*	*dose*	*time*	*drinks*
					water
					① ② ③ ④ ⑤ ⑥ ⑦ ⑧ ⑨ ⑩
					caffeine
					① ② ③ ④ ⑤ ⑥ ⑦ ⑧ ⑨ ⑩
					alcohol
					① ② ③ ④ ⑤ ⑥ ⑦ ⑧ ⑨ ⑩

HORMONES

☐ Menstruating ☐ Menopause
☐ PMS ☐ N/A | other

COMPUTER / MOBILE DEVICE / TV

☐ None ☐ Some ☐ A lot Total Time: ______
☐ Sitting ☐ Standing ☐ Mixture Breaks every: ______

PHYSICAL ACTIVITY

☐ None ☐ Minimal ☐ Some ☐ Sweatin' ☐ I'm beat DETAILS: ______________________

RELIEF MEASURES

☐ Medication ☐ Massage ☐ Sleep ☐ Exercise ☐ Water ☐ Cold/Ice
☐ Heat/Bath ☐ Other: ______________________________

Did it work? ☐ Nope ☐ A bit ☐ Mostly ☐ 100%

Notes

☐ *See back notes*

START:		END:		DURATION:		DATE		*Entry #44*

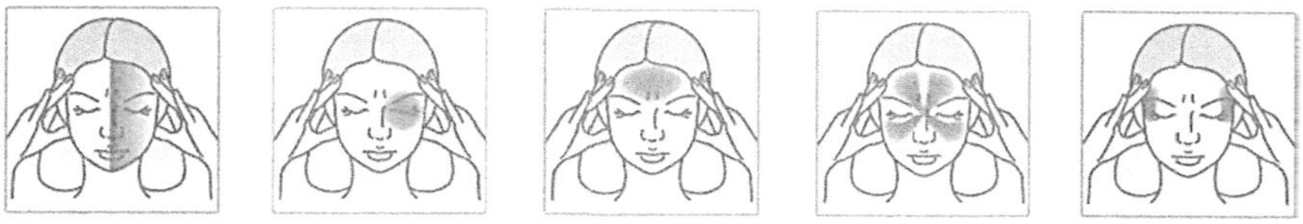

MIGRAINE | CLUSTER | TENSION | SINUS | TMJ

HOW WOULD YOU RATE...?

Mood	1	2	3	4	5
Energy	1	2	3	4	5
Mental clarity	1	2	3	4	5

PAIN LEVEL

1	2	3	4	5	6	7	8	9	10

Not too bad. *Well, I'm not enjoying this.* *Make it stop!*

ONSET

☐ Slow ☐ Average
☐ Rapid ☐ Sudden

DETAILED DESCRIPTION

☐ Constant ☐ Squeezing ☐ Throbbing ☐ Pounding ☐ Dull aching ☐ Burning
☐ Sharp ☐ Debilitating ☐ Other: ____________________

WHERE DOES IT HURT, EXACTLY?

OTHER SYMPTOMS

☐ Lightheaded ☐ Dizziness
☐ Light sensitivity ☐ Sound sensitivity
☐ Confusion ☐ Auras
☐ Muscle stiffness ☐ Muscle aches

FEELING SICK?

☐ Nausea ☐ Diarrhea ☐ Vomiting ☐ Sore throat ☐ Congestion ☐ Coughing
☐ Chills ☐ Fever ☐ Other: ____________________

SLEEP

hours ________ *quality* 1 2 3 4 5

WEATHER

☐ Cold ☐ Mild ☐ Hot Allergen levels: __________
☐ Dry ☐ Humid ☐ Wet BM Pressure: __________

STRESS LEVELS

None	Low	Medium	High	Max	@$#%!

item / meal	*time*	*meds / supplements*	*dose*	*time*	*drinks*
					water
					1 2 3 4 5 6 7 8 9 10
					caffeine
					1 2 3 4 5 6 7 8 9 10
					alcohol
					1 2 3 4 5 6 7 8 9 10

HORMONES

☐ Menstruating ☐ Menopause
☐ PMS ☐ N/A | other

COMPUTER / MOBILE DEVICE / TV

☐ None ☐ Some ☐ A lot Total Time: ______
☐ Sitting ☐ Standing ☐ Mixture Breaks every: ______

PHYSICAL ACTIVITY

☐ None ☐ Minimal ☐ Some ☐ Sweatin' ☐ I'm beat DETAILS: ____________________

RELIEF MEASURES

☐ Medication ☐ Massage ☐ Sleep ☐ Exercise ☐ Water ☐ Cold/Ice
☐ Heat/Bath ☐ Other: ____________________
Did it work? ☐ Nope ☐ A bit ☐ Mostly ☐ 100%

Notes ☐ *See back notes*

START:		END:		DURATION:		DATE		*Entry #45*

MIGRAINE

CLUSTER

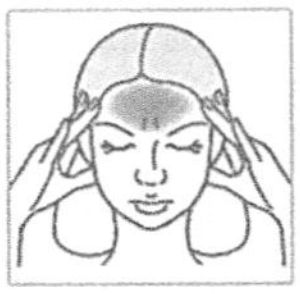
TENSION

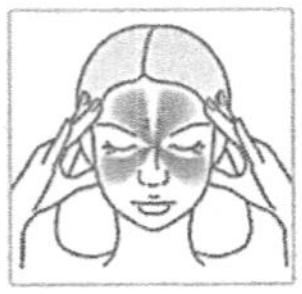
SINUS

TMJ

HOW WOULD YOU RATE...?					
Mood	①	②	③	④	⑤
Energy	①	②	③	④	⑤
Mental clarity	①	②	③	④	⑤

PAIN LEVEL

1	2	3	4	5	6	7	8	9	10

Not too bad. *Well, I'm not enjoying this.* *Make it stop!*

ONSET

☐ Slow ☐ Average
☐ Rapid ☐ Sudden

DETAILED DESCRIPTION

☐ Constant ☐ Squeezing ☐ Throbbing ☐ Pounding ☐ Dull aching ☐ Burning
☐ Sharp ☐ Debilitating ☐ Other: ______________________________

WHERE DOES IT HURT, EXACTLY?

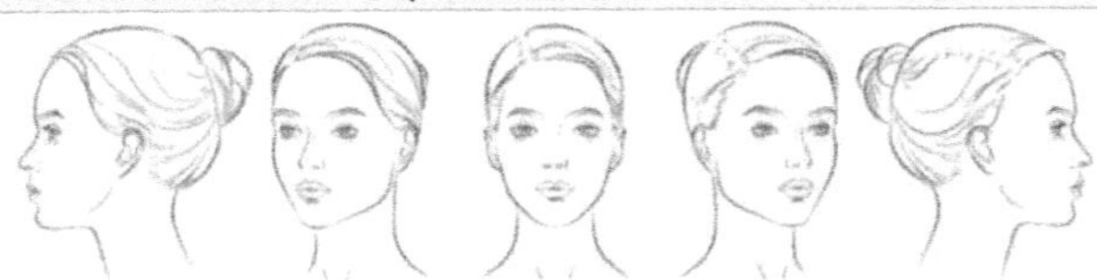

OTHER SYMPTOMS

☐ Lightheaded ☐ Dizziness
☐ Light sensitivity ☐ Sound sensitivity
☐ Confusion ☐ Auras
☐ Muscle stiffness ☐ Muscle aches

FEELING SICK?

☐ Nausea ☐ Diarrhea ☐ Vomiting ☐ Sore throat ☐ Congestion ☐ Coughing
☐ Chills ☐ Fever ☐ Other: ______________________________

SLEEP

hours ________ *quality* ① ② ③ ④ ⑤

WEATHER

☐ Cold ☐ Mild ☐ Hot Allergen levels: ____________
☐ Dry ☐ Humid ☐ Wet BM Pressure: ____________

STRESS LEVELS

None	Low	Medium	High	Max	@$#%!

item / meal	*time*	*meds / supplements*	*dose*	*time*	*drinks*
					water
					① ② ③ ④ ⑤ ⑥ ⑦ ⑧ ⑨ ⑩
					caffeine
					① ② ③ ④ ⑤ ⑥ ⑦ ⑧ ⑨ ⑩
					alcohol
					① ② ③ ④ ⑤ ⑥ ⑦ ⑧ ⑨ ⑩

HORMONES

☐ Menstruating ☐ Menopause
☐ PMS ☐ N/A | other

COMPUTER / MOBILE DEVICE / TV

☐ None ☐ Some ☐ A lot Total Time: _____
☐ Sitting ☐ Standing ☐ Mixture Breaks every: _____

PHYSICAL ACTIVITY

☐ None ☐ Minimal ☐ Some ☐ Sweatin' ☐ I'm beat DETAILS: ______________________

RELIEF MEASURES

☐ Medication ☐ Massage ☐ Sleep ☐ Exercise ☐ Water ☐ Cold/Ice
☐ Heat/Bath ☐ Other: ______________________________
Did it work? ☐ Nope ☐ A bit ☐ Mostly ☐ 100%

Notes ☐ *See back notes*

START:		END:		DURATION:		DATE		*Entry #46*

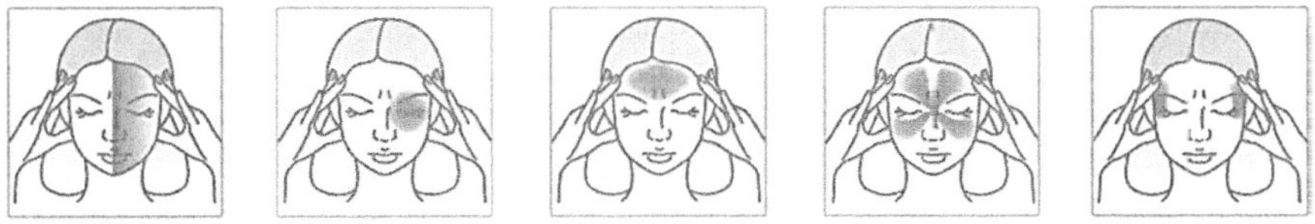

MIGRAINE CLUSTER TENSION SINUS TMJ

HOW WOULD YOU RATE...?

Mood	①	②	③	④	⑤
Energy	①	②	③	④	⑤
Mental clarity	①	②	③	④	⑤

PAIN LEVEL

1	2	3	4	5	6	7	8	9	10

Not too bad. *Well, I'm not enjoying this.* *Make it stop!*

ONSET

☐ Slow ☐ Average
☐ Rapid ☐ Sudden

DETAILED DESCRIPTION

☐ Constant ☐ Squeezing ☐ Throbbing ☐ Pounding ☐ Dull aching ☐ Burning
☐ Sharp ☐ Debilitating ☐ Other: ______

WHERE DOES IT HURT, EXACTLY?

OTHER SYMPTOMS

☐ Lightheaded ☐ Dizziness
☐ Light sensitivity ☐ Sound sensitivity
☐ Confusion ☐ Auras
☐ Muscle stiffness ☐ Muscle aches

FEELING SICK?

☐ Nausea ☐ Diarrhea ☐ Vomiting ☐ Sore throat ☐ Congestion ☐ Coughing
☐ Chills ☐ Fever ☐ Other: ______

SLEEP

hours ______ *quality* ① ② ③ ④ ⑤

WEATHER

☐ Cold ☐ Mild ☐ Hot Allergen levels: ______
☐ Dry ☐ Humid ☐ Wet BM Pressure: ______

STRESS LEVELS

None	Low	Medium	High	Max	@$#%!

item / meal	*time*	*meds / supplements*	*dose*	*time*	*drinks*
					water
					① ② ③ ④ ⑤ ⑥ ⑦ ⑧ ⑨ ⑩
					caffeine
					① ② ③ ④ ⑤ ⑥ ⑦ ⑧ ⑨ ⑩
					alcohol
					① ② ③ ④ ⑤ ⑥ ⑦ ⑧ ⑨ ⑩

HORMONES

☐ Menstruating ☐ Menopause
☐ PMS ☐ N/A | other

COMPUTER / MOBILE DEVICE / TV

☐ None ☐ Some ☐ A lot Total Time: ______
☐ Sitting ☐ Standing ☐ Mixture Breaks every: ______

PHYSICAL ACTIVITY

☐ None ☐ Minimal ☐ Some ☐ Sweatin' ☐ I'm beat DETAILS: ______

RELIEF MEASURES

☐ Medication ☐ Massage ☐ Sleep ☐ Exercise ☐ Water ☐ Cold/Ice
☐ Heat/Bath ☐ Other: ______
Did it work? ☐ Nope ☐ A bit ☐ Mostly ☐ 100%

Notes ☐ *See back notes*

START:		END:		DURATION:		DATE		*Entry #47*

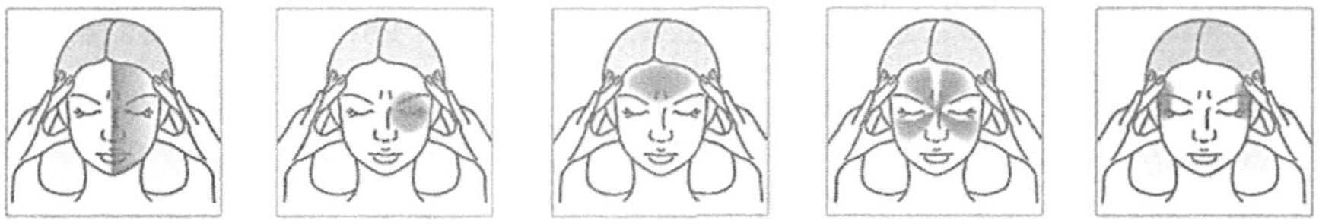

MIGRAINE CLUSTER TENSION SINUS TMJ

HOW WOULD YOU RATE…?

Mood	①	②	③	④	⑤
Energy	①	②	③	④	⑤
Mental clarity	①	②	③	④	⑤

PAIN LEVEL

1	2	3	4	5	6	7	8	9	10

Not too bad. *Well, I'm not enjoying this.* *Make it stop!*

ONSET

☐ Slow ☐ Average
☐ Rapid ☐ Sudden

DETAILED DESCRIPTION

☐ Constant ☐ Squeezing ☐ Throbbing ☐ Pounding ☐ Dull aching ☐ Burning
☐ Sharp ☐ Debilitating ☐ Other: ____________________

WHERE DOES IT HURT, EXACTLY?

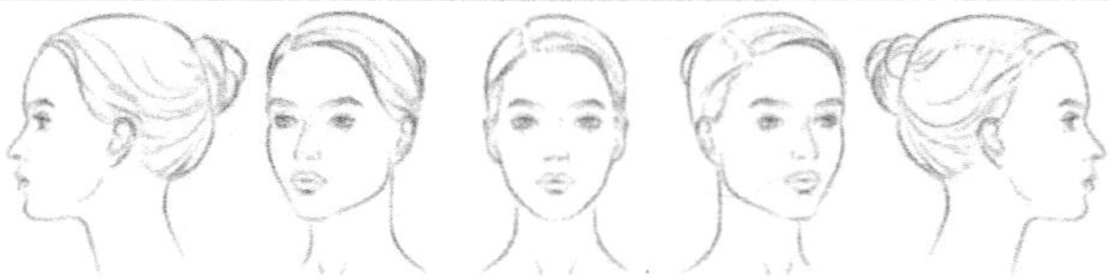

OTHER SYMPTOMS

☐ Lightheaded ☐ Dizziness
☐ Light sensitivity ☐ Sound sensitivity
☐ Confusion ☐ Auras
☐ Muscle stiffness ☐ Muscle aches

FEELING SICK?

☐ Nausea ☐ Diarrhea ☐ Vomiting ☐ Sore throat ☐ Congestion ☐ Coughing
☐ Chills ☐ Fever ☐ Other: ____________________

SLEEP

hours ________ *quality* ① ② ③ ④ ⑤

WEATHER

☐ Cold ☐ Mild ☐ Hot Allergen levels: ________
☐ Dry ☐ Humid ☐ Wet BM Pressure: ________

STRESS LEVELS

None	Low	Medium	High	Max	@$#%!

item / meal	*time*	*meds / supplements*	*dose*	*time*	*drinks*
					water
					① ② ③ ④ ⑤ ⑥ ⑦ ⑧ ⑨ ⑩
					caffeine
					① ② ③ ④ ⑤ ⑥ ⑦ ⑧ ⑨ ⑩
					alcohol
					① ② ③ ④ ⑤ ⑥ ⑦ ⑧ ⑨ ⑩

HORMONES

☐ Menstruating ☐ Menopause
☐ PMS ☐ N/A | other

COMPUTER / MOBILE DEVICE / TV

☐ None ☐ Some ☐ A lot Total Time: ______
☐ Sitting ☐ Standing ☐ Mixture Breaks every: ______

PHYSICAL ACTIVITY

☐ None ☐ Minimal ☐ Some ☐ Sweatin' ☐ I'm beat DETAILS: ____________________

RELIEF MEASURES

☐ Medication ☐ Massage ☐ Sleep ☐ Exercise ☐ Water ☐ Cold/Ice
☐ Heat/Bath ☐ Other: ____________________
Did it work? ☐ Nope ☐ A bit ☐ Mostly ☐ 100%

Notes

☐ *See back notes*

START: | END: | DURATION: | DATE | *Entry #48*

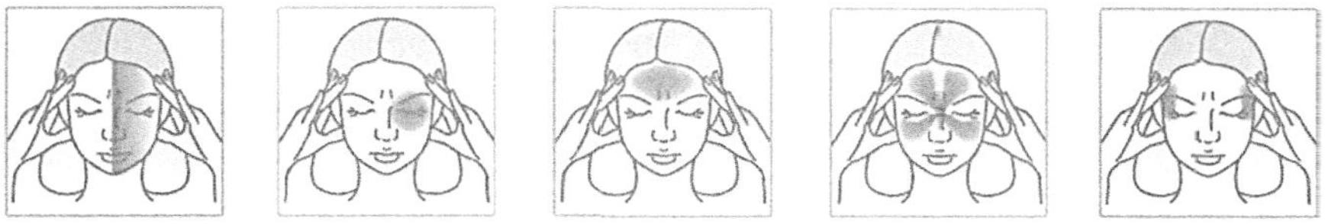

MIGRAINE | CLUSTER | TENSION | SINUS | TMJ

HOW WOULD YOU RATE...?

Mood	① ② ③ ④ ⑤
Energy	① ② ③ ④ ⑤
Mental clarity	① ② ③ ④ ⑤

PAIN LEVEL

1	2	3	4	5	6	7	8	9	10

Not too bad. *Well, I'm not enjoying this.* *Make it stop!*

ONSET

☐ Slow ☐ Average
☐ Rapid ☐ Sudden

DETAILED DESCRIPTION

☐ Constant ☐ Squeezing ☐ Throbbing ☐ Pounding ☐ Dull aching ☐ Burning
☐ Sharp ☐ Debilitating ☐ Other: ____________________

WHERE DOES IT HURT, EXACTLY?

OTHER SYMPTOMS

☐ Lightheaded ☐ Dizziness
☐ Light sensitivity ☐ Sound sensitivity
☐ Confusion ☐ Auras
☐ Muscle stiffness ☐ Muscle aches

FEELING SICK?

☐ Nausea ☐ Diarrhea ☐ Vomiting ☐ Sore throat ☐ Congestion ☐ Coughing
☐ Chills ☐ Fever ☐ Other: ____________________

SLEEP

hours ________ *quality* ① ② ③ ④ ⑤

WEATHER

☐ Cold ☐ Mild ☐ Hot Allergen levels: ____________
☐ Dry ☐ Humid ☐ Wet BM Pressure: ____________

STRESS LEVELS

None	Low	Medium	High	Max	@$#%!

item / meal	*time*	*meds / supplements*	*dose*	*time*	*drinks*
					water
					① ② ③ ④ ⑤ ⑥ ⑦ ⑧ ⑨ ⑩
					caffeine
					① ② ③ ④ ⑤ ⑥ ⑦ ⑧ ⑨ ⑩
					alcohol
					① ② ③ ④ ⑤ ⑥ ⑦ ⑧ ⑨ ⑩

HORMONES

☐ Menstruating ☐ Menopause
☐ PMS ☐ N/A | other

COMPUTER / MOBILE DEVICE / TV

☐ None ☐ Some ☐ A lot Total Time: ______
☐ Sitting ☐ Standing ☐ Mixture Breaks every: ______

PHYSICAL ACTIVITY

☐ None ☐ Minimal ☐ Some ☐ Sweatin' ☐ I'm beat DETAILS: ____________________

RELIEF MEASURES

☐ Medication ☐ Massage ☐ Sleep ☐ Exercise ☐ Water ☐ Cold/Ice
☐ Heat/Bath ☐ Other: ____________________
Did it work? ☐ Nope ☐ A bit ☐ Mostly ☐ 100%

Notes ☐ *See back notes*

START: ______ END: ______ DURATION: ______ DATE ______ *Entry #49*

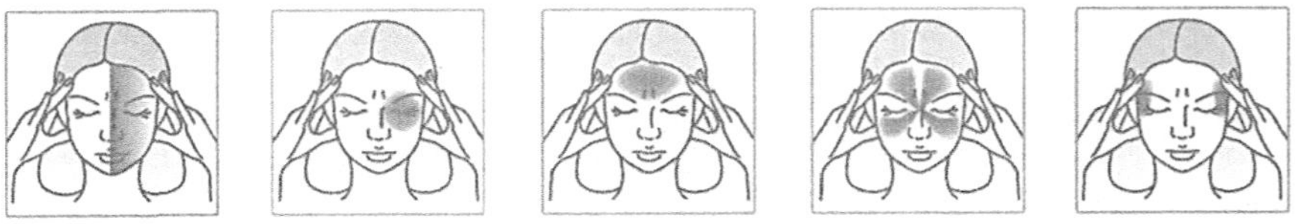

MIGRAINE | CLUSTER | TENSION | SINUS | TMJ

HOW WOULD YOU RATE...?

Mood	①	②	③	④	⑤
Energy	①	②	③	④	⑤
Mental clarity	①	②	③	④	⑤

PAIN LEVEL

1	2	3	4	5	6	7	8	9	10

Not too bad. *Well, I'm not enjoying this.* *Make it stop!*

ONSET

☐ Slow ☐ Average
☐ Rapid ☐ Sudden

DETAILED DESCRIPTION

☐ Constant ☐ Squeezing ☐ Throbbing ☐ Pounding ☐ Dull aching ☐ Burning
☐ Sharp ☐ Debilitating ☐ Other: ______

WHERE DOES IT HURT, EXACTLY?

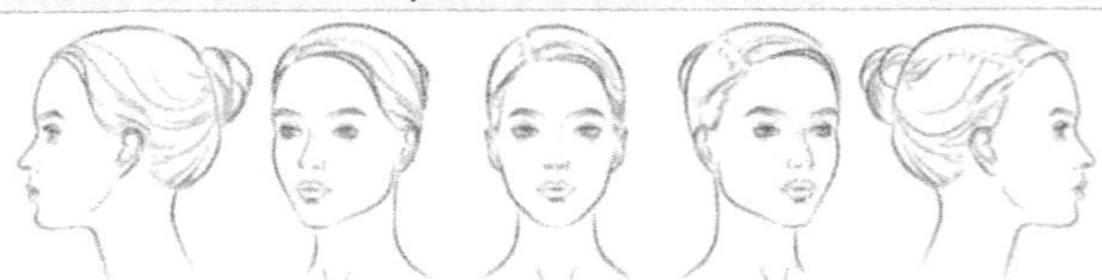

OTHER SYMPTOMS

☐ Lightheaded ☐ Dizziness
☐ Light sensitivity ☐ Sound sensitivity
☐ Confusion ☐ Auras
☐ Muscle stiffness ☐ Muscle aches

FEELING SICK?

☐ Nausea ☐ Diarrhea ☐ Vomiting ☐ Sore throat ☐ Congestion ☐ Coughing
☐ Chills ☐ Fever ☐ Other: ______

SLEEP

hours ______ *quality* ① ② ③ ④ ⑤

WEATHER

☐ Cold ☐ Mild ☐ Hot Allergen levels: ______
☐ Dry ☐ Humid ☐ Wet BM Pressure: ______

STRESS LEVELS

None	Low	Medium	High	Max	@$#%!

item / meal	*time*	*meds / supplements*	*dose*	*time*	*drinks*
					water
					① ② ③ ④ ⑤ ⑥ ⑦ ⑧ ⑨ ⑩
					caffeine
					① ② ③ ④ ⑤ ⑥ ⑦ ⑧ ⑨ ⑩
					alcohol
					① ② ③ ④ ⑤ ⑥ ⑦ ⑧ ⑨ ⑩

HORMONES

☐ Menstruating ☐ Menopause
☐ PMS ☐ N/A | other

COMPUTER / MOBILE DEVICE / TV

☐ None ☐ Some ☐ A lot Total Time: ______
☐ Sitting ☐ Standing ☐ Mixture Breaks every: ______

PHYSICAL ACTIVITY

☐ None ☐ Minimal ☐ Some ☐ Sweatin' ☐ I'm beat DETAILS: ______

RELIEF MEASURES

☐ Medication ☐ Massage ☐ Sleep ☐ Exercise ☐ Water ☐ Cold/Ice
☐ Heat/Bath ☐ Other: ______
Did it work? ☐ Nope ☐ A bit ☐ Mostly ☐ 100%

Notes ☐ *See back notes*

START:		END:		DURATION:		DATE		*Entry #50*

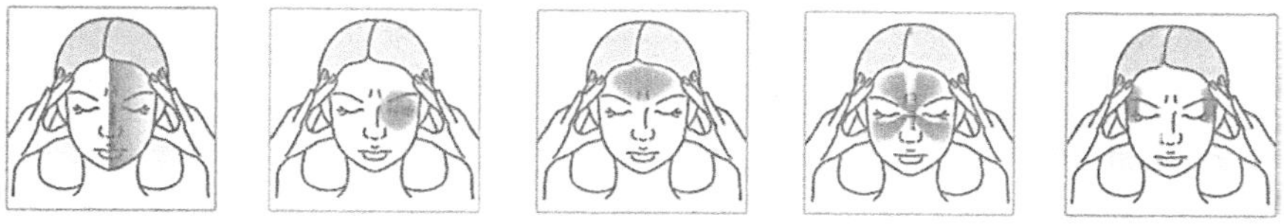

MIGRAINE | CLUSTER | TENSION | SINUS | TMJ

HOW WOULD YOU RATE...?

Mood	1	2	3	4	5
Energy	1	2	3	4	5
Mental clarity	1	2	3	4	5

PAIN LEVEL

1	2	3	4	5	6	7	8	9	10

Not too bad. *Well, I'm not enjoying this.* *Make it stop!*

ONSET

☐ Slow ☐ Average
☐ Rapid ☐ Sudden

DETAILED DESCRIPTION

☐ Constant ☐ Squeezing ☐ Throbbing ☐ Pounding ☐ Dull aching ☐ Burning
☐ Sharp ☐ Debilitating ☐ Other: ____________________

WHERE DOES IT HURT, EXACTLY?

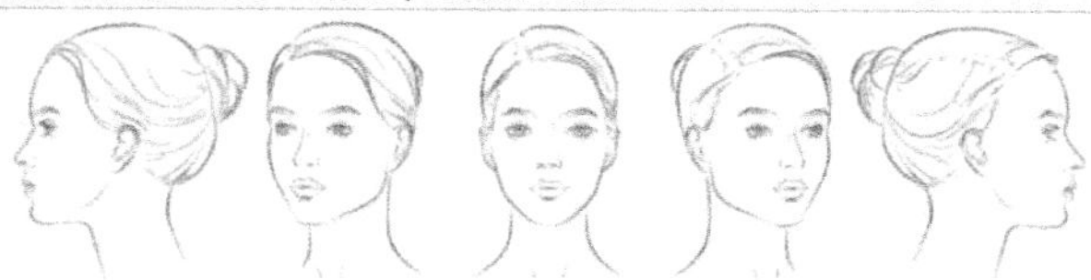

OTHER SYMPTOMS

☐ Lightheaded ☐ Dizziness
☐ Light sensitivity ☐ Sound sensitivity
☐ Confusion ☐ Auras
☐ Muscle stiffness ☐ Muscle aches

FEELING SICK?

☐ Nausea ☐ Diarrhea ☐ Vomiting ☐ Sore throat ☐ Congestion ☐ Coughing
☐ Chills ☐ Fever ☐ Other: ____________________

SLEEP

hours ________ *quality* 1 2 3 4 5

WEATHER

☐ Cold ☐ Mild ☐ Hot Allergen levels: ____________
☐ Dry ☐ Humid ☐ Wet BM Pressure: ____________

STRESS LEVELS

None	Low	Medium	High	Max	@$#%!

item / meal	*time*	*meds / supplements*	*dose*	*time*	*drinks*
					water
					1 2 3 4 5 6 7 8 9 10
					caffeine
					1 2 3 4 5 6 7 8 9 10
					alcohol
					1 2 3 4 5 6 7 8 9 10

HORMONES

☐ Menstruating ☐ Menopause
☐ PMS ☐ N/A | other

COMPUTER / MOBILE DEVICE / TV

☐ None ☐ Some ☐ A lot Total Time: ______
☐ Sitting ☐ Standing ☐ Mixture Breaks every: ______

PHYSICAL ACTIVITY

☐ None ☐ Minimal ☐ Some ☐ Sweatin' ☐ I'm beat DETAILS: ____________

RELIEF MEASURES

☐ Medication ☐ Massage ☐ Sleep ☐ Exercise ☐ Water ☐ Cold/Ice
☐ Heat/Bath ☐ Other: ____________________
Did it work? ☐ Nope ☐ A bit ☐ Mostly ☐ 100%

Notes ☐ *See back notes*

START:		END:		DURATION:		DATE		*Entry #51*

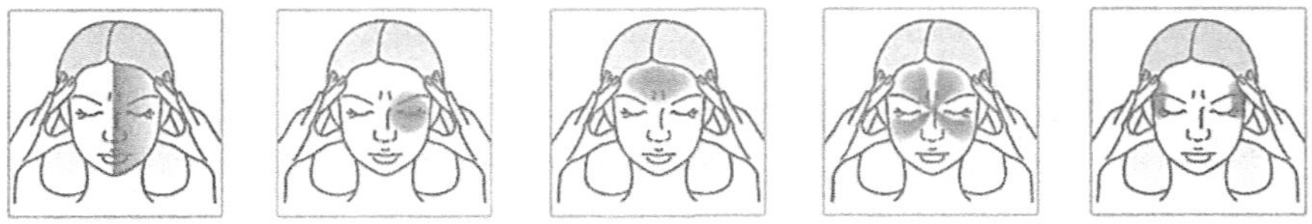

MIGRAINE | CLUSTER | TENSION | SINUS | TMJ

HOW WOULD YOU RATE...?

Mood	1	2	3	4	5
Energy	1	2	3	4	5
Mental clarity	1	2	3	4	5

PAIN LEVEL

1	2	3	4	5	6	7	8	9	10

Not too bad. *Well, I'm not enjoying this.* *Make it stop!*

ONSET

☐ Slow ☐ Average
☐ Rapid ☐ Sudden

DETAILED DESCRIPTION

☐ Constant ☐ Squeezing ☐ Throbbing ☐ Pounding ☐ Dull aching ☐ Burning
☐ Sharp ☐ Debilitating ☐ Other: ____________________

WHERE DOES IT HURT, EXACTLY?

OTHER SYMPTOMS

☐ Lightheaded ☐ Dizziness
☐ Light sensitivity ☐ Sound sensitivity
☐ Confusion ☐ Auras
☐ Muscle stiffness ☐ Muscle aches

FEELING SICK?

☐ Nausea ☐ Diarrhea ☐ Vomiting ☐ Sore throat ☐ Congestion ☐ Coughing
☐ Chills ☐ Fever ☐ Other: ____________________

SLEEP

hours ________ *quality* 1 2 3 4 5

WEATHER

☐ Cold ☐ Mild ☐ Hot Allergen levels: ____________
☐ Dry ☐ Humid ☐ Wet BM Pressure: ____________

STRESS LEVELS

None	Low	Medium	High	Max	@$#%!

item / meal	*time*	*meds / supplements*	*dose*	*time*	*drinks*
					water
					1 2 3 4 5 6 7 8 9 10
					caffeine
					1 2 3 4 5 6 7 8 9 10
					alcohol
					1 2 3 4 5 6 7 8 9 10

HORMONES

☐ Menstruating ☐ Menopause
☐ PMS ☐ N/A | other

COMPUTER / MOBILE DEVICE / TV

☐ None ☐ Some ☐ A lot Total Time: ______
☐ Sitting ☐ Standing ☐ Mixture Breaks every: ______

PHYSICAL ACTIVITY

☐ None ☐ Minimal ☐ Some ☐ Sweatin' ☐ I'm beat DETAILS: ____________________

RELIEF MEASURES

☐ Medication ☐ Massage ☐ Sleep ☐ Exercise ☐ Water ☐ Cold/Ice
☐ Heat/Bath ☐ Other: ____________________
Did it work? ☐ Nope ☐ A bit ☐ Mostly ☐ 100%

Notes ☐ *See back notes*

START:		END:		DURATION:		DATE		*Entry #52*

MIGRAINE | CLUSTER | TENSION | SINUS | TMJ

HOW WOULD YOU RATE...?					
Mood	1	2	3	4	5
Energy	1	2	3	4	5
Mental clarity	1	2	3	4	5

PAIN LEVEL

1	2	3	4	5	6	7	8	9	10

Not too bad. *Well, I'm not enjoying this.* *Make it stop!*

ONSET

☐ Slow ☐ Average
☐ Rapid ☐ Sudden

DETAILED DESCRIPTION

☐ Constant ☐ Squeezing ☐ Throbbing ☐ Pounding ☐ Dull aching ☐ Burning
☐ Sharp ☐ Debilitating ☐ Other: ____________________

WHERE DOES IT HURT, EXACTLY?

OTHER SYMPTOMS

☐ Lightheaded ☐ Dizziness
☐ Light sensitivity ☐ Sound sensitivity
☐ Confusion ☐ Auras
☐ Muscle stiffness ☐ Muscle aches

FEELING SICK?

☐ Nausea ☐ Diarrhea ☐ Vomiting ☐ Sore throat ☐ Congestion ☐ Coughing
☐ Chills ☐ Fever ☐ Other: ____________________

SLEEP

hours ________ *quality* 1 2 3 4 5

WEATHER

☐ Cold ☐ Mild ☐ Hot Allergen levels: ____________
☐ Dry ☐ Humid ☐ Wet BM Pressure: ____________

STRESS LEVELS

None	Low	Medium	High	Max	@$#%!

item / meal	*time*	*meds / supplements*	*dose*	*time*	*drinks*
					water
					1 2 3 4 5 6 7 8 9 10
					caffeine
					1 2 3 4 5 6 7 8 9 10
					alcohol
					1 2 3 4 5 6 7 8 9 10

HORMONES

☐ Menstruating ☐ Menopause
☐ PMS ☐ N/A | other

COMPUTER / MOBILE DEVICE / TV

☐ None ☐ Some ☐ A lot Total Time: ______
☐ Sitting ☐ Standing ☐ Mixture Breaks every: ______

PHYSICAL ACTIVITY

☐ None ☐ Minimal ☐ Some ☐ Sweatin' ☐ I'm beat DETAILS: ____________

RELIEF MEASURES

☐ Medication ☐ Massage ☐ Sleep ☐ Exercise ☐ Water ☐ Cold/Ice
☐ Heat/Bath ☐ Other: ____________________
Did it work? ☐ Nope ☐ A bit ☐ Mostly ☐ 100%

Notes ☐ *See back notes*

START:		END:		DURATION:		DATE		*Entry #53*

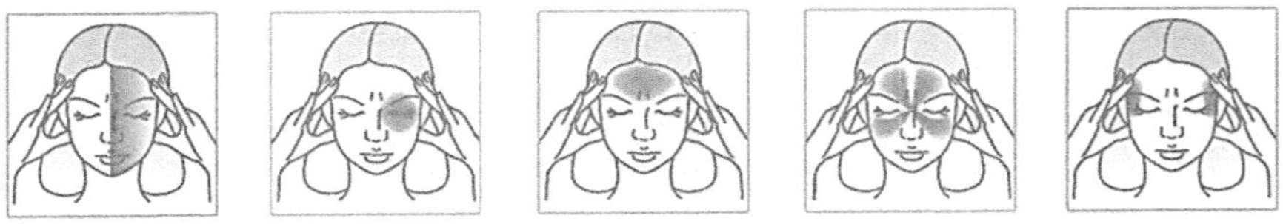

MIGRAINE CLUSTER TENSION SINUS TMJ

HOW WOULD YOU RATE...?

Mood	① ② ③ ④ ⑤
Energy	① ② ③ ④ ⑤
Mental clarity	① ② ③ ④ ⑤

PAIN LEVEL

1	2	3	4	5	6	7	8	9	10

Not too bad. *Well, I'm not enjoying this.* *Make it stop!*

ONSET

☐ Slow ☐ Average
☐ Rapid ☐ Sudden

DETAILED DESCRIPTION

☐ Constant ☐ Squeezing ☐ Throbbing ☐ Pounding ☐ Dull aching ☐ Burning
☐ Sharp ☐ Debilitating ☐ Other: ______________________________

WHERE DOES IT HURT, EXACTLY?

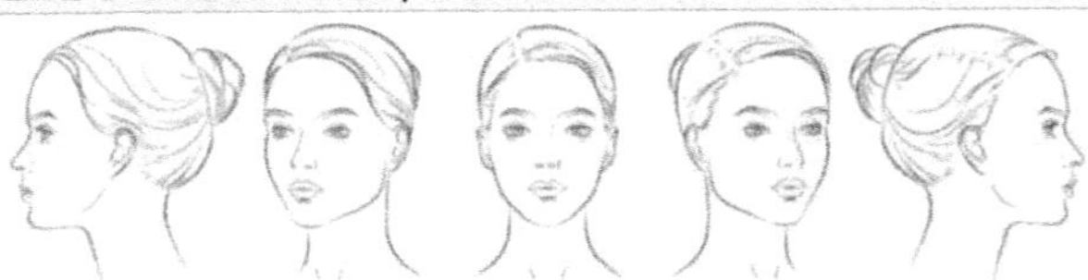

OTHER SYMPTOMS

☐ Lightheaded ☐ Dizziness
☐ Light sensitivity ☐ Sound sensitivity
☐ Confusion ☐ Auras
☐ Muscle stiffness ☐ Muscle aches

FEELING SICK?

☐ Nausea ☐ Diarrhea ☐ Vomiting ☐ Sore throat ☐ Congestion ☐ Coughing
☐ Chills ☐ Fever ☐ Other: ______________________________

SLEEP

hours ________ *quality* ① ② ③ ④ ⑤

WEATHER

☐ Cold ☐ Mild ☐ Hot Allergen levels: ____________
☐ Dry ☐ Humid ☐ Wet BM Pressure: ____________

STRESS LEVELS

None	Low	Medium	High	Max	@$#%!

item / meal	*time*	*meds / supplements*	*dose*	*time*	*drinks*
					water
					① ② ③ ④ ⑤ ⑥ ⑦ ⑧ ⑨ ⑩
					caffeine
					① ② ③ ④ ⑤ ⑥ ⑦ ⑧ ⑨ ⑩
					alcohol
					① ② ③ ④ ⑤ ⑥ ⑦ ⑧ ⑨ ⑩

HORMONES

☐ Menstruating ☐ Menopause
☐ PMS ☐ N/A | other

COMPUTER / MOBILE DEVICE / TV

☐ None ☐ Some ☐ A lot Total Time: ______
☐ Sitting ☐ Standing ☐ Mixture Breaks every: ______

PHYSICAL ACTIVITY

☐ None ☐ Minimal ☐ Some ☐ Sweatin' ☐ I'm beat DETAILS: ______________________

RELIEF MEASURES

☐ Medication ☐ Massage ☐ Sleep ☐ Exercise ☐ Water ☐ Cold/Ice
☐ Heat/Bath ☐ Other: ______________________________
Did it work? ☐ Nope ☐ A bit ☐ Mostly ☐ 100%

Notes ☐ *See back notes*

START:		END:		DURATION:		DATE		*Entry #54*

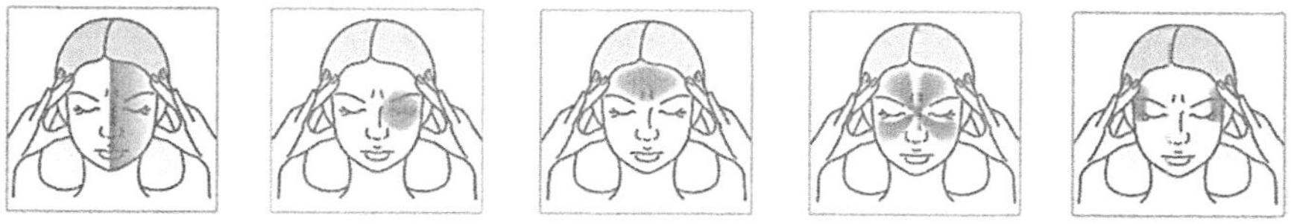

MIGRAINE CLUSTER TENSION SINUS TMJ

HOW WOULD YOU RATE...?

Mood ① ② ③ ④ ⑤

Energy ① ② ③ ④ ⑤

Mental clarity ① ② ③ ④ ⑤

PAIN LEVEL

1	2	3	4	5	6	7	8	9	10

Not too bad. *Well, I'm not enjoying this.* *Make it stop!*

ONSET

☐ Slow ☐ Average
☐ Rapid ☐ Sudden

DETAILED DESCRIPTION

☐ Constant ☐ Squeezing ☐ Throbbing ☐ Pounding ☐ Dull aching ☐ Burning
☐ Sharp ☐ Debilitating ☐ Other: ______________________

WHERE DOES IT HURT, EXACTLY?

OTHER SYMPTOMS

☐ Lightheaded ☐ Dizziness
☐ Light sensitivity ☐ Sound sensitivity
☐ Confusion ☐ Auras
☐ Muscle stiffness ☐ Muscle aches

FEELING SICK?

☐ Nausea ☐ Diarrhea ☐ Vomiting ☐ Sore throat ☐ Congestion ☐ Coughing
☐ Chills ☐ Fever ☐ Other: ______________________

SLEEP

hours ________ *quality* ① ② ③ ④ ⑤

WEATHER

☐ Cold ☐ Mild ☐ Hot Allergen levels: ____________
☐ Dry ☐ Humid ☐ Wet BM Pressure: ____________

STRESS LEVELS

None	Low	Medium	High	Max	@$#%!

item / meal	*time*	*meds / supplements*	*dose*	*time*	*drinks*
					water
					① ② ③ ④ ⑤ ⑥ ⑦ ⑧ ⑨ ⑩
					caffeine
					① ② ③ ④ ⑤ ⑥ ⑦ ⑧ ⑨ ⑩
					alcohol
					① ② ③ ④ ⑤ ⑥ ⑦ ⑧ ⑨ ⑩

HORMONES

☐ Menstruating ☐ Menopause
☐ PMS ☐ N/A | other

COMPUTER / MOBILE DEVICE / TV

☐ None ☐ Some ☐ A lot Total Time: ______
☐ Sitting ☐ Standing ☐ Mixture Breaks every: ______

PHYSICAL ACTIVITY

☐ None ☐ Minimal ☐ Some ☐ Sweatin' ☐ I'm beat DETAILS: ______________

RELIEF MEASURES

☐ Medication ☐ Massage ☐ Sleep ☐ Exercise ☐ Water ☐ Cold/Ice
☐ Heat/Bath ☐ Other: ______________________

Did it work? ☐ Nope ☐ A bit ☐ Mostly ☐ 100%

Notes ☐ *See back notes*

START:	END:	DURATION:	DATE	*Entry #55*

MIGRAINE CLUSTER TENSION SINUS TMJ

HOW WOULD YOU RATE...?

Mood	1	2	3	4	5
Energy	1	2	3	4	5
Mental clarity	1	2	3	4	5

PAIN LEVEL

1	2	3	4	5	6	7	8	9	10

Not too bad. *Well, I'm not enjoying this.* *Make it stop!*

ONSET

☐ Slow ☐ Average
☐ Rapid ☐ Sudden

DETAILED DESCRIPTION

☐ Constant ☐ Squeezing ☐ Throbbing ☐ Pounding ☐ Dull aching ☐ Burning
☐ Sharp ☐ Debilitating ☐ Other: ______________________________

WHERE DOES IT HURT, EXACTLY?

OTHER SYMPTOMS

☐ Lightheaded ☐ Dizziness
☐ Light sensitivity ☐ Sound sensitivity
☐ Confusion ☐ Auras
☐ Muscle stiffness ☐ Muscle aches

FEELING SICK?

☐ Nausea ☐ Diarrhea ☐ Vomiting ☐ Sore throat ☐ Congestion ☐ Coughing
☐ Chills ☐ Fever ☐ Other: ______________________________

SLEEP

hours _______ *quality* 1 2 3 4 5

WEATHER

☐ Cold ☐ Mild ☐ Hot Allergen levels: ___________
☐ Dry ☐ Humid ☐ Wet BM Pressure: ___________

STRESS LEVELS

None	Low	Medium	High	Max	@$#%!

item / meal	*time*	*meds / supplements*	*dose*	*time*	*drinks*
					water
					1 2 3 4 5 6 7 8 9 10
					caffeine
					1 2 3 4 5 6 7 8 9 10
					alcohol
					1 2 3 4 5 6 7 8 9 10

HORMONES

☐ Menstruating ☐ Menopause
☐ PMS ☐ N/A | other

COMPUTER / MOBILE DEVICE / TV

☐ None ☐ Some ☐ A lot Total Time: _____
☐ Sitting ☐ Standing ☐ Mixture Breaks every: _____

PHYSICAL ACTIVITY

☐ None ☐ Minimal ☐ Some ☐ Sweatin' ☐ I'm beat DETAILS: ______________

RELIEF MEASURES

☐ Medication ☐ Massage ☐ Sleep ☐ Exercise ☐ Water ☐ Cold/Ice
☐ Heat/Bath ☐ Other: ______________________________
Did it work? ☐ Nope ☐ A bit ☐ Mostly ☐ 100%

Notes

☐ *See back notes*

START:		END:		DURATION:		DATE		*Entry #56*

MIGRAINE CLUSTER TENSION SINUS TMJ

HOW WOULD YOU RATE...?

Mood	1	2	3	4	5
Energy	1	2	3	4	5
Mental clarity	1	2	3	4	5

PAIN LEVEL

1	2	3	4	5	6	7	8	9	10

Not too bad. *Well, I'm not enjoying this.* *Make it stop!*

ONSET

☐ Slow ☐ Average
☐ Rapid ☐ Sudden

DETAILED DESCRIPTION

☐ Constant ☐ Squeezing ☐ Throbbing ☐ Pounding ☐ Dull aching ☐ Burning
☐ Sharp ☐ Debilitating ☐ Other: ______________________________

WHERE DOES IT HURT, EXACTLY?

OTHER SYMPTOMS

☐ Lightheaded ☐ Dizziness
☐ Light sensitivity ☐ Sound sensitivity
☐ Confusion ☐ Auras
☐ Muscle stiffness ☐ Muscle aches

FEELING SICK?

☐ Nausea ☐ Diarrhea ☐ Vomiting ☐ Sore throat ☐ Congestion ☐ Coughing
☐ Chills ☐ Fever ☐ Other: ______________________________

SLEEP

hours ________ *quality* 1 2 3 4 5

WEATHER

☐ Cold ☐ Mild ☐ Hot Allergen levels: ____________
☐ Dry ☐ Humid ☐ Wet BM Pressure: ____________

STRESS LEVELS

None	Low	Medium	High	Max	@$#%!

item / meal	*time*	*meds / supplements*	*dose*	*time*	*drinks*
					water
					1 2 3 4 5 6 7 8 9 10
					caffeine
					1 2 3 4 5 6 7 8 9 10
					alcohol
					1 2 3 4 5 6 7 8 9 10

HORMONES

☐ Menstruating ☐ Menopause
☐ PMS ☐ N/A | other

COMPUTER / MOBILE DEVICE / TV

☐ None ☐ Some ☐ A lot Total Time: ______
☐ Sitting ☐ Standing ☐ Mixture Breaks every: ______

PHYSICAL ACTIVITY

☐ None ☐ Minimal ☐ Some ☐ Sweatin' ☐ I'm beat DETAILS: ______________________

RELIEF MEASURES

☐ Medication ☐ Massage ☐ Sleep ☐ Exercise ☐ Water ☐ Cold/Ice
☐ Heat/Bath ☐ Other: ______________________________
Did it work? ☐ Nope ☐ A bit ☐ Mostly ☐ 100%

Notes ☐ *See back notes*

START: | END: | DURATION: | DATE | *Entry #57*

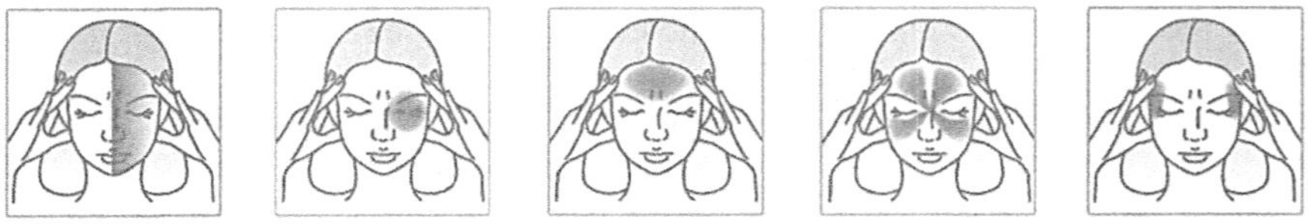

MIGRAINE CLUSTER TENSION SINUS TMJ

HOW WOULD YOU RATE...?

Mood	① ② ③ ④ ⑤
Energy	① ② ③ ④ ⑤
Mental clarity	① ② ③ ④ ⑤

PAIN LEVEL

1	2	3	4	5	6	7	8	9	10

Not too bad. *Well, I'm not enjoying this.* *Make it stop!*

ONSET

☐ Slow ☐ Average
☐ Rapid ☐ Sudden

DETAILED DESCRIPTION

☐ Constant ☐ Squeezing ☐ Throbbing ☐ Pounding ☐ Dull aching ☐ Burning
☐ Sharp ☐ Debilitating ☐ Other: ____________________

WHERE DOES IT HURT, EXACTLY?

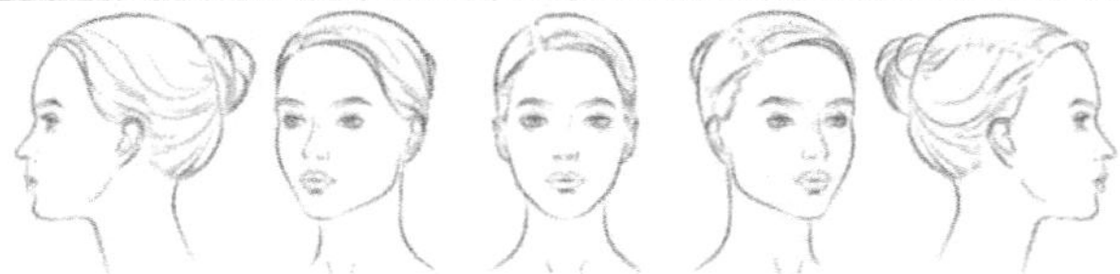

OTHER SYMPTOMS

☐ Lightheaded ☐ Dizziness
☐ Light sensitivity ☐ Sound sensitivity
☐ Confusion ☐ Auras
☐ Muscle stiffness ☐ Muscle aches

FEELING SICK?

☐ Nausea ☐ Diarrhea ☐ Vomiting ☐ Sore throat ☐ Congestion ☐ Coughing
☐ Chills ☐ Fever ☐ Other: ____________________

SLEEP

hours ________ *quality* ① ② ③ ④ ⑤

WEATHER

☐ Cold ☐ Mild ☐ Hot Allergen levels: __________
☐ Dry ☐ Humid ☐ Wet BM Pressure: __________

STRESS LEVELS

None	Low	Medium	High	Max	@$#%!

item / meal	*time*	*meds / supplements*	*dose*	*time*	*drinks*
					water
					① ② ③ ④ ⑤ ⑥ ⑦ ⑧ ⑨ ⑩
					caffeine
					① ② ③ ④ ⑤ ⑥ ⑦ ⑧ ⑨ ⑩
					alcohol
					① ② ③ ④ ⑤ ⑥ ⑦ ⑧ ⑨ ⑩

HORMONES

☐ Menstruating ☐ Menopause
☐ PMS ☐ N/A | other

COMPUTER / MOBILE DEVICE / TV

☐ None ☐ Some ☐ A lot Total Time: ______
☐ Sitting ☐ Standing ☐ Mixture Breaks every: ______

PHYSICAL ACTIVITY

☐ None ☐ Minimal ☐ Some ☐ Sweatin' ☐ I'm beat DETAILS: ____________

RELIEF MEASURES

☐ Medication ☐ Massage ☐ Sleep ☐ Exercise ☐ Water ☐ Cold/Ice
☐ Heat/Bath ☐ Other: ____________________
Did it work? ☐ Nope ☐ A bit ☐ Mostly ☐ 100%

Notes ☐ *See back notes*

START: | END: | DURATION: | DATE | *Entry #58*

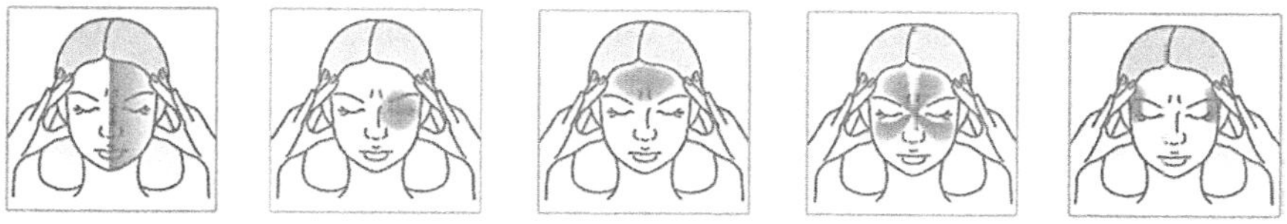

MIGRAINE | CLUSTER | TENSION | SINUS | TMJ

HOW WOULD YOU RATE...?

Mood	① ② ③ ④ ⑤
Energy	① ② ③ ④ ⑤
Mental clarity	① ② ③ ④ ⑤

PAIN LEVEL

1	2	3	4	5	6	7	8	9	10

Not too bad. *Well, I'm not enjoying this.* *Make it stop!*

ONSET

☐ Slow ☐ Average
☐ Rapid ☐ Sudden

DETAILED DESCRIPTION

☐ Constant ☐ Squeezing ☐ Throbbing ☐ Pounding ☐ Dull aching ☐ Burning
☐ Sharp ☐ Debilitating ☐ Other: ____________

WHERE DOES IT HURT, EXACTLY?

OTHER SYMPTOMS

☐ Lightheaded ☐ Dizziness
☐ Light sensitivity ☐ Sound sensitivity
☐ Confusion ☐ Auras
☐ Muscle stiffness ☐ Muscle aches

FEELING SICK?

☐ Nausea ☐ Diarrhea ☐ Vomiting ☐ Sore throat ☐ Congestion ☐ Coughing
☐ Chills ☐ Fever ☐ Other: ____________

SLEEP

hours ________ *quality* ① ② ③ ④ ⑤

WEATHER

☐ Cold ☐ Mild ☐ Hot Allergen levels: ________
☐ Dry ☐ Humid ☐ Wet BM Pressure: ________

STRESS LEVELS

None	Low	Medium	High	Max	@$#%!

item / meal	*time*	*meds / supplements*	*dose*	*time*	*drinks*
					water
					① ② ③ ④ ⑤ ⑥ ⑦ ⑧ ⑨ ⑩
					caffeine
					① ② ③ ④ ⑤ ⑥ ⑦ ⑧ ⑨ ⑩
					alcohol
					① ② ③ ④ ⑤ ⑥ ⑦ ⑧ ⑨ ⑩

HORMONES

☐ Menstruating ☐ Menopause
☐ PMS ☐ N/A | other

COMPUTER / MOBILE DEVICE / TV

☐ None ☐ Some ☐ A lot Total Time: ______
☐ Sitting ☐ Standing ☐ Mixture Breaks every: ______

PHYSICAL ACTIVITY

☐ None ☐ Minimal ☐ Some ☐ Sweatin' ☐ I'm beat DETAILS: ____________

RELIEF MEASURES

☐ Medication ☐ Massage ☐ Sleep ☐ Exercise ☐ Water ☐ Cold/Ice
☐ Heat/Bath ☐ Other: ____________
Did it work? ☐ Nope ☐ A bit ☐ Mostly ☐ 100%

Notes ☐ *See back notes*

START: ____ END: ____ DURATION: ____ DATE ____ *Entry #59*

MIGRAINE | CLUSTER | TENSION | SINUS | TMJ

HOW WOULD YOU RATE...?

Mood ① ② ③ ④ ⑤

Energy ① ② ③ ④ ⑤

Mental clarity ① ② ③ ④ ⑤

PAIN LEVEL

1	2	3	4	5	6	7	8	9	10

Not too bad. *Well, I'm not enjoying this.* *Make it stop!*

ONSET

☐ Slow ☐ Average
☐ Rapid ☐ Sudden

DETAILED DESCRIPTION

☐ Constant ☐ Squeezing ☐ Throbbing ☐ Pounding ☐ Dull aching ☐ Burning
☐ Sharp ☐ Debilitating ☐ Other: ______________________________

WHERE DOES IT HURT, EXACTLY?

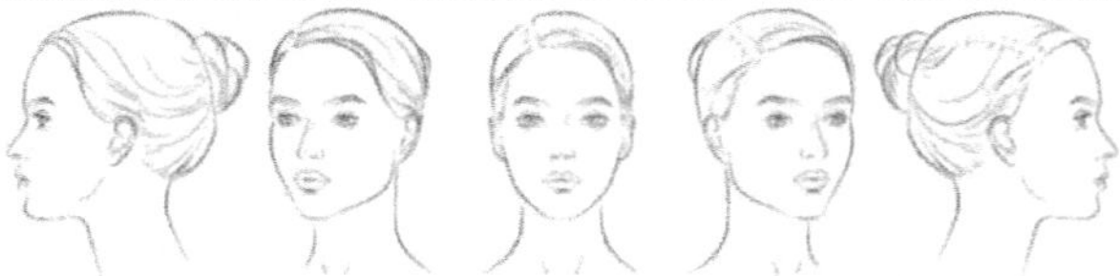

OTHER SYMPTOMS

☐ Lightheaded ☐ Dizziness
☐ Light sensitivity ☐ Sound sensitivity
☐ Confusion ☐ Auras
☐ Muscle stiffness ☐ Muscle aches

FEELING SICK?

☐ Nausea ☐ Diarrhea ☐ Vomiting ☐ Sore throat ☐ Congestion ☐ Coughing
☐ Chills ☐ Fever ☐ Other: ______________________________

SLEEP

hours ________ *quality* ① ② ③ ④ ⑤

WEATHER

☐ Cold ☐ Mild ☐ Hot Allergen levels: __________
☐ Dry ☐ Humid ☐ Wet BM Pressure: __________

STRESS LEVELS

None	Low	Medium	High	Max	@$#%!

item / meal	*time*	*meds / supplements*	*dose*	*time*	*drinks*
					water: ① ② ③ ④ ⑤ ⑥ ⑦ ⑧ ⑨ ⑩
					caffeine: ① ② ③ ④ ⑤ ⑥ ⑦ ⑧ ⑨ ⑩
					alcohol: ① ② ③ ④ ⑤ ⑥ ⑦ ⑧ ⑨ ⑩

HORMONES

☐ Menstruating ☐ Menopause
☐ PMS ☐ N/A | other

COMPUTER / MOBILE DEVICE / TV

☐ None ☐ Some ☐ A lot Total Time: ______
☐ Sitting ☐ Standing ☐ Mixture Breaks every: ______

PHYSICAL ACTIVITY

☐ None ☐ Minimal ☐ Some ☐ Sweatin' ☐ I'm beat DETAILS: ______________

RELIEF MEASURES

☐ Medication ☐ Massage ☐ Sleep ☐ Exercise ☐ Water ☐ Cold/Ice
☐ Heat/Bath ☐ Other: ______________________________

Did it work? ☐ Nope ☐ A bit ☐ Mostly ☐ 100%

Notes ☐ *See back notes*

START: | END: | DURATION: | DATE | *Entry #60*

MIGRAINE CLUSTER TENSION SINUS TMJ

HOW WOULD YOU RATE...?

Mood	1 2 3 4 5
Energy	1 2 3 4 5
Mental clarity	1 2 3 4 5

PAIN LEVEL

1	2	3	4	5	6	7	8	9	10

Not too bad. *Well, I'm not enjoying this.* *Make it stop!*

ONSET

☐ Slow ☐ Average
☐ Rapid ☐ Sudden

DETAILED DESCRIPTION

☐ Constant ☐ Squeezing ☐ Throbbing ☐ Pounding ☐ Dull aching ☐ Burning
☐ Sharp ☐ Debilitating ☐ Other: ______

WHERE DOES IT HURT, EXACTLY?

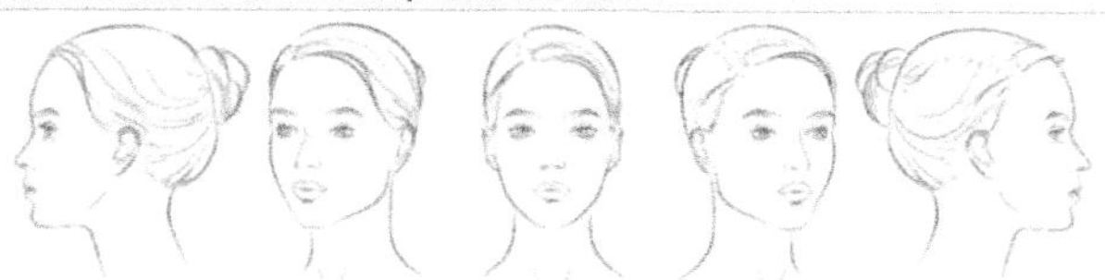

OTHER SYMPTOMS

☐ Lightheaded ☐ Dizziness
☐ Light sensitivity ☐ Sound sensitivity
☐ Confusion ☐ Auras
☐ Muscle stiffness ☐ Muscle aches

FEELING SICK?

☐ Nausea ☐ Diarrhea ☐ Vomiting ☐ Sore throat ☐ Congestion ☐ Coughing
☐ Chills ☐ Fever ☐ Other: ______

SLEEP

hours ______ *quality* 1 2 3 4 5

WEATHER

☐ Cold ☐ Mild ☐ Hot Allergen levels: ______
☐ Dry ☐ Humid ☐ Wet BM Pressure: ______

STRESS LEVELS

None	Low	Medium	High	Max	@$#%!

item / meal	*time*	*meds / supplements*	*dose*	*time*	*drinks*
					water
					1 2 3 4 5 6 7 8 9 10
					caffeine
					1 2 3 4 5 6 7 8 9 10
					alcohol
					1 2 3 4 5 6 7 8 9 10

HORMONES

☐ Menstruating ☐ Menopause
☐ PMS ☐ N/A | other

COMPUTER / MOBILE DEVICE / TV

☐ None ☐ Some ☐ A lot Total Time: ______
☐ Sitting ☐ Standing ☐ Mixture Breaks every: ______

PHYSICAL ACTIVITY

☐ None ☐ Minimal ☐ Some ☐ Sweatin' ☐ I'm beat DETAILS: ______

RELIEF MEASURES

☐ Medication ☐ Massage ☐ Sleep ☐ Exercise ☐ Water ☐ Cold/Ice
☐ Heat/Bath ☐ Other: ______
Did it work? ☐ Nope ☐ A bit ☐ Mostly ☐ 100%

Notes ☐ *See back notes*

START: ____ END: ____ DURATION: ____ DATE ____ *Entry #61*

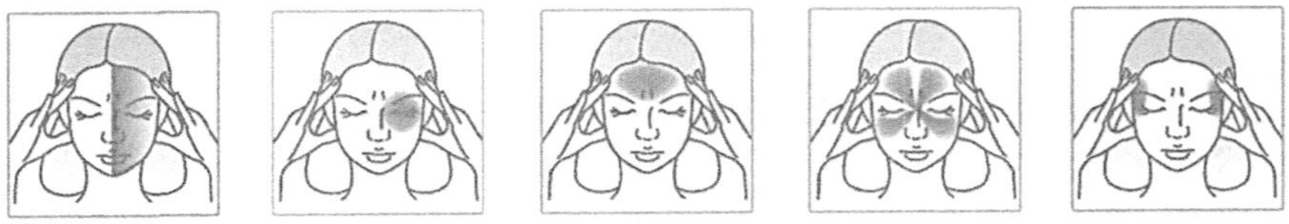

MIGRAINE CLUSTER TENSION SINUS TMJ

HOW WOULD YOU RATE...?

Mood	1	2	3	4	5
Energy	1	2	3	4	5
Mental clarity	1	2	3	4	5

PAIN LEVEL

1	2	3	4	5	6	7	8	9	10

Not too bad. *Well, I'm not enjoying this.* *Make it stop!*

ONSET

☐ Slow ☐ Average
☐ Rapid ☐ Sudden

DETAILED DESCRIPTION

☐ Constant ☐ Squeezing ☐ Throbbing ☐ Pounding ☐ Dull aching ☐ Burning
☐ Sharp ☐ Debilitating ☐ Other: ____

WHERE DOES IT HURT, EXACTLY?

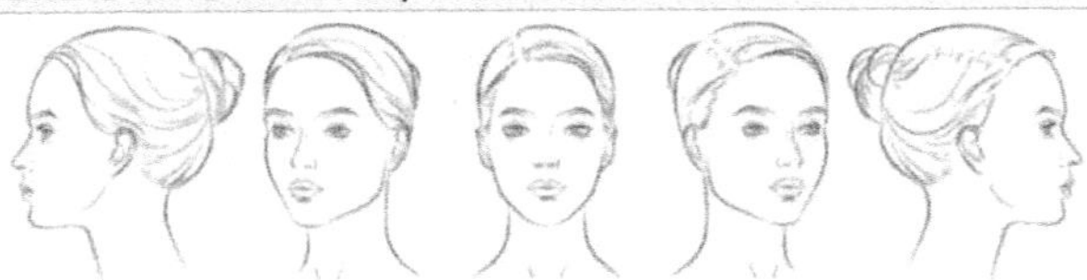

OTHER SYMPTOMS

☐ Lightheaded ☐ Dizziness
☐ Light sensitivity ☐ Sound sensitivity
☐ Confusion ☐ Auras
☐ Muscle stiffness ☐ Muscle aches

FEELING SICK?

☐ Nausea ☐ Diarrhea ☐ Vomiting ☐ Sore throat ☐ Congestion ☐ Coughing
☐ Chills ☐ Fever ☐ Other: ____

SLEEP

hours ____ *quality* 1 2 3 4 5

WEATHER

☐ Cold ☐ Mild ☐ Hot Allergen levels: ____
☐ Dry ☐ Humid ☐ Wet BM Pressure: ____

STRESS LEVELS

None	Low	Medium	High	Max	@$#%!

item / meal	*time*	*meds / supplements*	*dose*	*time*	*drinks*
					water: 1 2 3 4 5 6 7 8 9 10
					caffeine: 1 2 3 4 5 6 7 8 9 10
					alcohol: 1 2 3 4 5 6 7 8 9 10

HORMONES

☐ Menstruating ☐ Menopause
☐ PMS ☐ N/A | other

COMPUTER / MOBILE DEVICE / TV

☐ None ☐ Some ☐ A lot Total Time: ____
☐ Sitting ☐ Standing ☐ Mixture Breaks every: ____

PHYSICAL ACTIVITY

☐ None ☐ Minimal ☐ Some ☐ Sweatin' ☐ I'm beat DETAILS: ____

RELIEF MEASURES

☐ Medication ☐ Massage ☐ Sleep ☐ Exercise ☐ Water ☐ Cold/Ice
☐ Heat/Bath ☐ Other: ____
Did it work? ☐ Nope ☐ A bit ☐ Mostly ☐ 100%

Notes ☐ *See back notes*

START: | END: | DURATION: | DATE | *Entry #62*

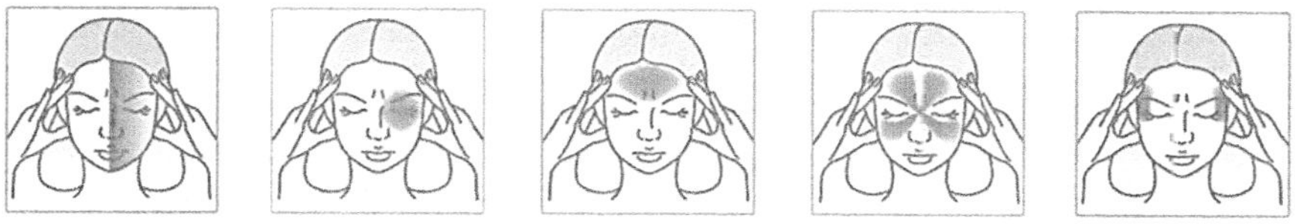

MIGRAINE | CLUSTER | TENSION | SINUS | TMJ

HOW WOULD YOU RATE...?

Mood	1	2	3	4	5
Energy	1	2	3	4	5
Mental clarity	1	2	3	4	5

PAIN LEVEL

1	2	3	4	5	6	7	8	9	10

Not too bad. *Well, I'm not enjoying this.* *Make it stop!*

ONSET

☐ Slow ☐ Average
☐ Rapid ☐ Sudden

DETAILED DESCRIPTION

☐ Constant ☐ Squeezing ☐ Throbbing ☐ Pounding ☐ Dull aching ☐ Burning
☐ Sharp ☐ Debilitating ☐ Other: ____________________

WHERE DOES IT HURT, EXACTLY?

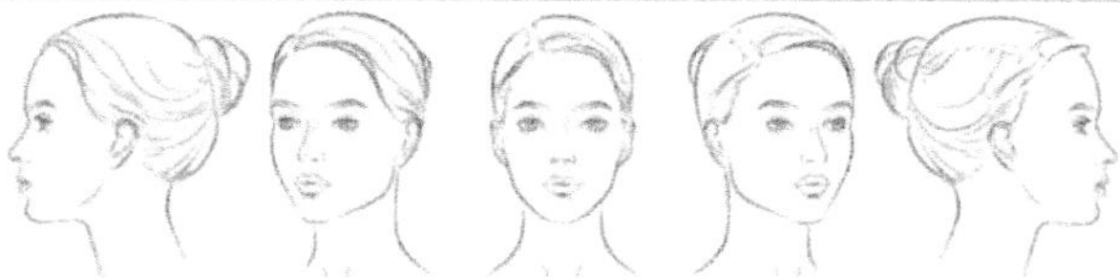

OTHER SYMPTOMS

☐ Lightheaded ☐ Dizziness
☐ Light sensitivity ☐ Sound sensitivity
☐ Confusion ☐ Auras
☐ Muscle stiffness ☐ Muscle aches

FEELING SICK?

☐ Nausea ☐ Diarrhea ☐ Vomiting ☐ Sore throat ☐ Congestion ☐ Coughing
☐ Chills ☐ Fever ☐ Other: ____________________

SLEEP

hours ________ *quality* 1 2 3 4 5

WEATHER

☐ Cold ☐ Mild ☐ Hot Allergen levels: __________
☐ Dry ☐ Humid ☐ Wet BM Pressure: __________

STRESS LEVELS

None	Low	Medium	High	Max	@$#%!

item / meal	*time*	*meds / supplements*	*dose*	*time*	*drinks*
					water: 1 2 3 4 5 6 7 8 9 10
					caffeine: 1 2 3 4 5 6 7 8 9 10
					alcohol: 1 2 3 4 5 6 7 8 9 10

HORMONES

☐ Menstruating ☐ Menopause
☐ PMS ☐ N/A | other

COMPUTER / MOBILE DEVICE / TV

☐ None ☐ Some ☐ A lot Total Time: _____
☐ Sitting ☐ Standing ☐ Mixture Breaks every: _____

PHYSICAL ACTIVITY

☐ None ☐ Minimal ☐ Some ☐ Sweatin' ☐ I'm beat DETAILS: __________

RELIEF MEASURES

☐ Medication ☐ Massage ☐ Sleep ☐ Exercise ☐ Water ☐ Cold/Ice
☐ Heat/Bath ☐ Other: ____________________
Did it work? ☐ Nope ☐ A bit ☐ Mostly ☐ 100%

Notes ☐ *See back notes*

START:	END:	DURATION:	DATE	*Entry #63*

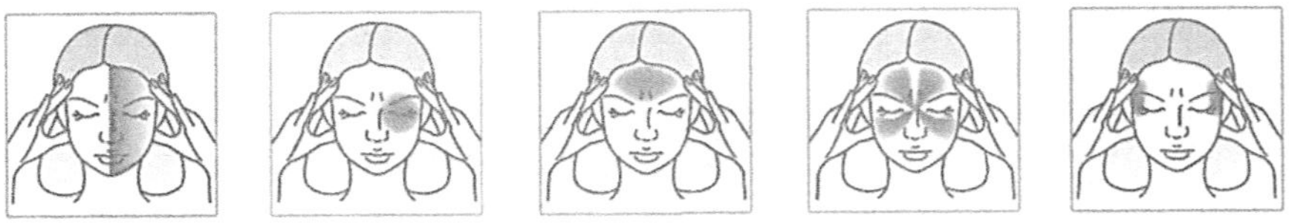

HOW WOULD YOU RATE...?

Mood	① ② ③ ④ ⑤
Energy	① ② ③ ④ ⑤
Mental clarity	① ② ③ ④ ⑤

PAIN LEVEL

1	2	3	4	5	6	7	8	9	10

Not too bad. *Well, I'm not enjoying this.* *Make it stop!*

ONSET

☐ Slow ☐ Average
☐ Rapid ☐ Sudden

DETAILED DESCRIPTION

☐ Constant ☐ Squeezing ☐ Throbbing ☐ Pounding ☐ Dull aching ☐ Burning
☐ Sharp ☐ Debilitating ☐ Other: ____________________

WHERE DOES IT HURT, EXACTLY?

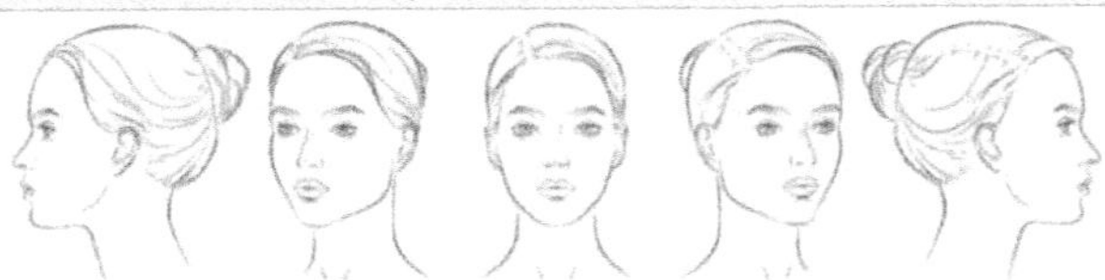

OTHER SYMPTOMS

☐ Lightheaded ☐ Dizziness
☐ Light sensitivity ☐ Sound sensitivity
☐ Confusion ☐ Auras
☐ Muscle stiffness ☐ Muscle aches

FEELING SICK?

☐ Nausea ☐ Diarrhea ☐ Vomiting ☐ Sore throat ☐ Congestion ☐ Coughing
☐ Chills ☐ Fever ☐ Other: ____________________

SLEEP

hours ________ *quality* ① ② ③ ④ ⑤

WEATHER

☐ Cold ☐ Mild ☐ Hot Allergen levels: __________
☐ Dry ☐ Humid ☐ Wet BM Pressure: __________

STRESS LEVELS

None	Low	Medium	High	Max	@$#%!

item / meal	*time*	*meds / supplements*	*dose*	*time*	*drinks*
					water ① ② ③ ④ ⑤ ⑥ ⑦ ⑧ ⑨ ⑩
					caffeine ① ② ③ ④ ⑤ ⑥ ⑦ ⑧ ⑨ ⑩
					alcohol ① ② ③ ④ ⑤ ⑥ ⑦ ⑧ ⑨ ⑩

HORMONES

☐ Menstruating ☐ Menopause
☐ PMS ☐ N/A | other

COMPUTER / MOBILE DEVICE / TV

☐ None ☐ Some ☐ A lot Total Time: ______
☐ Sitting ☐ Standing ☐ Mixture Breaks every: ______

PHYSICAL ACTIVITY

☐ None ☐ Minimal ☐ Some ☐ Sweatin' ☐ I'm beat DETAILS: ____________

RELIEF MEASURES

☐ Medication ☐ Massage ☐ Sleep ☐ Exercise ☐ Water ☐ Cold/Ice
☐ Heat/Bath ☐ Other: ____________________
Did it work? ☐ Nope ☐ A bit ☐ Mostly ☐ 100%

Notes ☐ *See back notes*

START:		END:		DURATION:		DATE		*Entry #64*

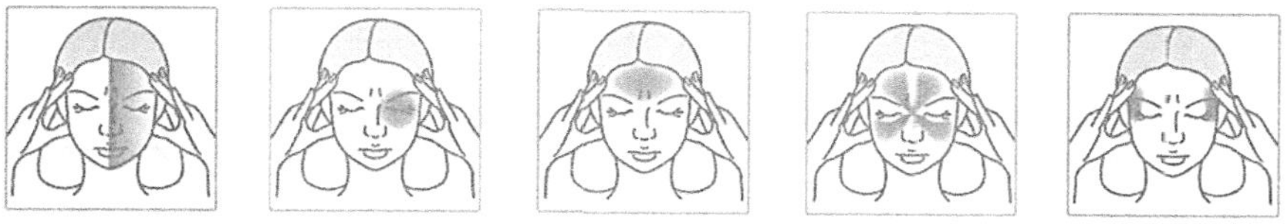

MIGRAINE CLUSTER TENSION SINUS TMJ

HOW WOULD YOU RATE...?

Mood	① ② ③ ④ ⑤
Energy	① ② ③ ④ ⑤
Mental clarity	① ② ③ ④ ⑤

PAIN LEVEL

1	2	3	4	5	6	7	8	9	10

Not too bad. *Well, I'm not enjoying this.* *Make it stop!*

ONSET

☐ Slow ☐ Average
☐ Rapid ☐ Sudden

DETAILED DESCRIPTION

☐ Constant ☐ Squeezing ☐ Throbbing ☐ Pounding ☐ Dull aching ☐ Burning
☐ Sharp ☐ Debilitating ☐ Other: ____________________

WHERE DOES IT HURT, EXACTLY?

OTHER SYMPTOMS

☐ Lightheaded ☐ Dizziness
☐ Light sensitivity ☐ Sound sensitivity
☐ Confusion ☐ Auras
☐ Muscle stiffness ☐ Muscle aches

FEELING SICK?

☐ Nausea ☐ Diarrhea ☐ Vomiting ☐ Sore throat ☐ Congestion ☐ Coughing
☐ Chills ☐ Fever ☐ Other: ____________________

SLEEP

hours ________ *quality* ① ② ③ ④ ⑤

WEATHER

☐ Cold ☐ Mild ☐ Hot Allergen levels: __________
☐ Dry ☐ Humid ☐ Wet BM Pressure: __________

STRESS LEVELS

None	Low	Medium	High	Max	@$#%!

item / meal	*time*	*meds / supplements*	*dose*	*time*	*drinks*
					water
					① ② ③ ④ ⑤ ⑥ ⑦ ⑧ ⑨ ⑩
					caffeine
					① ② ③ ④ ⑤ ⑥ ⑦ ⑧ ⑨ ⑩
					alcohol
					① ② ③ ④ ⑤ ⑥ ⑦ ⑧ ⑨ ⑩

HORMONES

☐ Menstruating ☐ Menopause
☐ PMS ☐ N/A | other

COMPUTER / MOBILE DEVICE / TV

☐ None ☐ Some ☐ A lot Total Time: ______
☐ Sitting ☐ Standing ☐ Mixture Breaks every: ______

PHYSICAL ACTIVITY

☐ None ☐ Minimal ☐ Some ☐ Sweatin' ☐ I'm beat DETAILS: ____________________

RELIEF MEASURES

☐ Medication ☐ Massage ☐ Sleep ☐ Exercise ☐ Water ☐ Cold/Ice
☐ Heat/Bath ☐ Other: ____________________
Did it work? ☐ Nope ☐ A bit ☐ Mostly ☐ 100%

Notes ☐ *See back notes*

START: ___ END: ___ DURATION: ___ DATE ___ *Entry #65*

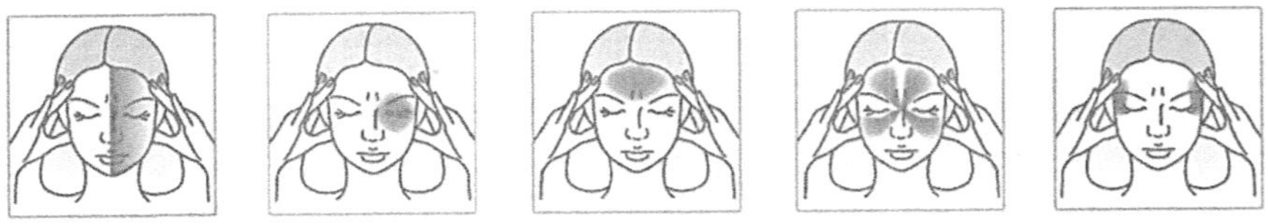

MIGRAINE | CLUSTER | TENSION | SINUS | TMJ

HOW WOULD YOU RATE...?

Mood	① ② ③ ④ ⑤
Energy	① ② ③ ④ ⑤
Mental clarity	① ② ③ ④ ⑤

PAIN LEVEL

1	2	3	4	5	6	7	8	9	10

Not too bad. *Well, I'm not enjoying this.* *Make it stop!*

ONSET

☐ Slow ☐ Average
☐ Rapid ☐ Sudden

DETAILED DESCRIPTION

☐ Constant ☐ Squeezing ☐ Throbbing ☐ Pounding ☐ Dull aching ☐ Burning
☐ Sharp ☐ Debilitating ☐ Other: ___

WHERE DOES IT HURT, EXACTLY?

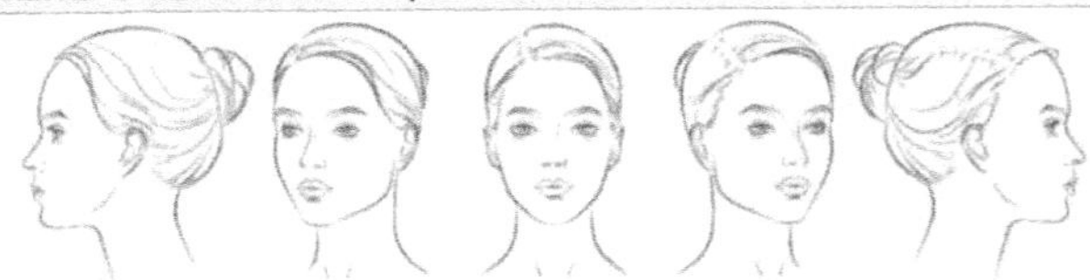

OTHER SYMPTOMS

☐ Lightheaded ☐ Dizziness
☐ Light sensitivity ☐ Sound sensitivity
☐ Confusion ☐ Auras
☐ Muscle stiffness ☐ Muscle aches

FEELING SICK?

☐ Nausea ☐ Diarrhea ☐ Vomiting ☐ Sore throat ☐ Congestion ☐ Coughing
☐ Chills ☐ Fever ☐ Other: ___

SLEEP

hours ___ *quality* ① ② ③ ④ ⑤

WEATHER

☐ Cold ☐ Mild ☐ Hot Allergen levels: ___
☐ Dry ☐ Humid ☐ Wet BM Pressure: ___

STRESS LEVELS

None	Low	Medium	High	Max	@$#%!

item / meal	*time*	*meds / supplements*	*dose*	*time*	*drinks*
					water
					① ② ③ ④ ⑤ ⑥ ⑦ ⑧ ⑨ ⑩
					caffeine
					① ② ③ ④ ⑤ ⑥ ⑦ ⑧ ⑨ ⑩
					alcohol
					① ② ③ ④ ⑤ ⑥ ⑦ ⑧ ⑨ ⑩

HORMONES

☐ Menstruating ☐ Menopause
☐ PMS ☐ N/A | other

COMPUTER / MOBILE DEVICE / TV

☐ None ☐ Some ☐ A lot Total Time: ___
☐ Sitting ☐ Standing ☐ Mixture Breaks every: ___

PHYSICAL ACTIVITY

☐ None ☐ Minimal ☐ Some ☐ Sweatin' ☐ I'm beat DETAILS: ___

RELIEF MEASURES

☐ Medication ☐ Massage ☐ Sleep ☐ Exercise ☐ Water ☐ Cold/Ice
☐ Heat/Bath ☐ Other: ___
Did it work? ☐ Nope ☐ A bit ☐ Mostly ☐ 100%

Notes ☐ *See back notes*

START:		END:		DURATION:		DATE		*Entry #66*

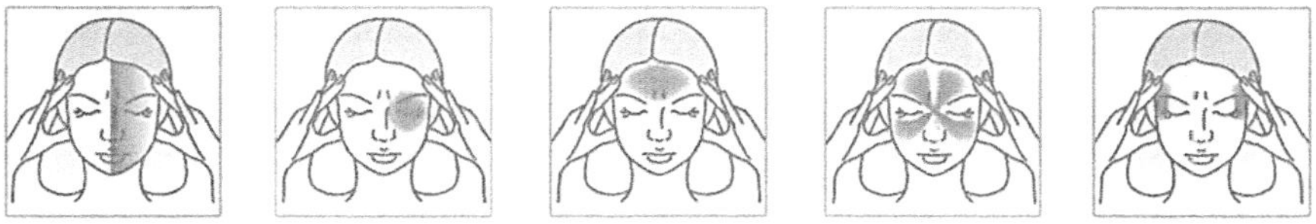

MIGRAINE CLUSTER TENSION SINUS TMJ

HOW WOULD YOU RATE...?

Mood	①	②	③	④	⑤
Energy	①	②	③	④	⑤
Mental clarity	①	②	③	④	⑤

PAIN LEVEL

1	2	3	4	5	6	7	8	9	10

Not too bad. *Well, I'm not enjoying this.* *Make it stop!*

ONSET

☐ Slow ☐ Average
☐ Rapid ☐ Sudden

DETAILED DESCRIPTION

☐ Constant ☐ Squeezing ☐ Throbbing ☐ Pounding ☐ Dull aching ☐ Burning
☐ Sharp ☐ Debilitating ☐ Other: ____________________

WHERE DOES IT HURT, EXACTLY?

OTHER SYMPTOMS

☐ Lightheaded ☐ Dizziness
☐ Light sensitivity ☐ Sound sensitivity
☐ Confusion ☐ Auras
☐ Muscle stiffness ☐ Muscle aches

FEELING SICK?

☐ Nausea ☐ Diarrhea ☐ Vomiting ☐ Sore throat ☐ Congestion ☐ Coughing
☐ Chills ☐ Fever ☐ Other: ____________________

SLEEP

hours ________ *quality* ① ② ③ ④ ⑤

WEATHER

☐ Cold ☐ Mild ☐ Hot Allergen levels: ____________
☐ Dry ☐ Humid ☐ Wet BM Pressure: ____________

STRESS LEVELS

None	Low	Medium	High	Max	@$#%!

item / meal	*time*	*meds / supplements*	*dose*	*time*	*drinks*
					water
					① ② ③ ④ ⑤ ⑥ ⑦ ⑧ ⑨ ⑩
					caffeine
					① ② ③ ④ ⑤ ⑥ ⑦ ⑧ ⑨ ⑩
					alcohol
					① ② ③ ④ ⑤ ⑥ ⑦ ⑧ ⑨ ⑩

HORMONES

☐ Menstruating ☐ Menopause
☐ PMS ☐ N/A | other

COMPUTER / MOBILE DEVICE / TV

☐ None ☐ Some ☐ A lot Total Time: ______
☐ Sitting ☐ Standing ☐ Mixture Breaks every: ______

PHYSICAL ACTIVITY

☐ None ☐ Minimal ☐ Some ☐ Sweatin' ☐ I'm beat DETAILS: ____________________

RELIEF MEASURES

☐ Medication ☐ Massage ☐ Sleep ☐ Exercise ☐ Water ☐ Cold/Ice
☐ Heat/Bath ☐ Other: ____________________
Did it work? ☐ Nope ☐ A bit ☐ Mostly ☐ 100%

Notes ☐ *See back notes*

START: ______ END: ______ DURATION: ______ DATE ______ *Entry #67*

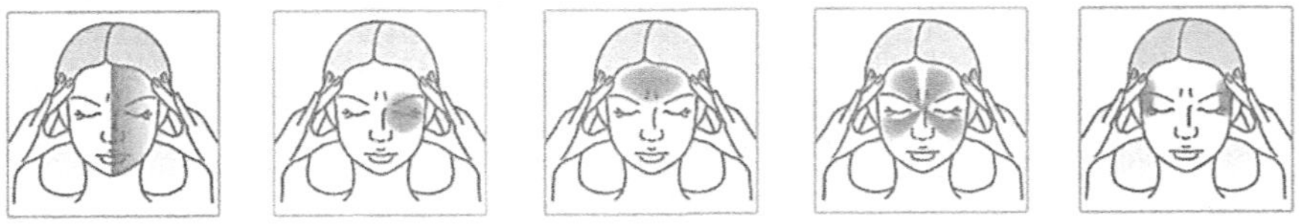

MIGRAINE | CLUSTER | TENSION | SINUS | TMJ

HOW WOULD YOU RATE...?

Mood ① ② ③ ④ ⑤

Energy ① ② ③ ④ ⑤

Mental clarity ① ② ③ ④ ⑤

PAIN LEVEL

1	2	3	4	5	6	7	8	9	10

Not too bad. *Well, I'm not enjoying this.* *Make it stop!*

ONSET

☐ Slow ☐ Average
☐ Rapid ☐ Sudden

DETAILED DESCRIPTION

☐ Constant ☐ Squeezing ☐ Throbbing ☐ Pounding ☐ Dull aching ☐ Burning
☐ Sharp ☐ Debilitating ☐ Other: ____________________

WHERE DOES IT HURT, EXACTLY?

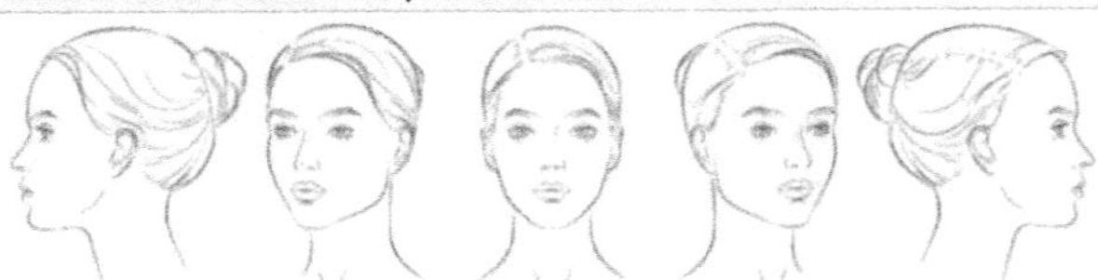

OTHER SYMPTOMS

☐ Lightheaded ☐ Dizziness
☐ Light sensitivity ☐ Sound sensitivity
☐ Confusion ☐ Auras
☐ Muscle stiffness ☐ Muscle aches

FEELING SICK?

☐ Nausea ☐ Diarrhea ☐ Vomiting ☐ Sore throat ☐ Congestion ☐ Coughing
☐ Chills ☐ Fever ☐ Other: ____________________

SLEEP

hours ______ *quality* ① ② ③ ④ ⑤

WEATHER

☐ Cold ☐ Mild ☐ Hot Allergen levels: ______
☐ Dry ☐ Humid ☐ Wet BM Pressure: ______

STRESS LEVELS

None	Low	Medium	High	Max	@$#%!

item / meal	*time*	*meds / supplements*	*dose*	*time*	*drinks*
					water ① ② ③ ④ ⑤ ⑥ ⑦ ⑧ ⑨ ⑩
					caffeine ① ② ③ ④ ⑤ ⑥ ⑦ ⑧ ⑨ ⑩
					alcohol ① ② ③ ④ ⑤ ⑥ ⑦ ⑧ ⑨ ⑩

HORMONES

☐ Menstruating ☐ Menopause
☐ PMS ☐ N/A | other

COMPUTER / MOBILE DEVICE / TV

☐ None ☐ Some ☐ A lot Total Time: ______
☐ Sitting ☐ Standing ☐ Mixture Breaks every: ______

PHYSICAL ACTIVITY

☐ None ☐ Minimal ☐ Some ☐ Sweatin' ☐ I'm beat DETAILS: ______

RELIEF MEASURES

☐ Medication ☐ Massage ☐ Sleep ☐ Exercise ☐ Water ☐ Cold/Ice
☐ Heat/Bath ☐ Other: ____________________
Did it work? ☐ Nope ☐ A bit ☐ Mostly ☐ 100%

Notes ☐ *See back notes*

START: | END: | DURATION: | DATE | *Entry #68*

HOW WOULD YOU RATE...?

Mood	1	2	3	4	5
Energy	1	2	3	4	5
Mental clarity	1	2	3	4	5

PAIN LEVEL

1	2	3	4	5	6	7	8	9	10

Not too bad. *Well, I'm not enjoying this.* *Make it stop!*

ONSET

☐ Slow ☐ Average
☐ Rapid ☐ Sudden

DETAILED DESCRIPTION

☐ Constant ☐ Squeezing ☐ Throbbing ☐ Pounding ☐ Dull aching ☐ Burning
☐ Sharp ☐ Debilitating ☐ Other: ______________________

WHERE DOES IT HURT, EXACTLY?

OTHER SYMPTOMS

☐ Lightheaded ☐ Dizziness
☐ Light sensitivity ☐ Sound sensitivity
☐ Confusion ☐ Auras
☐ Muscle stiffness ☐ Muscle aches

FEELING SICK?

☐ Nausea ☐ Diarrhea ☐ Vomiting ☐ Sore throat ☐ Congestion ☐ Coughing
☐ Chills ☐ Fever ☐ Other: ______________________

SLEEP

hours ________ *quality* 1 2 3 4 5

WEATHER

☐ Cold ☐ Mild ☐ Hot Allergen levels: ____________
☐ Dry ☐ Humid ☐ Wet BM Pressure: ____________

STRESS LEVELS

None	Low	Medium	High	Max	@$#%!

item / meal	*time*	*meds / supplements*	*dose*	*time*	*drinks*
					water
					1 2 3 4 5 6 7 8 9 10
					caffeine
					1 2 3 4 5 6 7 8 9 10
					alcohol
					1 2 3 4 5 6 7 8 9 10

HORMONES

☐ Menstruating ☐ Menopause
☐ PMS ☐ N/A | other

COMPUTER / MOBILE DEVICE / TV

☐ None ☐ Some ☐ A lot Total Time: _____
☐ Sitting ☐ Standing ☐ Mixture Breaks every: _____

PHYSICAL ACTIVITY

☐ None ☐ Minimal ☐ Some ☐ Sweatin' ☐ I'm bea DETAILS: ______________

RELIEF MEASURES

☐ Medication ☐ Massage ☐ Sleep ☐ Exercise ☐ Water ☐ Cold/Ice
☐ Heat/Bath ☐ Other: ______________________
Did it work? ☐ Nope ☐ A bit ☐ Mostly ☐ 100%

Notes ☐ *See back notes*

START:		END:		DURATION:		DATE		*Entry #69*

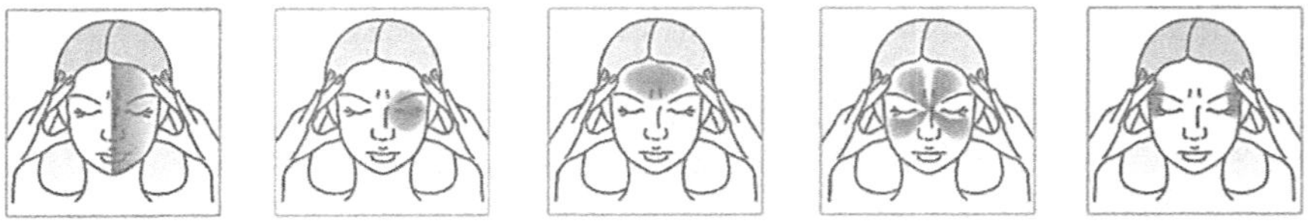

MIGRAINE | CLUSTER | TENSION | SINUS | TMJ

HOW WOULD YOU RATE...?

Mood	① ② ③ ④ ⑤
Energy	① ② ③ ④ ⑤
Mental clarity	① ② ③ ④ ⑤

PAIN LEVEL

1	2	3	4	5	6	7	8	9	10

Not too bad. *Well, I'm not enjoying this.* *Make it stop!*

ONSET

☐ Slow ☐ Average
☐ Rapid ☐ Sudden

DETAILED DESCRIPTION

☐ Constant ☐ Squeezing ☐ Throbbing ☐ Pounding ☐ Dull aching ☐ Burning
☐ Sharp ☐ Debilitating ☐ Other: ______________________________

WHERE DOES IT HURT, EXACTLY?

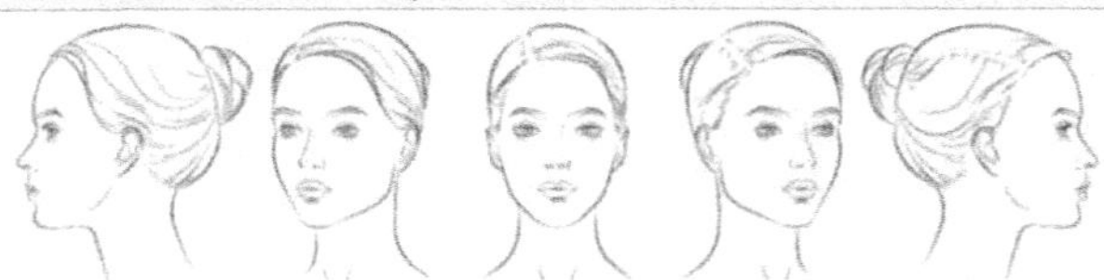

OTHER SYMPTOMS

☐ Lightheaded ☐ Dizziness
☐ Light sensitivity ☐ Sound sensitivity
☐ Confusion ☐ Auras
☐ Muscle stiffness ☐ Muscle aches

FEELING SICK?

☐ Nausea ☐ Diarrhea ☐ Vomiting ☐ Sore throat ☐ Congestion ☐ Coughing
☐ Chills ☐ Fever ☐ Other: ______________________________

SLEEP

hours ________ *quality* ① ② ③ ④ ⑤

WEATHER

☐ Cold ☐ Mild ☐ Hot Allergen levels: ____________
☐ Dry ☐ Humid ☐ Wet BM Pressure: ____________

STRESS LEVELS

None	Low	Medium	High	Max	@$#%!

item / meal	*time*	*meds / supplements*	*dose*	*time*	*drinks*
					water
					① ② ③ ④ ⑤ ⑥ ⑦ ⑧ ⑨ ⑩
					caffeine
					① ② ③ ④ ⑤ ⑥ ⑦ ⑧ ⑨ ⑩
					alcohol
					① ② ③ ④ ⑤ ⑥ ⑦ ⑧ ⑨ ⑩

HORMONES

☐ Menstruating ☐ Menopause
☐ PMS ☐ N/A | other

COMPUTER / MOBILE DEVICE / TV

☐ None ☐ Some ☐ A lot Total Time: ______
☐ Sitting ☐ Standing ☐ Mixture Breaks every: ______

PHYSICAL ACTIVITY

☐ None ☐ Minimal ☐ Some ☐ Sweatin' ☐ I'm beat DETAILS: ______________________

RELIEF MEASURES

☐ Medication ☐ Massage ☐ Sleep ☐ Exercise ☐ Water ☐ Cold/Ice
☐ Heat/Bath ☐ Other: ______________________________

Did it work? ☐ Nope ☐ A bit ☐ Mostly ☐ 100%

Notes

☐ *See back notes*

START:		END:		DURATION:		DATE		*Entry #70*

MIGRAINE

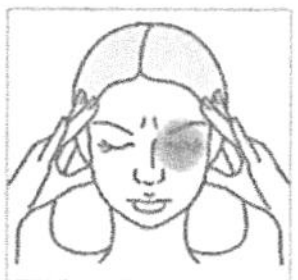
CLUSTER

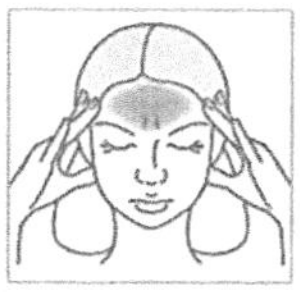
TENSION

SINUS

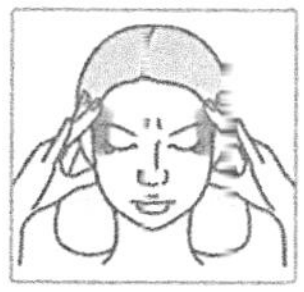
TMJ

HOW WOULD YOU RATE...?

Mood	①	②	③	④	⑤
Energy	①	②	③	④	⑤
Mental clarity	①	②	③	④	⑤

PAIN LEVEL

1	2	3	4	5	6	7	8	9	10

Not too bad. *Well, I'm not enjoying this.* *Make it stop!*

ONSET

☐ Slow ☐ Average
☐ Rapid ☐ Sudden

DETAILED DESCRIPTION

☐ Constant ☐ Squeezing ☐ Throbbing ☐ Pounding ☐ Dull aching ☐ Burning
☐ Sharp ☐ Debilitating ☐ Other: ____________________

WHERE DOES IT HURT, EXACTLY?

OTHER SYMPTOMS

☐ Lightheaded ☐ Dizziness
☐ Light sensitivity ☐ Sound sensitivity
☐ Confusion ☐ Auras
☐ Muscle stiffness ☐ Muscle aches

FEELING SICK?

☐ Nausea ☐ Diarrhea ☐ Vomiting ☐ Sore throat ☐ Congestion ☐ Coughing
☐ Chills ☐ Fever ☐ Other: ____________________

SLEEP

hours ________ *quality* ① ② ③ ④ ⑤

WEATHER

☐ Cold ☐ Mild ☐ Hot Allergen levels: __________
☐ Dry ☐ Humid ☐ Wet BM Pressure: __________

STRESS LEVELS

None	Low	Medium	High	Max	@$#%!

item / meal	*time*	*meds / supplements*	*dose*	*time*	*drinks*
					water
					① ② ③ ④ ⑤ ⑥ ⑦ ⑧ ⑨ ⑩
					caffeine
					① ② ③ ④ ⑤ ⑥ ⑦ ⑧ ⑨ ⑩
					alcohol
					① ② ③ ④ ⑤ ⑥ ⑦ ⑧ ⑨ ⑩

HORMONES

☐ Menstruating ☐ Menopause
☐ PMS ☐ N/A | other

COMPUTER / MOBILE DEVICE / TV

☐ None ☐ Some ☐ A lot Total Time: ______
☐ Sitting ☐ Standing ☐ Mixture Breaks every: ______

PHYSICAL ACTIVITY

☐ None ☐ Minimal ☐ Some ☐ Sweatin' ☐ I'm beat DETAILS: ____________________

RELIEF MEASURES

☐ Medication ☐ Massage ☐ Sleep ☐ Exercise ☐ Water ☐ Cold/Ice
☐ Heat/Bath ☐ Other: ____________________
Did it work? ☐ Nope ☐ A bit ☐ Mostly ☐ 100%

Notes ☐ *See back notes*

START:		END:		DURATION:		DATE		*Entry #71*

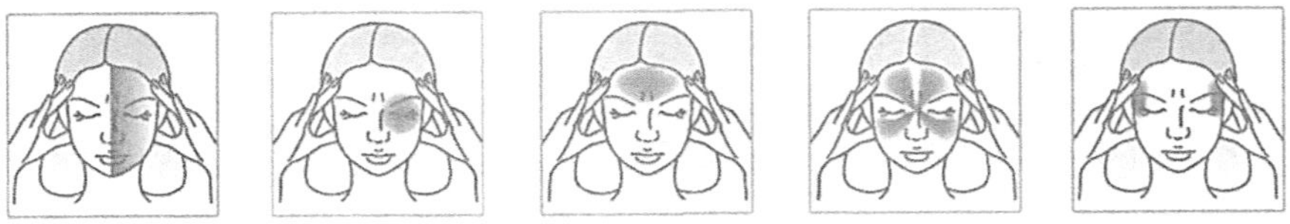

MIGRAINE CLUSTER TENSION SINUS TMJ

HOW WOULD YOU RATE...?

Mood ① ② ③ ④ ⑤

Energy ① ② ③ ④ ⑤

Mental clarity ① ② ③ ④ ⑤

PAIN LEVEL

1	2	3	4	5	6	7	8	9	10

Not too bad. *Well, I'm not enjoying this.* *Make it stop!*

ONSET

☐ Slow ☐ Average
☐ Rapid ☐ Sudden

DETAILED DESCRIPTION

☐ Constant ☐ Squeezing ☐ Throbbing ☐ Pounding ☐ Dull aching ☐ Burning
☐ Sharp ☐ Debilitating ☐ Other: ____________________

WHERE DOES IT HURT, EXACTLY?

OTHER SYMPTOMS

☐ Lightheaded ☐ Dizziness
☐ Light sensitivity ☐ Sound sensitivity
☐ Confusion ☐ Auras
☐ Muscle stiffness ☐ Muscle aches

FEELING SICK?

☐ Nausea ☐ Diarrhea ☐ Vomiting ☐ Sore throat ☐ Congestion ☐ Coughing
☐ Chills ☐ Fever ☐ Other: ____________________

SLEEP

hours *quality*
________ ① ② ③ ④ ⑤

WEATHER

☐ Cold ☐ Mild ☐ Hot Allergen levels: ____________
☐ Dry ☐ Humid ☐ Wet BM Pressure: ____________

STRESS LEVELS

None	Low	Medium	High	Max	@$#%!

item / meal	*time*	*meds / supplements*	*dose*	*time*	*drinks*
					water
					① ② ③ ④ ⑤ ⑥ ⑦ ⑧ ⑨ ⑩
					caffeine
					① ② ③ ④ ⑤ ⑥ ⑦ ⑧ ⑨ ⑩
					alcohol
					① ② ③ ④ ⑤ ⑥ ⑦ ⑧ ⑨ ⑩

HORMONES

☐ Menstruating ☐ Menopause
☐ PMS ☐ N/A | other

COMPUTER / MOBILE DEVICE / TV

☐ None ☐ Some ☐ A lot Total Time: ______
☐ Sitting ☐ Standing ☐ Mixture Breaks every: ______

PHYSICAL ACTIVITY

☐ None ☐ Minimal ☐ Some ☐ Sweatin' ☐ I'm beat DETAILS:____________________

RELIEF MEASURES

☐ Medication ☐ Massage ☐ Sleep ☐ Exercise ☐ Water ☐ Cold/Ice
☐ Heat/Bath ☐ Other: ____________________
Did it work? ☐ Nope ☐ A bit ☐ Mostly ☐ 100%

Notes ☐ *See back notes*

START: ______ END: ______ DURATION: ______ DATE ______ *Entry #72*

MIGRAINE | CLUSTER | TENSION | SINUS | TMJ

HOW WOULD YOU RATE...?

Mood	1	2	3	4	5
Energy	1	2	3	4	5
Mental clarity	1	2	3	4	5

PAIN LEVEL

1	2	3	4	5	6	7	8	9	10

Not too bad. *Well, I'm not enjoying this.* *Make it stop!*

ONSET

☐ Slow ☐ Average
☐ Rapid ☐ Sudden

DETAILED DESCRIPTION

☐ Constant ☐ Squeezing ☐ Throbbing ☐ Pounding ☐ Dull aching ☐ Burning
☐ Sharp ☐ Debilitating ☐ Other: ____________________

WHERE DOES IT HURT, EXACTLY?

OTHER SYMPTOMS

☐ Lightheaded ☐ Dizziness
☐ Light sensitivity ☐ Sound sensitivity
☐ Confusion ☐ Auras
☐ Muscle stiffness ☐ Muscle aches

FEELING SICK?

☐ Nausea ☐ Diarrhea ☐ Vomiting ☐ Sore throat ☐ Congestion ☐ Coughing
☐ Chills ☐ Fever ☐ Other: ____________________

SLEEP

hours ______ *quality* 1 2 3 4 5

WEATHER

☐ Cold ☐ Mild ☐ Hot Allergen levels: __________
☐ Dry ☐ Humid ☐ Wet BM Pressure: __________

STRESS LEVELS

None	Low	Medium	High	Max	@$#%!

item / meal	*time*	*meds / supplements*	*dose*	*time*	*drinks*
					water: 1 2 3 4 5 6 7 8 9 10
					caffeine: 1 2 3 4 5 6 7 8 9 10
					alcohol: 1 2 3 4 5 6 7 8 9 10

HORMONES

☐ Menstruating ☐ Menopause
☐ PMS ☐ N/A | other

COMPUTER / MOBILE DEVICE / TV

☐ None ☐ Some ☐ A lot Total Time: ______
☐ Sitting ☐ Standing ☐ Mixture Breaks every: ______

PHYSICAL ACTIVITY

☐ None ☐ Minimal ☐ Some ☐ Sweatin' ☐ I'm beat DETAILS: ____________________

RELIEF MEASURES

☐ Medication ☐ Massage ☐ Sleep ☐ Exercise ☐ Water ☐ Cold/Ice
☐ Heat/Bath ☐ Other: ____________________

Did it work? ☐ Nope ☐ A bit ☐ Mostly ☐ 100%

Notes ☐ *See back notes*

START:		END:		DURATION:		DATE		*Entry #73*

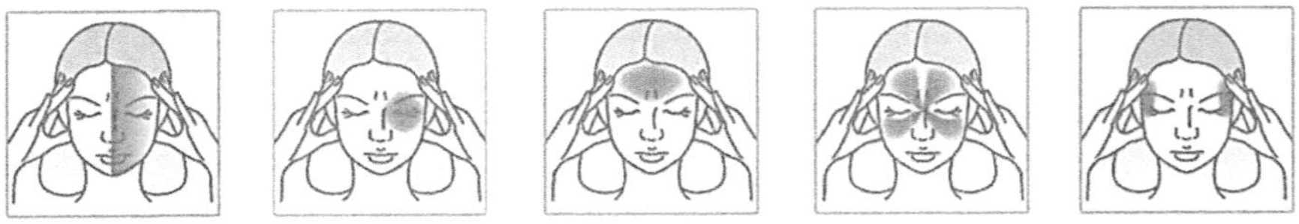

MIGRAINE CLUSTER TENSION SINUS TMJ

HOW WOULD YOU RATE...?

Mood	①	②	③	④	⑤
Energy	①	②	③	④	⑤
Mental clarity	①	②	③	④	⑤

PAIN LEVEL

1	2	3	4	5	6	7	8	9	10

Not too bad. *Well, I'm not enjoying this.* *Make it stop!*

ONSET

☐ Slow ☐ Average
☐ Rapid ☐ Sudden

DETAILED DESCRIPTION

☐ Constant ☐ Squeezing ☐ Throbbing ☐ Pounding ☐ Dull aching ☐ Burning
☐ Sharp ☐ Debilitating ☐ Other: ______________________________

WHERE DOES IT HURT, EXACTLY?

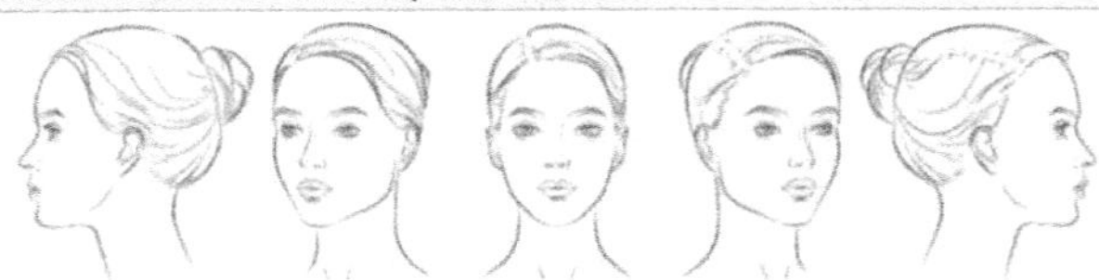

OTHER SYMPTOMS

☐ Lightheaded ☐ Dizziness
☐ Light sensitivity ☐ Sound sensitivity
☐ Confusion ☐ Auras
☐ Muscle stiffness ☐ Muscle aches

FEELING SICK?

☐ Nausea ☐ Diarrhea ☐ Vomiting ☐ Sore throat ☐ Congestion ☐ Coughing
☐ Chills ☐ Fever ☐ Other: ______________________________

SLEEP

hours ________ *quality* ① ② ③ ④ ⑤

WEATHER

☐ Cold ☐ Mild ☐ Hot Allergen levels: ____________
☐ Dry ☐ Humid ☐ Wet BM Pressure: ____________

STRESS LEVELS

None	Low	Medium	High	Max	@$#%!

item / meal	*time*	*meds / supplements*	*dose*	*time*	*drinks*
					water
					① ② ③ ④ ⑤ ⑥ ⑦ ⑧ ⑨ ⑩
					caffeine
					① ② ③ ④ ⑤ ⑥ ⑦ ⑧ ⑨ ⑩
					alcohol
					① ② ③ ④ ⑤ ⑥ ⑦ ⑧ ⑨ ⑩

HORMONES

☐ Menstruating ☐ Menopause
☐ PMS ☐ N/A | other

COMPUTER / MOBILE DEVICE / TV

☐ None ☐ Some ☐ A lot Total Time: ______
☐ Sitting ☐ Standing ☐ Mixture Breaks every: ______

PHYSICAL ACTIVITY

☐ None ☐ Minimal ☐ Some ☐ Sweatin' ☐ I'm beat DETAILS: ____________

RELIEF MEASURES

☐ Medication ☐ Massage ☐ Sleep ☐ Exercise ☐ Water ☐ Cold/Ice
☐ Heat/Bath ☐ Other: ______________________________

Did it work? ☐ Nope ☐ A bit ☐ Mostly ☐ 100%

Notes ☐ *See back notes*

START: | END: | DURATION: | DATE | *Entry #74*

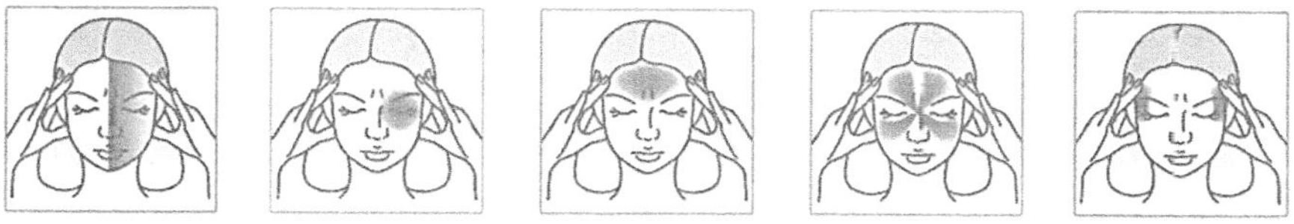

MIGRAINE | CLUSTER | TENSION | SINUS | TMJ

HOW WOULD YOU RATE...?

Mood	①	②	③	④	⑤
Energy	①	②	③	④	⑤
Mental clarity	①	②	③	④	⑤

PAIN LEVEL

1	2	3	4	5	6	7	8	9	10

Not too bad. *Well, I'm not enjoying this.* *Make it stop!*

ONSET

☐ Slow ☐ Average
☐ Rapid ☐ Sudden

DETAILED DESCRIPTION

☐ Constant ☐ Squeezing ☐ Throbbing ☐ Pounding ☐ Dull aching ☐ Burning
☐ Sharp ☐ Debilitating ☐ Other: ____________

WHERE DOES IT HURT, EXACTLY?

OTHER SYMPTOMS

☐ Lightheaded ☐ Dizziness
☐ Light sensitivity ☐ Sound sensitivity
☐ Confusion ☐ Auras
☐ Muscle stiffness ☐ Muscle aches

FEELING SICK?

☐ Nausea ☐ Diarrhea ☐ Vomiting ☐ Sore throat ☐ Congestion ☐ Coughing
☐ Chills ☐ Fever ☐ Other: ____________

SLEEP

hours ________ *quality* ① ② ③ ④ ⑤

WEATHER

☐ Cold ☐ Mild ☐ Hot Allergen levels: ________
☐ Dry ☐ Humid ☐ Wet BM Pressure: ________

STRESS LEVELS

None	Low	Medium	High	Max	@$#%!

item / meal	*time*	*meds / supplements*	*dose*	*time*	*drinks*
					water
					① ② ③ ④ ⑤ ⑥ ⑦ ⑧ ⑨ ⑩
					caffeine
					① ② ③ ④ ⑤ ⑥ ⑦ ⑧ ⑨ ⑩
					alcohol
					① ② ③ ④ ⑤ ⑥ ⑦ ⑧ ⑨ ⑩

HORMONES

☐ Menstruating ☐ Menopause
☐ PMS ☐ N/A | other

COMPUTER / MOBILE DEVICE / TV

☐ None ☐ Some ☐ A lot Total Time: ______
☐ Sitting ☐ Standing ☐ Mixture Breaks every: ______

PHYSICAL ACTIVITY

☐ None ☐ Minimal ☐ Some ☐ Sweatin' ☐ I'm beat DETAILS: ____________

RELIEF MEASURES

☐ Medication ☐ Massage ☐ Sleep ☐ Exercise ☐ Water ☐ Cold/Ice
☐ Heat/Bath ☐ Other: ____________
Did it work? ☐ Nope ☐ A bit ☐ Mostly ☐ 100%

Notes ☐ *See back notes*

START: | END: | DURATION: | DATE | *Entry #75*

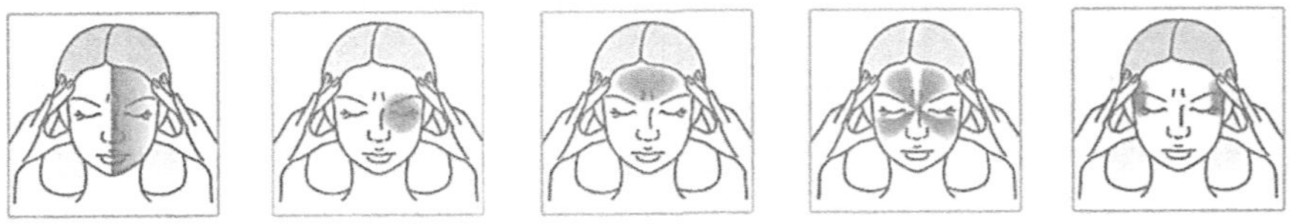

MIGRAINE | CLUSTER | TENSION | SINUS | TMJ

HOW WOULD YOU RATE...?

Mood ① ② ③ ④ ⑤

Energy ① ② ③ ④ ⑤

Mental clarity ① ② ③ ④ ⑤

PAIN LEVEL

1	2	3	4	5	6	7	8	9	10

Not too bad. *Well, I'm not enjoying this.* *Make it stop!*

ONSET

☐ Slow ☐ Average
☐ Rapid ☐ Sudden

DETAILED DESCRIPTION

☐ Constant ☐ Squeezing ☐ Throbbing ☐ Pounding ☐ Dull aching ☐ Burning
☐ Sharp ☐ Debilitating ☐ Other: ______

WHERE DOES IT HURT, EXACTLY?

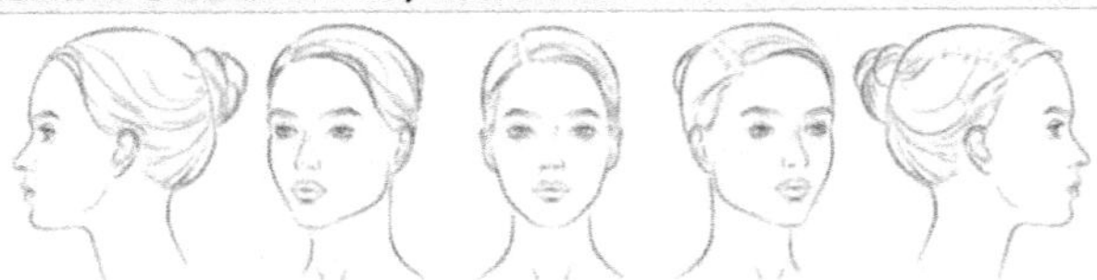

OTHER SYMPTOMS

☐ Lightheaded ☐ Dizziness
☐ Light sensitivity ☐ Sound sensitivity
☐ Confusion ☐ Auras
☐ Muscle stiffness ☐ Muscle aches

FEELING SICK?

☐ Nausea ☐ Diarrhea ☐ Vomiting ☐ Sore throat ☐ Congestion ☐ Coughing
☐ Chills ☐ Fever ☐ Other: ______

SLEEP

hours ______ *quality* ① ② ③ ④ ⑤

WEATHER

☐ Cold ☐ Mild ☐ Hot Allergen levels: ______
☐ Dry ☐ Humid ☐ Wet BM Pressure: ______

STRESS LEVELS

None	Low	Medium	High	Max	@$#%!

item / meal	*time*	*meds / supplements*	*dose*	*time*	*drinks*
					water ① ② ③ ④ ⑤ ⑥ ⑦ ⑧ ⑨ ⑩
					caffeine ① ② ③ ④ ⑤ ⑥ ⑦ ⑧ ⑨ ⑩
					alcohol ① ② ③ ④ ⑤ ⑥ ⑦ ⑧ ⑨ ⑩

HORMONES

☐ Menstruating ☐ Menopause
☐ PMS ☐ N/A | other

COMPUTER / MOBILE DEVICE / TV

☐ None ☐ Some ☐ A lot Total Time: ______
☐ Sitting ☐ Standing ☐ Mixture Breaks every: ______

PHYSICAL ACTIVITY

☐ None ☐ Minimal ☐ Some ☐ Sweatin' ☐ I'm beat DETAILS: ______

RELIEF MEASURES

☐ Medication ☐ Massage ☐ Sleep ☐ Exercise ☐ Water ☐ Cold/Ice
☐ Heat/Bath ☐ Other: ______
Did it work? ☐ Nope ☐ A bit ☐ Mostly ☐ 100%

Notes ☐ *See back notes*

START:		END:		DURATION:		DATE		*Entry #76*

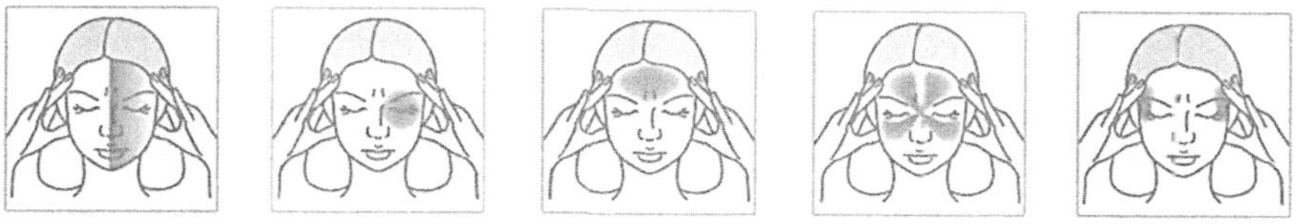

MIGRAINE | CLUSTER | TENSION | SINUS | TMJ

HOW WOULD YOU RATE...?

Mood	1	2	3	4	5
Energy	1	2	3	4	5
Mental clarity	1	2	3	4	5

PAIN LEVEL

1	2	3	4	5	6	7	8	9	10

Not too bad. *Well, I'm not enjoying this.* *Make it stop!*

ONSET

☐ Slow ☐ Average
☐ Rapid ☐ Sudden

DETAILED DESCRIPTION

☐ Constant ☐ Squeezing ☐ Throbbing ☐ Pounding ☐ Dull aching ☐ Burning
☐ Sharp ☐ Debilitating ☐ Other: ____________________

WHERE DOES IT HURT, EXACTLY?

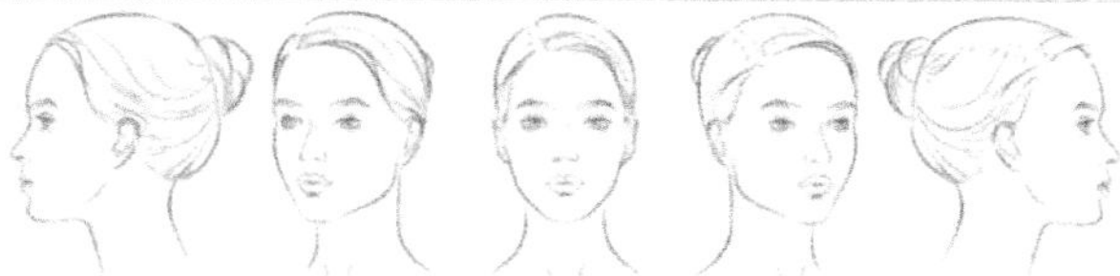

OTHER SYMPTOMS

☐ Lightheaded ☐ Dizziness
☐ Light sensitivity ☐ Sound sensitivity
☐ Confusion ☐ Auras
☐ Muscle stiffness ☐ Muscle aches

FEELING SICK?

☐ Nausea ☐ Diarrhea ☐ Vomiting ☐ Sore throat ☐ Congestion ☐ Coughing
☐ Chills ☐ Fever ☐ Other: ____________________

SLEEP

hours ________ *quality* 1 2 3 4 5

WEATHER

☐ Cold ☐ Mild ☐ Hot Allergen levels: __________
☐ Dry ☐ Humid ☐ Wet BM Pressure: __________

STRESS LEVELS

None	Low	Medium	High	Max	@$#%!

item / meal	*time*	*meds / supplements*	*dose*	*time*	*drinks*
					water
					1 2 3 4 5 6 7 8 9 10
					caffeine
					1 2 3 4 5 6 7 8 9 10
					alcohol
					1 2 3 4 5 6 7 8 9 10

HORMONES

☐ Menstruating ☐ Menopause
☐ PMS ☐ N/A | other

COMPUTER / MOBILE DEVICE / TV

☐ None ☐ Some ☐ A lot Total Time: ______
☐ Sitting ☐ Standing ☐ Mixture Breaks every: ______

PHYSICAL ACTIVITY

☐ None ☐ Minimal ☐ Some ☐ Sweatin' ☐ I'm beat DETAILS: ____________

RELIEF MEASURES

☐ Medication ☐ Massage ☐ Sleep ☐ Exercise ☐ Water ☐ Cold/Ice
☐ Heat/Bath ☐ Other: ____________________
Did it work? ☐ Nope ☐ A bit ☐ Mostly ☐ 100%

Notes ☐ *See back notes*

START:		END:		DURATION:		DATE		*Entry #77*

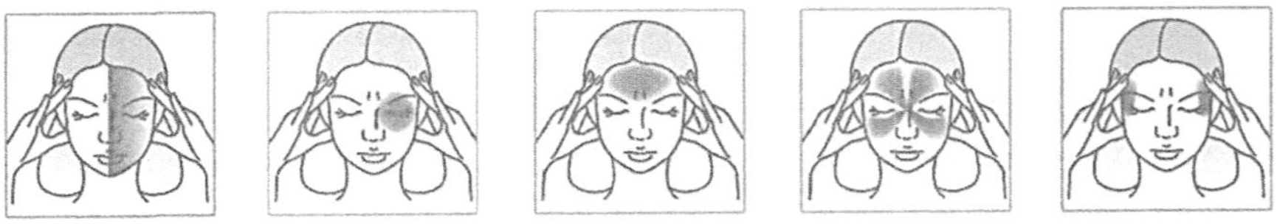

MIGRAINE　CLUSTER　TENSION　SINUS　TMJ

HOW WOULD YOU RATE...?					
Mood	①	②	③	④	⑤
Energy	①	②	③	④	⑤
Mental clarity	①	②	③	④	⑤

PAIN LEVEL

1	2	3	4	5	6	7	8	9	10

Not too bad.　*Well, I'm not enjoying this.*　*Make it stop!*

ONSET

☐ Slow　☐ Average
☐ Rapid　☐ Sudden

DETAILED DESCRIPTION

☐ Constant　☐ Squeezing　☐ Throbbing　☐ Pounding　☐ Dull aching　☐ Burning
☐ Sharp　☐ Debilitating　☐ Other: ____________________

WHERE DOES IT HURT, EXACTLY?

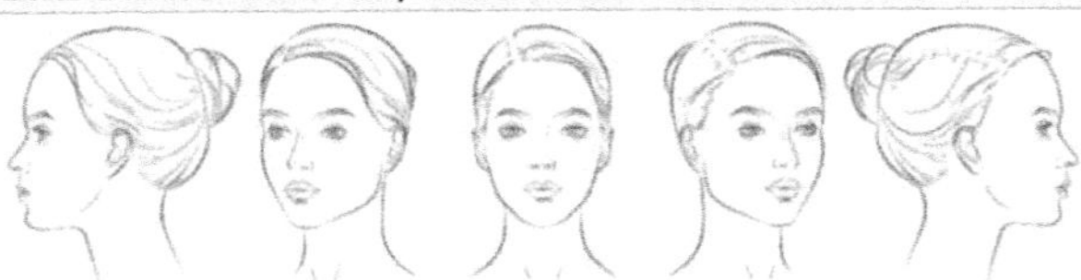

OTHER SYMPTOMS

☐ Lightheaded　☐ Dizziness
☐ Light sensitivity　☐ Sound sensitivity
☐ Confusion　☐ Auras
☐ Muscle stiffness　☐ Muscle aches

FEELING SICK?

☐ Nausea　☐ Diarrhea　☐ Vomiting　☐ Sore throat　☐ Congestion　☐ Coughing
☐ Chills　☐ Fever　☐ Other: ____________________

SLEEP

hours ________　*quality* ① ② ③ ④ ⑤

WEATHER

☐ Cold　☐ Mild　☐ Hot　Allergen levels: ________
☐ Dry　☐ Humid　☐ Wet　BM Pressure: ________

STRESS LEVELS

None	Low	Medium	High	Max	@$#%!

item / meal	*time*	*meds / supplements*	*dose*	*time*	*drinks*
					water
					① ② ③ ④ ⑤ ⑥ ⑦ ⑧ ⑨ ⑩
					caffeine
					① ② ③ ④ ⑤ ⑥ ⑦ ⑧ ⑨ ⑩
					alcohol
					① ② ③ ④ ⑤ ⑥ ⑦ ⑧ ⑨ ⑩

HORMONES

☐ Menstruating　☐ Menopause
☐ PMS　☐ N/A | other

COMPUTER / MOBILE DEVICE / TV

☐ None　☐ Some　☐ A lot　Total Time: ______
☐ Sitting　☐ Standing　☐ Mixture　Breaks every: ______

PHYSICAL ACTIVITY

☐ None　☐ Minimal　☐ Some　☐ Sweatin'　☐ I'm beat　DETAILS: ____________________

RELIEF MEASURES

☐ Medication　☐ Massage　☐ Sleep　☐ Exercise　☐ Water　☐ Cold/Ice
☐ Heat/Bath　☐ Other: ____________________
Did it work?　☐ Nope　☐ A bit　☐ Mostly　☐ 100%

Notes　☐ *See back notes*

START:	END:	DURATION:	DATE	*Entry #78*

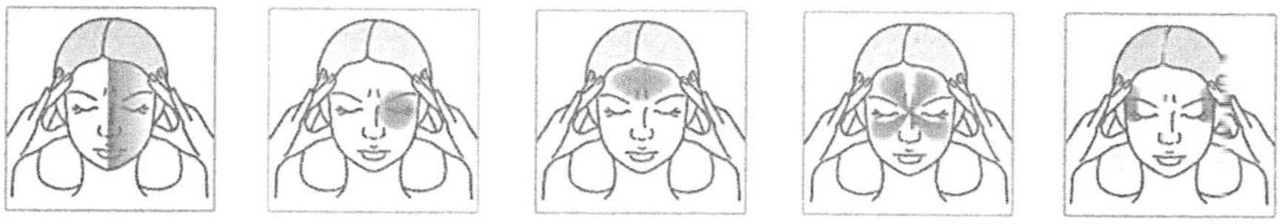

MIGRAINE | CLUSTER | TENSION | SINUS | TMJ

HOW WOULD YOU RATE...?

Mood	1	2	3	4	5
Energy	1	2	3	4	5
Mental clarity	1	2	3	4	5

PAIN LEVEL

1	2	3	4	5	6	7	8	9	10

Not too bad. *Well, I'm not enjoying this.* *Make it stop!*

ONSET

☐ Slow ☐ Average
☐ Rapid ☐ Sudden

DETAILED DESCRIPTION

☐ Constant ☐ Squeezing ☐ Throbbing ☐ Pounding ☐ Dull aching ☐ Burning
☐ Sharp ☐ Debilitating ☐ Other: ____________________

WHERE DOES IT HURT, EXACTLY?

OTHER SYMPTOMS

☐ Lightheaded ☐ Dizziness
☐ Light sensitivity ☐ Sound sensitivity
☐ Confusion ☐ Auras
☐ Muscle stiffness ☐ Muscle aches

FEELING SICK?

☐ Nausea ☐ Diarrhea ☐ Vomiting ☐ Sore throat ☐ Congestion ☐ Coughing
☐ Chills ☐ Fever ☐ Other: ____________________

SLEEP

hours ________ *quality* 1 2 3 4 5

WEATHER

☐ Cold ☐ Mild ☐ Hot Allergen levels: __________
☐ Dry ☐ Humid ☐ Wet BM Pressure: __________

STRESS LEVELS

None	Low	Medium	High	Max	@$#%!

item / meal	*time*	*meds / supplements*	*dose*	*time*	*drinks*
					water
					1 2 3 4 5 6 7 8 9 10
					caffeine
					1 2 3 4 5 6 7 8 9 10
					alcohol
					1 2 3 4 5 6 7 8 9 10

HORMONES

☐ Menstruating ☐ Menopause
☐ PMS ☐ N/A | other

COMPUTER / MOBILE DEVICE / TV

☐ None ☐ Some ☐ A lot Total Time: _____
☐ Sitting ☐ Standing ☐ Mixture Breaks every: _____

PHYSICAL ACTIVITY

☐ None ☐ Minimal ☐ Some ☐ Sweatin' ☐ I'm beat DETAILS: __________

RELIEF MEASURES

☐ Medication ☐ Massage ☐ Sleep ☐ Exercise ☐ Water ☐ Cold/Ice
☐ Heat/Bath ☐ Other: ____________________
Did it work? ☐ Nope ☐ A bit ☐ Mostly ☐ 100%

Notes ☐ *See back notes*

START:		END:		DURATION:		DATE		*Entry #79*

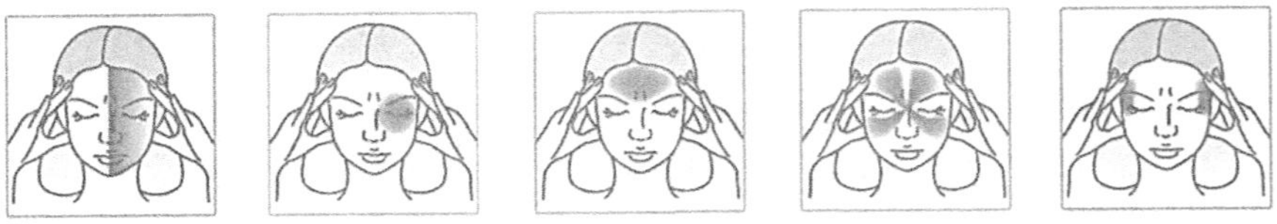

MIGRAINE | CLUSTER | TENSION | SINUS | TMJ

HOW WOULD YOU RATE...?

Mood	①	②	③	④	⑤
Energy	①	②	③	④	⑤
Mental clarity	①	②	③	④	⑤

PAIN LEVEL

1	2	3	4	5	6	7	8	9	10

Not too bad. *Well, I'm not enjoying this.* *Make it stop!*

ONSET

☐ Slow ☐ Average
☐ Rapid ☐ Sudden

DETAILED DESCRIPTION

☐ Constant ☐ Squeezing ☐ Throbbing ☐ Pounding ☐ Dull aching ☐ Burning
☐ Sharp ☐ Debilitating ☐ Other: ______________________

WHERE DOES IT HURT, EXACTLY?

OTHER SYMPTOMS

☐ Lightheaded ☐ Dizziness
☐ Light sensitivity ☐ Sound sensitivity
☐ Confusion ☐ Auras
☐ Muscle stiffness ☐ Muscle aches

FEELING SICK?

☐ Nausea ☐ Diarrhea ☐ Vomiting ☐ Sore throat ☐ Congestion ☐ Coughing
☐ Chills ☐ Fever ☐ Other: ______________________

SLEEP

hours ________ *quality* ① ② ③ ④ ⑤

WEATHER

☐ Cold ☐ Mild ☐ Hot Allergen levels: ____________
☐ Dry ☐ Humid ☐ Wet BM Pressure: ____________

STRESS LEVELS

None	Low	Medium	High	Max	@$#%!

item / meal	*time*	*meds / supplements*	*dose*	*time*	*drinks*
					water
					① ② ③ ④ ⑤ ⑥ ⑦ ⑧ ⑨ ⑩
					caffeine
					① ② ③ ④ ⑤ ⑥ ⑦ ⑧ ⑨ ⑩
					alcohol
					① ② ③ ④ ⑤ ⑥ ⑦ ⑧ ⑨ ⑩

HORMONES

☐ Menstruating ☐ Menopause
☐ PMS ☐ N/A | other

COMPUTER / MOBILE DEVICE / TV

☐ None ☐ Some ☐ A lot Total Time: ______
☐ Sitting ☐ Standing ☐ Mixture Breaks every: ______

PHYSICAL ACTIVITY

☐ None ☐ Minimal ☐ Some ☐ Sweatin' ☐ I'm beat DETAILS: ______________

RELIEF MEASURES

☐ Medication ☐ Massage ☐ Sleep ☐ Exercise ☐ Water ☐ Cold/Ice
☐ Heat/Bath ☐ Other: ______________________
Did it work? ☐ Nope ☐ A bit ☐ Mostly ☐ 100%

Notes ☐ *See back notes*

START: ______ END: ______ DURATION: ______ DATE ______ *Entry #80*

MIGRAINE CLUSTER TENSION SINUS TMJ

HOW WOULD YOU RATE...?

Mood	① ② ③ ④ ⑤
Energy	① ② ③ ④ ⑤
Mental clarity	① ② ③ ④ ⑤

PAIN LEVEL

1	2	3	4	5	6	7	8	9	10

Not too bad. *Well, I'm not enjoying this.* *Make it stop!*

ONSET

☐ Slow ☐ Average
☐ Rapid ☐ Sudden

DETAILED DESCRIPTION

☐ Constant ☐ Squeezing ☐ Throbbing ☐ Pounding ☐ Dull aching ☐ Burning
☐ Sharp ☐ Debilitating ☐ Other: ______

WHERE DOES IT HURT, EXACTLY?

OTHER SYMPTOMS

☐ Lightheaded ☐ Dizziness
☐ Light sensitivity ☐ Sound sensitivity
☐ Confusion ☐ Auras
☐ Muscle stiffness ☐ Muscle aches

FEELING SICK?

☐ Nausea ☐ Diarrhea ☐ Vomiting ☐ Sore throat ☐ Congestion ☐ Coughing
☐ Chills ☐ Fever ☐ Other: ______

SLEEP

hours ______ *quality* ① ② ③ ④ ⑤

WEATHER

☐ Cold ☐ Mild ☐ Hot Allergen levels: ______
☐ Dry ☐ Humid ☐ Wet BM Pressure: ______

STRESS LEVELS

None	Low	Medium	High	Max	@$#%!

item / meal	*time*	*meds / supplements*	*dose*	*time*	*drinks*
					water
					① ② ③ ④ ⑤ ⑥ ⑦ ⑧ ⑨ ⑩
					caffeine
					① ② ③ ④ ⑤ ⑥ ⑦ ⑧ ⑨ ⑩
					alcohol
					① ② ③ ④ ⑤ ⑥ ⑦ ⑧ ⑨ ⑩

HORMONES

☐ Menstruating ☐ Menopause
☐ PMS ☐ N/A other

COMPUTER / MOBILE DEVICE / TV

☐ None ☐ Some ☐ A lot Total Time: ______
☐ Sitting ☐ Standing ☐ Mixture Breaks every: ______

PHYSICAL ACTIVITY

☐ None ☐ Minimal ☐ Some ☐ Sweatin' ☐ I'm beat DETAILS: ______

RELIEF MEASURES

☐ Medication ☐ Massage ☐ Sleep ☐ Exercise ☐ Water ☐ Cold/Ice
☐ Heat/Bath ☐ Other: ______
Did it work? ☐ Nope ☐ A bit ☐ Mostly ☐ 100%

Notes ☐ *See back notes*

START:		END:		DURATION:		DATE		*Entry #81*

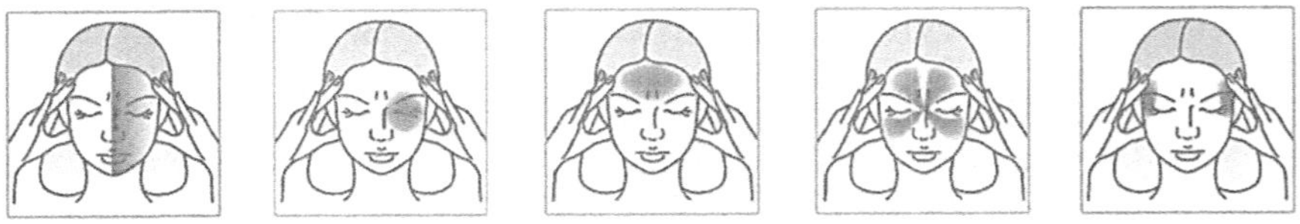

MIGRAINE | CLUSTER | TENSION | SINUS | TMJ

HOW WOULD YOU RATE...?

Mood	1	2	3	4	5
Energy	1	2	3	4	5
Mental clarity	1	2	3	4	5

PAIN LEVEL

1	2	3	4	5	6	7	8	9	10

Not too bad. *Well, I'm not enjoying this.* *Make it stop!*

ONSET

☐ Slow ☐ Average
☐ Rapid ☐ Sudden

DETAILED DESCRIPTION

☐ Constant ☐ Squeezing ☐ Throbbing ☐ Pounding ☐ Dull aching ☐ Burning
☐ Sharp ☐ Debilitating ☐ Other: ______

WHERE DOES IT HURT, EXACTLY?

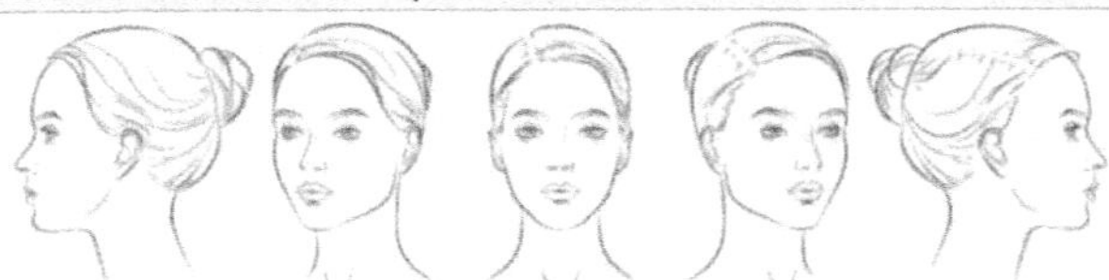

OTHER SYMPTOMS

☐ Lightheaded ☐ Dizziness
☐ Light sensitivity ☐ Sound sensitivity
☐ Confusion ☐ Auras
☐ Muscle stiffness ☐ Muscle aches

FEELING SICK?

☐ Nausea ☐ Diarrhea ☐ Vomiting ☐ Sore throat ☐ Congestion ☐ Coughing
☐ Chills ☐ Fever ☐ Other: ______

SLEEP

hours ______ *quality* 1 2 3 4 5

WEATHER

☐ Cold ☐ Mild ☐ Hot Allergen levels: ______
☐ Dry ☐ Humid ☐ Wet BM Pressure: ______

STRESS LEVELS

None	Low	Medium	High	Max	@$#%!

item / meal	*time*	*meds / supplements*	*dose*	*time*	*drinks*
					water
					1 2 3 4 5 6 7 8 9 10
					caffeine
					1 2 3 4 5 6 7 8 9 10
					alcohol
					1 2 3 4 5 6 7 8 9 10

HORMONES

☐ Menstruating ☐ Menopause
☐ PMS ☐ N/A | other

COMPUTER / MOBILE DEVICE / TV

☐ None ☐ Some ☐ A lot Total Time: ______
☐ Sitting ☐ Standing ☐ Mixture Breaks every: ______

PHYSICAL ACTIVITY

☐ None ☐ Minimal ☐ Some ☐ Sweatin' ☐ I'm beat DETAILS: ______

RELIEF MEASURES

☐ Medication ☐ Massage ☐ Sleep ☐ Exercise ☐ Water ☐ Cold/Ice
☐ Heat/Bath ☐ Other: ______
Did it work? ☐ Nope ☐ A bit ☐ Mostly ☐ 100%

Notes ☐ *See back notes*

START:		END:		DURATION:		DATE		*Entry #82*

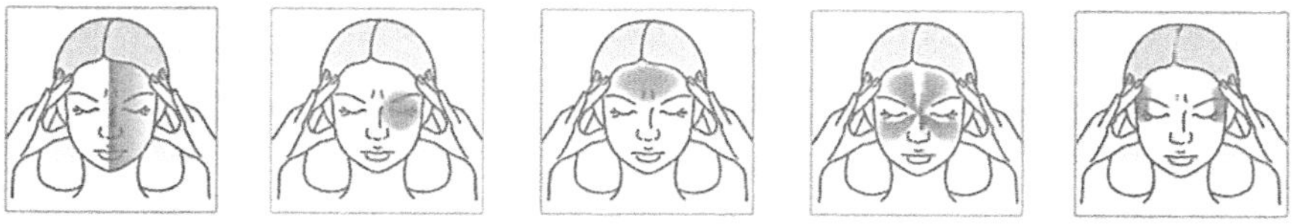

MIGRAINE	CLUSTER	TENSION	SINUS	TMJ

HOW WOULD YOU RATE...?

- Mood ① ② ③ ④ ⑤
- Energy ① ② ③ ④ ⑤
- Mental clarity ① ② ③ ④ ⑤

PAIN LEVEL

1	2	3	4	5	6	7	8	9	10

Not too bad. *Well, I'm not enjoying this.* *Make it stop!*

ONSET

☐ Slow ☐ Average
☐ Rapid ☐ Sudden

DETAILED DESCRIPTION

☐ Constant ☐ Squeezing ☐ Throbbing ☐ Pounding ☐ Dull aching ☐ Burning
☐ Sharp ☐ Debilitating ☐ Other: ____________________

WHERE DOES IT HURT, EXACTLY?

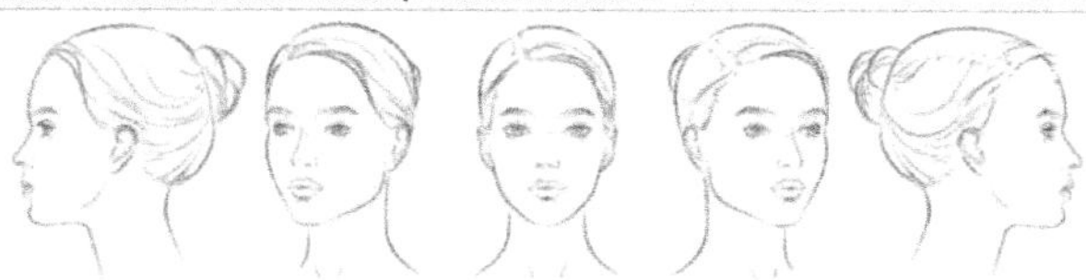

OTHER SYMPTOMS

☐ Lightheaded ☐ Dizziness
☐ Light sensitivity ☐ Sound sensitivity
☐ Confusion ☐ Auras
☐ Muscle stiffness ☐ Muscle aches

FEELING SICK?

☐ Nausea ☐ Diarrhea ☐ Vomiting ☐ Sore throat ☐ Congestion ☐ Coughing
☐ Chills ☐ Fever ☐ Other: ____________________

SLEEP

hours ________ *quality* ① ② ③ ④ ⑤

WEATHER

☐ Cold ☐ Mild ☐ Hot Allergen levels: ____________
☐ Dry ☐ Humid ☐ Wet BM Pressure: ____________

STRESS LEVELS

None	Low	Medium	High	Max	@$#%!

item / meal	*time*	*meds / supplements*	*dose*	*time*	*drinks*
					water
					① ② ③ ④ ⑤ ⑥ ⑦ ⑧ ⑨ ⑩
					caffeine
					① ② ③ ④ ⑤ ⑥ ⑦ ⑧ ⑨ ⑩
					alcohol
					① ② ③ ④ ⑤ ⑥ ⑦ ⑧ ⑨ ⑩

HORMONES

☐ Menstruating ☐ Menopause
☐ PMS ☐ N/A | other

COMPUTER / MOBILE DEVICE / TV

☐ None ☐ Some ☐ A lot Total Time: _____
☐ Sitting ☐ Standing ☐ Mixture Breaks every: _____

PHYSICAL ACTIVITY

☐ None ☐ Minimal ☐ Some ☐ Sweatin' ☐ I'm beat DETAILS: ____________

RELIEF MEASURES

☐ Medication ☐ Massage ☐ Sleep ☐ Exercise ☐ Water ☐ Cold/Ice
☐ Heat/Bath ☐ Other: ____________________
Did it work? ☐ Nope ☐ A bit ☐ Mostly ☐ 100%

Notes ☐ *See back notes*

START: ____ END: ____ DURATION: ____ DATE ____ *Entry #83*

HOW WOULD YOU RATE...?	
Mood	① ② ③ ④ ⑤
Energy	① ② ③ ④ ⑤
Mental clarity	① ② ③ ④ ⑤

MIGRAINE

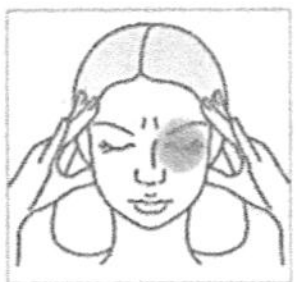
CLUSTER

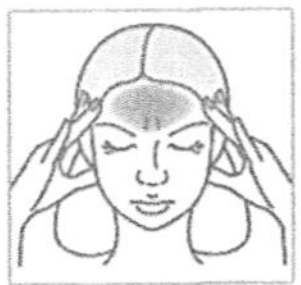
TENSION

SINUS

TMJ

PAIN LEVEL

1	2	3	4	5	6	7	8	9	10

Not too bad. *Well, I'm not enjoying this.* *Make it stop!*

ONSET

☐ Slow ☐ Average
☐ Rapid ☐ Sudden

DETAILED DESCRIPTION

☐ Constant ☐ Squeezing ☐ Throbbing ☐ Pounding ☐ Dull aching ☐ Burning
☐ Sharp ☐ Debilitating ☐ Other: ____

WHERE DOES IT HURT, EXACTLY?

OTHER SYMPTOMS

☐ Lightheaded ☐ Dizziness
☐ Light sensitivity ☐ Sound sensitivity
☐ Confusion ☐ Auras
☐ Muscle stiffness ☐ Muscle aches

FEELING SICK?

☐ Nausea ☐ Diarrhea ☐ Vomiting ☐ Sore throat ☐ Congestion ☐ Coughing
☐ Chills ☐ Fever ☐ Other: ____

SLEEP

hours ____ *quality* ① ② ③ ④ ⑤

WEATHER

☐ Cold ☐ Mild ☐ Hot Allergen levels: ____
☐ Dry ☐ Humid ☐ Wet BM Pressure: ____

STRESS LEVELS

None	Low	Medium	High	Max	@$#%!

item / meal	*time*	*meds / supplements*	*dose*	*time*	*drinks*
					water
					① ② ③ ④ ⑤ ⑥ ⑦ ⑧ ⑨ ⑩
					caffeine
					① ② ③ ④ ⑤ ⑥ ⑦ ⑧ ⑨ ⑩
					alcohol
					① ② ③ ④ ⑤ ⑥ ⑦ ⑧ ⑨ ⑩

HORMONES

☐ Menstruating ☐ Menopause
☐ PMS ☐ N/A | other

COMPUTER / MOBILE DEVICE / TV

☐ None ☐ Some ☐ A lot Total Time: ____
☐ Sitting ☐ Standing ☐ Mixture Breaks every: ____

PHYSICAL ACTIVITY

☐ None ☐ Minimal ☐ Some ☐ Sweatin' ☐ I'm beat DETAILS: ____

RELIEF MEASURES

☐ Medication ☐ Massage ☐ Sleep ☐ Exercise ☐ Water ☐ Cold/Ice
☐ Heat/Bath ☐ Other: ____
Did it work? ☐ Nope ☐ A bit ☐ Mostly ☐ 100%

Notes ☐ *See back notes*

START:		END:		DURATION:		DATE		*Entry #84*

MIGRAINE

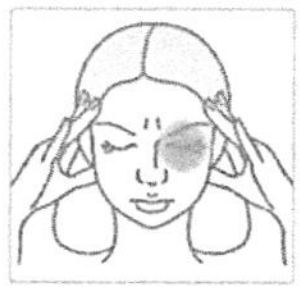
CLUSTER

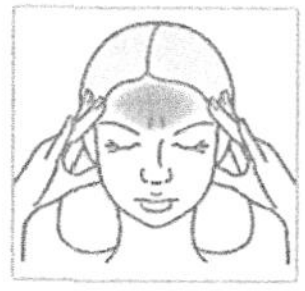
TENSION

SINUS

TMJ

HOW WOULD YOU RATE...?

Mood	① ② ③ ④ ⑤
Energy	① ② ③ ④ ⑤
Mental clarity	① ② ③ ④ ⑤

PAIN LEVEL

1	2	3	4	5	6	7	8	9	10

Not too bad. *Well, I'm not enjoying this.* *Make it stop!*

ONSET

☐ Slow ☐ Average
☐ Rapid ☐ Sudden

DETAILED DESCRIPTION

☐ Constant ☐ Squeezing ☐ Throbbing ☐ Pounding ☐ Dull aching ☐ Burning
☐ Sharp ☐ Debilitating ☐ Other: ____________________

WHERE DOES IT HURT, EXACTLY?

OTHER SYMPTOMS

☐ Lightheaded ☐ Dizziness
☐ Light sensitivity ☐ Sound sensitivity
☐ Confusion ☐ Auras
☐ Muscle stiffness ☐ Muscle aches

FEELING SICK?

☐ Nausea ☐ Diarrhea ☐ Vomiting ☐ Sore throat ☐ Congestion ☐ Coughing
☐ Chills ☐ Fever ☐ Other: ____________________

SLEEP

hours ________ *quality* ① ② ③ ④ ⑤

WEATHER

☐ Cold ☐ Mild ☐ Hot Allergen levels: __________
☐ Dry ☐ Humid ☐ Wet BM Pressure: __________

STRESS LEVELS

None	Low	Medium	High	Max	@$#%!

item / meal	*time*	*meds / supplements*	*dose*	*time*	*drinks*
					water
					① ② ③ ④ ⑤ ⑥ ⑦ ⑧ ⑨ ⑩
					caffeine
					① ② ③ ④ ⑤ ⑥ ⑦ ⑧ ⑨ ⑩
					alcohol
					① ② ③ ④ ⑤ ⑥ ⑦ ⑧ ⑨ ⑩

HORMONES

☐ Menstruating ☐ Menopause
☐ PMS ☐ N/A | other

COMPUTER / MOBILE DEVICE / TV

☐ None ☐ Some ☐ A lot Total Time: ______
☐ Sitting ☐ Standing ☐ Mixture Breaks every: ______

PHYSICAL ACTIVITY

☐ None ☐ Minimal ☐ Some ☐ Sweatin' ☐ I'm beat DETAILS: ____________________

RELIEF MEASURES

☐ Medication ☐ Massage ☐ Sleep ☐ Exercise ☐ Water ☐ Cold/Ice
☐ Heat/Bath ☐ Other: ____________________
Did it work? ☐ Nope ☐ A bit ☐ Mostly ☐ 100%

Notes ☐ *See back notes*

START:		END:		DURATION:		DATE		*Entry #85*

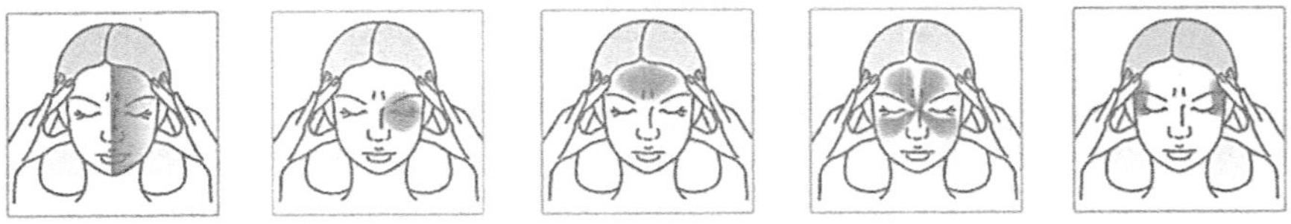

MIGRAINE CLUSTER TENSION SINUS TMJ

HOW WOULD YOU RATE...?

Mood	1	2	3	4	5
Energy	1	2	3	4	5
Mental clarity	1	2	3	4	5

PAIN LEVEL

1	2	3	4	5	6	7	8	9	10

Not too bad. *Well, I'm not enjoying this.* *Make it stop!*

ONSET

☐ Slow ☐ Average
☐ Rapid ☐ Sudden

DETAILED DESCRIPTION

☐ Constant ☐ Squeezing ☐ Throbbing ☐ Pounding ☐ Dull aching ☐ Burning
☐ Sharp ☐ Debilitating ☐ Other: ______

WHERE DOES IT HURT, EXACTLY?

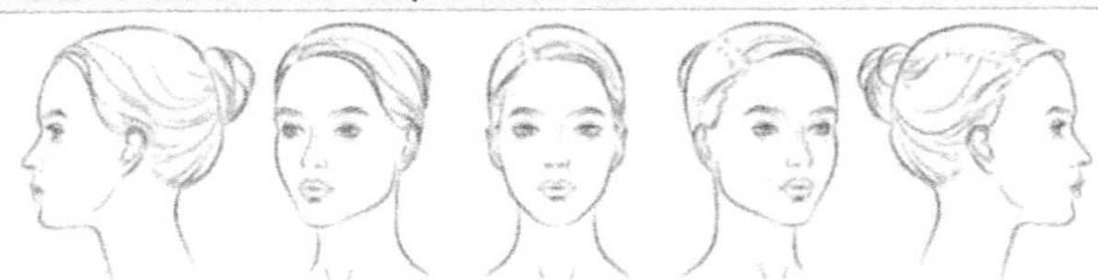

OTHER SYMPTOMS

☐ Lightheaded ☐ Dizziness
☐ Light sensitivity ☐ Sound sensitivity
☐ Confusion ☐ Auras
☐ Muscle stiffness ☐ Muscle aches

FEELING SICK?

☐ Nausea ☐ Diarrhea ☐ Vomiting ☐ Sore throat ☐ Congestion ☐ Coughing
☐ Chills ☐ Fever ☐ Other: ______

SLEEP

hours ______ *quality* 1 2 3 4 5

WEATHER

☐ Cold ☐ Mild ☐ Hot Allergen levels: ______
☐ Dry ☐ Humid ☐ Wet BM Pressure: ______

STRESS LEVELS

None	Low	Medium	High	Max	@$#%!

item / meal	*time*	*meds / supplements*	*dose*	*time*	*drinks*
					water: 1 2 3 4 5 6 7 8 9 10
					caffeine: 1 2 3 4 5 6 7 8 9 10
					alcohol: 1 2 3 4 5 6 7 8 9 10

HORMONES

☐ Menstruating ☐ Menopause
☐ PMS ☐ N/A | other

COMPUTER / MOBILE DEVICE / TV

☐ None ☐ Some ☐ A lot Total Time: ______
☐ Sitting ☐ Standing ☐ Mixture Breaks every: ______

PHYSICAL ACTIVITY

☐ None ☐ Minimal ☐ Some ☐ Sweatin' ☐ I'm beat DETAILS: ______

RELIEF MEASURES

☐ Medication ☐ Massage ☐ Sleep ☐ Exercise ☐ Water ☐ Cold/Ice
☐ Heat/Bath ☐ Other: ______
Did it work? ☐ Nope ☐ A bit ☐ Mostly ☐ 100%

Notes ☐ *See back notes*

START:		END:		DURATION:		DATE		*Entry #86*

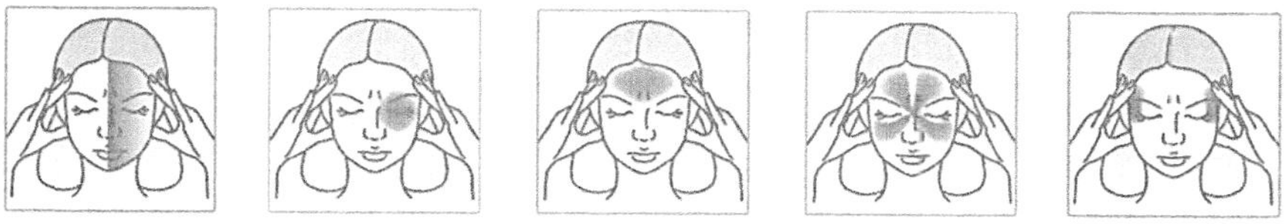

MIGRAINE CLUSTER TENSION SINUS TMJ

HOW WOULD YOU RATE...?

Mood	①	②	③	④	⑤
Energy	①	②	③	④	⑤
Mental clarity	①	②	③	④	⑤

PAIN LEVEL

1	2	3	4	5	6	7	8	9	10

Not too bad. *Well, I'm not enjoying this.* *Make it stop!*

ONSET

☐ Slow ☐ Average
☐ Rapid ☐ Sudden

DETAILED DESCRIPTION

☐ Constant ☐ Squeezing ☐ Throbbing ☐ Pounding ☐ Dull aching ☐ Burning
☐ Sharp ☐ Debilitating ☐ Other: ____________________

WHERE DOES IT HURT, EXACTLY?

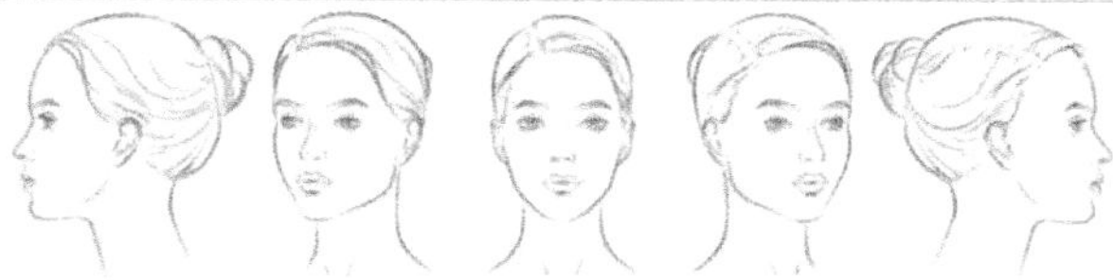

OTHER SYMPTOMS

☐ Lightheaded ☐ Dizziness
☐ Light sensitivity ☐ Sound sensitivity
☐ Confusion ☐ Auras
☐ Muscle stiffness ☐ Muscle aches

FEELING SICK?

☐ Nausea ☐ Diarrhea ☐ Vomiting ☐ Sore throat ☐ Congestion ☐ Coughing
☐ Chills ☐ Fever ☐ Other: ____________________

SLEEP

hours ________ *quality* ① ② ③ ④ ⑤

WEATHER

☐ Cold ☐ Mild ☐ Hot Allergen levels: ____________
☐ Dry ☐ Humid ☐ Wet BM Pressure: ____________

STRESS LEVELS

None	Low	Medium	High	Max	@$#%!

item / meal	*time*	*meds / supplements*	*dose*	*time*	*drinks*
					water
					① ② ③ ④ ⑤ ⑥ ⑦ ⑧ ⑨ ⑩
					caffeine
					① ② ③ ④ ⑤ ⑥ ⑦ ⑧ ⑨ ⑩
					alcohol
					① ② ③ ④ ⑤ ⑥ ⑦ ⑧ ⑨ ⑩

HORMONES

☐ Menstruating ☐ Menopause
☐ PMS ☐ N/A | other

COMPUTER / MOBILE DEVICE / TV

☐ None ☐ Some ☐ A lot Total Time: ______
☐ Sitting ☐ Standing ☐ Mixture Breaks every: ______

PHYSICAL ACTIVITY

☐ None ☐ Minimal ☐ Some ☐ Sweatin' ☐ I'm beat DETAILS: ____________

RELIEF MEASURES

☐ Medication ☐ Massage ☐ Sleep ☐ Exercise ☐ Water ☐ Cold/Ice
☐ Heat/Bath ☐ Other: ____________________
Did it work? ☐ Nope ☐ A bit ☐ Mostly ☐ 100%

Notes ☐ *See back notes*

START:		END:		DURATION:		DATE		*Entry #87*

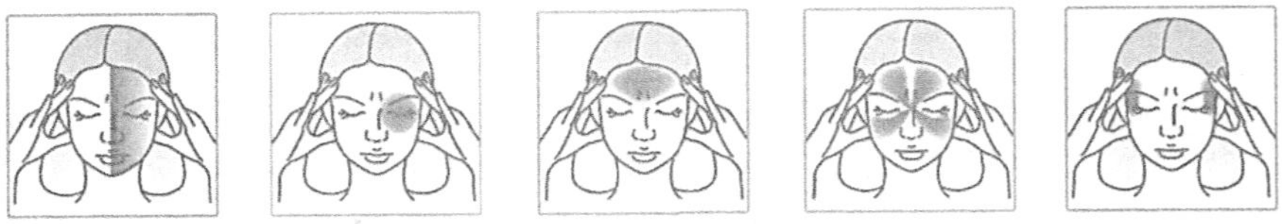

MIGRAINE CLUSTER TENSION SINUS TMJ

HOW WOULD YOU RATE...?

Mood	①	②	③	④	⑤
Energy	①	②	③	④	⑤
Mental clarity	①	②	③	④	⑤

PAIN LEVEL

1	2	3	4	5	6	7	8	9	10

Not too bad. *Well, I'm not enjoying this.* *Make it stop!*

ONSET

☐ Slow ☐ Average
☐ Rapid ☐ Sudden

DETAILED DESCRIPTION

☐ Constant ☐ Squeezing ☐ Throbbing ☐ Pounding ☐ Dull aching ☐ Burning
☐ Sharp ☐ Debilitating ☐ Other: ____________________

WHERE DOES IT HURT, EXACTLY?

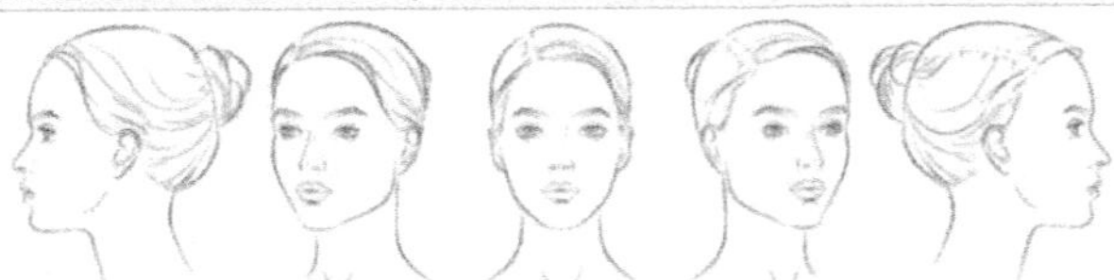

OTHER SYMPTOMS

☐ Lightheaded ☐ Dizziness
☐ Light sensitivity ☐ Sound sensitivity
☐ Confusion ☐ Auras
☐ Muscle stiffness ☐ Muscle aches

FEELING SICK?

☐ Nausea ☐ Diarrhea ☐ Vomiting ☐ Sore throat ☐ Congestion ☐ Coughing
☐ Chills ☐ Fever ☐ Other: ____________________

SLEEP

hours ________ *quality* ① ② ③ ④ ⑤

WEATHER

☐ Cold ☐ Mild ☐ Hot Allergen levels: __________
☐ Dry ☐ Humid ☐ Wet BM Pressure: __________

STRESS LEVELS

None	Low	Medium	High	Max	@$#%!

item / meal	*time*	*meds / supplements*	*dose*	*time*	*drinks*
					water
					① ② ③ ④ ⑤ ⑥ ⑦ ⑧ ⑨ ⑩
					caffeine
					① ② ③ ④ ⑤ ⑥ ⑦ ⑧ ⑨ ⑩
					alcohol
					① ② ③ ④ ⑤ ⑥ ⑦ ⑧ ⑨ ⑩

HORMONES

☐ Menstruating ☐ Menopause
☐ PMS ☐ N/A | other

COMPUTER / MOBILE DEVICE / TV

☐ None ☐ Some ☐ A lot Total Time: ______
☐ Sitting ☐ Standing ☐ Mixture Breaks every: ______

PHYSICAL ACTIVITY

☐ None ☐ Minimal ☐ Some ☐ Sweatin' ☐ I'm beat DETAILS: ____________________

RELIEF MEASURES

☐ Medication ☐ Massage ☐ Sleep ☐ Exercise ☐ Water ☐ Cold/Ice
☐ Heat/Bath ☐ Other: ____________________
Did it work? ☐ Nope ☐ A bit ☐ Mostly ☐ 100%

Notes ☐ *See back notes*

START: | END: | DURATION: | DATE | *Entry #88*

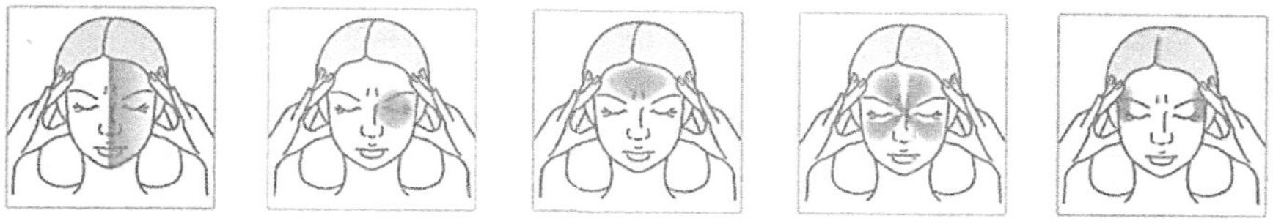

MIGRAINE | CLUSTER | TENSION | SINUS | TMJ

HOW WOULD YOU RATE...?

Mood	1	2	3	4	5
Energy	1	2	3	4	5
Mental clarity	1	2	3	4	5

PAIN LEVEL

1	2	3	4	5	6	7	8	9	10

Not too bad. *Well, I'm not enjoying this.* *Make it stop!*

ONSET

☐ Slow ☐ Average
☐ Rapid ☐ Sudden

DETAILED DESCRIPTION

☐ Constant ☐ Squeezing ☐ Throbbing ☐ Pounding ☐ Dull aching ☐ Burning
☐ Sharp ☐ Debilitating ☐ Other: ______

WHERE DOES IT HURT, EXACTLY?

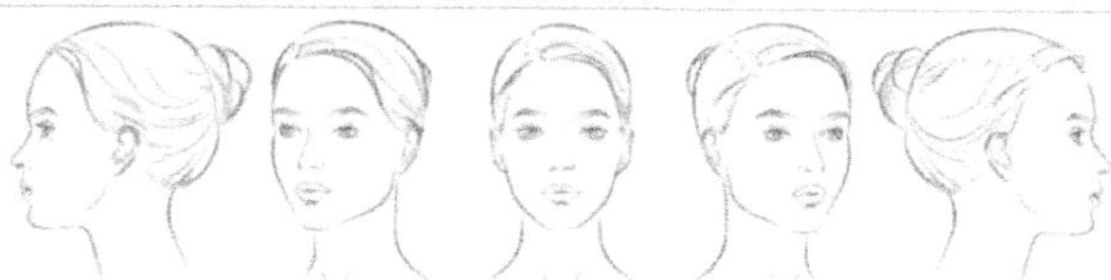

OTHER SYMPTOMS

☐ Lightheaded ☐ Dizziness
☐ Light sensitivity ☐ Sound sensitivity
☐ Confusion ☐ Auras
☐ Muscle stiffness ☐ Muscle aches

FEELING SICK?

☐ Nausea ☐ Diarrhea ☐ Vomiting ☐ Sore throat ☐ Congestion ☐ Coughing
☐ Chills ☐ Fever ☐ Other: ______

SLEEP

hours ______ *quality* 1 2 3 4 5

WEATHER

☐ Cold ☐ Mild ☐ Hot Allergen levels: ______
☐ Dry ☐ Humid ☐ Wet BM Pressure: ______

STRESS LEVELS

None	Low	Medium	High	Max	@$#%!

item / meal	*time*	*meds / supplements*	*dose*	*time*	*drinks*
					water
					1 2 3 4 5 6 7 8 9 10
					caffeine
					1 2 3 4 5 6 7 8 9 10
					alcohol
					1 2 3 4 5 6 7 8 9 10

HORMONES

☐ Menstruating ☐ Menopause
☐ PMS ☐ N/A | other

COMPUTER / MOBILE DEVICE / TV

☐ None ☐ Some ☐ A lot Total Time: ______
☐ Sitting ☐ Standing ☐ Mixture Breaks every: ______

PHYSICAL ACTIVITY

☐ None ☐ Minimal ☐ Some ☐ Sweatin' ☐ I'm beat DETAILS: ______

RELIEF MEASURES

☐ Medication ☐ Massage ☐ Sleep ☐ Exercise ☐ Water ☐ Cold/Ice
☐ Heat/Bath ☐ Other: ______
Did it work? ☐ Nope ☐ A bit ☐ Mostly ☐ 100%

Notes ☐ *See back notes*

START:		END:		DURATION:		DATE		*Entry #89*

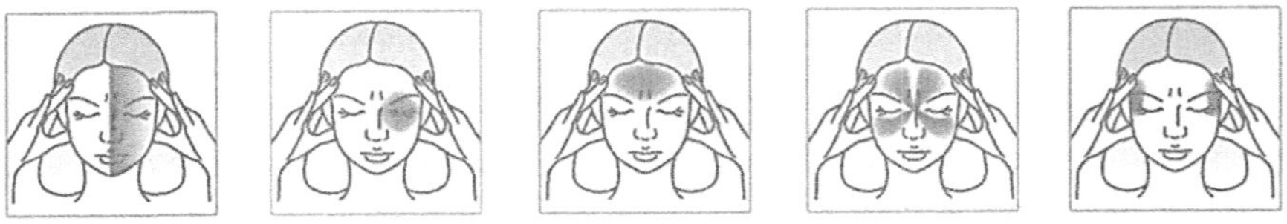

MIGRAINE | CLUSTER | TENSION | SINUS | TMJ

HOW WOULD YOU RATE...?

Mood	1	2	3	4	5
Energy	1	2	3	4	5
Mental clarity	1	2	3	4	5

PAIN LEVEL

1	2	3	4	5	6	7	8	9	10

Not too bad. *Well, I'm not enjoying this.* *Make it stop!*

ONSET

☐ Slow ☐ Average
☐ Rapid ☐ Sudden

DETAILED DESCRIPTION

☐ Constant ☐ Squeezing ☐ Throbbing ☐ Pounding ☐ Dull aching ☐ Burning
☐ Sharp ☐ Debilitating ☐ Other: ____________________

WHERE DOES IT HURT, EXACTLY?

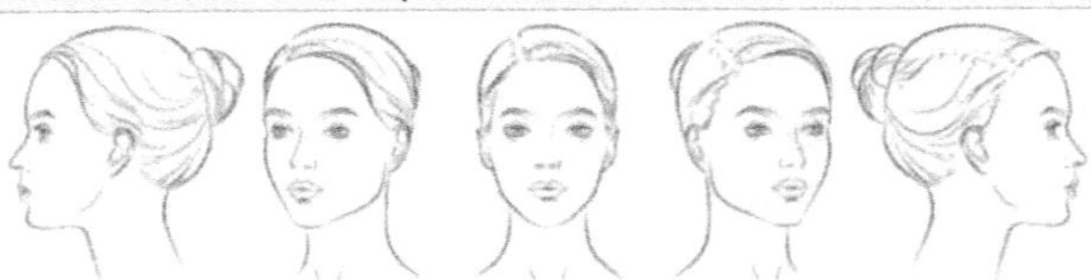

OTHER SYMPTOMS

☐ Lightheaded ☐ Dizziness
☐ Light sensitivity ☐ Sound sensitivity
☐ Confusion ☐ Auras
☐ Muscle stiffness ☐ Muscle aches

FEELING SICK?

☐ Nausea ☐ Diarrhea ☐ Vomiting ☐ Sore throat ☐ Congestion ☐ Coughing
☐ Chills ☐ Fever ☐ Other: ____________________

SLEEP

hours ________ *quality* 1 2 3 4 5

WEATHER

☐ Cold ☐ Mild ☐ Hot Allergen levels: ____________
☐ Dry ☐ Humid ☐ Wet BM Pressure: ____________

STRESS LEVELS

None	Low	Medium	High	Max	@$#%!

item / meal	*time*	*meds / supplements*	*dose*	*time*	*drinks*
					water
					1 2 3 4 5 6 7 8 9 10
					caffeine
					1 2 3 4 5 6 7 8 9 10
					alcohol
					1 2 3 4 5 6 7 8 9 10

HORMONES

☐ Menstruating ☐ Menopause
☐ PMS ☐ N/A | other

COMPUTER / MOBILE DEVICE / TV

☐ None ☐ Some ☐ A lot Total Time: ______
☐ Sitting ☐ Standing ☐ Mixture Breaks every: ______

PHYSICAL ACTIVITY

☐ None ☐ Minimal ☐ Some ☐ Sweatin' ☐ I'm beat DETAILS: ____________________

RELIEF MEASURES

☐ Medication ☐ Massage ☐ Sleep ☐ Exercise ☐ Water ☐ Cold/Ice
☐ Heat/Bath ☐ Other: ____________________

Did it work? ☐ Nope ☐ A bit ☐ Mostly ☐ 100%

Notes ☐ *See back notes*

START: ____ END: ____ DURATION: ____ DATE ____ *Entry #90*

MIGRAINE

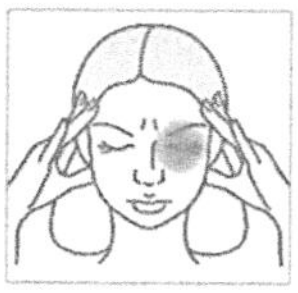

CLUSTER

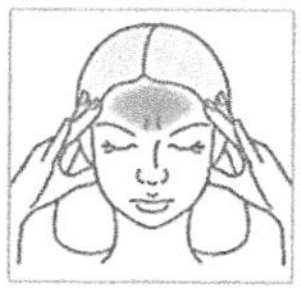

TENSION

SINUS

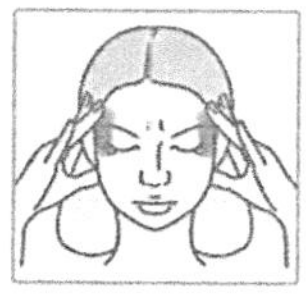

TMJ

HOW WOULD YOU RATE...?	
Mood	① ② ③ ④ ⑤
Energy	① ② ③ ④ ⑤
Mental clarity	① ② ③ ④ ⑤

PAIN LEVEL

1	2	3	4	5	6	7	8	9	10

Not too bad. *Well, I'm not enjoying this.* *Make it stop!*

ONSET

☐ Slow ☐ Average
☐ Rapid ☐ Sudden

DETAILED DESCRIPTION

☐ Constant ☐ Squeezing ☐ Throbbing ☐ Pounding ☐ Dull aching ☐ Burning
☐ Sharp ☐ Debilitating ☐ Other: ____________________

WHERE DOES IT HURT, EXACTLY?

OTHER SYMPTOMS

☐ Lightheaded ☐ Dizziness
☐ Light sensitivity ☐ Sound sensitivity
☐ Confusion ☐ Auras
☐ Muscle stiffness ☐ Muscle aches

FEELING SICK?

☐ Nausea ☐ Diarrhea ☐ Vomiting ☐ Sore throat ☐ Congestion ☐ Coughing
☐ Chills ☐ Fever ☐ Other: ____________________

SLEEP

hours ________ *quality* ① ② ③ ④ ⑤

WEATHER

☐ Cold ☐ Mild ☐ Hot Allergen levels: ________
☐ Dry ☐ Humid ☐ Wet BM Pressure: ________

STRESS LEVELS

None	Low	Medium	High	Max	@$#%!

item / meal	*time*	*meds / supplements*	*dose*	*time*	*drinks*
					water
					① ② ③ ④ ⑤ ⑥ ⑦ ⑧ ⑨ ⑩
					caffeine
					① ② ③ ④ ⑤ ⑥ ⑦ ⑧ ⑨ ⑩
					alcohol
					① ② ③ ④ ⑤ ⑥ ⑦ ⑧ ⑨ ⑩

HORMONES

☐ Menstruating ☐ Menopause
☐ PMS ☐ N/A | other

COMPUTER / MOBILE DEVICE / TV

☐ None ☐ Some ☐ A lot Total Time: ______
☐ Sitting ☐ Standing ☐ Mixture Breaks every: ______

PHYSICAL ACTIVITY

☐ None ☐ Minimal ☐ Some ☐ Sweatin' ☐ I'm beat DETAILS: ____________

RELIEF MEASURES

☐ Medication ☐ Massage ☐ Sleep ☐ Exercise ☐ Water ☐ Cold/Ice
☐ Heat/Bath ☐ Other: ____________________
Did it work? ☐ Nope ☐ A bit ☐ Mostly ☐ 100%

Notes ☐ *See back notes*

START: | END: | DURATION: | DATE | *Entry #91*

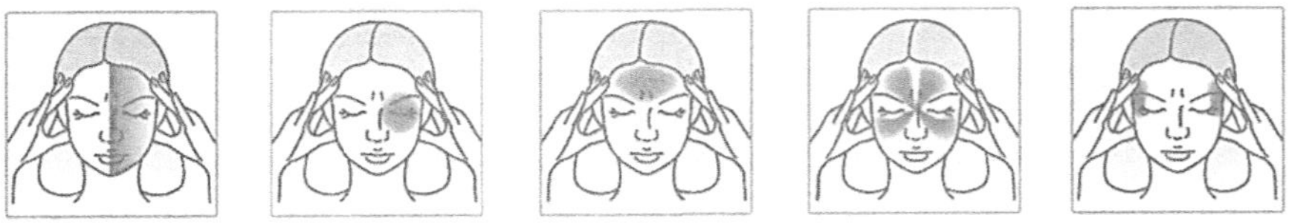

MIGRAINE | CLUSTER | TENSION | SINUS | TMJ

HOW WOULD YOU RATE...?

Mood	①	②	③	④	⑤
Energy	①	②	③	④	⑤
Mental clarity	①	②	③	④	⑤

PAIN LEVEL

1	2	3	4	5	6	7	8	9	10

Not too bad. *Well, I'm not enjoying this.* *Make it stop!*

ONSET

☐ Slow ☐ Average
☐ Rapid ☐ Sudden

DETAILED DESCRIPTION

☐ Constant ☐ Squeezing ☐ Throbbing ☐ Pounding ☐ Dull aching ☐ Burning
☐ Sharp ☐ Debilitating ☐ Other: ______

WHERE DOES IT HURT, EXACTLY?

OTHER SYMPTOMS

☐ Lightheaded ☐ Dizziness
☐ Light sensitivity ☐ Sound sensitivity
☐ Confusion ☐ Auras
☐ Muscle stiffness ☐ Muscle aches

FEELING SICK?

☐ Nausea ☐ Diarrhea ☐ Vomiting ☐ Sore throat ☐ Congestion ☐ Coughing
☐ Chills ☐ Fever ☐ Other: ______

SLEEP

hours ______ *quality* ① ② ③ ④ ⑤

WEATHER

☐ Cold ☐ Mild ☐ Hot Allergen levels: ______
☐ Dry ☐ Humid ☐ Wet BM Pressure: ______

STRESS LEVELS

None	Low	Medium	High	Max	@$#%!

item / meal	*time*	*meds / supplements*	*dose*	*time*	*drinks*
					water
					① ② ③ ④ ⑤ ⑥ ⑦ ⑧ ⑨ ⑩
					caffeine
					① ② ③ ④ ⑤ ⑥ ⑦ ⑧ ⑨ ⑩
					alcohol
					① ② ③ ④ ⑤ ⑥ ⑦ ⑧ ⑨ ⑩

HORMONES

☐ Menstruating ☐ Menopause
☐ PMS ☐ N/A | other

COMPUTER / MOBILE DEVICE / TV

☐ None ☐ Some ☐ A lot Total Time: ______
☐ Sitting ☐ Standing ☐ Mixture Breaks every: ______

PHYSICAL ACTIVITY

☐ None ☐ Minimal ☐ Some ☐ Sweatin' ☐ I'm beat DETAILS: ______

RELIEF MEASURES

☐ Medication ☐ Massage ☐ Sleep ☐ Exercise ☐ Water ☐ Cold/Ice
☐ Heat/Bath ☐ Other: ______

Did it work? ☐ Nope ☐ A bit ☐ Mostly ☐ 100%

Notes ☐ *See back notes*

START: | END: | DURATION: | DATE | *Entry #92*

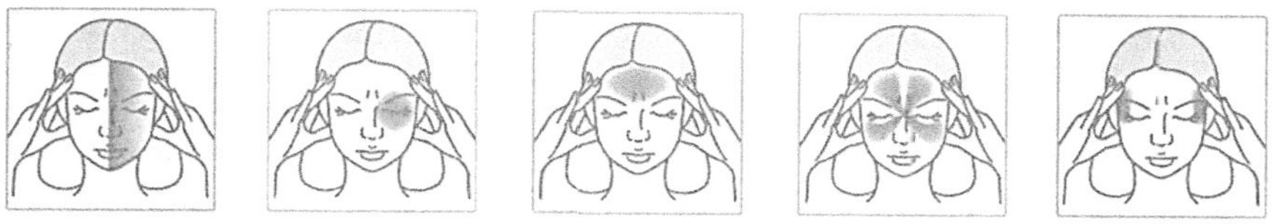

MIGRAINE CLUSTER TENSION SINUS TMJ

HOW WOULD YOU RATE...?

Mood	① ② ③ ④ ⑤
Energy	① ② ③ ④ ⑤
Mental clarity	① ② ③ ④ ⑤

PAIN LEVEL

1	2	3	4	5	6	7	8	9	10

Not too bad. *Well, I'm not enjoying this.* *Make it stop!*

ONSET

☐ Slow ☐ Average
☐ Rapid ☐ Sudden

DETAILED DESCRIPTION

☐ Constant ☐ Squeezing ☐ Throbbing ☐ Pounding ☐ Dull aching ☐ Burning
☐ Sharp ☐ Debilitating ☐ Other: ____________________

WHERE DOES IT HURT, EXACTLY?

OTHER SYMPTOMS

☐ Lightheaded ☐ Dizziness
☐ Light sensitivity ☐ Sound sensitivity
☐ Confusion ☐ Auras
☐ Muscle stiffness ☐ Muscle aches

FEELING SICK?

☐ Nausea ☐ Diarrhea ☐ Vomiting ☐ Sore throat ☐ Congestion ☐ Coughing
☐ Chills ☐ Fever ☐ Other: ____________________

SLEEP

hours ________ *quality* ① ② ③ ④ ⑤

WEATHER

☐ Cold ☐ Mild ☐ Hot Allergen levels: ____________
☐ Dry ☐ Humid ☐ Wet BM Pressure: ____________

STRESS LEVELS

None	Low	Medium	High	Max	@$#%!

item / meal	*time*	*meds / supplements*	*dose*	*time*	*drinks*
					water
					① ② ③ ④ ⑤ ⑥ ⑦ ⑧ ⑨ ⑩
					caffeine
					① ② ③ ④ ⑤ ⑥ ⑦ ⑧ ⑨ ⑩
					alcohol
					① ② ③ ④ ⑤ ⑥ ⑦ ⑧ ⑨ ⑩

HORMONES

☐ Menstruating ☐ Menopause
☐ PMS ☐ N/A | other

COMPUTER / MOBILE DEVICE / TV

☐ None ☐ Some ☐ A lot Total Time: ______
☐ Sitting ☐ Standing ☐ Mixture Breaks every: ______

PHYSICAL ACTIVITY

☐ None ☐ Minimal ☐ Some ☐ Sweatin' ☐ I'm beat DETAILS: ____________

RELIEF MEASURES

☐ Medication ☐ Massage ☐ Sleep ☐ Exercise ☐ Water ☐ Cold/Ice
☐ Heat/Bath ☐ Other: ____________________
Did it work? ☐ Nope ☐ A bit ☐ Mostly ☐ 100%

Notes ☐ *See back notes*

START: | END: | DURATION: | DATE | *Entry #93*

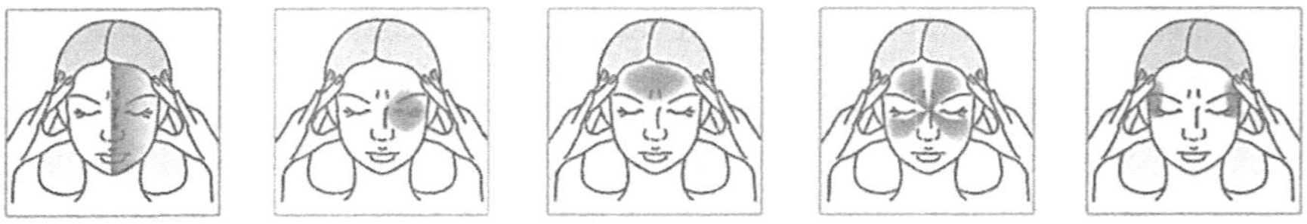

MIGRAINE CLUSTER TENSION SINUS TMJ

HOW WOULD YOU RATE...?

Mood	① ② ③ ④ ⑤
Energy	① ② ③ ④ ⑤
Mental clarity	① ② ③ ④ ⑤

PAIN LEVEL

1	2	3	4	5	6	7	8	9	10

Not too bad. *Well, I'm not enjoying this.* *Make it stop!*

ONSET

☐ Slow ☐ Average
☐ Rapid ☐ Sudden

DETAILED DESCRIPTION

☐ Constant ☐ Squeezing ☐ Throbbing ☐ Pounding ☐ Dull aching ☐ Burning
☐ Sharp ☐ Debilitating ☐ Other: ____________

WHERE DOES IT HURT, EXACTLY?

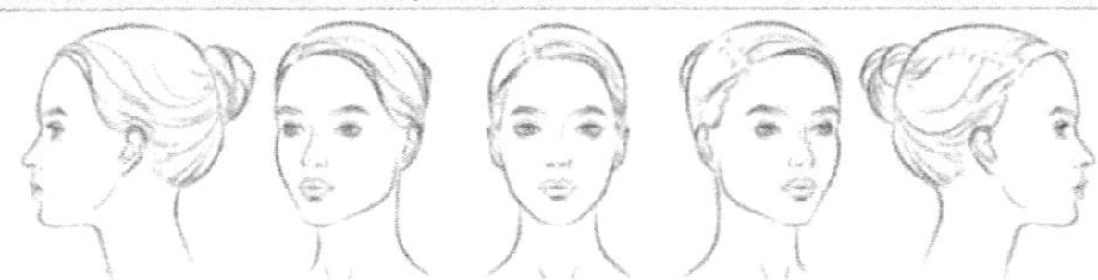

OTHER SYMPTOMS

☐ Lightheaded ☐ Dizziness
☐ Light sensitivity ☐ Sound sensitivity
☐ Confusion ☐ Auras
☐ Muscle stiffness ☐ Muscle aches

FEELING SICK?

☐ Nausea ☐ Diarrhea ☐ Vomiting ☐ Sore throat ☐ Congestion ☐ Coughing
☐ Chills ☐ Fever ☐ Other: ____________

SLEEP

hours ________ *quality* ① ② ③ ④ ⑤

WEATHER

☐ Cold ☐ Mild ☐ Hot Allergen levels: ________
☐ Dry ☐ Humid ☐ Wet BM Pressure: ________

STRESS LEVELS

None	Low	Medium	High	Max	@$#%!

item / meal	*time*	*meds / supplements*	*dose*	*time*	*drinks*
					water
					① ② ③ ④ ⑤ ⑥ ⑦ ⑧ ⑨ ⑩
					caffeine
					① ② ③ ④ ⑤ ⑥ ⑦ ⑧ ⑨ ⑩
					alcohol
					① ② ③ ④ ⑤ ⑥ ⑦ ⑧ ⑨ ⑩

HORMONES

☐ Menstruating ☐ Menopause
☐ PMS ☐ N/A | other

COMPUTER / MOBILE DEVICE / TV

☐ None ☐ Some ☐ A lot Total Time: ______
☐ Sitting ☐ Standing ☐ Mixture Breaks every: ______

PHYSICAL ACTIVITY

☐ None ☐ Minimal ☐ Some ☐ Sweatin' ☐ I'm beat DETAILS: ____________

RELIEF MEASURES

☐ Medication ☐ Massage ☐ Sleep ☐ Exercise ☐ Water ☐ Cold/Ice
☐ Heat/Bath ☐ Other: ____________
Did it work? ☐ Nope ☐ A bit ☐ Mostly ☐ 100%

Notes ☐ *See back notes*

START:		END:		DURATION:		DATE		*Entry #94*

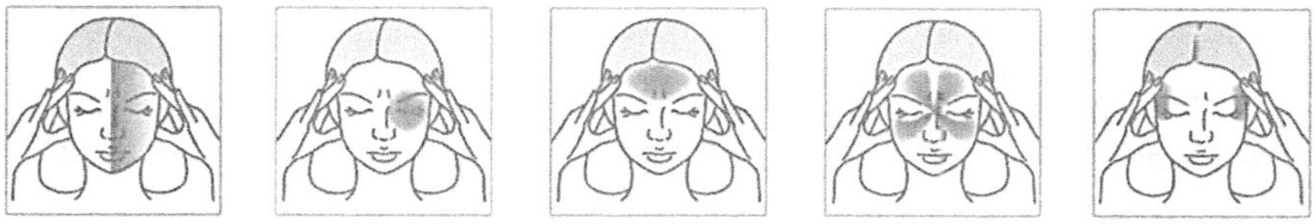

MIGRAINE CLUSTER TENSION SINUS TMJ

HOW WOULD YOU RATE...?

Mood	1	2	3	4	5
Energy	1	2	3	4	5
Mental clarity	1	2	3	4	5

PAIN LEVEL

1	2	3	4	5	6	7	8	9	10

Not too bad. *Well, I'm not enjoying this.* *Make it stop!*

ONSET

☐ Slow ☐ Average
☐ Rapid ☐ Sudden

DETAILED DESCRIPTION

☐ Constant ☐ Squeezing ☐ Throbbing ☐ Pounding ☐ Dull aching ☐ Burning
☐ Sharp ☐ Debilitating ☐ Other: ____________________

WHERE DOES IT HURT, EXACTLY?

OTHER SYMPTOMS

☐ Lightheaded ☐ Dizziness
☐ Light sensitivity ☐ Sound sensitivity
☐ Confusion ☐ Auras
☐ Muscle stiffness ☐ Muscle aches

FEELING SICK?

☐ Nausea ☐ Diarrhea ☐ Vomiting ☐ Sore throat ☐ Congestion ☐ Coughing
☐ Chills ☐ Fever ☐ Other: ____________________

SLEEP

hours ________ *quality* 1 2 3 4 5

WEATHER

☐ Cold ☐ Mild ☐ Hot Allergen levels: ____________
☐ Dry ☐ Humid ☐ Wet BM Pressure: ____________

STRESS LEVELS

None	Low	Medium	High	Max	@$#%!

item / meal	*time*	*meds / supplements*	*dose*	*time*	*drinks*
					water
					1 2 3 4 5 6 7 8 9 10
					caffeine
					1 2 3 4 5 6 7 8 9 10
					alcohol
					1 2 3 4 5 6 7 8 9 10

HORMONES

☐ Menstruating ☐ Menopause
☐ PMS ☐ N/A | other

COMPUTER / MOBILE DEVICE / TV

☐ None ☐ Some ☐ A lot Total Time: ______
☐ Sitting ☐ Standing ☐ Mixture Breaks every: ______

PHYSICAL ACTIVITY

☐ None ☐ Minimal ☐ Some ☐ Sweatin' ☐ I'm beat DETAILS: ____________

RELIEF MEASURES

☐ Medication ☐ Massage ☐ Sleep ☐ Exercise ☐ Water ☐ Cold/Ice
☐ Heat/Bath ☐ Other: ____________________
Did it work? ☐ Nope ☐ A bit ☐ Mostly ☐ 100%

Notes ☐ *See back notes*

START:		END:		DURATION:		DATE		*Entry #95*

MIGRAINE CLUSTER TENSION SINUS TMJ

HOW WOULD YOU RATE...?

Mood	①	②	③	④	⑤
Energy	①	②	③	④	⑤
Mental clarity	①	②	③	④	⑤

PAIN LEVEL

1	2	3	4	5	6	7	8	9	10

Not too bad. *Well, I'm not enjoying this.* *Make it stop!*

ONSET

☐ Slow ☐ Average
☐ Rapid ☐ Sudden

DETAILED DESCRIPTION

☐ Constant ☐ Squeezing ☐ Throbbing ☐ Pounding ☐ Dull aching ☐ Burning
☐ Sharp ☐ Debilitating ☐ Other: ______________________________

WHERE DOES IT HURT, EXACTLY?

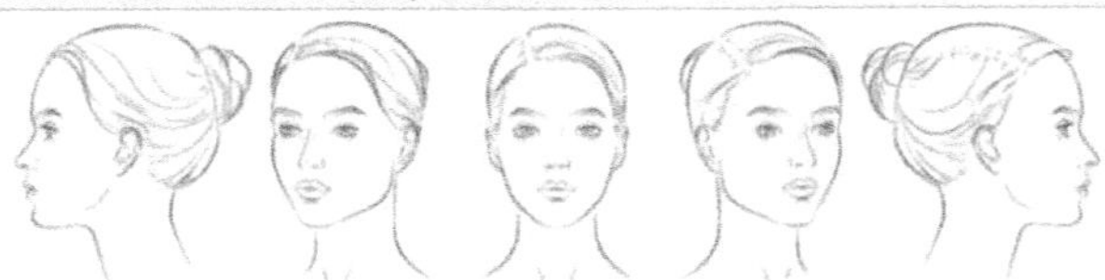

OTHER SYMPTOMS

☐ Lightheaded ☐ Dizziness
☐ Light sensitivity ☐ Sound sensitivity
☐ Confusion ☐ Auras
☐ Muscle stiffness ☐ Muscle aches

FEELING SICK?

☐ Nausea ☐ Diarrhea ☐ Vomiting ☐ Sore throat ☐ Congestion ☐ Coughing
☐ Chills ☐ Fever ☐ Other: ______________________________

SLEEP

hours ________ *quality* ① ② ③ ④ ⑤

WEATHER

☐ Cold ☐ Mild ☐ Hot Allergen levels: ____________
☐ Dry ☐ Humid ☐ Wet BM Pressure: ____________

STRESS LEVELS

None	Low	Medium	High	Max	@$#%!

item / meal	*time*	*meds / supplements*	*dose*	*time*	*drinks*
					water
					① ② ③ ④ ⑤ ⑥ ⑦ ⑧ ⑨ ⑩
					caffeine
					① ② ③ ④ ⑤ ⑥ ⑦ ⑧ ⑨ ⑩
					alcohol
					① ② ③ ④ ⑤ ⑥ ⑦ ⑧ ⑨ ⑩

HORMONES

☐ Menstruating ☐ Menopause
☐ PMS ☐ N/A | other

COMPUTER / MOBILE DEVICE / TV

☐ None ☐ Some ☐ A lot Total Time: _____
☐ Sitting ☐ Standing ☐ Mixture Breaks every: _____

PHYSICAL ACTIVITY

☐ None ☐ Minimal ☐ Some ☐ Sweatin' ☐ I'm beat DETAILS: ______________

RELIEF MEASURES

☐ Medication ☐ Massage ☐ Sleep ☐ Exercise ☐ Water ☐ Cold/Ice
☐ Heat/Bath ☐ Other: ______________________________
Did it work? ☐ Nope ☐ A bit ☐ Mostly ☐ 100%

Notes ☐ *See back notes*

START:		END:		DURATION:		DATE		*Entry #96*

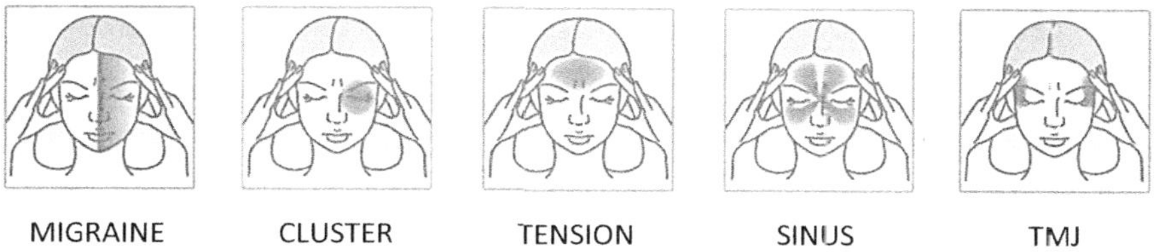

HOW WOULD YOU RATE...?

Mood	1	2	3	4	5
Energy	1	2	3	4	5
Mental clarity	1	2	3	4	5

PAIN LEVEL

1	2	3	4	5	6	7	8	9	10

Not too bad. *Well, I'm not enjoying this.* *Make it stop!*

ONSET

☐ Slow ☐ Average
☐ Rapid ☐ Sudden

DETAILED DESCRIPTION

☐ Constant ☐ Squeezing ☐ Throbbing ☐ Pounding ☐ Dull aching ☐ Burning
☐ Sharp ☐ Debilitating ☐ Other: ____________________

WHERE DOES IT HURT, EXACTLY?

OTHER SYMPTOMS

☐ Lightheaded ☐ Dizziness
☐ Light sensitivity ☐ Sound sensitivity
☐ Confusion ☐ Auras
☐ Muscle stiffness ☐ Muscle aches

FEELING SICK?

☐ Nausea ☐ Diarrhea ☐ Vomiting ☐ Sore throat ☐ Congestion ☐ Coughing
☐ Chills ☐ Fever ☐ Other: ____________________

SLEEP

hours ________ *quality* 1 2 3 4 5

WEATHER

☐ Cold ☐ Mild ☐ Hot Allergen levels: ____________
☐ Dry ☐ Humid ☐ Wet BM Pressure: ____________

STRESS LEVELS

None	Low	Medium	High	Max	@$#%!

item / meal	*time*	*meds / supplements*	*dose*	*time*	*drinks*
					water
					1 2 3 4 5 6 7 8 9 10
					caffeine
					1 2 3 4 5 6 7 8 9 10
					alcohol
					1 2 3 4 5 6 7 8 9 10

HORMONES

☐ Menstruating ☐ Menopause
☐ PMS ☐ N/A | other

COMPUTER / MOBILE DEVICE / TV

☐ None ☐ Some ☐ A lot Total Time: ______
☐ Sitting ☐ Standing ☐ Mixture Breaks every: ______

PHYSICAL ACTIVITY

☐ None ☐ Minimal ☐ Some ☐ Sweatin' ☐ I'm beat DETAILS: ____________________

RELIEF MEASURES

☐ Medication ☐ Massage ☐ Sleep ☐ Exercise ☐ Water ☐ Cold/Ice
☐ Heat/Bath ☐ Other: ____________________
Did it work? ☐ Nope ☐ A bit ☐ Mostly ☐ 100%

Notes ☐ *See back notes*

START:		END:		DURATION:		DATE		*Entry #97*

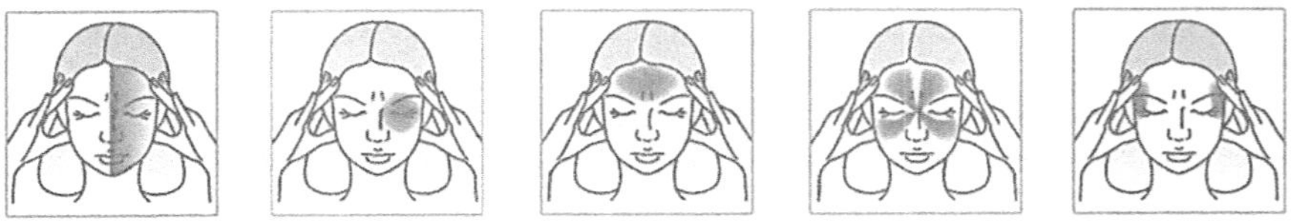

MIGRAINE CLUSTER TENSION SINUS TMJ

HOW WOULD YOU RATE...?

Mood	① ② ③ ④ ⑤
Energy	① ② ③ ④ ⑤
Mental clarity	① ② ③ ④ ⑤

PAIN LEVEL

1	2	3	4	5	6	7	8	9	10

Not too bad. *Well, I'm not enjoying this.* *Make it stop!*

ONSET

☐ Slow ☐ Average
☐ Rapid ☐ Sudden

DETAILED DESCRIPTION

☐ Constant ☐ Squeezing ☐ Throbbing ☐ Pounding ☐ Dull aching ☐ Burning
☐ Sharp ☐ Debilitating ☐ Other: ____________________

WHERE DOES IT HURT, EXACTLY?

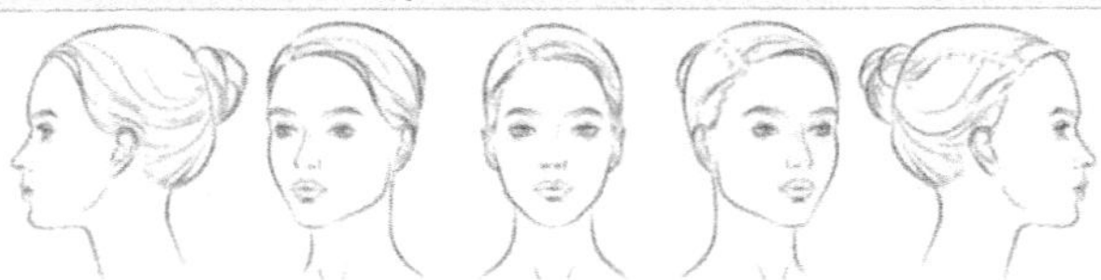

OTHER SYMPTOMS

☐ Lightheaded ☐ Dizziness
☐ Light sensitivity ☐ Sound sensitivity
☐ Confusion ☐ Auras
☐ Muscle stiffness ☐ Muscle aches

FEELING SICK?

☐ Nausea ☐ Diarrhea ☐ Vomiting ☐ Sore throat ☐ Congestion ☐ Coughing
☐ Chills ☐ Fever ☐ Other: ____________________

SLEEP

hours ________ *quality* ① ② ③ ④ ⑤

WEATHER

☐ Cold ☐ Mild ☐ Hot Allergen levels: ____________
☐ Dry ☐ Humid ☐ Wet BM Pressure: ____________

STRESS LEVELS

None	Low	Medium	High	Max	@$#%!

item / meal	*time*	*meds / supplements*	*dose*	*time*	*drinks*
					water
					① ② ③ ④ ⑤ ⑥ ⑦ ⑧ ⑨ ⑩
					caffeine
					① ② ③ ④ ⑤ ⑥ ⑦ ⑧ ⑨ ⑩
					alcohol
					① ② ③ ④ ⑤ ⑥ ⑦ ⑧ ⑨ ⑩

HORMONES

☐ Menstruating ☐ Menopause
☐ PMS ☐ N/A | other

COMPUTER / MOBILE DEVICE / TV

☐ None ☐ Some ☐ A lot Total Time: ______
☐ Sitting ☐ Standing ☐ Mixture Breaks every: ______

PHYSICAL ACTIVITY

☐ None ☐ Minimal ☐ Some ☐ Sweatin' ☐ I'm beat DETAILS: ____________________

RELIEF MEASURES

☐ Medication ☐ Massage ☐ Sleep ☐ Exercise ☐ Water ☐ Cold/Ice
☐ Heat/Bath ☐ Other: ____________________

Did it work? ☐ Nope ☐ A bit ☐ Mostly ☐ 100%

Notes

☐ *See back notes*

START:		END:		DURATION:		DATE		*Entry #98*

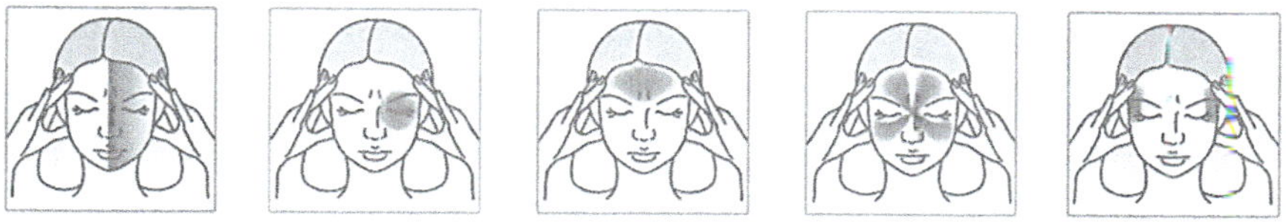

MIGRAINE	CLUSTER	TENSION	SINUS	TMJ

HOW WOULD YOU RATE...?

Mood	①	②	③	④	⑤
Energy	①	②	③	④	⑤
Mental clarity	①	②	③	④	⑤

PAIN LEVEL

1	2	3	4	5	6	7	8	9	10

Not too bad. *Well, I'm not enjoying this.* *Make it stop!*

ONSET

☐ Slow ☐ Average
☐ Rapid ☐ Sudden

DETAILED DESCRIPTION

☐ Constant ☐ Squeezing ☐ Throbbing ☐ Pounding ☐ Dull aching ☐ Burning
☐ Sharp ☐ Debilitating ☐ Other: ____________________

WHERE DOES IT HURT, EXACTLY?

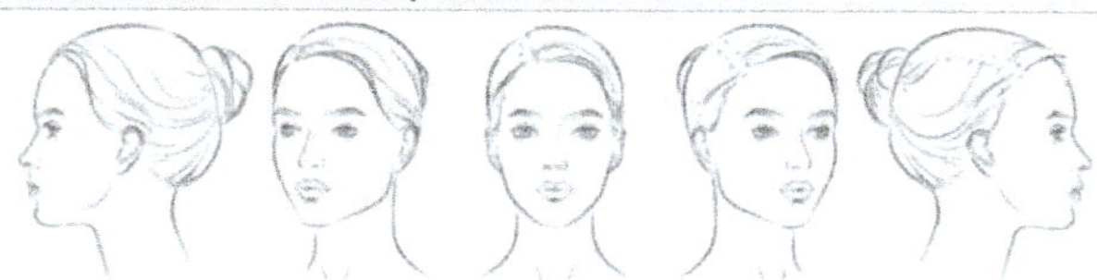

OTHER SYMPTOMS

☐ Lightheaded ☐ Dizziness
☐ Light sensitivity ☐ Sound sensitivity
☐ Confusion ☐ Auras
☐ Muscle stiffness ☐ Muscle aches

FEELING SICK?

☐ Nausea ☐ Diarrhea ☐ Vomiting ☐ Sore throat ☐ Congestion ☐ Coughing
☐ Chills ☐ Fever ☐ Other: ____________________

SLEEP

hours ________ *quality* ① ② ③ ④ ⑤

WEATHER

☐ Cold ☐ Mild ☐ Hot Allergen levels: __________
☐ Dry ☐ Humid ☐ Wet BM Pressure: __________

STRESS LEVELS

None	Low	Medium	High	Max	@$#%!

item / meal	*time*	*meds / supplements*	*dose*	*time*	*drinks*
					water: ① ② ③ ④ ⑤ ⑥ ⑦ ⑧ ⑨ ⑩
					caffeine: ① ② ③ ④ ⑤ ⑥ ⑦ ⑧ ⑨ ⑩
					alcohol: ① ② ③ ④ ⑤ ⑥ ⑦ ⑧ ⑨ ⑩

HORMONES

☐ Menstruating ☐ Menopause
☐ PMS ☐ N/A | other

COMPUTER / MOBILE DEVICE / TV

☐ None ☐ Some ☐ A lot Total Time: ______
☐ Sitting ☐ Standing ☐ Mixture Breaks every: ______

PHYSICAL ACTIVITY

☐ None ☐ Minimal ☐ Some ☐ Sweatin' ☐ I'm beat DETAILS: ____________________

RELIEF MEASURES

☐ Medication ☐ Massage ☐ Sleep ☐ Exercise ☐ Water ☐ Cold/Ice
☐ Heat/Bath ☐ Other: ____________________
Did it work? ☐ Nope ☐ A bit ☐ Mostly ☐ 100%

Notes ☐ *See back notes*

START:		END:		DURATION:		DATE		*Entry #99*

 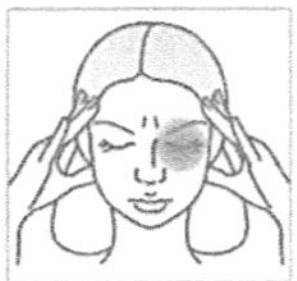 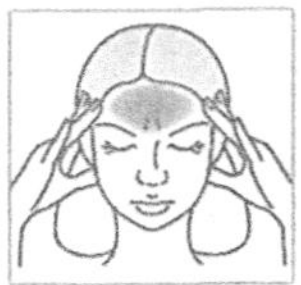  

MIGRAINE CLUSTER TENSION SINUS TMJ

HOW WOULD YOU RATE...?

Mood	① ② ③ ④ ⑤
Energy	① ② ③ ④ ⑤
Mental clarity	① ② ③ ④ ⑤

PAIN LEVEL

1	2	3	4	5	6	7	8	9	10

Not too bad. *Well, I'm not enjoying this.* *Make it stop!*

ONSET

☐ Slow ☐ Average
☐ Rapid ☐ Sudden

DETAILED DESCRIPTION

☐ Constant ☐ Squeezing ☐ Throbbing ☐ Pounding ☐ Dull aching ☐ Burning
☐ Sharp ☐ Debilitating ☐ Other: ____________________

WHERE DOES IT HURT, EXACTLY?

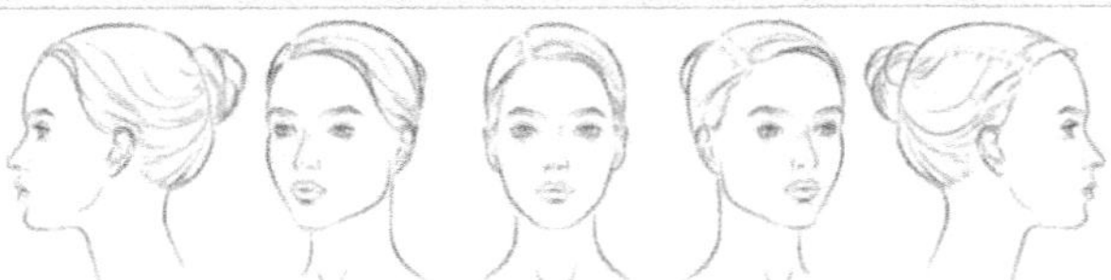

OTHER SYMPTOMS

☐ Lightheaded ☐ Dizziness
☐ Light sensitivity ☐ Sound sensitivity
☐ Confusion ☐ Auras
☐ Muscle stiffness ☐ Muscle aches

FEELING SICK?

☐ Nausea ☐ Diarrhea ☐ Vomiting ☐ Sore throat ☐ Congestion ☐ Coughing
☐ Chills ☐ Fever ☐ Other: ____________________

SLEEP

hours ________ *quality* ① ② ③ ④ ⑤

WEATHER

☐ Cold ☐ Mild ☐ Hot Allergen levels: __________
☐ Dry ☐ Humid ☐ Wet BM Pressure: __________

STRESS LEVELS

None	Low	Medium	High	Max	@$#%!

item / meal	*time*	*meds / supplements*	*dose*	*time*	*drinks*
					water
					① ② ③ ④ ⑤ ⑥ ⑦ ⑧ ⑨ ⑩
					caffeine
					① ② ③ ④ ⑤ ⑥ ⑦ ⑧ ⑨ ⑩
					alcohol
					① ② ③ ④ ⑤ ⑥ ⑦ ⑧ ⑨ ⑩

HORMONES

☐ Menstruating ☐ Menopause
☐ PMS ☐ N/A | other

COMPUTER / MOBILE DEVICE / TV

☐ None ☐ Some ☐ A lot Total Time: ______
☐ Sitting ☐ Standing ☐ Mixture Breaks every: ______

PHYSICAL ACTIVITY

☐ None ☐ Minimal ☐ Some ☐ Sweatin' ☐ I'm beat DETAILS: __________

RELIEF MEASURES

☐ Medication ☐ Massage ☐ Sleep ☐ Exercise ☐ Water ☐ Cold/Ice
☐ Heat/Bath ☐ Other: ____________________

Did it work? ☐ Nope ☐ A bit ☐ Mostly ☐ 100%

Notes ☐ *See back notes*

START:		END:		DURATION:		DATE		*Entry #100*

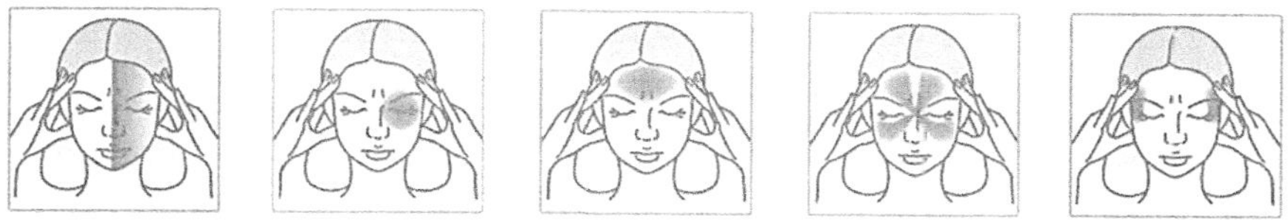

MIGRAINE | CLUSTER | TENSION | SINUS | TMJ

HOW WOULD YOU RATE...?

Mood	1	2	3	4	5
Energy	1	2	3	4	5
Mental clarity	1	2	3	4	5

PAIN LEVEL

1	2	3	4	5	6	7	8	9	10

Not too bad. *Well, I'm not enjoying this.* *Make it stop!*

ONSET

☐ Slow ☐ Average
☐ Rapid ☐ Sudden

DETAILED DESCRIPTION

☐ Constant ☐ Squeezing ☐ Throbbing ☐ Pounding ☐ Dull aching ☐ Burning
☐ Sharp ☐ Debilitating ☐ Other: ______________________________

WHERE DOES IT HURT, EXACTLY?

OTHER SYMPTOMS

☐ Lightheaded ☐ Dizziness
☐ Light sensitivity ☐ Sound sensitivity
☐ Confusion ☐ Auras
☐ Muscle stiffness ☐ Muscle aches

FEELING SICK?

☐ Nausea ☐ Diarrhea ☐ Vomiting ☐ Sore throat ☐ Congestion ☐ Coughing
☐ Chills ☐ Fever ☐ Other: ______________________________

SLEEP

hours ________ *quality* 1 2 3 4 5

WEATHER

☐ Cold ☐ Mild ☐ Hot Allergen levels: ____________
☐ Dry ☐ Humid ☐ Wet BM Pressure: ____________

STRESS LEVELS

None	Low	Medium	High	Max	@$#%!

item / meal	*time*	*meds / supplements*	*dose*	*time*	*drinks*
					water
					1 2 3 4 5 6 7 8 9 10
					caffeine
					1 2 3 4 5 6 7 8 9 10
					alcohol
					1 2 3 4 5 6 7 8 9 10

HORMONES

☐ Menstruating ☐ Menopause
☐ PMS ☐ N/A | other

COMPUTER / MOBILE DEVICE / TV

☐ None ☐ Some ☐ A lot Total Time: ______
☐ Sitting ☐ Standing ☐ Mixture Breaks every: ______

PHYSICAL ACTIVITY

☐ None ☐ Minimal ☐ Some ☐ Sweatin' ☐ I'm beat DETAILS: ____________________

RELIEF MEASURES

☐ Medication ☐ Massage ☐ Sleep ☐ Exercise ☐ Water ☐ Cold/Ice
☐ Heat/Bath ☐ Other: ______________________________
Did it work? ☐ Nope ☐ A bit ☐ Mostly ☐ 100%

Notes ☐ *See back notes*

START: ____ END: ____ DURATION: ____ DATE ____ *Entry #101*

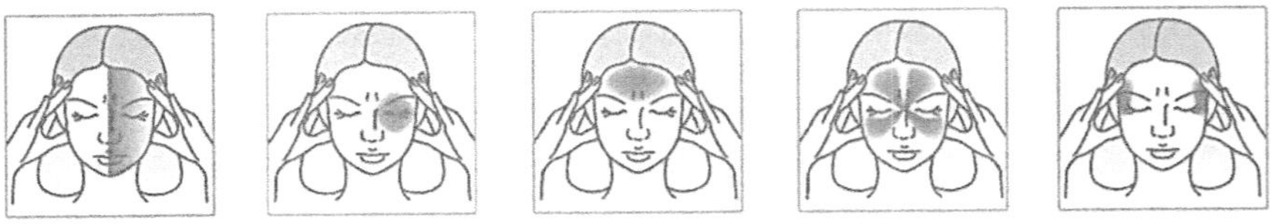

MIGRAINE CLUSTER TENSION SINUS TMJ

HOW WOULD YOU RATE...?

Mood	① ② ③ ④ ⑤
Energy	① ② ③ ④ ⑤
Mental clarity	① ② ③ ④ ⑤

PAIN LEVEL

1	2	3	4	5	6	7	8	9	10

Not too bad. *Well, I'm not enjoying this.* *Make it stop!*

ONSET

☐ Slow ☐ Average
☐ Rapid ☐ Sudden

DETAILED DESCRIPTION

☐ Constant ☐ Squeezing ☐ Throbbing ☐ Pounding ☐ Dull aching ☐ Burning
☐ Sharp ☐ Debilitating ☐ Other: ____________

WHERE DOES IT HURT, EXACTLY?

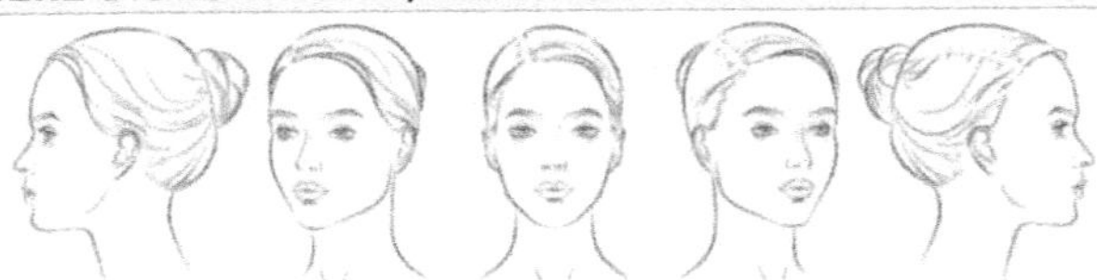

OTHER SYMPTOMS

☐ Lightheaded ☐ Dizziness
☐ Light sensitivity ☐ Sound sensitivity
☐ Confusion ☐ Auras
☐ Muscle stiffness ☐ Muscle aches

FEELING SICK?

☐ Nausea ☐ Diarrhea ☐ Vomiting ☐ Sore throat ☐ Congestion ☐ Coughing
☐ Chills ☐ Fever ☐ Other: ____________

SLEEP

hours ______ *quality* ① ② ③ ④ ⑤

WEATHER

☐ Cold ☐ Mild ☐ Hot Allergen levels: ______
☐ Dry ☐ Humid ☐ Wet BM Pressure: ______

STRESS LEVELS

None	Low	Medium	High	Max	@$#%!

item / meal	*time*	*meds / supplements*	*dose*	*time*	*drinks*
					water ① ② ③ ④ ⑤ ⑥ ⑦ ⑧ ⑨ ⑩
					caffeine ① ② ③ ④ ⑤ ⑥ ⑦ ⑧ ⑨ ⑩
					alcohol ① ② ③ ④ ⑤ ⑥ ⑦ ⑧ ⑨ ⑩

HORMONES

☐ Menstruating ☐ Menopause
☐ PMS ☐ N/A | other

COMPUTER / MOBILE DEVICE / TV

☐ None ☐ Some ☐ A lot Total Time: ______
☐ Sitting ☐ Standing ☐ Mixture Breaks every: ______

PHYSICAL ACTIVITY

☐ None ☐ Minimal ☐ Some ☐ Sweatin' ☐ I'm beat DETAILS: ____________

RELIEF MEASURES

☐ Medication ☐ Massage ☐ Sleep ☐ Exercise ☐ Water ☐ Cold/Ice
☐ Heat/Bath ☐ Other: ____________
Did it work? ☐ Nope ☐ A bit ☐ Mostly ☐ 100%

Notes ☐ *See back notes*

START: | END: | DURATION: | DATE | *Entry #102*

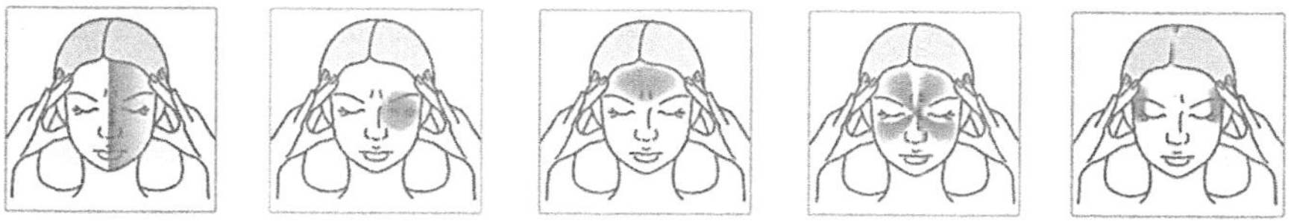

MIGRAINE | CLUSTER | TENSION | SINUS | TMJ

HOW WOULD YOU RATE...?

Mood	1	2	3	4	5
Energy	1	2	3	4	5
Mental clarity	1	2	3	4	5

PAIN LEVEL

1	2	3	4	5	6	7	8	9	10

Not too bad. *Well, I'm not enjoying this.* *Make it stop!*

ONSET

☐ Slow ☐ Average
☐ Rapid ☐ Sudden

DETAILED DESCRIPTION

☐ Constant ☐ Squeezing ☐ Throbbing ☐ Pounding ☐ Dull aching ☐ Burning
☐ Sharp ☐ Debilitating ☐ Other: ____________________

WHERE DOES IT HURT, EXACTLY?

OTHER SYMPTOMS

☐ Lightheaded ☐ Dizziness
☐ Light sensitivity ☐ Sound sensitivity
☐ Confusion ☐ Auras
☐ Muscle stiffness ☐ Muscle aches

FEELING SICK?

☐ Nausea ☐ Diarrhea ☐ Vomiting ☐ Sore throat ☐ Congestion ☐ Coughing
☐ Chills ☐ Fever ☐ Other: ____________________

SLEEP

hours ________ *quality* 1 2 3 4 5

WEATHER

☐ Cold ☐ Mild ☐ Hot Allergen levels: __________
☐ Dry ☐ Humid ☐ Wet BM Pressure: __________

STRESS LEVELS

None	Low	Medium	High	Max	@$#%!

item / meal	*time*	*meds / supplements*	*dose*	*time*	*drinks*
					water: 1 2 3 4 5 6 7 8 9 10
					caffeine: 1 2 3 4 5 6 7 8 9 10
					alcohol: 1 2 3 4 5 6 7 8 9 10

HORMONES

☐ Menstruating ☐ Menopause
☐ PMS ☐ N/A | other

COMPUTER / MOBILE DEVICE / TV

☐ None ☐ Some ☐ A lot Total Time: ______
☐ Sitting ☐ Standing ☐ Mixture Breaks every: ______

PHYSICAL ACTIVITY

☐ None ☐ Minimal ☐ Some ☐ Sweatin' ☐ I'm beat DETAILS: ____________________

RELIEF MEASURES

☐ Medication ☐ Massage ☐ Sleep ☐ Exercise ☐ Water ☐ Cold/Ice
☐ Heat/Bath ☐ Other: ____________________
Did it work? ☐ Nope ☐ A bit ☐ Mostly ☐ 100%

Notes ☐ *See back notes*

START:		END:		DURATION:		DATE		*Entry #103*

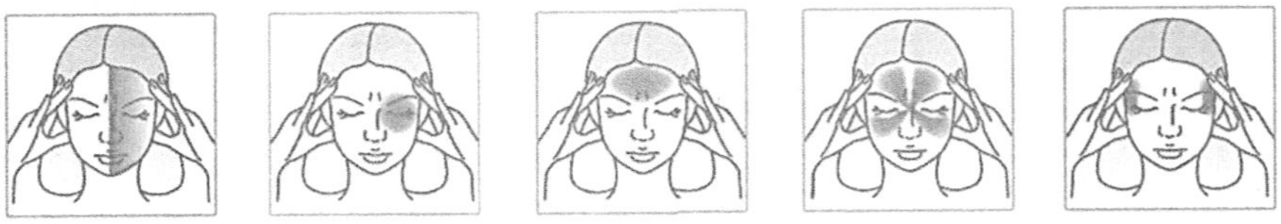

MIGRAINE | CLUSTER | TENSION | SINUS | TMJ

HOW WOULD YOU RATE...?

Mood	1	2	3	4	5
Energy	1	2	3	4	5
Mental clarity	1	2	3	4	5

PAIN LEVEL

1	2	3	4	5	6	7	8	9	10

Not too bad. *Well, I'm not enjoying this.* *Make it stop!*

ONSET

☐ Slow ☐ Average
☐ Rapid ☐ Sudden

DETAILED DESCRIPTION

☐ Constant ☐ Squeezing ☐ Throbbing ☐ Pounding ☐ Dull aching ☐ Burning
☐ Sharp ☐ Debilitating ☐ Other: ______________________________

WHERE DOES IT HURT, EXACTLY?

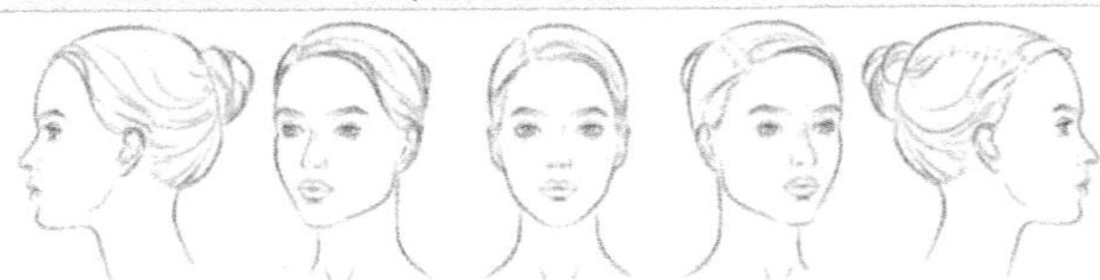

OTHER SYMPTOMS

☐ Lightheaded ☐ Dizziness
☐ Light sensitivity ☐ Sound sensitivity
☐ Confusion ☐ Auras
☐ Muscle stiffness ☐ Muscle aches

FEELING SICK?

☐ Nausea ☐ Diarrhea ☐ Vomiting ☐ Sore throat ☐ Congestion ☐ Coughing
☐ Chills ☐ Fever ☐ Other: ______________________________

SLEEP

hours ________ *quality* 1 2 3 4 5

WEATHER

☐ Cold ☐ Mild ☐ Hot Allergen levels: ____________
☐ Dry ☐ Humid ☐ Wet BM Pressure: ____________

STRESS LEVELS

None	Low	Medium	High	Max	@$#%!

item / meal	*time*	*meds / supplements*	*dose*	*time*	*drinks*
					water
					1 2 3 4 5 6 7 8 9 10
					caffeine
					1 2 3 4 5 6 7 8 9 10
					alcohol
					1 2 3 4 5 6 7 8 9 10

HORMONES

☐ Menstruating ☐ Menopause
☐ PMS ☐ N/A | other

COMPUTER / MOBILE DEVICE / TV

☐ None ☐ Some ☐ A lot Total Time: _____
☐ Sitting ☐ Standing ☐ Mixture Breaks every: _____

PHYSICAL ACTIVITY

☐ None ☐ Minimal ☐ Some ☐ Sweatin' ☐ I'm beat DETAILS: ______________

RELIEF MEASURES

☐ Medication ☐ Massage ☐ Sleep ☐ Exercise ☐ Water ☐ Cold/Ice
☐ Heat/Bath ☐ Other: ______________________________
Did it work? ☐ Nope ☐ A bit ☐ Mostly ☐ 100%

Notes ☐ *See back notes*

START:		END:		DURATION:		DATE		*Entry #104*

MIGRAINE | CLUSTER | TENSION | SINUS | TMJ

HOW WOULD YOU RATE...?

Mood	1	2	3	4	5
Energy	1	2	3	4	5
Mental clarity	1	2	3	4	5

PAIN LEVEL

1	2	3	4	5	6	7	8	9	10

Not too bad. *Well. I'm not enjoying this.* *Make it stop!*

ONSET

☐ Slow ☐ Average
☐ Rapid ☐ Sudden

DETAILED DESCRIPTION

☐ Constant ☐ Squeezing ☐ Throbbing ☐ Pounding ☐ Dull aching ☐ Burning
☐ Sharp ☐ Debilitating ☐ Other: ______________________

WHERE DOES IT HURT, EXACTLY?

OTHER SYMPTOMS

☐ Lightheaded ☐ Dizziness
☐ Light sensitivity ☐ Sound sensitivity
☐ Confusion ☐ Auras
☐ Muscle stiffness ☐ Muscle aches

FEELING SICK?

☐ Nausea ☐ Diarrhea ☐ Vomiting ☐ Sore throat ☐ Congestion ☐ Coughing
☐ Chills ☐ Fever ☐ Other: ______________________

SLEEP

hours ________ *quality* 1 2 3 4 5

WEATHER

☐ Cold ☐ Mild ☐ Hot Allergen levels: ____________
☐ Dry ☐ Humid ☐ Wet BM Pressure: ____________

STRESS LEVELS

None	Low	Medium	High	Max	@$#%!

item / meal	*time*	*meds / supplements*	*dose*	*time*	*drinks*
					water
					1 2 3 4 5 6 7 8 9 10
					caffeine
					1 2 3 4 5 6 7 8 9 10
					alcohol
					1 2 3 4 5 6 7 8 9 10

HORMONES

☐ Menstruating ☐ Menopause
☐ PMS ☐ N/A | other

COMPUTER / MOBILE DEVICE / TV

☐ None ☐ Some ☐ A lot Total Time: ______
☐ Sitting ☐ Standing ☐ Mixture Breaks every: ______

PHYSICAL ACTIVITY

☐ None ☐ Minimal ☐ Some ☐ Sweatin' ☐ I'm beat DETAILS: ______________

RELIEF MEASURES

☐ Medication ☐ Massage ☐ Sleep ☐ Exercise ☐ Water ☐ Cold/Ice
☐ Heat/Bath ☐ Other: ______________________
Did it work? ☐ Nope ☐ A bit ☐ Mostly ☐ 100%

Notes ☐ *See back notes*

START: | END: | DURATION: | DATE | *Entry #105*

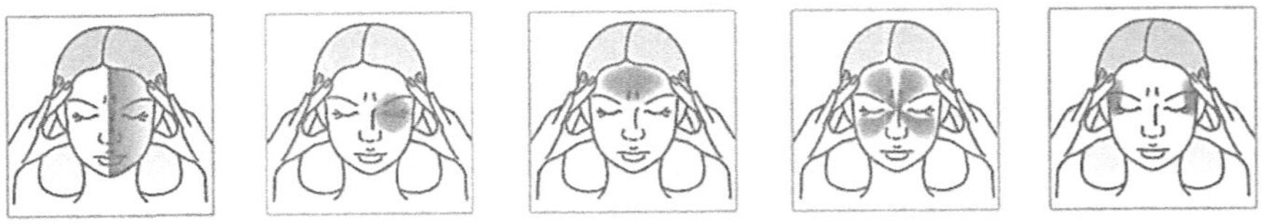

MIGRAINE | CLUSTER | TENSION | SINUS | TMJ

HOW WOULD YOU RATE...?

Mood	1	2	3	4	5
Energy	1	2	3	4	5
Mental clarity	1	2	3	4	5

PAIN LEVEL

1	2	3	4	5	6	7	8	9	10

Not too bad. *Well, I'm not enjoying this.* *Make it stop!*

ONSET

☐ Slow ☐ Average
☐ Rapid ☐ Sudden

DETAILED DESCRIPTION

☐ Constant ☐ Squeezing ☐ Throbbing ☐ Pounding ☐ Dull aching ☐ Burning
☐ Sharp ☐ Debilitating ☐ Other: ______

WHERE DOES IT HURT, EXACTLY?

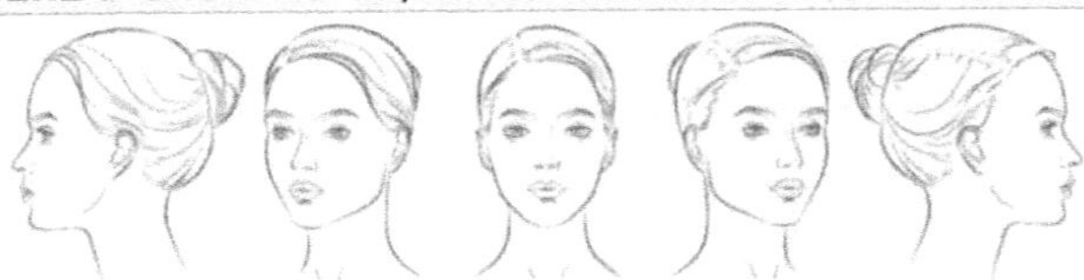

OTHER SYMPTOMS

☐ Lightheaded ☐ Dizziness
☐ Light sensitivity ☐ Sound sensitivity
☐ Confusion ☐ Auras
☐ Muscle stiffness ☐ Muscle aches

FEELING SICK?

☐ Nausea ☐ Diarrhea ☐ Vomiting ☐ Sore throat ☐ Congestion ☐ Coughing
☐ Chills ☐ Fever ☐ Other: ______

SLEEP

hours ______ *quality* 1 2 3 4 5

WEATHER

☐ Cold ☐ Mild ☐ Hot Allergen levels: ______
☐ Dry ☐ Humid ☐ Wet BM Pressure: ______

STRESS LEVELS

None	Low	Medium	High	Max	@$#%!

item / meal	*time*	*meds / supplements*	*dose*	*time*	*drinks*
					water: 1 2 3 4 5 6 7 8 9 10
					caffeine: 1 2 3 4 5 6 7 8 9 10
					alcohol: 1 2 3 4 5 6 7 8 9 10

HORMONES

☐ Menstruating ☐ Menopause
☐ PMS ☐ N/A | other

COMPUTER / MOBILE DEVICE / TV

☐ None ☐ Some ☐ A lot Total Time: ______
☐ Sitting ☐ Standing ☐ Mixture Breaks every: ______

PHYSICAL ACTIVITY

☐ None ☐ Minimal ☐ Some ☐ Sweatin' ☐ I'm beat DETAILS: ______

RELIEF MEASURES

☐ Medication ☐ Massage ☐ Sleep ☐ Exercise ☐ Water ☐ Cold/Ice
☐ Heat/Bath ☐ Other: ______
Did it work? ☐ Nope ☐ A bit ☐ Mostly ☐ 100%

Notes ☐ *See back notes*

START: ______ END: ______ DURATION: ______ DATE ______ *Entry #106*

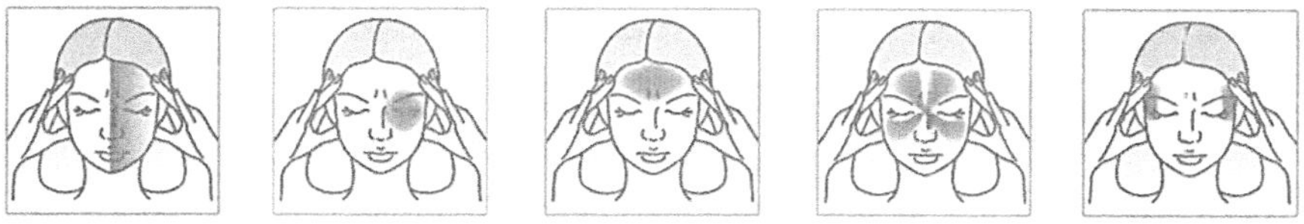

HOW WOULD YOU RATE...?

Mood	1	2	3	4	5
Energy	1	2	3	4	5
Mental clarity	1	2	3	4	5

PAIN LEVEL

1	2	3	4	5	6	7	8	9	10

Not too bad. *Well, I'm not enjoying this.* *Make it stop!*

ONSET

☐ Slow ☐ Average
☐ Rapid ☐ Sudden

DETAILED DESCRIPTION

☐ Constant ☐ Squeezing ☐ Throbbing ☐ Pounding ☐ Dull aching ☐ Burning
☐ Sharp ☐ Debilitating ☐ Other: ____________________

WHERE DOES IT HURT, EXACTLY?

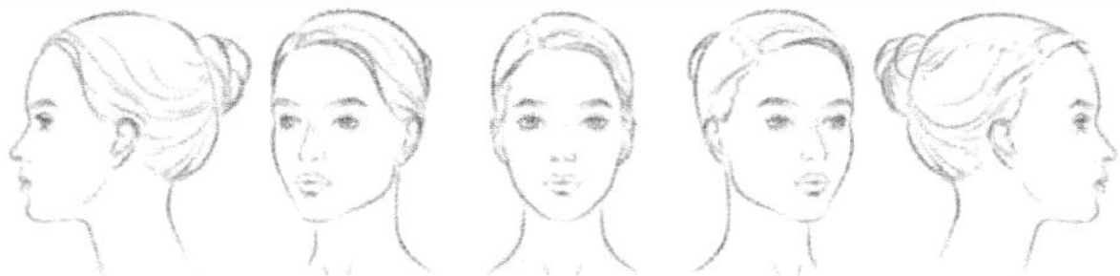

OTHER SYMPTOMS

☐ Lightheaded ☐ Dizziness
☐ Light sensitivity ☐ Sound sensitivity
☐ Confusion ☐ Auras
☐ Muscle stiffness ☐ Muscle aches

FEELING SICK?

☐ Nausea ☐ Diarrhea ☐ Vomiting ☐ Sore throat ☐ Congestion ☐ Coughing
☐ Chills ☐ Fever ☐ Other: ____________________

SLEEP

hours ________ *quality* 1 2 3 4 5

WEATHER

☐ Cold ☐ Mild ☐ Hot Allergen levels: __________
☐ Dry ☐ Humid ☐ Wet BM Pressure: __________

STRESS LEVELS

None	Low	Medium	High	Max	@$#%!

item / meal	*time*	*meds / supplements*	*dose*	*time*	*drinks*
					water: 1 2 3 4 5 6 7 8 9 10
					caffeine: 1 2 3 4 5 6 7 8 9 10
					alcohol: 1 2 3 4 5 6 7 8 9 10

HORMONES

☐ Menstruating ☐ Menopause
☐ PMS ☐ N/A | other

COMPUTER / MOBILE DEVICE / TV

☐ None ☐ Some ☐ A lot Total Time: ______
☐ Sitting ☐ Standing ☐ Mixture Breaks every: ______

PHYSICAL ACTIVITY

☐ None ☐ Minimal ☐ Some ☐ Sweatin' ☐ I'm beat DETAILS: ____________________

RELIEF MEASURES

☐ Medication ☐ Massage ☐ Sleep ☐ Exercise ☐ Water ☐ Cold/Ice
☐ Heat/Bath ☐ Other: ____________________
Did it work? ☐ Nope ☐ A bit ☐ Mostly ☐ 100%

Notes ☐ *See back notes*

START:		END:		DURATION:		DATE		*Entry #107*

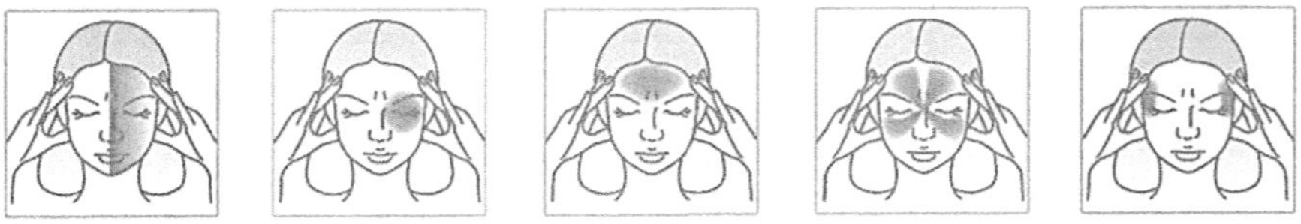

MIGRAINE CLUSTER TENSION SINUS TMJ

HOW WOULD YOU RATE...?

Mood	① ② ③ ④ ⑤
Energy	① ② ③ ④ ⑤
Mental clarity	① ② ③ ④ ⑤

PAIN LEVEL

1	2	3	4	5	6	7	8	9	10

Not too bad. *Well, I'm not enjoying this.* *Make it stop!*

ONSET

☐ Slow ☐ Average
☐ Rapid ☐ Sudden

DETAILED DESCRIPTION

☐ Constant ☐ Squeezing ☐ Throbbing ☐ Pounding ☐ Dull aching ☐ Burning
☐ Sharp ☐ Debilitating ☐ Other: ______________________________

WHERE DOES IT HURT, EXACTLY?

OTHER SYMPTOMS

☐ Lightheaded ☐ Dizziness
☐ Light sensitivity ☐ Sound sensitivity
☐ Confusion ☐ Auras
☐ Muscle stiffness ☐ Muscle aches

FEELING SICK?

☐ Nausea ☐ Diarrhea ☐ Vomiting ☐ Sore throat ☐ Congestion ☐ Coughing
☐ Chills ☐ Fever ☐ Other: ______________________________

SLEEP

hours ________ *quality* ① ② ③ ④ ⑤

WEATHER

☐ Cold ☐ Mild ☐ Hot Allergen levels: ____________
☐ Dry ☐ Humid ☐ Wet BM Pressure: ____________

STRESS LEVELS

None	Low	Medium	High	Max	@$#%!

item / meal	*time*	*meds / supplements*	*dose*	*time*	*drinks*
					water
					① ② ③ ④ ⑤ ⑥ ⑦ ⑧ ⑨ ⑩
					caffeine
					① ② ③ ④ ⑤ ⑥ ⑦ ⑧ ⑨ ⑩
					alcohol
					① ② ③ ④ ⑤ ⑥ ⑦ ⑧ ⑨ ⑩

HORMONES

☐ Menstruating ☐ Menopause
☐ PMS ☐ N/A | other

COMPUTER / MOBILE DEVICE / TV

☐ None ☐ Some ☐ A lot Total Time: _____
☐ Sitting ☐ Standing ☐ Mixture Breaks every: _____

PHYSICAL ACTIVITY

☐ None ☐ Minimal ☐ Some ☐ Sweatin' ☐ I'm beat DETAILS: ______________________

RELIEF MEASURES

☐ Medication ☐ Massage ☐ Sleep ☐ Exercise ☐ Water ☐ Cold/Ice
☐ Heat/Bath ☐ Other: ______________________________
Did it work? ☐ Nope ☐ A bit ☐ Mostly ☐ 100%

Notes ☐ *See back notes*

START:		END:		DURATION:		DATE		*Entry #108*

MIGRAINE CLUSTER TENSION SINUS TMJ

HOW WOULD YOU RATE...?

Mood	① ② ③ ④ ⑤
Energy	① ② ③ ④ ⑤
Mental clarity	① ② ③ ④ ⑤

PAIN LEVEL

1	2	3	4	5	6	7	8	9	10

Not too bad. *Well. I'm not enjoying this.* *Make it stop!*

ONSET

☐ Slow ☐ Average
☐ Rapid ☐ Sudden

DETAILED DESCRIPTION

☐ Constant ☐ Squeezing ☐ Throbbing ☐ Pouncing ☐ Dull aching ☐ Burning
☐ Sharp ☐ Debilitating ☐ Other: ______

WHERE DOES IT HURT, EXACTLY?

OTHER SYMPTOMS

☐ Lightheaded ☐ Dizziness
☐ Light sensitivity ☐ Sound sensitivity
☐ Confusion ☐ Auras
☐ Muscle stiffness ☐ Muscle aches

FEELING SICK?

☐ Nausea ☐ Diarrhea ☐ Vomiting ☐ Sore throat ☐ Congestion ☐ Coughing
☐ Chills ☐ Fever ☐ Other: ______

SLEEP

hours ______ *quality* ① ② ③ ④ ⑤

WEATHER

☐ Cold ☐ Mild ☐ Hot Allergen levels: ______
☐ Dry ☐ Humid ☐ Wet BM Pressure: ______

STRESS LEVELS

None	Low	Medium	High	Max	@$#%!

item / meal	*time*	*meds / supplements*	*dose*	*time*	*drinks*
					water
					① ② ③ ④ ⑤ ⑥ ⑦ ⑧ ⑨ ⑩
					caffeine
					① ② ③ ④ ⑤ ⑥ ⑦ ⑧ ⑨ ⑩
					alcohol
					① ② ③ ④ ⑤ ⑥ ⑦ ⑧ ⑨ ⑩

HORMONES

☐ Menstruating ☐ Menopause
☐ PMS ☐ N/A | other

COMPUTER / MOBILE DEVICE / TV

☐ None ☐ Some ☐ A lot Total Time: ______
☐ Sitting ☐ Standing ☐ Mixture Breaks every: ______

PHYSICAL ACTIVITY

☐ None ☐ Minimal ☐ Some ☐ Sweatin' ☐ I'm beat DETAILS: ______

RELIEF MEASURES

☐ Medication ☐ Massage ☐ Sleep ☐ Exercise ☐ Water ☐ Cold/Ice
☐ Heat/Bath ☐ Other: ______
Did it work? ☐ Nope ☐ A bit ☐ Mostly ☐ 100%

Notes ☐ *See back notes*

START:	END:	DURATION:	DATE	*Entry #109*

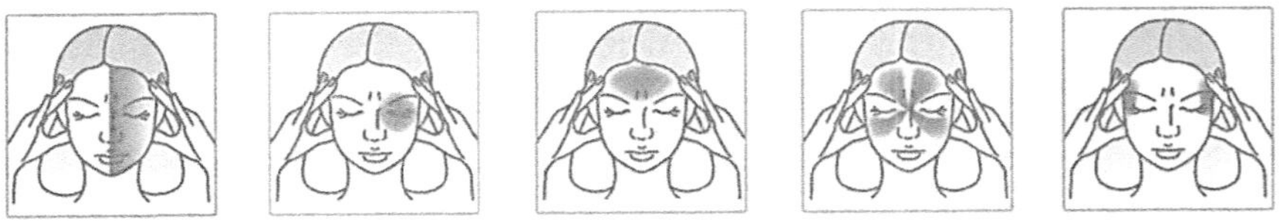

MIGRAINE | CLUSTER | TENSION | SINUS | TMJ

HOW WOULD YOU RATE...?

Mood	1	2	3	4	5
Energy	1	2	3	4	5
Mental clarity	1	2	3	4	5

PAIN LEVEL

1	2	3	4	5	6	7	8	9	10

Not too bad. *Well, I'm not enjoying this.* *Make it stop!*

ONSET

☐ Slow ☐ Average
☐ Rapid ☐ Sudden

DETAILED DESCRIPTION

☐ Constant ☐ Squeezing ☐ Throbbing ☐ Pounding ☐ Dull aching ☐ Burning
☐ Sharp ☐ Debilitating ☐ Other: ____________________

WHERE DOES IT HURT, EXACTLY?

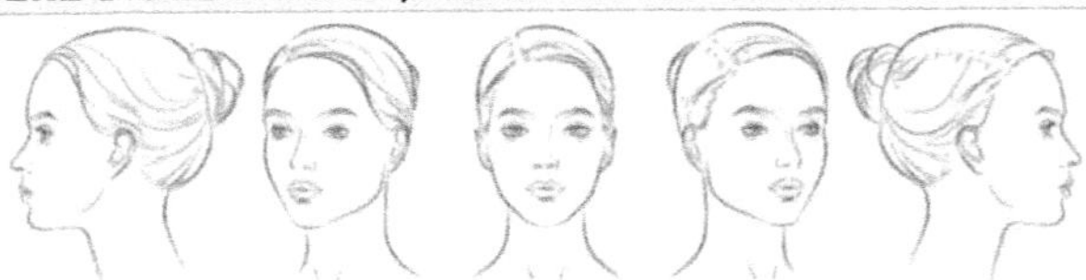

OTHER SYMPTOMS

☐ Lightheaded ☐ Dizziness
☐ Light sensitivity ☐ Sound sensitivity
☐ Confusion ☐ Auras
☐ Muscle stiffness ☐ Muscle aches

FEELING SICK?

☐ Nausea ☐ Diarrhea ☐ Vomiting ☐ Sore throat ☐ Congestion ☐ Coughing
☐ Chills ☐ Fever ☐ Other: ____________________

SLEEP

hours ________ *quality* 1 2 3 4 5

WEATHER

☐ Cold ☐ Mild ☐ Hot Allergen levels: __________
☐ Dry ☐ Humid ☐ Wet BM Pressure: __________

STRESS LEVELS

None	Low	Medium	High	Max	@$#%!

item / meal	*time*	*meds / supplements*	*dose*	*time*	*drinks*
					water
					1 2 3 4 5 6 7 8 9 10
					caffeine
					1 2 3 4 5 6 7 8 9 10
					alcohol
					1 2 3 4 5 6 7 8 9 10

HORMONES

☐ Menstruating ☐ Menopause
☐ PMS ☐ N/A | other

COMPUTER / MOBILE DEVICE / TV

☐ None ☐ Some ☐ A lot Total Time: ______
☐ Sitting ☐ Standing ☐ Mixture Breaks every: ______

PHYSICAL ACTIVITY

☐ None ☐ Minimal ☐ Some ☐ Sweatin' ☐ I'm beat DETAILS: ____________________

RELIEF MEASURES

☐ Medication ☐ Massage ☐ Sleep ☐ Exercise ☐ Water ☐ Cold/Ice
☐ Heat/Bath ☐ Other: ____________________
Did it work? ☐ Nope ☐ A bit ☐ Mostly ☐ 100%

Notes ☐ *See back notes*

START:		END:		DURATION:		DATE		*Entry #110*

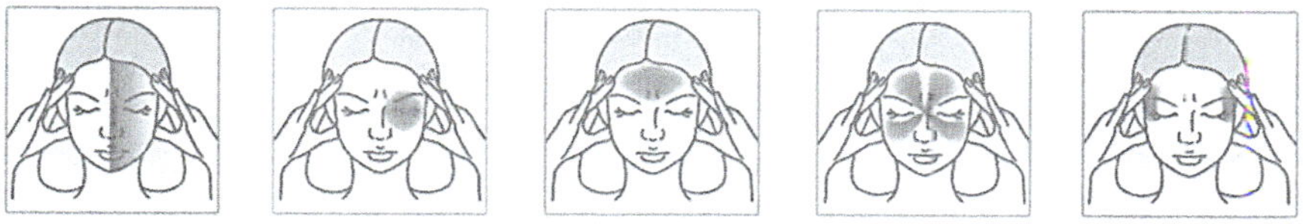

MIGRAINE CLUSTER TENSION SINUS TMJ

HOW WOULD YOU RATE...?

Mood	1	2	3	4	5
Energy	1	2	3	4	5
Mental clarity	1	2	3	4	5

PAIN LEVEL

1	2	3	4	5	6	7	8	9	10

Not too bad. *Well, I'm not enjoying this.* *Make it stop!*

ONSET

☐ Slow ☐ Average
☐ Rapid ☐ Sudden

DETAILED DESCRIPTION

☐ Constant ☐ Squeezing ☐ Throbbing ☐ Pounding ☐ Dull aching ☐ Burning
☐ Sharp ☐ Debilitating ☐ Other: ____________________

WHERE DOES IT HURT, EXACTLY?

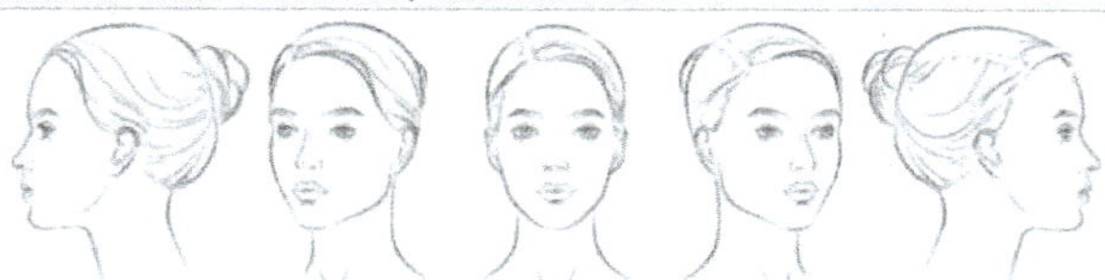

OTHER SYMPTOMS

☐ Lightheaded ☐ Dizziness
☐ Light sensitivity ☐ Sound sensitivity
☐ Confusion ☐ Auras
☐ Muscle stiffness ☐ Muscle aches

FEELING SICK?

☐ Nausea ☐ Diarrhea ☐ Vomiting ☐ Sore throat ☐ Congestion ☐ Coughing
☐ Chills ☐ Fever ☐ Other: ____________________

SLEEP

hours ________ *quality* 1 2 3 4 5

WEATHER

☐ Cold ☐ Mild ☐ Hot Allergen levels: ____________
☐ Dry ☐ Humid ☐ Wet BM Pressure: ____________

STRESS LEVELS

None	Low	Medium	High	Max	@$#%!

item / meal	*time*	*meds / supplements*	*dose*	*time*	*drinks*
					water
					1 2 3 4 5 6 7 8 9 10
					caffeine
					1 2 3 4 5 6 7 8 9 10
					alcohol
					1 2 3 4 5 6 7 8 9 10

HORMONES

☐ Menstruating ☐ Menopause
☐ PMS ☐ N/A | other

COMPUTER / MOBILE DEVICE / TV

☐ None ☐ Some ☐ A lot Total Time: ______
☐ Sitting ☐ Standing ☐ Mixture Breaks every: ______

PHYSICAL ACTIVITY

☐ None ☐ Minimal ☐ Some ☐ Sweatin' ☐ I'm beat DETAILS: ____________

RELIEF MEASURES

☐ Medication ☐ Massage ☐ Sleep ☐ Exercise ☐ Water ☐ Cold/Ice
☐ Heat/Bath ☐ Other: ____________________

Did it work? ☐ Nope ☐ A bit ☐ Mostly ☐ 100%

Notes ☐ *See back notes*

START: | END: | DURATION: | DATE | *Entry #111*

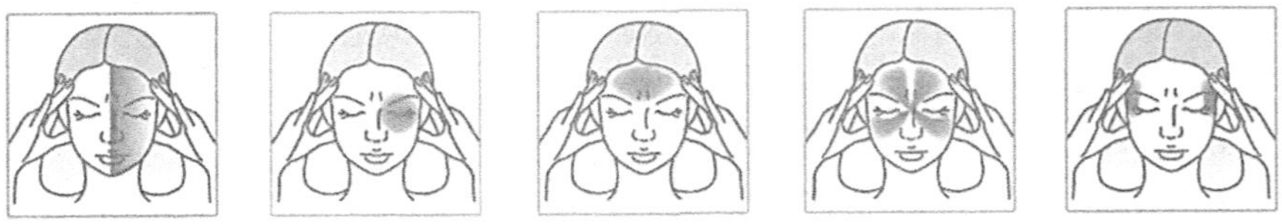

MIGRAINE | CLUSTER | TENSION | SINUS | TMJ

HOW WOULD YOU RATE...?

Mood	① ② ③ ④ ⑤
Energy	① ② ③ ④ ⑤
Mental clarity	① ② ③ ④ ⑤

PAIN LEVEL

1	2	3	4	5	6	7	8	9	10

Not too bad. *Well, I'm not enjoying this.* *Make it stop!*

ONSET

☐ Slow ☐ Average
☐ Rapid ☐ Sudden

DETAILED DESCRIPTION

☐ Constant ☐ Squeezing ☐ Throbbing ☐ Pounding ☐ Dull aching ☐ Burning
☐ Sharp ☐ Debilitating ☐ Other: ____________________

WHERE DOES IT HURT, EXACTLY?

OTHER SYMPTOMS

☐ Lightheaded ☐ Dizziness
☐ Light sensitivity ☐ Sound sensitivity
☐ Confusion ☐ Auras
☐ Muscle stiffness ☐ Muscle aches

FEELING SICK?

☐ Nausea ☐ Diarrhea ☐ Vomiting ☐ Sore throat ☐ Congestion ☐ Coughing
☐ Chills ☐ Fever ☐ Other: ____________________

SLEEP

hours ________ *quality* ① ② ③ ④ ⑤

WEATHER

☐ Cold ☐ Mild ☐ Hot Allergen levels: ____________
☐ Dry ☐ Humid ☐ Wet BM Pressure: ____________

STRESS LEVELS

None	Low	Medium	High	Max	@$#%!

item / meal	*time*	*meds / supplements*	*dose*	*time*	*drinks*
					water
					① ② ③ ④ ⑤ ⑥ ⑦ ⑧ ⑨ ⑩
					caffeine
					① ② ③ ④ ⑤ ⑥ ⑦ ⑧ ⑨ ⑩
					alcohol
					① ② ③ ④ ⑤ ⑥ ⑦ ⑧ ⑨ ⑩

HORMONES

☐ Menstruating ☐ Menopause
☐ PMS ☐ N/A | other

COMPUTER / MOBILE DEVICE / TV

☐ None ☐ Some ☐ A lot Total Time: _____
☐ Sitting ☐ Standing ☐ Mixture Breaks every: _____

PHYSICAL ACTIVITY

☐ None ☐ Minimal ☐ Some ☐ Sweatin' ☐ I'm beat DETAILS: ____________

RELIEF MEASURES

☐ Medication ☐ Massage ☐ Sleep ☐ Exercise ☐ Water ☐ Cold/Ice
☐ Heat/Bath ☐ Other: ____________________
Did it work? ☐ Nope ☐ A bit ☐ Mostly ☐ 100%

Notes ☐ *See back notes*

START: | END: | DURATION: | DATE | *Entry #112*

MIGRAINE | CLUSTER | TENSION | SINUS | TMJ

HOW WOULD YOU RATE...?

Mood	① ② ③ ④ ⑤
Energy	① ② ③ ④ ⑤
Mental clarity	① ② ③ ④ ⑤

PAIN LEVEL

1	2	3	4	5	6	7	8	9	10

Not too bad. *Well, I'm not enjoying this.* *Make it stop!*

ONSET

☐ Slow ☐ Average
☐ Rapid ☐ Sudden

DETAILED DESCRIPTION

☐ Constant ☐ Squeezing ☐ Throbbing ☐ Pouncing ☐ Dull aching ☐ Burning
☐ Sharp ☐ Debilitating ☐ Other: ____________________

WHERE DOES IT HURT, EXACTLY?

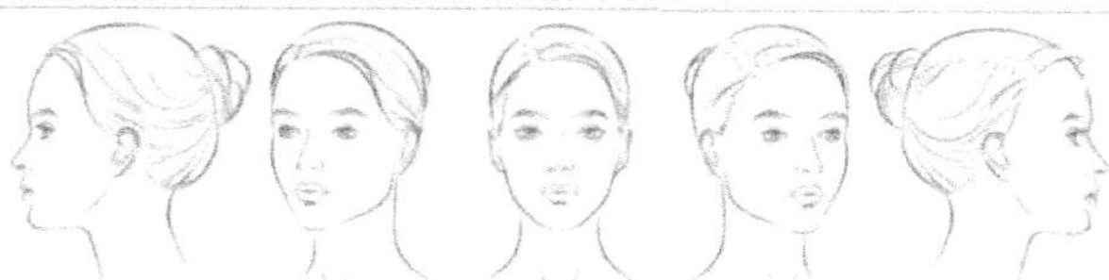

OTHER SYMPTOMS

☐ Lightheaded ☐ Dizziness
☐ Light sensitivity ☐ Sound sensitivity
☐ Confusion ☐ Auras
☐ Muscle stiffness ☐ Muscle aches

FEELING SICK?

☐ Nausea ☐ Diarrhea ☐ Vomiting ☐ Sore throat ☐ Congestion ☐ Coughing
☐ Chills ☐ Fever ☐ Other: ____________________

SLEEP

hours ______ *quality* ① ② ③ ④ ⑤

WEATHER

☐ Cold ☐ Mild ☐ Hot Allergen levels: ______
☐ Dry ☐ Humid ☐ Wet BM Pressure: ______

STRESS LEVELS

None	Low	Medium	High	Max	@$#%!

item / meal	*time*	*meds / supplements*	*dose*	*time*	*drinks*
					water
					① ② ③ ④ ⑤ ⑥ ⑦ ⑧ ⑨ ⑩
					caffeine
					① ② ③ ④ ⑤ ⑥ ⑦ ⑧ ⑨ ⑩
					alcohol
					① ② ③ ④ ⑤ ⑥ ⑦ ⑧ ⑨ ⑩

HORMONES

☐ Menstruating ☐ Menopause
☐ PMS ☐ N/A | other

COMPUTER / MOBILE DEVICE / TV

☐ None ☐ Some ☐ A lot Total Time: ______
☐ Sitting ☐ Standing ☐ Mixture Breaks every: ______

PHYSICAL ACTIVITY

☐ None ☐ Minimal ☐ Some ☐ Sweatin' ☐ I'm beat DETAILS: ____________

RELIEF MEASURES

☐ Medication ☐ Massage ☐ Sleep ☐ Exercise ☐ Water ☐ Cold/Ice
☐ Heat/Bath ☐ Other: ____________________
Did it work? ☐ Nope ☐ A bit ☐ Mostly ☐ 100%

Notes ☐ *See back notes*

START:		END:		DURATION:		DATE		*Entry #113*

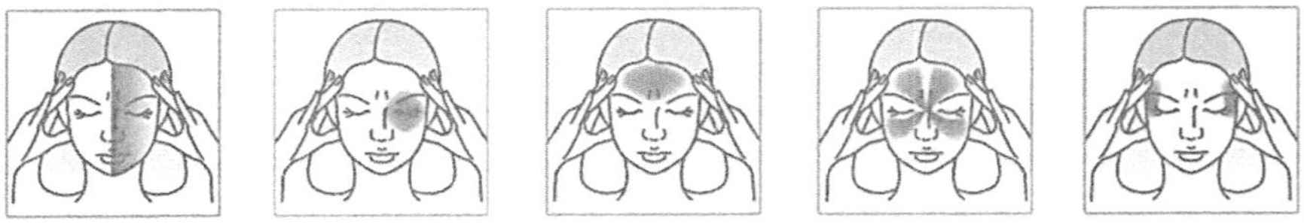

MIGRAINE | CLUSTER | TENSION | SINUS | TMJ

HOW WOULD YOU RATE...?

Mood	① ② ③ ④ ⑤
Energy	① ② ③ ④ ⑤
Mental clarity	① ② ③ ④ ⑤

PAIN LEVEL

1	2	3	4	5	6	7	8	9	10

Not too bad. *Well, I'm not enjoying this.* *Make it stop!*

ONSET

☐ Slow ☐ Average
☐ Rapid ☐ Sudden

DETAILED DESCRIPTION

☐ Constant ☐ Squeezing ☐ Throbbing ☐ Pounding ☐ Dull aching ☐ Burning
☐ Sharp ☐ Debilitating ☐ Other: ________________

WHERE DOES IT HURT, EXACTLY?

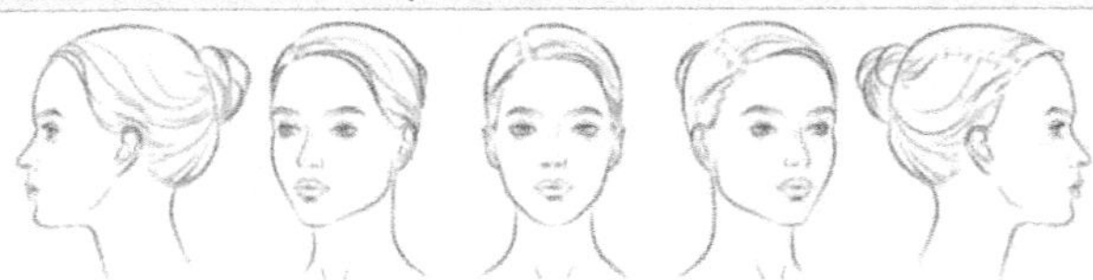

OTHER SYMPTOMS

☐ Lightheaded ☐ Dizziness
☐ Light sensitivity ☐ Sound sensitivity
☐ Confusion ☐ Auras
☐ Muscle stiffness ☐ Muscle aches

FEELING SICK?

☐ Nausea ☐ Diarrhea ☐ Vomiting ☐ Sore throat ☐ Congestion ☐ Coughing
☐ Chills ☐ Fever ☐ Other: ________________

SLEEP

hours ________ *quality* ① ② ③ ④ ⑤

WEATHER

☐ Cold ☐ Mild ☐ Hot Allergen levels: ________
☐ Dry ☐ Humid ☐ Wet BM Pressure: ________

STRESS LEVELS

None	Low	Medium	High	Max	@$#%!

item / meal	*time*	*meds / supplements*	*dose*	*time*	*drinks*
					water: ① ② ③ ④ ⑤ ⑥ ⑦ ⑧ ⑨ ⑩
					caffeine: ① ② ③ ④ ⑤ ⑥ ⑦ ⑧ ⑨ ⑩
					alcohol: ① ② ③ ④ ⑤ ⑥ ⑦ ⑧ ⑨ ⑩

HORMONES

☐ Menstruating ☐ Menopause
☐ PMS ☐ N/A | other

COMPUTER / MOBILE DEVICE / TV

☐ None ☐ Some ☐ A lot Total Time: ______
☐ Sitting ☐ Standing ☐ Mixture Breaks every: ______

PHYSICAL ACTIVITY

☐ None ☐ Minimal ☐ Some ☐ Sweatin' ☐ I'm beat DETAILS: ________________

RELIEF MEASURES

☐ Medication ☐ Massage ☐ Sleep ☐ Exercise ☐ Water ☐ Cold/Ice
☐ Heat/Bath ☐ Other: ________________
Did it work? ☐ Nope ☐ A bit ☐ Mostly ☐ 100%

Notes ☐ *See back notes*

START: ______ END: ______ DURATION: ______ DATE ______ *Entry #114*

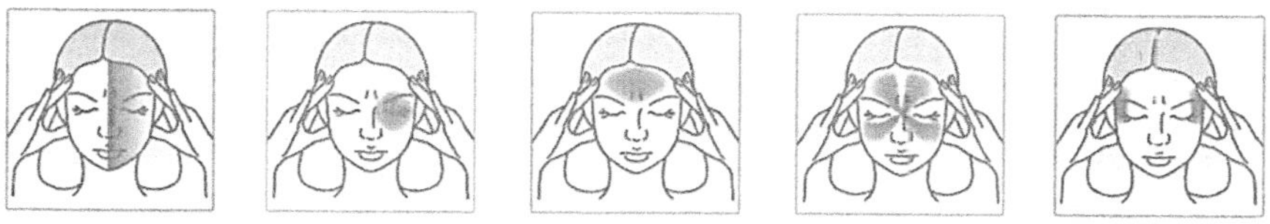

MIGRAINE CLUSTER TENSION SINUS TMJ

HOW WOULD YOU RATE...?

Mood	① ② ③ ④ ⑤
Energy	① ② ③ ④ ⑤
Mental clarity	① ② ③ ④ ⑤

PAIN LEVEL

1	2	3	4	5	6	7	8	9	10

Not too bad. *Well, I'm not enjoying this.* *Make it stop!*

ONSET

☐ Slow ☐ Average
☐ Rapid ☐ Sudden

DETAILED DESCRIPTION

☐ Constant ☐ Squeezing ☐ Throbbing ☐ Pounding ☐ Dull aching ☐ Burning
☐ Sharp ☐ Debilitating ☐ Other: ______________________

WHERE DOES IT HURT, EXACTLY?

OTHER SYMPTOMS

☐ Lightheaded ☐ Dizziness
☐ Light sensitivity ☐ Sound sensitivity
☐ Confusion ☐ Auras
☐ Muscle stiffness ☐ Muscle aches

FEELING SICK?

☐ Nausea ☐ Diarrhea ☐ Vomiting ☐ Sore throat ☐ Congestion ☐ Coughing
☐ Chills ☐ Fever ☐ Other: ______________________

SLEEP

hours ______ *quality* ① ② ③ ④ ⑤

WEATHER

☐ Cold ☐ Mild ☐ Hot Allergen levels: ______
☐ Dry ☐ Humid ☐ Wet BM Pressure: ______

STRESS LEVELS

None	Low	Medium	High	Max	@$#%!

item / meal	*time*	*meds / supplements*	*dose*	*time*	*drinks*
					water
					① ② ③ ④ ⑤ ⑥ ⑦ ⑧ ⑨ ⑩
					caffeine
					① ② ③ ④ ⑤ ⑥ ⑦ ⑧ ⑨ ⑩
					alcohol
					① ② ③ ④ ⑤ ⑥ ⑦ ⑧ ⑨ ⑩

HORMONES

☐ Menstruating ☐ Menopause
☐ PMS ☐ N/A | other

COMPUTER / MOBILE DEVICE / TV

☐ None ☐ Some ☐ A lot Total Time: ______
☐ Sitting ☐ Standing ☐ Mixture Breaks every: ______

PHYSICAL ACTIVITY

☐ None ☐ Minimal ☐ Some ☐ Sweatin' ☐ I'm beat DETAILS: ______

RELIEF MEASURES

☐ Medication ☐ Massage ☐ Sleep ☐ Exercise ☐ Water ☐ Cold/Ice
☐ Heat/Bath ☐ Other ______________________
Did it work? ☐ Nope ☐ A bit ☐ Mostly ☐ 100%

Notes ☐ *See back notes*

START:		END:		DURATION:		DATE		*Entry #115*

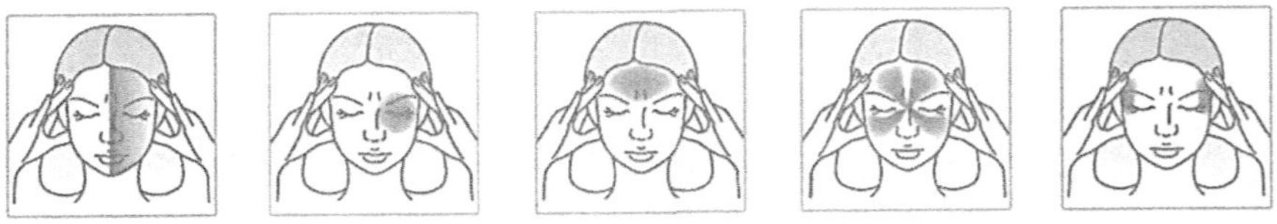

MIGRAINE | CLUSTER | TENSION | SINUS | TMJ

HOW WOULD YOU RATE...?

Mood	1	2	3	4	5
Energy	1	2	3	4	5
Mental clarity	1	2	3	4	5

PAIN LEVEL

1	2	3	4	5	6	7	8	9	10

Not too bad. *Well, I'm not enjoying this.* *Make it stop!*

ONSET

☐ Slow ☐ Average
☐ Rapid ☐ Sudden

DETAILED DESCRIPTION

☐ Constant ☐ Squeezing ☐ Throbbing ☐ Pounding ☐ Dull aching ☐ Burning
☐ Sharp ☐ Debilitating ☐ Other: ____________________

WHERE DOES IT HURT, EXACTLY?

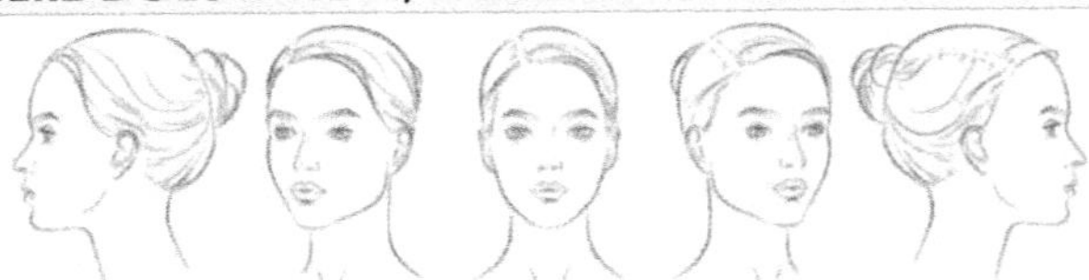

OTHER SYMPTOMS

☐ Lightheaded ☐ Dizziness
☐ Light sensitivity ☐ Sound sensitivity
☐ Confusion ☐ Auras
☐ Muscle stiffness ☐ Muscle aches

FEELING SICK?

☐ Nausea ☐ Diarrhea ☐ Vomiting ☐ Sore throat ☐ Congestion ☐ Coughing
☐ Chills ☐ Fever ☐ Other: ____________________

SLEEP

hours ______ *quality* 1 2 3 4 5

WEATHER

☐ Cold ☐ Mild ☐ Hot Allergen levels: __________
☐ Dry ☐ Humid ☐ Wet BM Pressure: __________

STRESS LEVELS

None	Low	Medium	High	Max	@$#%!

item / meal	*time*	*meds / supplements*	*dose*	*time*	*drinks*
					water 1 2 3 4 5 6 7 8 9 10
					caffeine 1 2 3 4 5 6 7 8 9 10
					alcohol 1 2 3 4 5 6 7 8 9 10

HORMONES

☐ Menstruating ☐ Menopause
☐ PMS ☐ N/A | other

COMPUTER / MOBILE DEVICE / TV

☐ None ☐ Some ☐ A lot Total Time: ______
☐ Sitting ☐ Standing ☐ Mixture Breaks every: ______

PHYSICAL ACTIVITY

☐ None ☐ Minimal ☐ Some ☐ Sweatin' ☐ I'm beat DETAILS: ____________________

RELIEF MEASURES

☐ Medication ☐ Massage ☐ Sleep ☐ Exercise ☐ Water ☐ Cold/Ice
☐ Heat/Bath ☐ Other: ____________________
Did it work? ☐ Nope ☐ A bit ☐ Mostly ☐ 100%

Notes ☐ *See back notes*

START: ______ END: ______ DURATION: ______ DATE ______ *Entry #116*

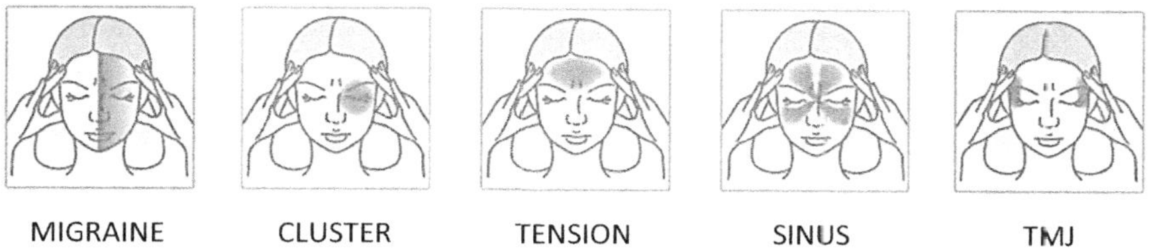

HOW WOULD YOU RATE...?

Mood	1	2	3	4	5
Energy	1	2	3	4	5
Mental clarity	1	2	3	4	5

PAIN LEVEL

1	2	3	4	5	6	7	8	9	10

Not too bad. *Well. I'm not enjoying this.* *Make it stop!*

ONSET

☐ Slow ☐ Average
☐ Rapid ☐ Sudden

DETAILED DESCRIPTION

☐ Constant ☐ Squeezing ☐ Throbbing ☐ Pounding ☐ Dull aching ☐ Burning
☐ Sharp ☐ Debilitating ☐ Other: ______

WHERE DOES IT HURT, EXACTLY?

OTHER SYMPTOMS

☐ Lightheaded ☐ Dizziness
☐ Light sensitivity ☐ Sound sensitivity
☐ Confusion ☐ Auras
☐ Muscle stiffness ☐ Muscle aches

FEELING SICK?

☐ Nausea ☐ Diarrhea ☐ Vomiting ☐ Sore throat ☐ Congestion ☐ Coughing
☐ Chills ☐ Fever ☐ Other: ______

SLEEP

hours ______ *quality* 1 2 3 4 5

WEATHER

☐ Cold ☐ Mild ☐ Hot Allergen levels: ______
☐ Dry ☐ Humid ☐ Wet BM Pressure: ______

STRESS LEVELS

None	Low	Medium	High	Max	@$#%!

item / meal	*time*	*meds / supplements*	*dose*	*time*	*drinks*
					water: 1 2 3 4 5 6 7 8 9 10
					caffeine: 1 2 3 4 5 6 7 8 9 10
					alcohol: 1 2 3 4 5 6 7 8 9 10

HORMONES

☐ Menstruating ☐ Menopause
☐ PMS ☐ N/A | other

COMPUTER / MOBILE DEVICE / TV

☐ None ☐ Some ☐ A lot Total Time: ______
☐ Sitting ☐ Standing ☐ Mixture Breaks every: ______

PHYSICAL ACTIVITY

☐ None ☐ Minimal ☐ Some ☐ Sweatin' ☐ I'm bea DETAILS: ______

RELIEF MEASURES

☐ Medication ☐ Massage ☐ Sleep ☐ Exercise ☐ Water ☐ Cold/Ice
☐ Heat/Bath ☐ Other: ______
Did it work? ☐ Nope ☐ A bit ☐ Mostly ☐ 100%

Notes ☐ *See back notes*

START:		END:		DURATION:		DATE		*Entry #117*

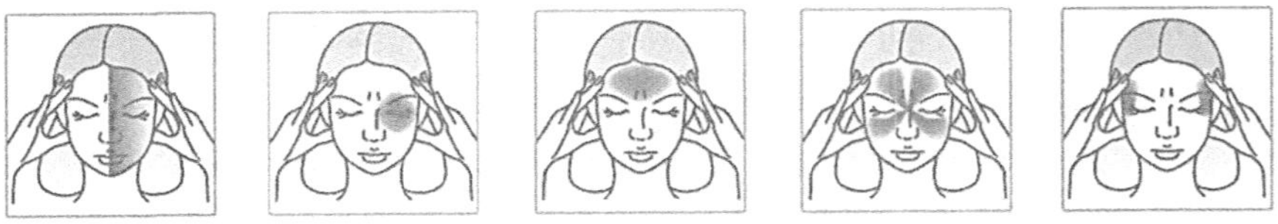

MIGRAINE | CLUSTER | TENSION | SINUS | TMJ

HOW WOULD YOU RATE...?

Mood	1	2	3	4	5
Energy	1	2	3	4	5
Mental clarity	1	2	3	4	5

PAIN LEVEL

1	2	3	4	5	6	7	8	9	10

Not too bad. *Well, I'm not enjoying this.* *Make it stop!*

ONSET

☐ Slow ☐ Average
☐ Rapid ☐ Sudden

DETAILED DESCRIPTION

☐ Constant ☐ Squeezing ☐ Throbbing ☐ Pounding ☐ Dull aching ☐ Burning
☐ Sharp ☐ Debilitating ☐ Other: ____________________

WHERE DOES IT HURT, EXACTLY?

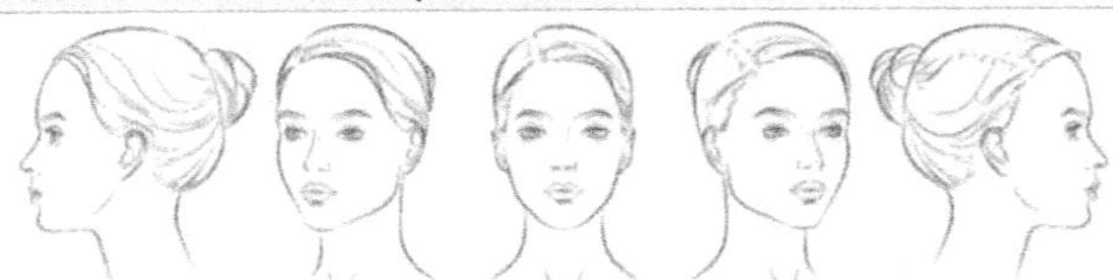

OTHER SYMPTOMS

☐ Lightheaded ☐ Dizziness
☐ Light sensitivity ☐ Sound sensitivity
☐ Confusion ☐ Auras
☐ Muscle stiffness ☐ Muscle aches

FEELING SICK?

☐ Nausea ☐ Diarrhea ☐ Vomiting ☐ Sore throat ☐ Congestion ☐ Coughing
☐ Chills ☐ Fever ☐ Other: ____________________

SLEEP

hours ________ *quality* 1 2 3 4 5

WEATHER

☐ Cold ☐ Mild ☐ Hot Allergen levels: ____________
☐ Dry ☐ Humid ☐ Wet BM Pressure: ____________

STRESS LEVELS

None	Low	Medium	High	Max	@$#%!

item / meal	*time*	*meds / supplements*	*dose*	*time*	*drinks*
					water: 1 2 3 4 5 6 7 8 9 10
					caffeine: 1 2 3 4 5 6 7 8 9 10
					alcohol: 1 2 3 4 5 6 7 8 9 10

HORMONES

☐ Menstruating ☐ Menopause
☐ PMS ☐ N/A | other

COMPUTER / MOBILE DEVICE / TV

☐ None ☐ Some ☐ A lot Total Time: ______
☐ Sitting ☐ Standing ☐ Mixture Breaks every: ______

PHYSICAL ACTIVITY

☐ None ☐ Minimal ☐ Some ☐ Sweatin' ☐ I'm beat DETAILS: ____________

RELIEF MEASURES

☐ Medication ☐ Massage ☐ Sleep ☐ Exercise ☐ Water ☐ Cold/Ice
☐ Heat/Bath ☐ Other: ____________________
Did it work? ☐ Nope ☐ A bit ☐ Mostly ☐ 100%

Notes ☐ *See back notes*

START:		END:		DURATION:		DATE		*Entry #118*

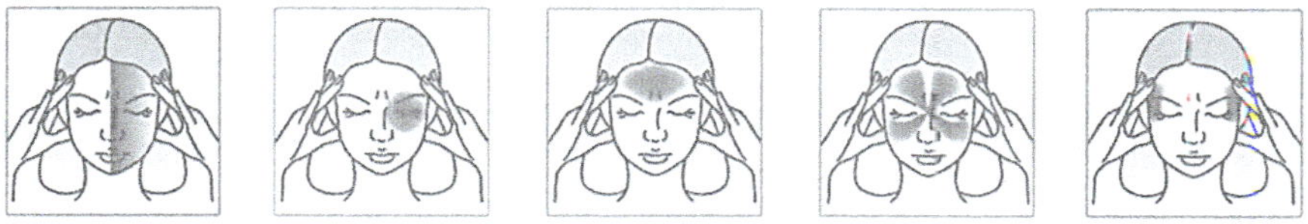

MIGRAINE | CLUSTER | TENSION | SINUS | TMJ

HOW WOULD YOU RATE...?

Mood	1	2	3	4	5
Energy	1	2	3	4	5
Mental clarity	1	2	3	4	5

PAIN LEVEL

1	2	3	4	5	6	7	8	9	10

Not too bad. *Well, I'm not enjoying this.* *Make it stop!*

ONSET

☐ Slow ☐ Average
☐ Rapid ☐ Sudden

DETAILED DESCRIPTION

☐ Constant ☐ Squeezing ☐ Throbbing ☐ Pounding ☐ Dull aching ☐ Burning
☐ Sharp ☐ Debilitating ☐ Other: ____________________

WHERE DOES IT HURT, EXACTLY?

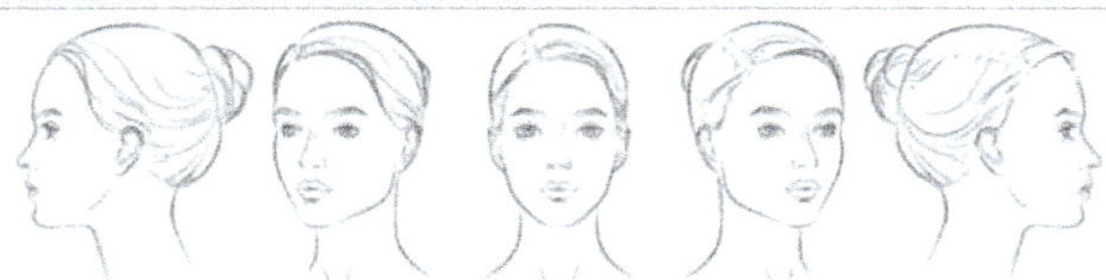

OTHER SYMPTOMS

☐ Lightheaded ☐ Dizziness
☐ Light sensitivity ☐ Sound sensitivity
☐ Confusion ☐ Auras
☐ Muscle stiffness ☐ Muscle aches

FEELING SICK?

☐ Nausea ☐ Diarrhea ☐ Vomiting ☐ Sore throat ☐ Congestion ☐ Coughing
☐ Chills ☐ Fever ☐ Other: ____________________

SLEEP

hours ________ *quality* 1 2 3 4 5

WEATHER

☐ Cold ☐ Mild ☐ Hot Allergen levels: __________
☐ Dry ☐ Humid ☐ Wet BM Pressure: __________

STRESS LEVELS

None	Low	Medium	High	Max	@$#%!

item / meal	*time*	*meds / supplements*	*dose*	*time*	*drinks*
					water
					1 2 3 4 5 6 7 8 9 10
					caffeine
					1 2 3 4 5 6 7 8 9 10
					alcohol
					1 2 3 4 5 6 7 8 9 10

HORMONES

☐ Menstruating ☐ Menopause
☐ PMS ☐ N/A | other

COMPUTER / MOBILE DEVICE / TV

☐ None ☐ Some ☐ A lot Total Time: ______
☐ Sitting ☐ Standing ☐ Mixture Breaks every: ______

PHYSICAL ACTIVITY

☐ None ☐ Minimal ☐ Some ☐ Sweatin' ☐ I'm beat DETAILS: ____________________

RELIEF MEASURES

☐ Medication ☐ Massage ☐ Sleep ☐ Exercise ☐ Water ☐ Cold/Ice
☐ Heat/Bath ☐ Other: ____________________

Did it work? ☐ Nope ☐ A bit ☐ Mostly ☐ 100%

Notes ☐ *See back notes*

START:		END:		DURATION:		DATE		*Entry #119*

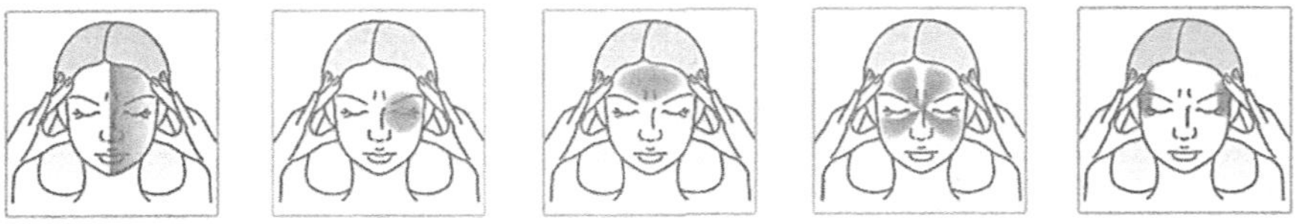

MIGRAINE | CLUSTER | TENSION | SINUS | TMJ

HOW WOULD YOU RATE...?

Mood	1	2	3	4	5
Energy	1	2	3	4	5
Mental clarity	1	2	3	4	5

PAIN LEVEL

1	2	3	4	5	6	7	8	9	10

Not too bad. *Well, I'm not enjoying this.* *Make it stop!*

ONSET

☐ Slow ☐ Average
☐ Rapid ☐ Sudden

DETAILED DESCRIPTION

☐ Constant ☐ Squeezing ☐ Throbbing ☐ Pounding ☐ Dull aching ☐ Burning
☐ Sharp ☐ Debilitating ☐ Other: ____________

WHERE DOES IT HURT, EXACTLY?

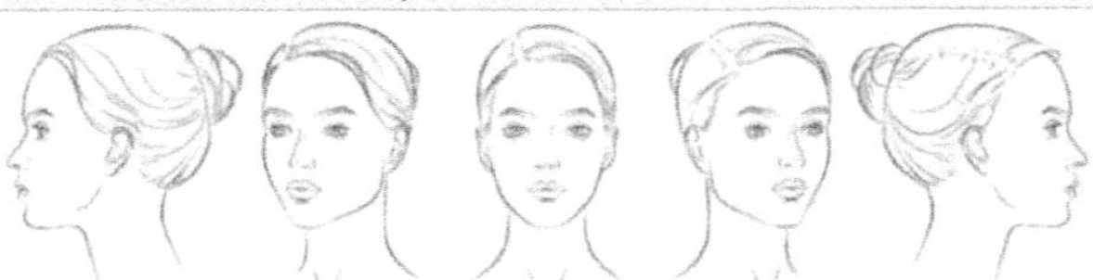

OTHER SYMPTOMS

☐ Lightheaded ☐ Dizziness
☐ Light sensitivity ☐ Sound sensitivity
☐ Confusion ☐ Auras
☐ Muscle stiffness ☐ Muscle aches

FEELING SICK?

☐ Nausea ☐ Diarrhea ☐ Vomiting ☐ Sore throat ☐ Congestion ☐ Coughing
☐ Chills ☐ Fever ☐ Other: ____________

SLEEP

hours ________ *quality* 1 2 3 4 5

WEATHER

☐ Cold ☐ Mild ☐ Hot Allergen levels: ________
☐ Dry ☐ Humid ☐ Wet BM Pressure: ________

STRESS LEVELS

None	Low	Medium	High	Max	@$#%!

item / meal	*time*	*meds / supplements*	*dose*	*time*	*drinks*
					water: 1 2 3 4 5 6 7 8 9 10
					caffeine: 1 2 3 4 5 6 7 8 9 10
					alcohol: 1 2 3 4 5 6 7 8 9 10

HORMONES

☐ Menstruating ☐ Menopause
☐ PMS ☐ N/A | other

COMPUTER / MOBILE DEVICE / TV

☐ None ☐ Some ☐ A lot Total Time: ______
☐ Sitting ☐ Standing ☐ Mixture Breaks every: ______

PHYSICAL ACTIVITY

☐ None ☐ Minimal ☐ Some ☐ Sweatin' ☐ I'm beat DETAILS: ____________

RELIEF MEASURES

☐ Medication ☐ Massage ☐ Sleep ☐ Exercise ☐ Water ☐ Cold/Ice
☐ Heat/Bath ☐ Other: ____________
Did it work? ☐ Nope ☐ A bit ☐ Mostly ☐ 100%

Notes ☐ *See back notes*

START:		END:		DURATION:		DATE		*Entry #120*

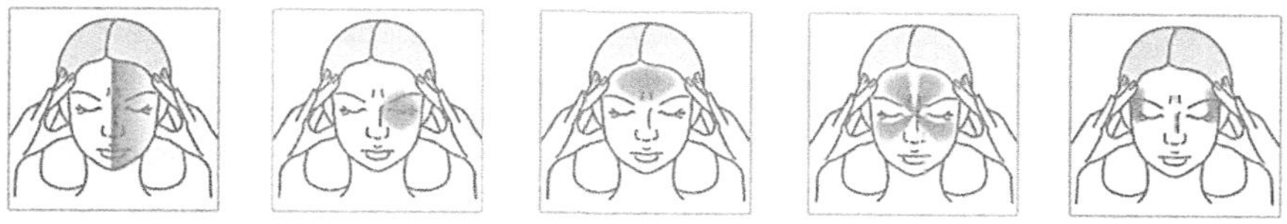

MIGRAINE | CLUSTER | TENSION | SINUS | TMJ

HOW WOULD YOU RATE...?					
Mood	①	②	③	④	⑤
Energy	①	②	③	④	⑤
Mental clarity	①	②	③	④	⑤

PAIN LEVEL

1	2	3	4	5	6	7	8	9	10

Not too bad. *Well. I'm not enjoying this.* *Make it stop!*

ONSET

☐ Slow ☐ Average
☐ Rapid ☐ Sudden

DETAILED DESCRIPTION

☐ Constant ☐ Squeezing ☐ Throbbing ☐ Pouncing ☐ Dull aching ☐ Burning
☐ Sharp ☐ Debilitating ☐ Other: ______________________________

WHERE DOES IT HURT, EXACTLY?

OTHER SYMPTOMS

☐ Lightheaded ☐ Dizziness
☐ Light sensitivity ☐ Sound sensitivity
☐ Confusion ☐ Auras
☐ Muscle stiffness ☐ Muscle aches

FEELING SICK?

☐ Nausea ☐ Diarrhea ☐ Vomiting ☐ Sore throat ☐ Congestion ☐ Coughing
☐ Chills ☐ Fever ☐ Other: ______________________________

SLEEP

hours ________ *quality* ① ② ③ ④ ⑤

WEATHER

☐ Cold ☐ Mild ☐ Hot Allergen levels: ____________
☐ Dry ☐ Humid ☐ Wet BM Pressure: ____________

STRESS LEVELS

None	Low	Medium	High	Max	@$#%!

item / meal	*time*	*meds / supplements*	*dose*	*time*	*drinks*
					water
					① ② ③ ④ ⑤ ⑥ ⑦ ⑧ ⑨ ⑩
					caffeine
					① ② ③ ④ ⑤ ⑥ ⑦ ⑧ ⑨ ⑩
					alcohol
					① ② ③ ④ ⑤ ⑥ ⑦ ⑧ ⑨ ⑩

HORMONES

☐ Menstruating ☐ Menopause
☐ PMS ☐ N/A | other

COMPUTER / MOBILE DEVICE / TV

☐ None ☐ Some ☐ A lot Total Time: ______
☐ Sitting ☐ Standing ☐ Mixture Breaks every: ______

PHYSICAL ACTIVITY

☐ None ☐ Minimal ☐ Some ☐ Sweatin' ☐ I'm beat DETAILS: ______________________

RELIEF MEASURES

☐ Medication ☐ Massage ☐ Sleep ☐ Exercise ☐ Water ☐ Cold/Ice
☐ Heat/Bath ☐ Other: ______________________________
Did it work? ☐ Nope ☐ A bit ☐ Mostly ☐ 100%

Notes ☐ *See back notes*

START:		END:		DURATION:		DATE		*Entry #121*

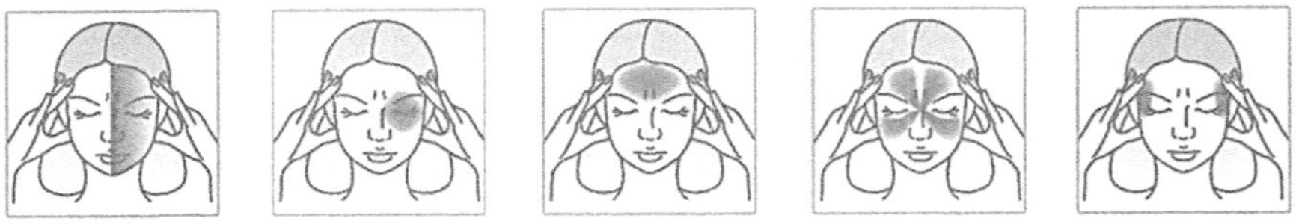

MIGRAINE CLUSTER TENSION SINUS TMJ

HOW WOULD YOU RATE...?

Mood	① ② ③ ④ ⑤
Energy	① ② ③ ④ ⑤
Mental clarity	① ② ③ ④ ⑤

PAIN LEVEL

1	2	3	4	5	6	7	8	9	10

Not too bad. *Well, I'm not enjoying this.* *Make it stop!*

ONSET

☐ Slow ☐ Average
☐ Rapid ☐ Sudden

DETAILED DESCRIPTION

☐ Constant ☐ Squeezing ☐ Throbbing ☐ Pounding ☐ Dull aching ☐ Burning
☐ Sharp ☐ Debilitating ☐ Other: ____________________

WHERE DOES IT HURT, EXACTLY?

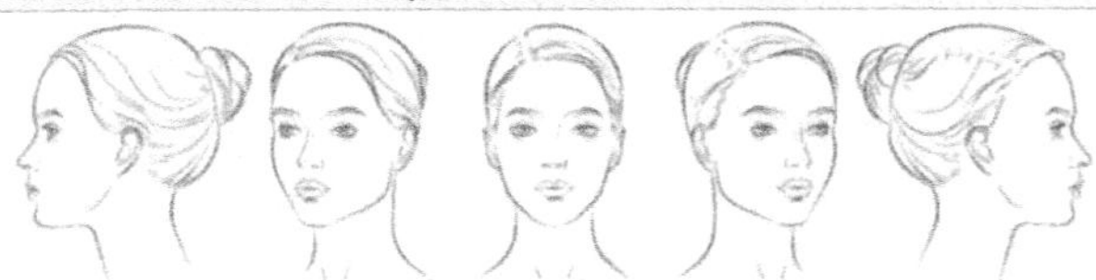

OTHER SYMPTOMS

☐ Lightheaded ☐ Dizziness
☐ Light sensitivity ☐ Sound sensitivity
☐ Confusion ☐ Auras
☐ Muscle stiffness ☐ Muscle aches

FEELING SICK?

☐ Nausea ☐ Diarrhea ☐ Vomiting ☐ Sore throat ☐ Congestion ☐ Coughing
☐ Chills ☐ Fever ☐ Other: ____________________

SLEEP

hours ________ *quality* ① ② ③ ④ ⑤

WEATHER

☐ Cold ☐ Mild ☐ Hot Allergen levels: __________
☐ Dry ☐ Humid ☐ Wet BM Pressure: __________

STRESS LEVELS

None	Low	Medium	High	Max	@$#%!

item / meal	*time*	*meds / supplements*	*dose*	*time*	*drinks*
					water: ① ② ③ ④ ⑤ ⑥ ⑦ ⑧ ⑨ ⑩
					caffeine: ① ② ③ ④ ⑤ ⑥ ⑦ ⑧ ⑨ ⑩
					alcohol: ① ② ③ ④ ⑤ ⑥ ⑦ ⑧ ⑨ ⑩

HORMONES

☐ Menstruating ☐ Menopause
☐ PMS ☐ N/A | other

COMPUTER / MOBILE DEVICE / TV

☐ None ☐ Some ☐ A lot Total Time: ______
☐ Sitting ☐ Standing ☐ Mixture Breaks every: ______

PHYSICAL ACTIVITY

☐ None ☐ Minimal ☐ Some ☐ Sweatin' ☐ I'm beat DETAILS: __________

RELIEF MEASURES

☐ Medication ☐ Massage ☐ Sleep ☐ Exercise ☐ Water ☐ Cold/Ice
☐ Heat/Bath ☐ Other: ____________________
Did it work? ☐ Nope ☐ A bit ☐ Mostly ☐ 100%

Notes ☐ *See back notes*

START: ______ END: ______ DURATION: ______ DATE ______ *Entry #122*

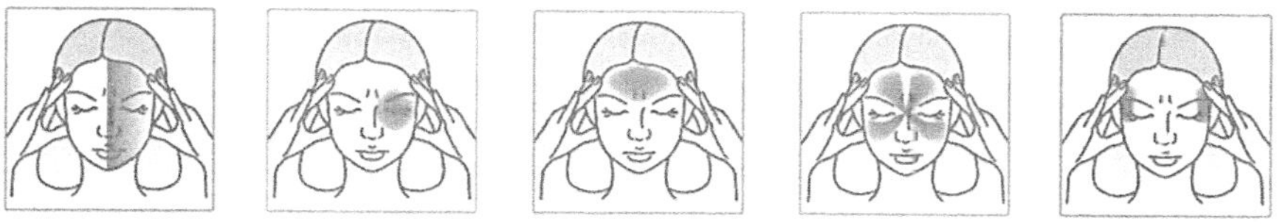

MIGRAINE CLUSTER TENSION SINUS TMJ

HOW WOULD YOU RATE...?

Mood	① ② ③ ④ ⑤
Energy	① ② ③ ④ ⑤
Mental clarity	① ② ③ ④ ⑤

PAIN LEVEL

1	2	3	4	5	6	7	8	9	10

Not too bad. *Well, I'm not enjoying this.* *Make it stop!*

ONSET

☐ Slow ☐ Average
☐ Rapid ☐ Sudden

DETAILED DESCRIPTION

☐ Constant ☐ Squeezing ☐ Throbbing ☐ Pounding ☐ Dull aching ☐ Burning
☐ Sharp ☐ Debilitating ☐ Other: ______________________

WHERE DOES IT HURT, EXACTLY?

OTHER SYMPTOMS

☐ Lightheaded ☐ Dizziness
☐ Light sensitivity ☐ Sound sensitivity
☐ Confusion ☐ Auras
☐ Muscle stiffness ☐ Muscle aches

FEELING SICK?

☐ Nausea ☐ Diarrhea ☐ Vomiting ☐ Sore throat ☐ Congestion ☐ Coughing
☐ Chills ☐ Fever ☐ Other: ______________________

SLEEP

hours ______ *quality* ① ② ③ ④ ⑤

WEATHER

☐ Cold ☐ Mild ☐ Hot Allergen levels: ______
☐ Dry ☐ Humid ☐ Wet BM Pressure: ______

STRESS LEVELS

None	Low	Medium	High	Max	@$#%!

item / meal	*time*	*meds / supplements*	*dose*	*time*	*drinks*
					water ① ② ③ ④ ⑤ ⑥ ⑦ ⑧ ⑨ ⑩
					caffeine ① ② ③ ④ ⑤ ⑥ ⑦ ⑧ ⑨ ⑩
					alcohol ① ② ③ ④ ⑤ ⑥ ⑦ ⑧ ⑨ ⑩

HORMONES

☐ Menstruating ☐ Menopause
☐ PMS ☐ N/A | other

COMPUTER / MOBILE DEVICE / TV

☐ None ☐ Some ☐ A lot Total Time: ______
☐ Sitting ☐ Standing ☐ Mixture Breaks every: ______

PHYSICAL ACTIVITY

☐ None ☐ Minimal ☐ Some ☐ Sweatin' ☐ I'm beat DETAILS: ______

RELIEF MEASURES

☐ Medication ☐ Massage ☐ Sleep ☐ Exercise ☐ Water ☐ Cold/Ice
☐ Heat/Bath ☐ Other: ______________________
Did it work? ☐ Nope ☐ A bit ☐ Mostly ☐ 100%

Notes ☐ *See back notes*

START:		END:		DURATION:		DATE		*Entry #123*

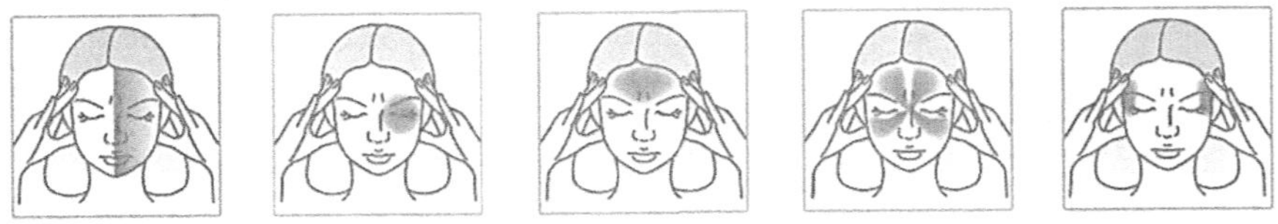

MIGRAINE CLUSTER TENSION SINUS TMJ

HOW WOULD YOU RATE...?	
Mood	① ② ③ ④ ⑤
Energy	① ② ③ ④ ⑤
Mental clarity	① ② ③ ④ ⑤

PAIN LEVEL

1	2	3	4	5	6	7	8	9	10

Not too bad. *Well, I'm not enjoying this.* *Make it stop!*

ONSET

☐ Slow ☐ Average
☐ Rapid ☐ Sudden

DETAILED DESCRIPTION

☐ Constant ☐ Squeezing ☐ Throbbing ☐ Pounding ☐ Dull aching ☐ Burning
☐ Sharp ☐ Debilitating ☐ Other: ______________________________

WHERE DOES IT HURT, EXACTLY?

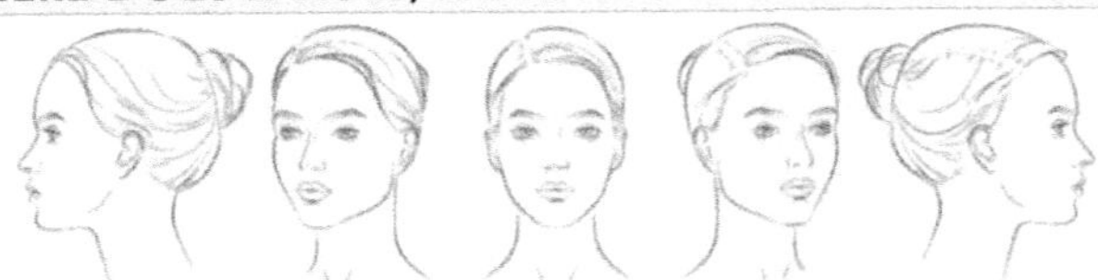

OTHER SYMPTOMS

☐ Lightheaded ☐ Dizziness
☐ Light sensitivity ☐ Sound sensitivity
☐ Confusion ☐ Auras
☐ Muscle stiffness ☐ Muscle aches

FEELING SICK?

☐ Nausea ☐ Diarrhea ☐ Vomiting ☐ Sore throat ☐ Congestion ☐ Coughing
☐ Chills ☐ Fever ☐ Other: ______________________________

SLEEP

hours ________ *quality* ① ② ③ ④ ⑤

WEATHER

☐ Cold ☐ Mild ☐ Hot Allergen levels: __________
☐ Dry ☐ Humid ☐ Wet BM Pressure: __________

STRESS LEVELS

None	Low	Medium	High	Max	@$#%!

item / meal	*time*	*meds / supplements*	*dose*	*time*	*drinks*
					water
					① ② ③ ④ ⑤ ⑥ ⑦ ⑧ ⑨ ⑩
					caffeine
					① ② ③ ④ ⑤ ⑥ ⑦ ⑧ ⑨ ⑩
					alcohol
					① ② ③ ④ ⑤ ⑥ ⑦ ⑧ ⑨ ⑩

HORMONES

☐ Menstruating ☐ Menopause
☐ PMS ☐ N/A | other

COMPUTER / MOBILE DEVICE / TV

☐ None ☐ Some ☐ A lot Total Time: _____
☐ Sitting ☐ Standing ☐ Mixture Breaks every: _____

PHYSICAL ACTIVITY

☐ None ☐ Minimal ☐ Some ☐ Sweatin' ☐ I'm beat DETAILS: ______________

RELIEF MEASURES

☐ Medication ☐ Massage ☐ Sleep ☐ Exercise ☐ Water ☐ Cold/Ice
☐ Heat/Bath ☐ Other: ______________________________
Did it work? ☐ Nope ☐ A bit ☐ Mostly ☐ 100%

Notes ☐ *See back notes*

START:		END:		DURATION:		DATE		*Entry #124*

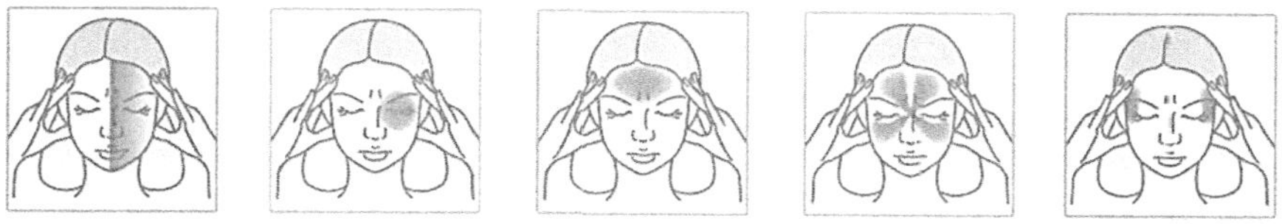

MIGRAINE | CLUSTER | TENSION | SINUS | TMJ

HOW WOULD YOU RATE...?

Mood	1	2	3	4	5
Energy	1	2	3	4	5
Mental clarity	1	2	3	4	5

PAIN LEVEL

1	2	3	4	5	6	7	8	9	10

Not too bad. *Well, I'm not enjoying this.* *Make it stop!*

ONSET

☐ Slow ☐ Average
☐ Rapid ☐ Sudden

DETAILED DESCRIPTION

☐ Constant ☐ Squeezing ☐ Throbbing ☐ Pouncing ☐ Dull aching ☐ Burning
☐ Sharp ☐ Debilitating ☐ Other: ____________________

WHERE DOES IT HURT, EXACTLY?

OTHER SYMPTOMS

☐ Lightheaded ☐ Dizziness
☐ Light sensitivity ☐ Sound sensitivity
☐ Confusion ☐ Auras
☐ Muscle stiffness ☐ Muscle aches

FEELING SICK?

☐ Nausea ☐ Diarrhea ☐ Vomiting ☐ Sore throat ☐ Congestion ☐ Coughing
☐ Chills ☐ Fever ☐ Other: ____________________

SLEEP

hours ________ *quality* 1 2 3 4 5

WEATHER

☐ Cold ☐ Mild ☐ Hot Allergen levels: __________
☐ Dry ☐ Humid ☐ Wet BM Pressure: __________

STRESS LEVELS

None	Low	Medium	High	Max	@$#%!

item / meal	*time*	*meds / supplements*	*dose*	*time*	*drinks*
					water 1 2 3 4 5 6 7 8 9 10
					caffeine 1 2 3 4 5 6 7 8 9 10
					alcohol 1 2 3 4 5 6 7 8 9 10

HORMONES

☐ Menstruating ☐ Menopause
☐ PMS ☐ N/A | other

COMPUTER / MOBILE DEVICE / TV

☐ None ☐ Some ☐ A lot Total Time: ______
☐ Sitting ☐ Standing ☐ Mixture Breaks every: ______

PHYSICAL ACTIVITY

☐ None ☐ Minimal ☐ Some ☐ Sweatin' ☐ I'm beat DETAILS: ____________________

RELIEF MEASURES

☐ Medication ☐ Massage ☐ Sleep ☐ Exercise ☐ Water ☐ Cold/Ice
☐ Heat/Bath ☐ Other: ____________________
Did it work? ☐ Nope ☐ A bit ☐ Mostly ☐ 100%

Notes ☐ *See back notes*

START: ______ END: ______ DURATION: ______ DATE ______ *Entry #125*

MIGRAINE

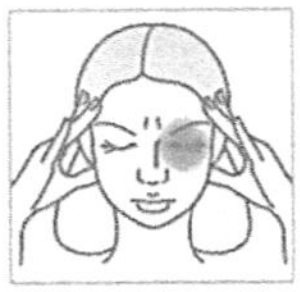
CLUSTER

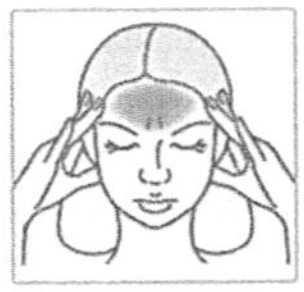
TENSION

SINUS

TMJ

HOW WOULD YOU RATE...?

Mood	① ② ③ ④ ⑤
Energy	① ② ③ ④ ⑤
Mental clarity	① ② ③ ④ ⑤

PAIN LEVEL

1	2	3	4	5	6	7	8	9	10

Not too bad. *Well, I'm not enjoying this.* *Make it stop!*

ONSET

☐ Slow ☐ Average
☐ Rapid ☐ Sudden

DETAILED DESCRIPTION

☐ Constant ☐ Squeezing ☐ Throbbing ☐ Pounding ☐ Dull aching ☐ Burning
☐ Sharp ☐ Debilitating ☐ Other: ____________________

WHERE DOES IT HURT, EXACTLY?

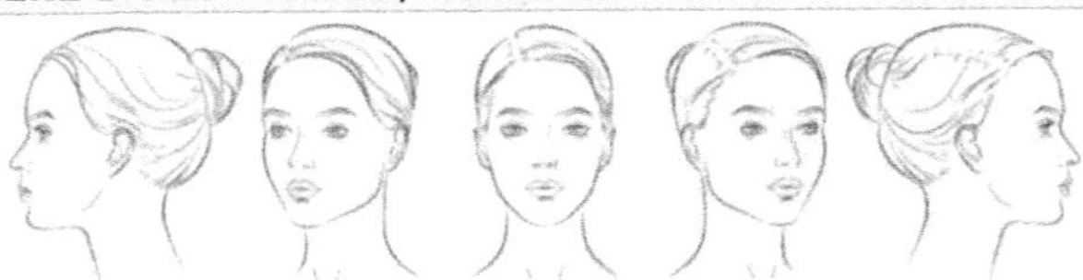

OTHER SYMPTOMS

☐ Lightheaded ☐ Dizziness
☐ Light sensitivity ☐ Sound sensitivity
☐ Confusion ☐ Auras
☐ Muscle stiffness ☐ Muscle aches

FEELING SICK?

☐ Nausea ☐ Diarrhea ☐ Vomiting ☐ Sore throat ☐ Congestion ☐ Coughing
☐ Chills ☐ Fever ☐ Other: ____________________

SLEEP

hours ______ *quality* ① ② ③ ④ ⑤

WEATHER

☐ Cold ☐ Mild ☐ Hot Allergen levels: ______
☐ Dry ☐ Humid ☐ Wet BM Pressure: ______

STRESS LEVELS

None	Low	Medium	High	Max	@$#%!

item / meal	*time*	*meds / supplements*	*dose*	*time*	*drinks*
					water
					① ② ③ ④ ⑤ ⑥ ⑦ ⑧ ⑨ ⑩
					caffeine
					① ② ③ ④ ⑤ ⑥ ⑦ ⑧ ⑨ ⑩
					alcohol
					① ② ③ ④ ⑤ ⑥ ⑦ ⑧ ⑨ ⑩

HORMONES

☐ Menstruating ☐ Menopause
☐ PMS ☐ N/A | other

COMPUTER / MOBILE DEVICE / TV

☐ None ☐ Some ☐ A lot Total Time: ______
☐ Sitting ☐ Standing ☐ Mixture Breaks every: ______

PHYSICAL ACTIVITY

☐ None ☐ Minimal ☐ Some ☐ Sweatin' ☐ I'm beat DETAILS: ______

RELIEF MEASURES

☐ Medication ☐ Massage ☐ Sleep ☐ Exercise ☐ Water ☐ Cold/Ice
☐ Heat/Bath ☐ Other: ____________________
Did it work? ☐ Nope ☐ A bit ☐ Mostly ☐ 100%

Notes ☐ *See back notes*

START: | END: | DURATION: | DATE | *Entry #126*

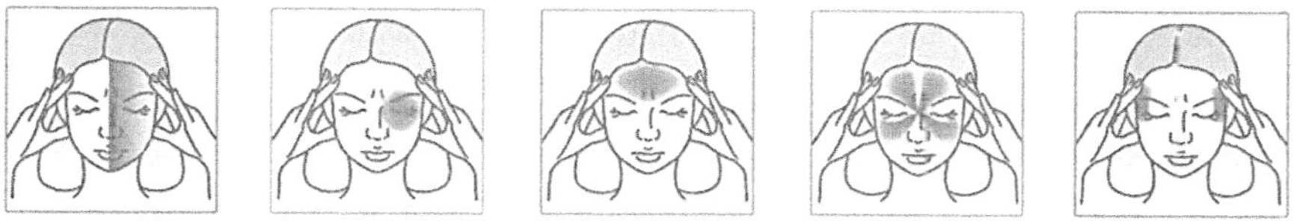

MIGRAINE | CLUSTER | TENSION | SINUS | TMJ

HOW WOULD YOU RATE...?

Mood	① ② ③ ④ ⑤
Energy	① ② ③ ④ ⑤
Mental clarity	① ② ③ ④ ⑤

PAIN LEVEL

1	2	3	4	5	6	7	8	9	10

Not too bad. *Well, I'm not enjoying this.* *Make it stop!*

ONSET

☐ Slow ☐ Average
☐ Rapid ☐ Sudden

DETAILED DESCRIPTION

☐ Constant ☐ Squeezing ☐ Throbbing ☐ Pounding ☐ Dull aching ☐ Burning
☐ Sharp ☐ Debilitating ☐ Other: ____________________

WHERE DOES IT HURT, EXACTLY?

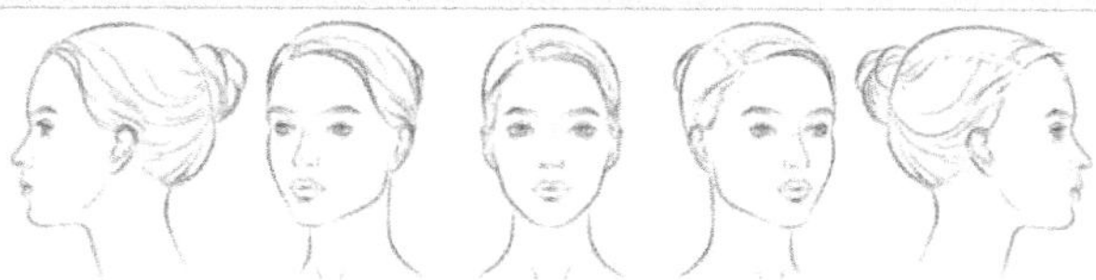

OTHER SYMPTOMS

☐ Lightheaded ☐ Dizziness
☐ Light sensitivity ☐ Sound sensitivity
☐ Confusion ☐ Auras
☐ Muscle stiffness ☐ Muscle aches

FEELING SICK?

☐ Nausea ☐ Diarrhea ☐ Vomiting ☐ Sore throat ☐ Congestion ☐ Coughing
☐ Chills ☐ Fever ☐ Other: ____________________

SLEEP

hours ________ *quality* ① ② ③ ④ ⑤

WEATHER

☐ Cold ☐ Mild ☐ Hot Allergen levels: ____________
☐ Dry ☐ Humid ☐ Wet BM Pressure: ____________

STRESS LEVELS

None	Low	Medium	High	Max	@$#%!

item / meal	*time*	*meds / supplements*	*dose*	*time*	*drinks*
					water
					① ② ③ ④ ⑤ ⑥ ⑦ ⑧ ⑨ ⑩
					caffeine
					① ② ③ ④ ⑤ ⑥ ⑦ ⑧ ⑨ ⑩
					alcohol
					① ② ③ ④ ⑤ ⑥ ⑦ ⑧ ⑨ ⑩

HORMONES

☐ Menstruating ☐ Menopause
☐ PMS ☐ N/A | other

COMPUTER / MOBILE DEVICE / TV

☐ None ☐ Some ☐ A lot Total Time: ______
☐ Sitting ☐ Standing ☐ Mixture Breaks every: ______

PHYSICAL ACTIVITY

☐ None ☐ Minimal ☐ Some ☐ Sweatin' ☐ I'm beat DETAILS: ____________

RELIEF MEASURES

☐ Medication ☐ Massage ☐ Sleep ☐ Exercise ☐ Water ☐ Cold/Ice
☐ Heat/Bath ☐ Other: ____________________

Did it work? ☐ Nope ☐ A bit ☐ Mostly ☐ 100%

Notes ☐ *See back notes*

START: | END: | DURATION: | DATE | *Entry #127*

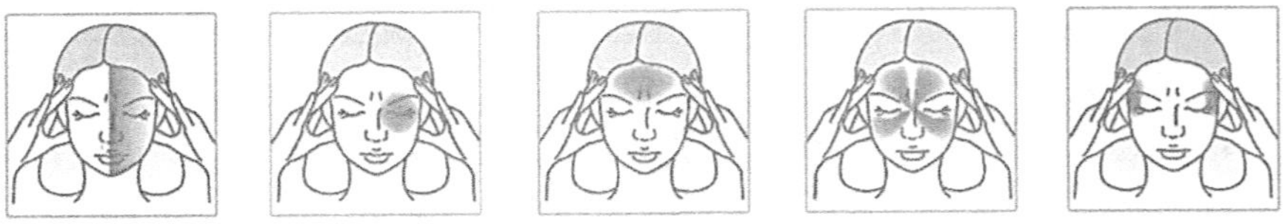

MIGRAINE CLUSTER TENSION SINUS TMJ

HOW WOULD YOU RATE...?

Mood	① ② ③ ④ ⑤
Energy	① ② ③ ④ ⑤
Mental clarity	① ② ③ ④ ⑤

PAIN LEVEL

1	2	3	4	5	6	7	8	9	10

Not too bad. *Well, I'm not enjoying this.* *Make it stop!*

ONSET

☐ Slow ☐ Average
☐ Rapid ☐ Sudden

DETAILED DESCRIPTION

☐ Constant ☐ Squeezing ☐ Throbbing ☐ Pounding ☐ Dull aching ☐ Burning
☐ Sharp ☐ Debilitating ☐ Other: ____________

WHERE DOES IT HURT, EXACTLY?

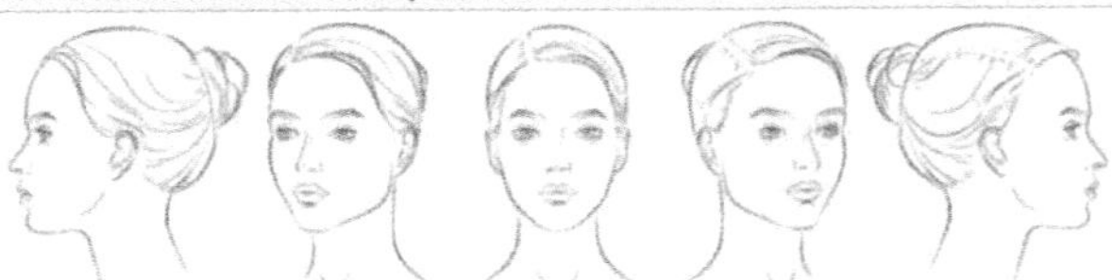

OTHER SYMPTOMS

☐ Lightheaded ☐ Dizziness
☐ Light sensitivity ☐ Sound sensitivity
☐ Confusion ☐ Auras
☐ Muscle stiffness ☐ Muscle aches

FEELING SICK?

☐ Nausea ☐ Diarrhea ☐ Vomiting ☐ Sore throat ☐ Congestion ☐ Coughing
☐ Chills ☐ Fever ☐ Other: ____________

SLEEP

hours ______ *quality* ① ② ③ ④ ⑤

WEATHER

☐ Cold ☐ Mild ☐ Hot Allergen levels: ______
☐ Dry ☐ Humid ☐ Wet BM Pressure: ______

STRESS LEVELS

None	Low	Medium	High	Max	@$#%!

item / meal	*time*	*meds / supplements*	*dose*	*time*	*drinks*
					water
					① ② ③ ④ ⑤ ⑥ ⑦ ⑧ ⑨ ⑩
					caffeine
					① ② ③ ④ ⑤ ⑥ ⑦ ⑧ ⑨ ⑩
					alcohol
					① ② ③ ④ ⑤ ⑥ ⑦ ⑧ ⑨ ⑩

HORMONES

☐ Menstruating ☐ Menopause
☐ PMS ☐ N/A | other

COMPUTER / MOBILE DEVICE / TV

☐ None ☐ Some ☐ A lot Total Time: ______
☐ Sitting ☐ Standing ☐ Mixture Breaks every: ______

PHYSICAL ACTIVITY

☐ None ☐ Minimal ☐ Some ☐ Sweatin' ☐ I'm beat DETAILS: ____________

RELIEF MEASURES

☐ Medication ☐ Massage ☐ Sleep ☐ Exercise ☐ Water ☐ Cold/Ice
☐ Heat/Bath ☐ Other: ____________
Did it work? ☐ Nope ☐ A bit ☐ Mostly ☐ 100%

Notes ☐ *See back notes*

START: | END: | DURATION: | DATE | *Entry #128*

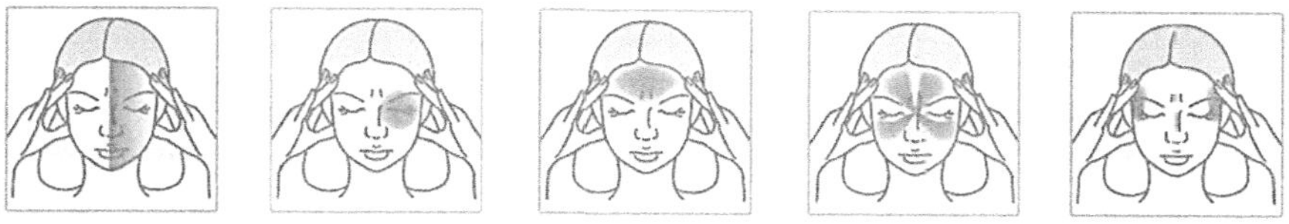

MIGRAINE | CLUSTER | TENSION | SINUS | TMJ

HOW WOULD YOU RATE...?

Mood	1	2	3	4	5
Energy	1	2	3	4	5
Mental clarity	1	2	3	4	5

PAIN LEVEL

1	2	3	4	5	6	7	8	9	10

Not too bad. *Well, I'm not enjoying this.* *Make it stop!*

ONSET

☐ Slow ☐ Average
☐ Rapid ☐ Sudden

DETAILED DESCRIPTION

☐ Constant ☐ Squeezing ☐ Throbbing ☐ Pounding ☐ Dull aching ☐ Burning
☐ Sharp ☐ Debilitating ☐ Other: ______

WHERE DOES IT HURT, EXACTLY?

OTHER SYMPTOMS

☐ Lightheaded ☐ Dizziness
☐ Light sensitivity ☐ Sound sensitivity
☐ Confusion ☐ Auras
☐ Muscle stiffness ☐ Muscle aches

FEELING SICK?

☐ Nausea ☐ Diarrhea ☐ Vomiting ☐ Sore throat ☐ Congestion ☐ Coughing
☐ Chills ☐ Fever ☐ Other: ______

SLEEP

hours ______ *quality* 1 2 3 4 5

WEATHER

☐ Cold ☐ Mild ☐ Hot Allergen levels: ______
☐ Dry ☐ Humid ☐ Wet BM Pressure: ______

STRESS LEVELS

None	Low	Medium	High	Max	@$#%!

item / meal	*time*	*meds / supplements*	*dose*	*time*	*drinks*
					water: 1 2 3 4 5 6 7 8 9 10
					caffeine: 1 2 3 4 5 6 7 8 9 10
					alcohol: 1 2 3 4 5 6 7 8 9 10

HORMONES

☐ Menstruating ☐ Menopause
☐ PMS ☐ N/A | other

COMPUTER / MOBILE DEVICE / TV

☐ None ☐ Some ☐ A lot Total Time: ______
☐ Sitting ☐ Standing ☐ Mixture Breaks every: ______

PHYSICAL ACTIVITY

☐ None ☐ Minimal ☐ Some ☐ Sweatin' ☐ I'm beat DETAILS: ______

RELIEF MEASURES

☐ Medication ☐ Massage ☐ Sleep ☐ Exercise ☐ Water ☐ Cold/Ice
☐ Heat/Bath ☐ Other: ______
Did it work? ☐ Nope ☐ A bit ☐ Mostly ☐ 100%

Notes ☐ *See back notes*

START: | END: | DURATION: | DATE | *Entry #129*

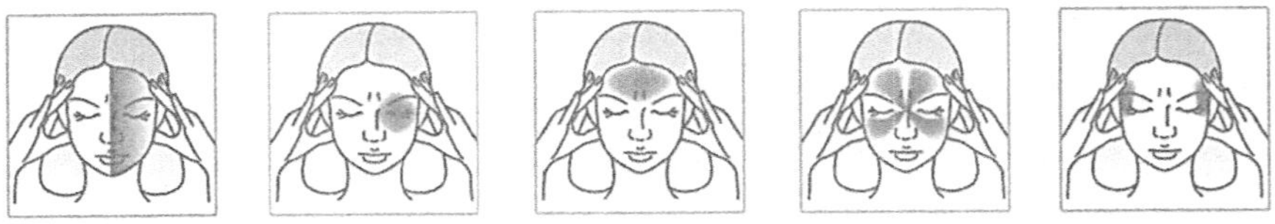

MIGRAINE CLUSTER TENSION SINUS TMJ

HOW WOULD YOU RATE...?

Mood ① ② ③ ④ ⑤

Energy ① ② ③ ④ ⑤

Mental clarity ① ② ③ ④ ⑤

PAIN LEVEL

1	2	3	4	5	6	7	8	9	10

Not too bad. *Well, I'm not enjoying this.* *Make it stop!*

ONSET

☐ Slow ☐ Average
☐ Rapid ☐ Sudden

DETAILED DESCRIPTION

☐ Constant ☐ Squeezing ☐ Throbbing ☐ Pounding ☐ Dull aching ☐ Burning
☐ Sharp ☐ Debilitating ☐ Other: ____________

WHERE DOES IT HURT, EXACTLY?

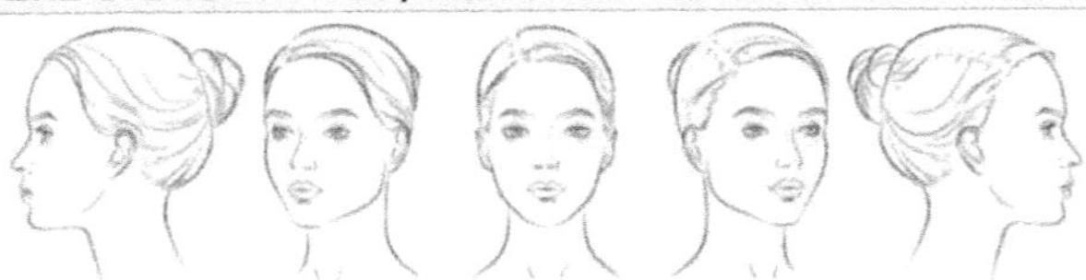

OTHER SYMPTOMS

☐ Lightheaded ☐ Dizziness
☐ Light sensitivity ☐ Sound sensitivity
☐ Confusion ☐ Auras
☐ Muscle stiffness ☐ Muscle aches

FEELING SICK?

☐ Nausea ☐ Diarrhea ☐ Vomiting ☐ Sore throat ☐ Congestion ☐ Coughing
☐ Chills ☐ Fever ☐ Other: ____________

SLEEP

hours ______ *quality* ① ② ③ ④ ⑤

WEATHER

☐ Cold ☐ Mild ☐ Hot Allergen levels: ____________
☐ Dry ☐ Humid ☐ Wet BM Pressure: ____________

STRESS LEVELS

None	Low	Medium	High	Max	@$#%!

item / meal	*time*	*meds / supplements*	*dose*	*time*	*drinks*
					water
					① ② ③ ④ ⑤ ⑥ ⑦ ⑧ ⑨ ⑩
					caffeine
					① ② ③ ④ ⑤ ⑥ ⑦ ⑧ ⑨ ⑩
					alcohol
					① ② ③ ④ ⑤ ⑥ ⑦ ⑧ ⑨ ⑩

HORMONES

☐ Menstruating ☐ Menopause
☐ PMS ☐ N/A | other

COMPUTER / MOBILE DEVICE / TV

☐ None ☐ Some ☐ A lot Total Time: ______
☐ Sitting ☐ Standing ☐ Mixture Breaks every: ______

PHYSICAL ACTIVITY

☐ None ☐ Minimal ☐ Some ☐ Sweatin' ☐ I'm beat DETAILS: ____________

RELIEF MEASURES

☐ Medication ☐ Massage ☐ Sleep ☐ Exercise ☐ Water ☐ Cold/Ice
☐ Heat/Bath ☐ Other: ____________
Did it work? ☐ Nope ☐ A bit ☐ Mostly ☐ 100%

Notes ☐ *See back notes*

START: | END: | DURATION: | DATE | *Entry #130*

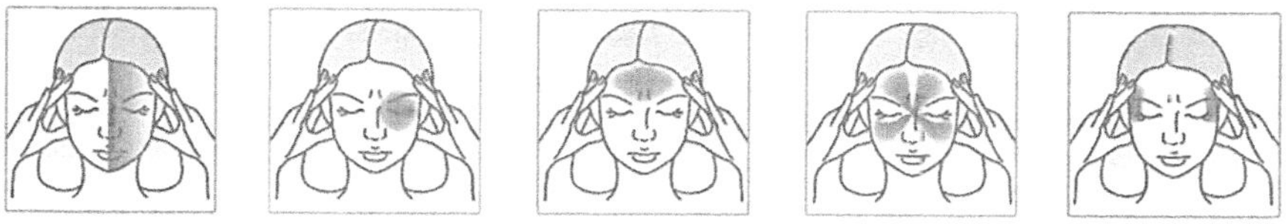

MIGRAINE | CLUSTER | TENSION | SINUS | TMJ

HOW WOULD YOU RATE...?

Mood	① ② ③ ④ ⑤
Energy	① ② ③ ④ ⑤
Mental clarity	① ② ③ ④ ⑤

PAIN LEVEL

1	2	3	4	5	6	7	8	9	10

Not too bad. *Well, I'm not enjoying this.* *Make it stop!*

ONSET

☐ Slow ☐ Average
☐ Rapid ☐ Sudden

DETAILED DESCRIPTION

☐ Constant ☐ Squeezing ☐ Throbbing ☐ Pounding ☐ Dull aching ☐ Burning
☐ Sharp ☐ Debilitating ☐ Other: ____________________

WHERE DOES IT HURT, EXACTLY?

OTHER SYMPTOMS

☐ Lightheaded ☐ Dizziness
☐ Light sensitivity ☐ Sound sensitivity
☐ Confusion ☐ Auras
☐ Muscle stiffness ☐ Muscle aches

FEELING SICK?

☐ Nausea ☐ Diarrhea ☐ Vomiting ☐ Sore throat ☐ Congestion ☐ Coughing
☐ Chills ☐ Fever ☐ Other: ____________________

SLEEP

hours ________ *quality* ① ② ③ ④ ⑤

WEATHER

☐ Cold ☐ Mild ☐ Hot Allergen levels: __________
☐ Dry ☐ Humid ☐ Wet BM Pressure: __________

STRESS LEVELS

None	Low	Medium	High	Max	@$#%!

item / meal	*time*	*meds / supplements*	*dose*	*time*	*drinks*
					water
					① ② ③ ④ ⑤ ⑥ ⑦ ⑧ ⑨ ⑩
					caffeine
					① ② ③ ④ ⑤ ⑥ ⑦ ⑧ ⑨ ⑩
					alcohol
					① ② ③ ④ ⑤ ⑥ ⑦ ⑧ ⑨ ⑩

HORMONES

☐ Menstruating ☐ Menopause
☐ PMS ☐ N/A | other

COMPUTER / MOBILE DEVICE / TV

☐ None ☐ Some ☐ A lot Total Time: ______
☐ Sitting ☐ Standing ☐ Mixture Breaks every: ______

PHYSICAL ACTIVITY

☐ None ☐ Minimal ☐ Some ☐ Sweatin' ☐ I'm beat DETAILS: ____________________

RELIEF MEASURES

☐ Medication ☐ Massage ☐ Sleep ☐ Exercise ☐ Water ☐ Cold/Ice
☐ Heat/Bath ☐ Other: ____________________
Did it work? ☐ Nope ☐ A bit ☐ Mostly ☐ 100%

Notes ☐ *See back notes*

START: ______ END: ______ DURATION: ______ DATE ______ *Entry #131*

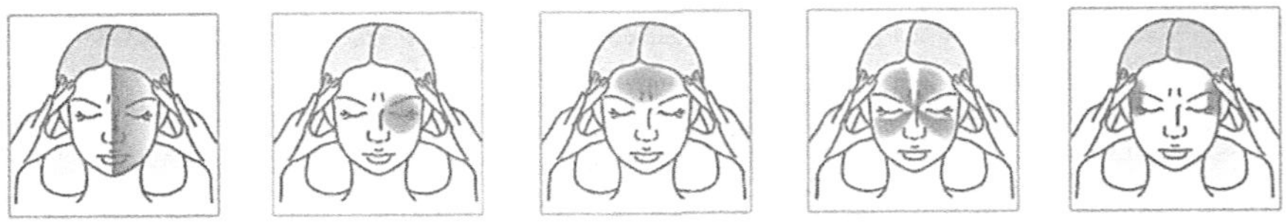

MIGRAINE CLUSTER TENSION SINUS TMJ

HOW WOULD YOU RATE...?

Mood	① ② ③ ④ ⑤
Energy	① ② ③ ④ ⑤
Mental clarity	① ② ③ ④ ⑤

PAIN LEVEL

1	2	3	4	5	6	7	8	9	10

Not too bad. *Well, I'm not enjoying this.* *Make it stop!*

ONSET

☐ Slow ☐ Average
☐ Rapid ☐ Sudden

DETAILED DESCRIPTION

☐ Constant ☐ Squeezing ☐ Throbbing ☐ Pounding ☐ Dull aching ☐ Burning
☐ Sharp ☐ Debilitating ☐ Other: ______________________

WHERE DOES IT HURT, EXACTLY?

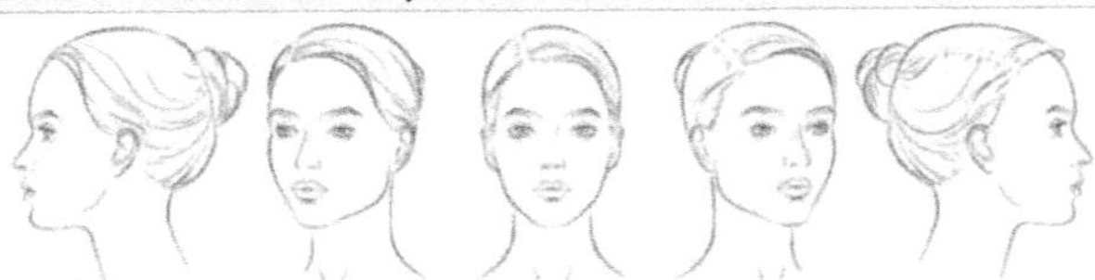

OTHER SYMPTOMS

☐ Lightheaded ☐ Dizziness
☐ Light sensitivity ☐ Sound sensitivity
☐ Confusion ☐ Auras
☐ Muscle stiffness ☐ Muscle aches

FEELING SICK?

☐ Nausea ☐ Diarrhea ☐ Vomiting ☐ Sore throat ☐ Congestion ☐ Coughing
☐ Chills ☐ Fever ☐ Other: ______________________

SLEEP

hours ______ *quality* ① ② ③ ④ ⑤

WEATHER

☐ Cold ☐ Mild ☐ Hot Allergen levels: __________
☐ Dry ☐ Humid ☐ Wet BM Pressure: __________

STRESS LEVELS

None	Low	Medium	High	Max	@$#%!

item / meal	*time*	*meds / supplements*	*dose*	*time*	*drinks*
					water
					① ② ③ ④ ⑤ ⑥ ⑦ ⑧ ⑨ ⑩
					caffeine
					① ② ③ ④ ⑤ ⑥ ⑦ ⑧ ⑨ ⑩
					alcohol
					① ② ③ ④ ⑤ ⑥ ⑦ ⑧ ⑨ ⑩

HORMONES

☐ Menstruating ☐ Menopause
☐ PMS ☐ N/A | other

COMPUTER / MOBILE DEVICE / TV

☐ None ☐ Some ☐ A lot Total Time: ______
☐ Sitting ☐ Standing ☐ Mixture Breaks every: ______

PHYSICAL ACTIVITY

☐ None ☐ Minimal ☐ Some ☐ Sweatin' ☐ I'm beat DETAILS: ______________

RELIEF MEASURES

☐ Medication ☐ Massage ☐ Sleep ☐ Exercise ☐ Water ☐ Cold/Ice
☐ Heat/Bath ☐ Other: ______________________
Did it work? ☐ Nope ☐ A bit ☐ Mostly ☐ 100%

Notes ☐ *See back notes*

START: | END: | DURATION: | DATE | *Entry #132*

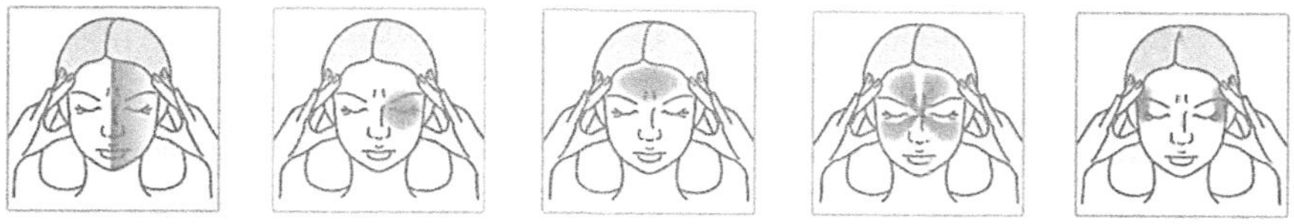

MIGRAINE | CLUSTER | TENSION | SINUS | TMJ

HOW WOULD YOU RATE...?

Mood	① ② ③ ④ ⑤
Energy	① ② ③ ④ ⑤
Mental clarity	① ② ③ ④ ⑤

PAIN LEVEL

1	2	3	4	5	6	7	8	9	10

Not too bad. *Well. I'm not enjoying this.* *Make it stop!*

ONSET

☐ Slow ☐ Average
☐ Rapid ☐ Sudden

DETAILED DESCRIPTION

☐ Constant ☐ Squeezing ☐ Throbbing ☐ Pouncing ☐ Dull aching ☐ Burning
☐ Sharp ☐ Debilitating ☐ Other: ____________________

WHERE DOES IT HURT, EXACTLY?

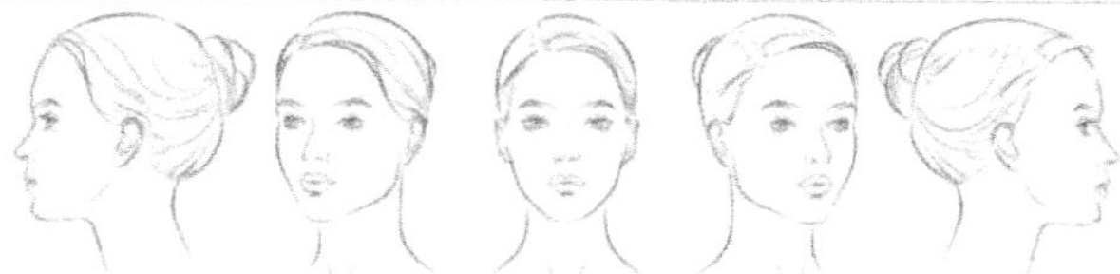

OTHER SYMPTOMS

☐ Lightheaded ☐ Dizziness
☐ Light sensitivity ☐ Sound sensitivity
☐ Confusion ☐ Auras
☐ Muscle stiffness ☐ Muscle aches

FEELING SICK?

☐ Nausea ☐ Diarrhea ☐ Vomiting ☐ Sore throat ☐ Congestion ☐ Coughing
☐ Chills ☐ Fever ☐ Other: ____________________

SLEEP

hours ______ *quality* ① ② ③ ④ ⑤

WEATHER

☐ Cold ☐ Mild ☐ Hot Allergen levels: __________
☐ Dry ☐ Humid ☐ Wet BM Pressure: __________

STRESS LEVELS

None	Low	Medium	High	Max	@$#%!

item / meal	*time*	*meds / supplements*	*dose*	*time*	*drinks*
					water
					① ② ③ ④ ⑤ ⑥ ⑦ ⑧ ⑨ ⑩
					caffeine
					① ② ③ ④ ⑤ ⑥ ⑦ ⑧ ⑨ ⑩
					alcohol
					① ② ③ ④ ⑤ ⑥ ⑦ ⑧ ⑨ ⑩

HORMONES

☐ Menstruating ☐ Menopause
☐ PMS ☐ N/A | other

COMPUTER / MOBILE DEVICE / TV

☐ None ☐ Some ☐ A lot Total Time: ______
☐ Sitting ☐ Standing ☐ Mixture Breaks every: ______

PHYSICAL ACTIVITY

☐ None ☐ Minimal ☐ Some ☐ Sweatin' ☐ I'm beat DETAILS: __________

RELIEF MEASURES

☐ Medication ☐ Massage ☐ Sleep ☐ Exercise ☐ Water ☐ Cold/Ice
☐ Heat/Bath ☐ Other: ____________________
Did it work? ☐ Nope ☐ A bit ☐ Mostly ☐ 100%

Notes ☐ *See back notes*

START:		END:		DURATION:		DATE		*Entry #133*

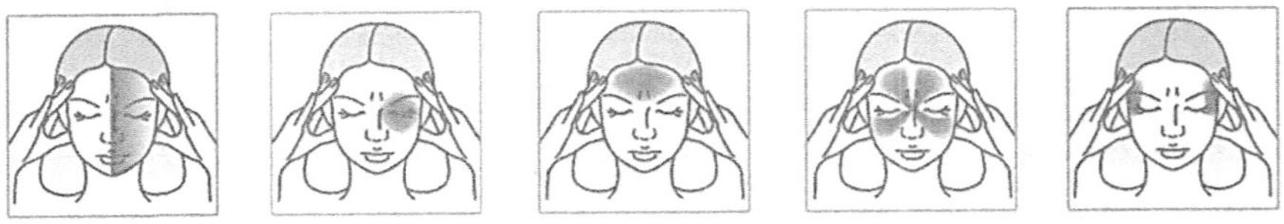

MIGRAINE | CLUSTER | TENSION | SINUS | TMJ

HOW WOULD YOU RATE...?

Mood	1	2	3	4	5
Energy	1	2	3	4	5
Mental clarity	1	2	3	4	5

PAIN LEVEL

1	2	3	4	5	6	7	8	9	10

Not too bad. *Well, I'm not enjoying this.* *Make it stop!*

ONSET

☐ Slow ☐ Average
☐ Rapid ☐ Sudden

DETAILED DESCRIPTION

☐ Constant ☐ Squeezing ☐ Throbbing ☐ Pounding ☐ Dull aching ☐ Burning
☐ Sharp ☐ Debilitating ☐ Other: ____________________

WHERE DOES IT HURT, EXACTLY?

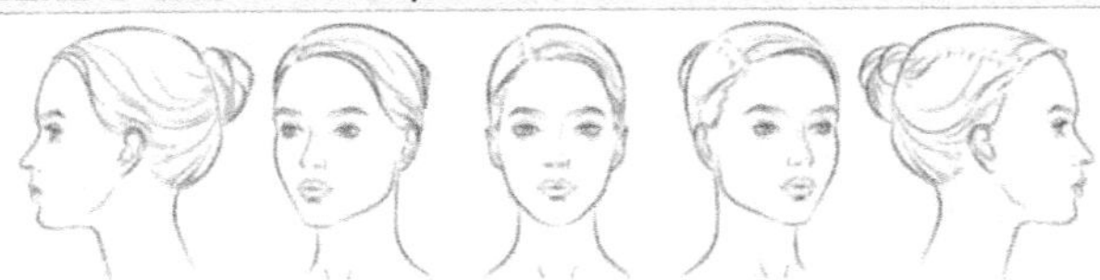

OTHER SYMPTOMS

☐ Lightheaded ☐ Dizziness
☐ Light sensitivity ☐ Sound sensitivity
☐ Confusion ☐ Auras
☐ Muscle stiffness ☐ Muscle aches

FEELING SICK?

☐ Nausea ☐ Diarrhea ☐ Vomiting ☐ Sore throat ☐ Congestion ☐ Coughing
☐ Chills ☐ Fever ☐ Other: ____________________

SLEEP

hours ________ *quality* 1 2 3 4 5

WEATHER

☐ Cold ☐ Mild ☐ Hot Allergen levels: __________
☐ Dry ☐ Humid ☐ Wet BM Pressure: __________

STRESS LEVELS

None	Low	Medium	High	Max	@$#%!

item / meal	*time*	*meds / supplements*	*dose*	*time*	*drinks*
					water: 1 2 3 4 5 6 7 8 9 10
					caffeine: 1 2 3 4 5 6 7 8 9 10
					alcohol: 1 2 3 4 5 6 7 8 9 10

HORMONES

☐ Menstruating ☐ Menopause
☐ PMS ☐ N/A | other

COMPUTER / MOBILE DEVICE / TV

☐ None ☐ Some ☐ A lot Total Time: ______
☐ Sitting ☐ Standing ☐ Mixture Breaks every: ______

PHYSICAL ACTIVITY

☐ None ☐ Minimal ☐ Some ☐ Sweatin' ☐ I'm beat DETAILS: ____________________

RELIEF MEASURES

☐ Medication ☐ Massage ☐ Sleep ☐ Exercise ☐ Water ☐ Cold/Ice
☐ Heat/Bath ☐ Other: ____________________
Did it work? ☐ Nope ☐ A bit ☐ Mostly ☐ 100%

Notes ☐ *See back notes*

START: | END: | DURATION: | DATE | *Entry #134*

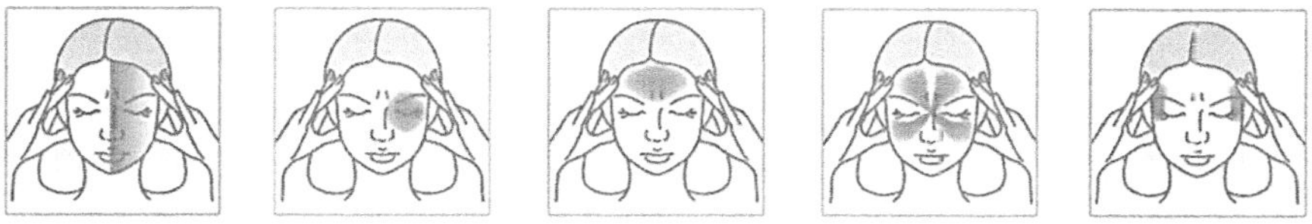

MIGRAINE CLUSTER TENSION SINUS TMJ

HOW WOULD YOU RATE...?

Mood	① ② ③ ④ ⑤
Energy	① ② ③ ④ ⑤
Mental clarity	① ② ③ ④ ⑤

PAIN LEVEL

1	2	3	4	5	6	7	8	9	10

Not too bad. *Well, I'm not enjoying this.* *Make it stop!*

ONSET

☐ Slow ☐ Average
☐ Rapid ☐ Sudden

DETAILED DESCRIPTION

☐ Constant ☐ Squeezing ☐ Throbbing ☐ Pounding ☐ Dull aching ☐ Burning
☐ Sharp ☐ Debilitating ☐ Other: ______

WHERE DOES IT HURT, EXACTLY?

OTHER SYMPTOMS

☐ Lightheaded ☐ Dizziness
☐ Light sensitivity ☐ Sound sensitivity
☐ Confusion ☐ Auras
☐ Muscle stiffness ☐ Muscle aches

FEELING SICK?

☐ Nausea ☐ Diarrhea ☐ Vomiting ☐ Sore throat ☐ Congestion ☐ Coughing
☐ Chills ☐ Fever ☐ Other: ______

SLEEP

hours ______ *quality* ① ② ③ ④ ⑤

WEATHER

☐ Cold ☐ Mild ☐ Hot Allergen levels: ______
☐ Dry ☐ Humid ☐ Wet BM Pressure: ______

STRESS LEVELS

None	Low	Medium	High	Max	@$#%!

item / meal	*time*	*meds / supplements*	*dose*	*time*	*drinks*
					water
					① ② ③ ④ ⑤ ⑥ ⑦ ⑧ ⑨ ⑩
					caffeine
					① ② ③ ④ ⑤ ⑥ ⑦ ⑧ ⑨ ⑩
					alcohol
					① ② ③ ④ ⑤ ⑥ ⑦ ⑧ ⑨ ⑩

HORMONES

☐ Menstruating ☐ Menopause
☐ PMS ☐ N/A | other

COMPUTER / MOBILE DEVICE / TV

☐ None ☐ Some ☐ A lot Total Time: ______
☐ Sitting ☐ Standing ☐ Mixture Breaks every: ______

PHYSICAL ACTIVITY

☐ None ☐ Minimal ☐ Some ☐ Sweatin' ☐ I'm beat DETAILS: ______

RELIEF MEASURES

☐ Medication ☐ Massage ☐ Sleep ☐ Exercise ☐ Water ☐ Cold/Ice
☐ Heat/Bath ☐ Other: ______
Did it work? ☐ Nope ☐ A bit ☐ Mostly ☐ 100%

Notes ☐ *See back notes*

START:		END:		DURATION:		DATE		*Entry #135*

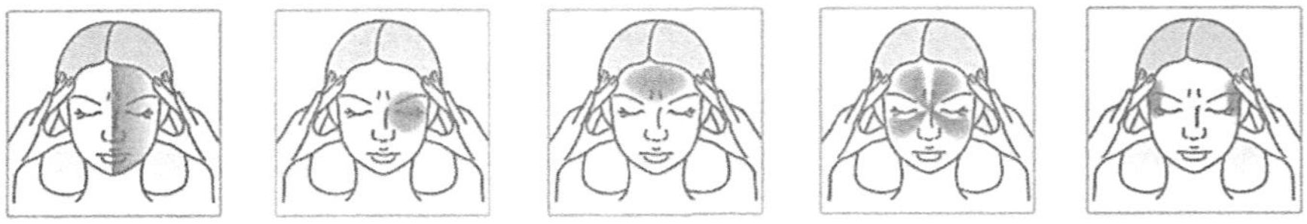

MIGRAINE CLUSTER TENSION SINUS TMJ

HOW WOULD YOU RATE...?

Mood	1	2	3	4	5
Energy	1	2	3	4	5
Mental clarity	1	2	3	4	5

PAIN LEVEL

1	2	3	4	5	6	7	8	9	10

Not too bad. *Well, I'm not enjoying this.* *Make it stop!*

ONSET

☐ Slow ☐ Average
☐ Rapid ☐ Sudden

DETAILED DESCRIPTION

☐ Constant ☐ Squeezing ☐ Throbbing ☐ Pounding ☐ Dull aching ☐ Burning
☐ Sharp ☐ Debilitating ☐ Other: ____________________

WHERE DOES IT HURT, EXACTLY?

OTHER SYMPTOMS

☐ Lightheaded ☐ Dizziness
☐ Light sensitivity ☐ Sound sensitivity
☐ Confusion ☐ Auras
☐ Muscle stiffness ☐ Muscle aches

FEELING SICK?

☐ Nausea ☐ Diarrhea ☐ Vomiting ☐ Sore throat ☐ Congestion ☐ Coughing
☐ Chills ☐ Fever ☐ Other: ____________________

SLEEP

hours ________ *quality* 1 2 3 4 5

WEATHER

☐ Cold ☐ Mild ☐ Hot Allergen levels: ____________
☐ Dry ☐ Humid ☐ Wet BM Pressure: ____________

STRESS LEVELS

None	Low	Medium	High	Max	@$#%!

item / meal	*time*	*meds / supplements*	*dose*	*time*	*drinks*
					water
					1 2 3 4 5 6 7 8 9 10
					caffeine
					1 2 3 4 5 6 7 8 9 10
					alcohol
					1 2 3 4 5 6 7 8 9 10

HORMONES

☐ Menstruating ☐ Menopause
☐ PMS ☐ N/A | other

COMPUTER / MOBILE DEVICE / TV

☐ None ☐ Some ☐ A lot Total Time: _____
☐ Sitting ☐ Standing ☐ Mixture Breaks every: _____

PHYSICAL ACTIVITY

☐ None ☐ Minimal ☐ Some ☐ Sweatin' ☐ I'm beat DETAILS: ____________

RELIEF MEASURES

☐ Medication ☐ Massage ☐ Sleep ☐ Exercise ☐ Water ☐ Cold/Ice
☐ Heat/Bath ☐ Other: ____________________
Did it work? ☐ Nope ☐ A bit ☐ Mostly ☐ 100%

Notes ☐ *See back notes*

START:		END:		DURATION:		DATE		*Entry #136*

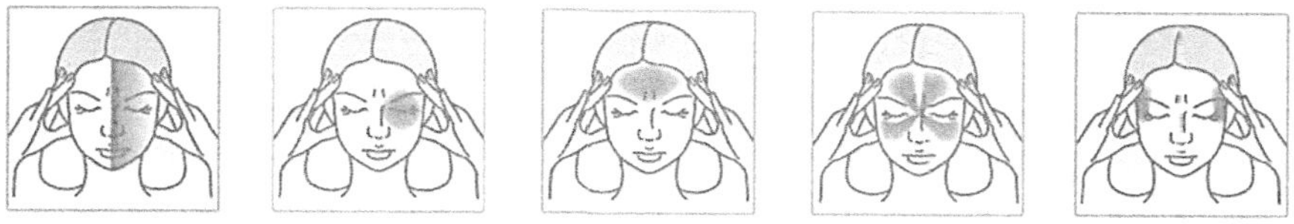

MIGRAINE | CLUSTER | TENSION | SINUS | TMJ

HOW WOULD YOU RATE...?

Mood	① ② ③ ④ ⑤
Energy	① ② ③ ④ ⑤
Mental clarity	① ② ③ ④ ⑤

PAIN LEVEL

1	2	3	4	5	6	7	8	9	10

Not too bad. *Well. I'm not enjoying this.* *Make it stop!*

ONSET

☐ Slow ☐ Average
☐ Rapid ☐ Sudden

DETAILED DESCRIPTION

☐ Constant ☐ Squeezing ☐ Throbbing ☐ Pouncing ☐ Dull aching ☐ Burning
☐ Sharp ☐ Debilitating ☐ Other: ______________________________

WHERE DOES IT HURT, EXACTLY?

OTHER SYMPTOMS

☐ Lightheaded ☐ Dizziness
☐ Light sensitivity ☐ Sound sensitivity
☐ Confusion ☐ Auras
☐ Muscle stiffness ☐ Muscle aches

FEELING SICK?

☐ Nausea ☐ Diarrhea ☐ Vomiting ☐ Sore throat ☐ Congestion ☐ Coughing
☐ Chills ☐ Fever ☐ Other: ______________________________

SLEEP

hours ________ *quality* ① ② ③ ④ ⑤

WEATHER

☐ Cold ☐ Mild ☐ Hot Allergen levels: ____________
☐ Dry ☐ Humid ☐ Wet BM Pressure: ____________

STRESS LEVELS

None	Low	Medium	High	Max	@$#%!

item / meal	*time*	*meds / supplements*	*dose*	*time*	*drinks*
					water
					① ② ③ ④ ⑤ ⑥ ⑦ ⑧ ⑨ ⑩
					caffeine
					① ② ③ ④ ⑤ ⑥ ⑦ ⑧ ⑨ ⑩
					alcohol
					① ② ③ ④ ⑤ ⑥ ⑦ ⑧ ⑨ ⑩

HORMONES

☐ Menstruating ☐ Menopause
☐ PMS ☐ N/A | other

COMPUTER / MOBILE DEVICE / TV

☐ None ☐ Some ☐ A lot Total Time: _____
☐ Sitting ☐ Standing ☐ Mixture Breaks every: _____

PHYSICAL ACTIVITY

☐ None ☐ Minimal ☐ Some ☐ Sweatin' ☐ I'm beat DETAILS: ____________

RELIEF MEASURES

☐ Medication ☐ Massage ☐ Sleep ☐ Exercise ☐ Water ☐ Cold/Ice
☐ Heat/Bath ☐ Other: ______________________________
Did it work? ☐ Nope ☐ A bit ☐ Mostly ☐ 100%

Notes ☐ *See back notes*

START: ____ END: ____ DURATION: ____ DATE ____ *Entry #137*

MIGRAINE

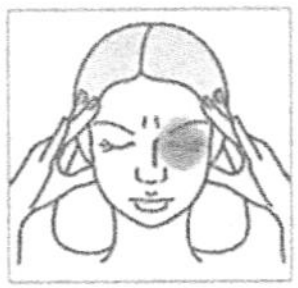

CLUSTER

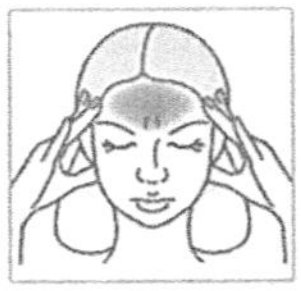

TENSION

SINUS

TMJ

HOW WOULD YOU RATE...?

Mood	1	2	3	4	5
Energy	1	2	3	4	5
Mental clarity	1	2	3	4	5

PAIN LEVEL

1	2	3	4	5	6	7	8	9	10

Not too bad. *Well, I'm not enjoying this.* *Make it stop!*

ONSET

☐ Slow ☐ Average
☐ Rapid ☐ Sudden

DETAILED DESCRIPTION

☐ Constant ☐ Squeezing ☐ Throbbing ☐ Pounding ☐ Dull aching ☐ Burning
☐ Sharp ☐ Debilitating ☐ Other: ____

WHERE DOES IT HURT, EXACTLY?

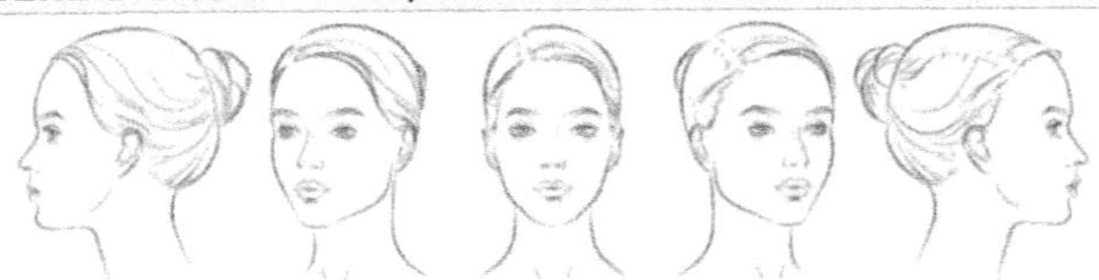

OTHER SYMPTOMS

☐ Lightheaded ☐ Dizziness
☐ Light sensitivity ☐ Sound sensitivity
☐ Confusion ☐ Auras
☐ Muscle stiffness ☐ Muscle aches

FEELING SICK?

☐ Nausea ☐ Diarrhea ☐ Vomiting ☐ Sore throat ☐ Congestion ☐ Coughing
☐ Chills ☐ Fever ☐ Other: ____

SLEEP

hours ____ *quality* 1 2 3 4 5

WEATHER

☐ Cold ☐ Mild ☐ Hot Allergen levels: ____
☐ Dry ☐ Humid ☐ Wet BM Pressure: ____

STRESS LEVELS

None	Low	Medium	High	Max	@$#%!

item / meal	*time*	*meds / supplements*	*dose*	*time*	*drinks*
					water: 1 2 3 4 5 6 7 8 9 10
					caffeine: 1 2 3 4 5 6 7 8 9 10
					alcohol: 1 2 3 4 5 6 7 8 9 10

HORMONES

☐ Menstruating ☐ Menopause
☐ PMS ☐ N/A | other

COMPUTER / MOBILE DEVICE / TV

☐ None ☐ Some ☐ A lot Total Time: ____
☐ Sitting ☐ Standing ☐ Mixture Breaks every: ____

PHYSICAL ACTIVITY

☐ None ☐ Minimal ☐ Some ☐ Sweatin' ☐ I'm beat DETAILS: ____

RELIEF MEASURES

☐ Medication ☐ Massage ☐ Sleep ☐ Exercise ☐ Water ☐ Cold/Ice
☐ Heat/Bath ☐ Other: ____
Did it work? ☐ Nope ☐ A bit ☐ Mostly ☐ 100%

Notes ☐ *See back notes*

START:		END:		DURATION:		DATE		*Entry #138*

MIGRAINE

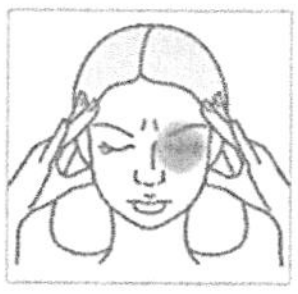
CLUSTER

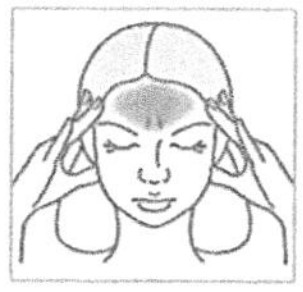
TENSION

SINUS

TMJ

HOW WOULD YOU RATE...?	
Mood	① ② ③ ④ ⑤
Energy	① ② ③ ④ ⑤
Mental clarity	① ② ③ ④ ⑤

PAIN LEVEL

1	2	3	4	5	6	7	8	9	10

Not too bad. *Well. I'm not enjoying this.* *Make it stop!*

ONSET

☐ Slow ☐ Average
☐ Rapid ☐ Sudden

DETAILED DESCRIPTION

☐ Constant ☐ Squeezing ☐ Throbbing ☐ Pouncing ☐ Dull aching ☐ Burning
☐ Sharp ☐ Debilitating ☐ Other: ______________________________

WHERE DOES IT HURT, EXACTLY?

OTHER SYMPTOMS

☐ Lightheaded ☐ Dizziness
☐ Light sensitivity ☐ Sound sensitivity
☐ Confusion ☐ Auras
☐ Muscle stiffness ☐ Muscle aches

FEELING SICK?

☐ Nausea ☐ Diarrhea ☐ Vomiting ☐ Sore throat ☐ Congestion ☐ Coughing
☐ Chills ☐ Fever ☐ Other: ______________________________

SLEEP

hours ________ *quality* ① ② ③ ④ ⑤

WEATHER

☐ Cold ☐ Mild ☐ Hot Allergen levels: ____________
☐ Dry ☐ Humid ☐ Wet BM Pressure: ____________

STRESS LEVELS

None	Low	Medium	High	Max	@$#%!

item / meal	*time*	*meds / supplements*	*dose*	*time*	*drinks*
					water
					① ② ③ ④ ⑤ ⑥ ⑦ ⑧ ⑨ ⑩
					caffeine
					① ② ③ ④ ⑤ ⑥ ⑦ ⑧ ⑨ ⑩
					alcohol
					① ② ③ ④ ⑤ ⑥ ⑦ ⑧ ⑨ ⑩

HORMONES

☐ Menstruating ☐ Menopause
☐ PMS ☐ N/A | other

COMPUTER / MOBILE DEVICE / TV

☐ None ☐ Some ☐ A lot Total Time: ______
☐ Sitting ☐ Standing ☐ Mixture Breaks every: ______

PHYSICAL ACTIVITY

☐ None ☐ Minimal ☐ Some ☐ Sweatin' ☐ I'm beat DETAILS: ______________

RELIEF MEASURES

☐ Medication ☐ Massage ☐ Sleep ☐ Exercise ☐ Water ☐ Cold/Ice
☐ Heat/Bath ☐ Other: ______________________________
Did it work? ☐ Nope ☐ A bit ☐ Mostly ☐ 100%

Notes ☐ *See back notes*

START:		END:		DURATION:		DATE		*Entry #139*

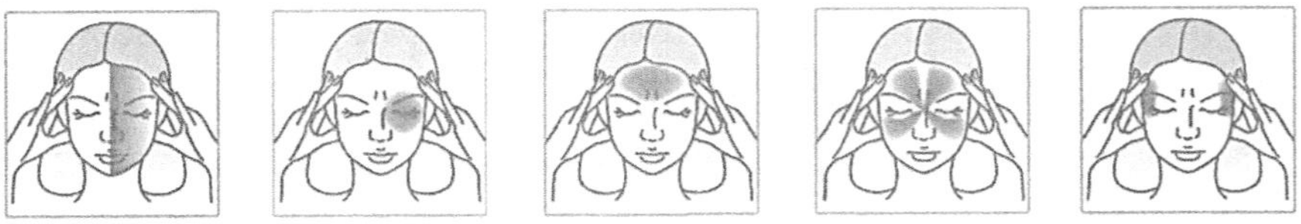

MIGRAINE | CLUSTER | TENSION | SINUS | TMJ

HOW WOULD YOU RATE...?

Mood	①	②	③	④	⑤
Energy	①	②	③	④	⑤
Mental clarity	①	②	③	④	⑤

PAIN LEVEL

1	2	3	4	5	6	7	8	9	10

Not too bad. *Well, I'm not enjoying this.* *Make it stop!*

ONSET

☐ Slow ☐ Average
☐ Rapid ☐ Sudden

DETAILED DESCRIPTION

☐ Constant ☐ Squeezing ☐ Throbbing ☐ Pounding ☐ Dull aching ☐ Burning
☐ Sharp ☐ Debilitating ☐ Other: ____________

WHERE DOES IT HURT, EXACTLY?

OTHER SYMPTOMS

☐ Lightheaded ☐ Dizziness
☐ Light sensitivity ☐ Sound sensitivity
☐ Confusion ☐ Auras
☐ Muscle stiffness ☐ Muscle aches

FEELING SICK?

☐ Nausea ☐ Diarrhea ☐ Vomiting ☐ Sore throat ☐ Congestion ☐ Coughing
☐ Chills ☐ Fever ☐ Other: ____________

SLEEP

hours ________ *quality* ① ② ③ ④ ⑤

WEATHER

☐ Cold ☐ Mild ☐ Hot Allergen levels: ____________
☐ Dry ☐ Humid ☐ Wet BM Pressure: ____________

STRESS LEVELS

None	Low	Medium	High	Max	@$#%!

item / meal	*time*	*meds / supplements*	*dose*	*time*	*drinks*
					water
					① ② ③ ④ ⑤ ⑥ ⑦ ⑧ ⑨ ⑩
					caffeine
					① ② ③ ④ ⑤ ⑥ ⑦ ⑧ ⑨ ⑩
					alcohol
					① ② ③ ④ ⑤ ⑥ ⑦ ⑧ ⑨ ⑩

HORMONES

☐ Menstruating ☐ Menopause
☐ PMS ☐ N/A | other

COMPUTER / MOBILE DEVICE / TV

☐ None ☐ Some ☐ A lot Total Time: ______
☐ Sitting ☐ Standing ☐ Mixture Breaks every: ______

PHYSICAL ACTIVITY

☐ None ☐ Minimal ☐ Some ☐ Sweatin' ☐ I'm beat DETAILS: ____________

RELIEF MEASURES

☐ Medication ☐ Massage ☐ Sleep ☐ Exercise ☐ Water ☐ Cold/Ice
☐ Heat/Bath ☐ Other: ____________

Did it work? ☐ Nope ☐ A bit ☐ Mostly ☐ 100%

Notes ☐ *See back notes*

START:		END:		DURATION:		DATE		*Entry #140*

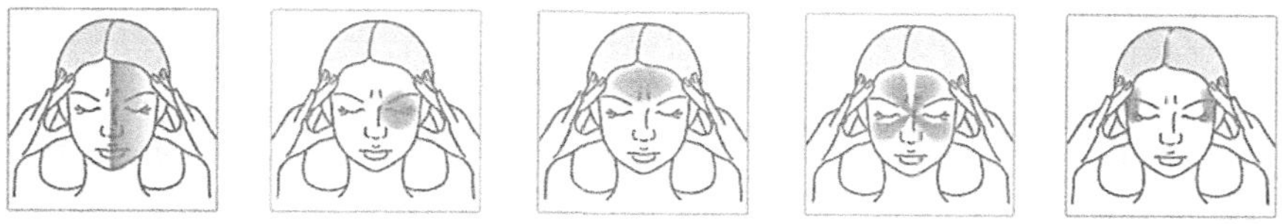

MIGRAINE CLUSTER TENSION SINUS TMJ

HOW WOULD YOU RATE...?

Mood	1	2	3	4	5
Energy	1	2	3	4	5
Mental clarity	1	2	3	4	5

PAIN LEVEL

1	2	3	4	5	6	7	8	9	10

Not too bad. *Well, I'm not enjoying this.* *Make it stop!*

ONSET

☐ Slow ☐ Average
☐ Rapid ☐ Sudden

DETAILED DESCRIPTION

☐ Constant ☐ Squeezing ☐ Throbbing ☐ Pounding ☐ Dull aching ☐ Burning
☐ Sharp ☐ Debilitating ☐ Other: ____________________

WHERE DOES IT HURT, EXACTLY?

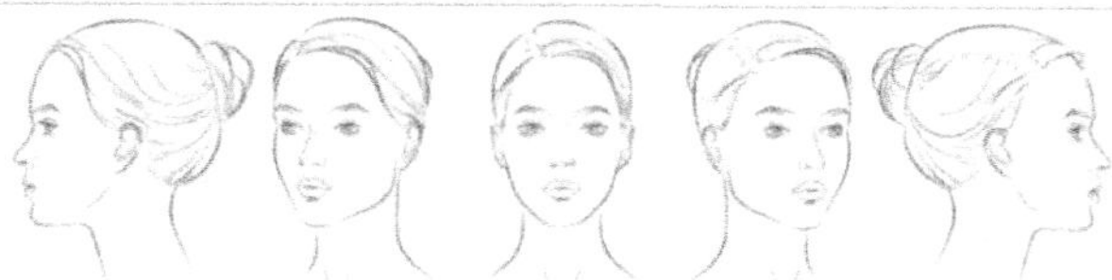

OTHER SYMPTOMS

☐ Lightheaded ☐ Dizziness
☐ Light sensitivity ☐ Sound sensitivity
☐ Confusion ☐ Auras
☐ Muscle stiffness ☐ Muscle aches

FEELING SICK?

☐ Nausea ☐ Diarrhea ☐ Vomiting ☐ Sore throat ☐ Congestion ☐ Coughing
☐ Chills ☐ Fever ☐ Other: ____________________

SLEEP

hours ________ *quality* 1 2 3 4 5

WEATHER

☐ Cold ☐ Mild ☐ Hot Allergen levels: __________
☐ Dry ☐ Humid ☐ Wet BM Pressure: __________

STRESS LEVELS

None	Low	Medium	High	Max	@$#%!

item / meal	*time*	*meds / supplements*	*dose*	*time*	*drinks*
					water: 1 2 3 4 5 6 7 8 9 10
					caffeine: 1 2 3 4 5 6 7 8 9 10
					alcohol: 1 2 3 4 5 6 7 8 9 10

HORMONES

☐ Menstruating ☐ Menopause
☐ PMS ☐ N/A | other

COMPUTER / MOBILE DEVICE / TV

☐ None ☐ Some ☐ A lot Total Time: ______
☐ Sitting ☐ Standing ☐ Mixture Breaks every: ______

PHYSICAL ACTIVITY

☐ None ☐ Minimal ☐ Some ☐ Sweatin' ☐ I'm beat DETAILS: ____________________

RELIEF MEASURES

☐ Medication ☐ Massage ☐ Sleep ☐ Exercise ☐ Water ☐ Cold/Ice
☐ Heat/Bath ☐ Other: ____________________
Did it work? ☐ Nope ☐ A bit ☐ Mostly ☐ 100%

Notes ☐ *See back notes*

START: | END: | DURATION: | DATE | *Entry #141*

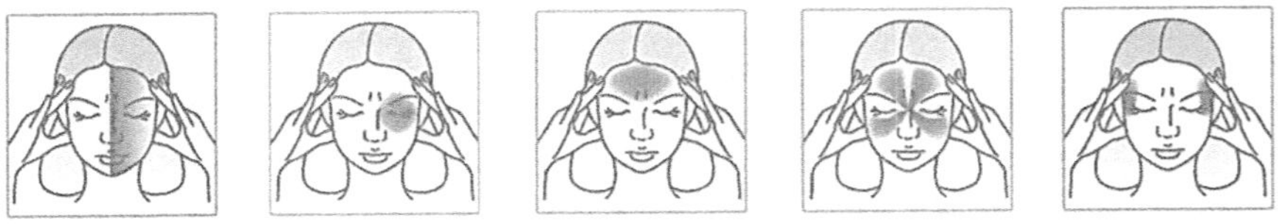

MIGRAINE | CLUSTER | TENSION | SINUS | TMJ

HOW WOULD YOU RATE...?

Mood	① ② ③ ④ ⑤
Energy	① ② ③ ④ ⑤
Mental clarity	① ② ③ ④ ⑤

PAIN LEVEL

1	2	3	4	5	6	7	8	9	10

Not too bad. *Well, I'm not enjoying this.* *Make it stop!*

ONSET

☐ Slow ☐ Average
☐ Rapid ☐ Sudden

DETAILED DESCRIPTION

☐ Constant ☐ Squeezing ☐ Throbbing ☐ Pounding ☐ Dull aching ☐ Burning
☐ Sharp ☐ Debilitating ☐ Other: ____________

WHERE DOES IT HURT, EXACTLY?

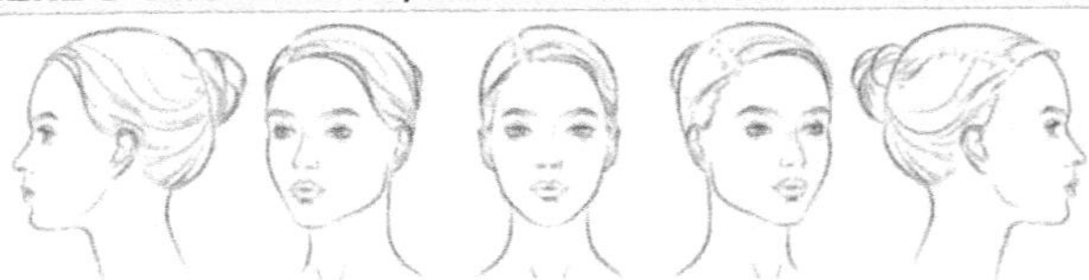

OTHER SYMPTOMS

☐ Lightheaded ☐ Dizziness
☐ Light sensitivity ☐ Sound sensitivity
☐ Confusion ☐ Auras
☐ Muscle stiffness ☐ Muscle aches

FEELING SICK?

☐ Nausea ☐ Diarrhea ☐ Vomiting ☐ Sore throat ☐ Congestion ☐ Coughing
☐ Chills ☐ Fever ☐ Other: ____________

SLEEP

hours ______ *quality* ① ② ③ ④ ⑤

WEATHER

☐ Cold ☐ Mild ☐ Hot Allergen levels: ________
☐ Dry ☐ Humid ☐ Wet BM Pressure: ________

STRESS LEVELS

None	Low	Medium	High	Max	@$#%!

item / meal	*time*	*meds / supplements*	*dose*	*time*	*drinks*
					water ① ② ③ ④ ⑤ ⑥ ⑦ ⑧ ⑨ ⑩
					caffeine ① ② ③ ④ ⑤ ⑥ ⑦ ⑧ ⑨ ⑩
					alcohol ① ② ③ ④ ⑤ ⑥ ⑦ ⑧ ⑨ ⑩

HORMONES

☐ Menstruating ☐ Menopause
☐ PMS ☐ N/A | other

COMPUTER / MOBILE DEVICE / TV

☐ None ☐ Some ☐ A lot Total Time: ______
☐ Sitting ☐ Standing ☐ Mixture Breaks every: ______

PHYSICAL ACTIVITY

☐ None ☐ Minimal ☐ Some ☐ Sweatin' ☐ I'm beat DETAILS: ____________

RELIEF MEASURES

☐ Medication ☐ Massage ☐ Sleep ☐ Exercise ☐ Water ☐ Cold/Ice
☐ Heat/Bath ☐ Other: ____________
Did it work? ☐ Nope ☐ A bit ☐ Mostly ☐ 100%

Notes ☐ *See back notes*

START:		END:		DURATION:		DATE		*Entry #142*

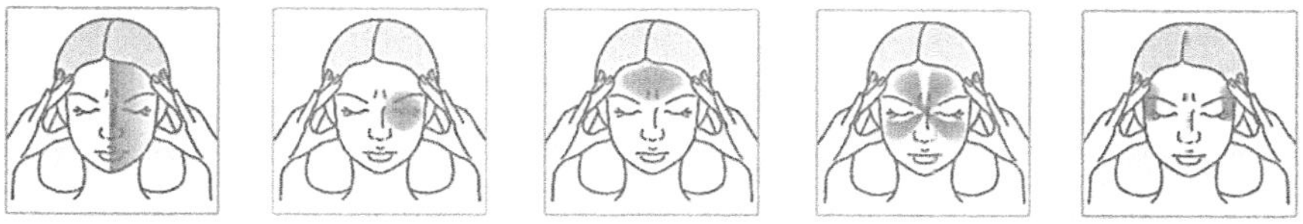

MIGRAINE CLUSTER TENSION SINUS TMJ

HOW WOULD YOU RATE...?

Mood	1	2	3	4	5
Energy	1	2	3	4	5
Mental clarity	1	2	3	4	5

PAIN LEVEL

1	2	3	4	5	6	7	8	9	10

Not too bad. *Well. I'm not enjoying this.* *Make it stop!*

ONSET

☐ Slow ☐ Average
☐ Rapid ☐ Sudden

DETAILED DESCRIPTION

☐ Constant ☐ Squeezing ☐ Throbbing ☐ Pouncing ☐ Dull aching ☐ Burning
☐ Sharp ☐ Debilitating ☐ Other: ____________________

WHERE DOES IT HURT, EXACTLY?

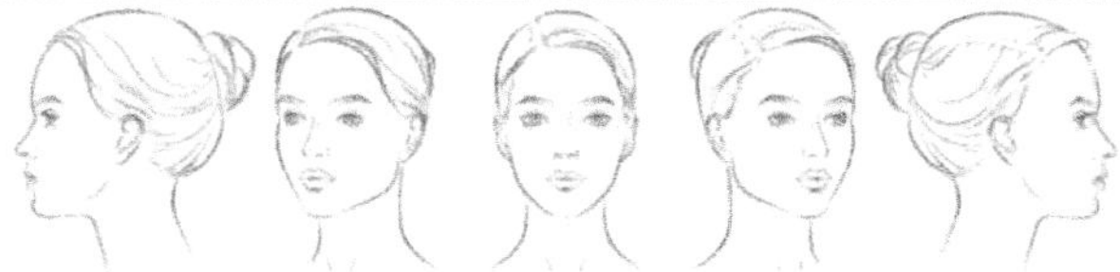

OTHER SYMPTOMS

☐ Lightheaded ☐ Dizziness
☐ Light sensitivity ☐ Sound sensitivity
☐ Confusion ☐ Auras
☐ Muscle stiffness ☐ Muscle aches

FEELING SICK?

☐ Nausea ☐ Diarrhea ☐ Vomiting ☐ Sore throat ☐ Congestion ☐ Coughing
☐ Chills ☐ Fever ☐ Other: ____________________

SLEEP

hours ________ *quality* 1 2 3 4 5

WEATHER

☐ Cold ☐ Mild ☐ Hot Allergen levels: ____________
☐ Dry ☐ Humid ☐ Wet BM Pressure: ____________

STRESS LEVELS

None	Low	Medium	High	Max	@$#%!

item / meal	*time*	*meds / supplements*	*dose*	*time*	*drinks*
					water 1 2 3 4 5 6 7 8 9 10
					caffeine 1 2 3 4 5 6 7 8 9 10
					alcohol 1 2 3 4 5 6 7 8 9 10

HORMONES

☐ Menstruating ☐ Menopause
☐ PMS ☐ N/A | other

COMPUTER / MOBILE DEVICE / TV

☐ None ☐ Some ☐ A lot Total Time: ______
☐ Sitting ☐ Standing ☐ Mixture Breaks every: ______

PHYSICAL ACTIVITY

☐ None ☐ Minimal ☐ Some ☐ Sweatin' ☐ I'm beat DETAILS: ____________________

RELIEF MEASURES

☐ Medication ☐ Massage ☐ Sleep ☐ Exercise ☐ Water ☐ Cold/Ice
☐ Heat/Bath ☐ Other: ____________________
Did it work? ☐ Nope ☐ A bit ☐ Mostly ☐ 100%

Notes ☐ *See back notes*

START:		END:		DURATION:		DATE		*Entry #143*

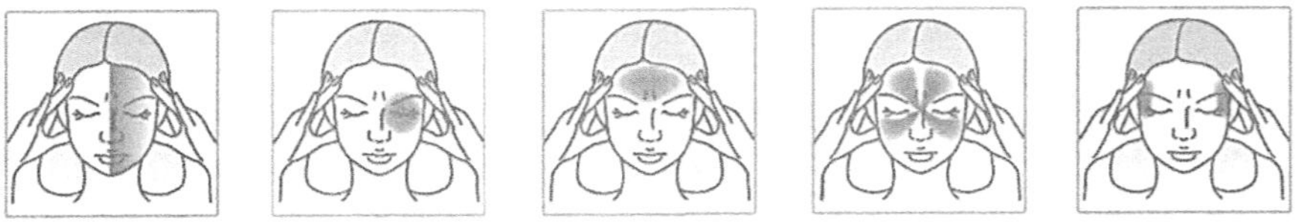

MIGRAINE CLUSTER TENSION SINUS TMJ

HOW WOULD YOU RATE...?

Mood	1	2	3	4	5
Energy	1	2	3	4	5
Mental clarity	1	2	3	4	5

PAIN LEVEL

1	2	3	4	5	6	7	8	9	10

Not too bad. *Well, I'm not enjoying this.* *Make it stop!*

ONSET

☐ Slow ☐ Average
☐ Rapid ☐ Sudden

DETAILED DESCRIPTION

☐ Constant ☐ Squeezing ☐ Throbbing ☐ Pounding ☐ Dull aching ☐ Burning
☐ Sharp ☐ Debilitating ☐ Other: ______

WHERE DOES IT HURT, EXACTLY?

OTHER SYMPTOMS

☐ Lightheaded ☐ Dizziness
☐ Light sensitivity ☐ Sound sensitivity
☐ Confusion ☐ Auras
☐ Muscle stiffness ☐ Muscle aches

FEELING SICK?

☐ Nausea ☐ Diarrhea ☐ Vomiting ☐ Sore throat ☐ Congestion ☐ Coughing
☐ Chills ☐ Fever ☐ Other: ______

SLEEP

hours ______ *quality* 1 2 3 4 5

WEATHER

☐ Cold ☐ Mild ☐ Hot Allergen levels: ______
☐ Dry ☐ Humid ☐ Wet BM Pressure: ______

STRESS LEVELS

None	Low	Medium	High	Max	@$#%!

item / meal	*time*	*meds / supplements*	*dose*	*time*	*drinks*
					water
					1 2 3 4 5 6 7 8 9 10
					caffeine
					1 2 3 4 5 6 7 8 9 10
					alcohol
					1 2 3 4 5 6 7 8 9 10

HORMONES

☐ Menstruating ☐ Menopause
☐ PMS ☐ N/A | other

COMPUTER / MOBILE DEVICE / TV

☐ None ☐ Some ☐ A lot Total Time: ______
☐ Sitting ☐ Standing ☐ Mixture Breaks every: ______

PHYSICAL ACTIVITY

☐ None ☐ Minimal ☐ Some ☐ Sweatin' ☐ I'm beat DETAILS: ______

RELIEF MEASURES

☐ Medication ☐ Massage ☐ Sleep ☐ Exercise ☐ Water ☐ Cold/Ice
☐ Heat/Bath ☐ Other: ______
Did it work? ☐ Nope ☐ A bit ☐ Mostly ☐ 100%

Notes ☐ *See back notes*

START:		END:		DURATION:		DATE		*Entry #144*

HOW WOULD YOU RATE...?					
Mood	1	2	3	4	5
Energy	1	2	3	4	5
Mental clarity	1	2	3	4	5

PAIN LEVEL

1	2	3	4	5	6	7	8	9	10

Not too bad. *Well, I'm not enjoying this.* *Make it stop!*

ONSET

☐ Slow ☐ Average
☐ Rapid ☐ Sudden

DETAILED DESCRIPTION

☐ Constant ☐ Squeezing ☐ Throbbing ☐ Pounding ☐ Dull aching ☐ Burning
☐ Sharp ☐ Debilitating ☐ Other: ____________

WHERE DOES IT HURT, EXACTLY?

OTHER SYMPTOMS

☐ Lightheaded ☐ Dizziness
☐ Light sensitivity ☐ Sound sensitivity
☐ Confusion ☐ Auras
☐ Muscle stiffness ☐ Muscle aches

FEELING SICK?

☐ Nausea ☐ Diarrhea ☐ Vomiting ☐ Sore throat ☐ Congestion ☐ Coughing
☐ Chills ☐ Fever ☐ Other: ____________

SLEEP

hours ________ *quality* 1 2 3 4 5

WEATHER

☐ Cold ☐ Mild ☐ Hot Allergen levels: ________
☐ Dry ☐ Humid ☐ Wet BM Pressure: ________

STRESS LEVELS

None	Low	Medium	High	Max	@$#%!

item / meal	*time*	*meds / supplements*	*dose*	*time*	*drinks*
					water
					1 2 3 4 5 6 7 8 9 10
					caffeine
					1 2 3 4 5 6 7 8 9 10
					alcohol
					1 2 3 4 5 6 7 8 9 10

HORMONES

☐ Menstruating ☐ Menopause
☐ PMS ☐ N/A | other

COMPUTER / MOBILE DEVICE / TV

☐ None ☐ Some ☐ A lot Total Time: ______
☐ Sitting ☐ Standing ☐ Mixture Breaks every: ______

PHYSICAL ACTIVITY

☐ None ☐ Minimal ☐ Some ☐ Sweatin' ☐ I'm beat DETAILS: ____________

RELIEF MEASURES

☐ Medication ☐ Massage ☐ Sleep ☐ Exercise ☐ Water ☐ Cold/Ice
☐ Heat/Bath ☐ Other: ____________
Did it work? ☐ Nope ☐ A bit ☐ Mostly ☐ 100%

Notes ☐ *See back notes*

START:		END:		DURATION:		DATE		*Entry #145*

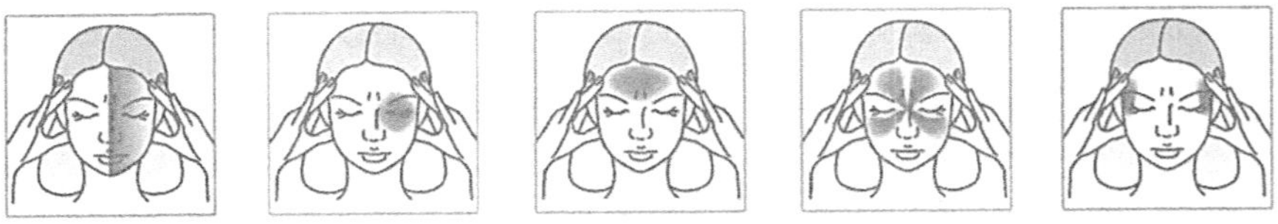

MIGRAINE | CLUSTER | TENSION | SINUS | TMJ

HOW WOULD YOU RATE...?

Mood	①	②	③	④	⑤
Energy	①	②	③	④	⑤
Mental clarity	①	②	③	④	⑤

PAIN LEVEL

1	2	3	4	5	6	7	8	9	10

Not too bad. *Well, I'm not enjoying this.* *Make it stop!*

ONSET

☐ Slow ☐ Average
☐ Rapid ☐ Sudden

DETAILED DESCRIPTION

☐ Constant ☐ Squeezing ☐ Throbbing ☐ Pounding ☐ Dull aching ☐ Burning
☐ Sharp ☐ Debilitating ☐ Other: ______________________________

WHERE DOES IT HURT, EXACTLY?

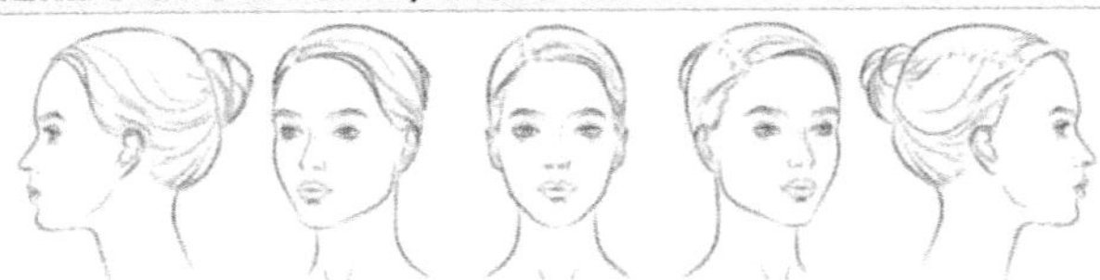

OTHER SYMPTOMS

☐ Lightheaded ☐ Dizziness
☐ Light sensitivity ☐ Sound sensitivity
☐ Confusion ☐ Auras
☐ Muscle stiffness ☐ Muscle aches

FEELING SICK?

☐ Nausea ☐ Diarrhea ☐ Vomiting ☐ Sore throat ☐ Congestion ☐ Coughing
☐ Chills ☐ Fever ☐ Other: ______________________________

SLEEP

hours ________ *quality* ① ② ③ ④ ⑤

WEATHER

☐ Cold ☐ Mild ☐ Hot Allergen levels: ____________
☐ Dry ☐ Humid ☐ Wet BM Pressure: ____________

STRESS LEVELS

None	Low	Medium	High	Max	@$#%!

item / meal	*time*	*meds / supplements*	*dose*	*time*	*drinks*
					water
					① ② ③ ④ ⑤ ⑥ ⑦ ⑧ ⑨ ⑩
					caffeine
					① ② ③ ④ ⑤ ⑥ ⑦ ⑧ ⑨ ⑩
					alcohol
					① ② ③ ④ ⑤ ⑥ ⑦ ⑧ ⑨ ⑩

HORMONES

☐ Menstruating ☐ Menopause
☐ PMS ☐ N/A | other

COMPUTER / MOBILE DEVICE / TV

☐ None ☐ Some ☐ A lot Total Time: ______
☐ Sitting ☐ Standing ☐ Mixture Breaks every: ______

PHYSICAL ACTIVITY

☐ None ☐ Minimal ☐ Some ☐ Sweatin' ☐ I'm beat DETAILS: ____________________

RELIEF MEASURES

☐ Medication ☐ Massage ☐ Sleep ☐ Exercise ☐ Water ☐ Cold/Ice
☐ Heat/Bath ☐ Other: ______________________________
Did it work? ☐ Nope ☐ A bit ☐ Mostly ☐ 100%

Notes ☐ *See back notes*

START:		END:		DURATION:		DATE		*Entry #146*

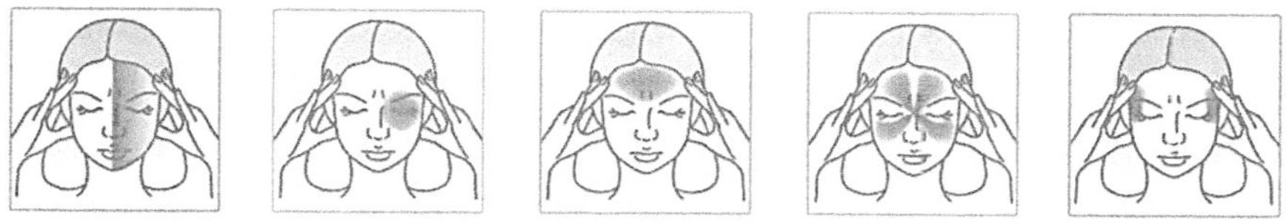

MIGRAINE	CLUSTER	TENSION	SINUS	TMJ

HOW WOULD YOU RATE...?

Mood	1	2	3	4	5
Energy	1	2	3	4	5
Mental clarity	1	2	3	4	5

PAIN LEVEL

1	2	3	4	5	6	7	8	9	10

Not too bad. *Well, I'm not enjoying this.* *Make it stop!*

ONSET

☐ Slow ☐ Average
☐ Rapid ☐ Sudden

DETAILED DESCRIPTION

☐ Constant ☐ Squeezing ☐ Throbbing ☐ Pounding ☐ Dull aching ☐ Burning
☐ Sharp ☐ Debilitating ☐ Other: ____________________

WHERE DOES IT HURT, EXACTLY?

OTHER SYMPTOMS

☐ Lightheaded ☐ Dizziness
☐ Light sensitivity ☐ Sound sensitivity
☐ Confusion ☐ Auras
☐ Muscle stiffness ☐ Muscle aches

FEELING SICK?

☐ Nausea ☐ Diarrhea ☐ Vomiting ☐ Sore throat ☐ Congestion ☐ Coughing
☐ Chills ☐ Fever ☐ Other: ____________________

SLEEP

hours ________ *quality* 1 2 3 4 5

WEATHER

☐ Cold ☐ Mild ☐ Hot Allergen levels: __________
☐ Dry ☐ Humid ☐ Wet BM Pressure: __________

STRESS LEVELS

None	Low	Medium	High	Max	@$#%!

item / meal	*time*	*meds / supplements*	*dose*	*time*	*drinks*
					water: 1 2 3 4 5 6 7 8 9 10
					caffeine: 1 2 3 4 5 6 7 8 9 10
					alcohol: 1 2 3 4 5 6 7 8 9 10

HORMONES

☐ Menstruating ☐ Menopause
☐ PMS ☐ N/A | other

COMPUTER / MOBILE DEVICE / TV

☐ None ☐ Some ☐ A lot Total Time: _____
☐ Sitting ☐ Standing ☐ Mixture Breaks every: _____

PHYSICAL ACTIVITY

☐ None ☐ Minimal ☐ Some ☐ Sweatin' ☐ I'm beat DETAILS: ____________________

RELIEF MEASURES

☐ Medication ☐ Massage ☐ Sleep ☐ Exercise ☐ Water ☐ Cold/Ice
☐ Heat/Bath ☐ Other: ____________________
Did it work? ☐ Nope ☐ A bit ☐ Mostly ☐ 100%

Notes ☐ *See back notes*

START: ____ END: ____ DURATION: ____ DATE ____ *Entry #147*

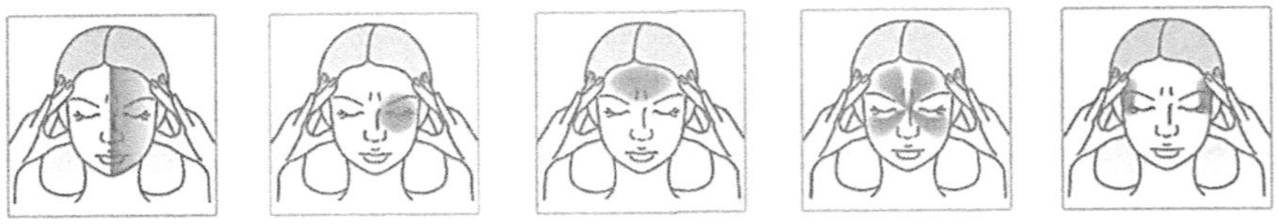

MIGRAINE | CLUSTER | TENSION | SINUS | TMJ

HOW WOULD YOU RATE...?

Mood	①	②	③	④	⑤
Energy	①	②	③	④	⑤
Mental clarity	①	②	③	④	⑤

PAIN LEVEL

1	2	3	4	5	6	7	8	9	10

Not too bad. *Well, I'm not enjoying this.* *Make it stop!*

ONSET

☐ Slow ☐ Average
☐ Rapid ☐ Sudden

DETAILED DESCRIPTION

☐ Constant ☐ Squeezing ☐ Throbbing ☐ Pounding ☐ Dull aching ☐ Burning
☐ Sharp ☐ Debilitating ☐ Other: ____

WHERE DOES IT HURT, EXACTLY?

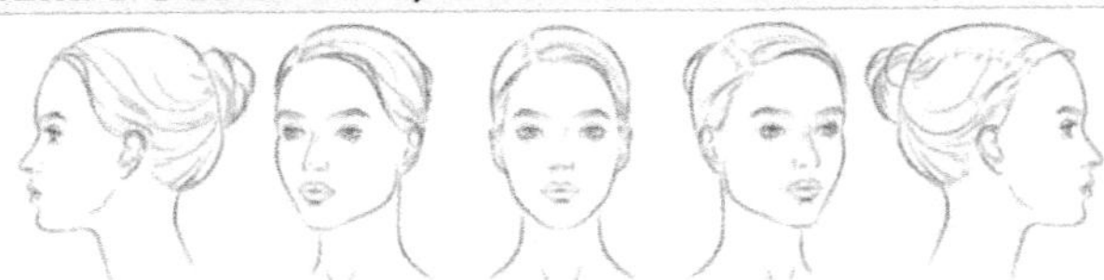

OTHER SYMPTOMS

☐ Lightheaded ☐ Dizziness
☐ Light sensitivity ☐ Sound sensitivity
☐ Confusion ☐ Auras
☐ Muscle stiffness ☐ Muscle aches

FEELING SICK?

☐ Nausea ☐ Diarrhea ☐ Vomiting ☐ Sore throat ☐ Congestion ☐ Coughing
☐ Chills ☐ Fever ☐ Other: ____

SLEEP

hours ____ *quality* ① ② ③ ④ ⑤

WEATHER

☐ Cold ☐ Mild ☐ Hot Allergen levels: ____
☐ Dry ☐ Humid ☐ Wet BM Pressure: ____

STRESS LEVELS

None	Low	Medium	High	Max	@$#%!

item / meal	*time*	*meds / supplements*	*dose*	*time*	*drinks*
					water
					① ② ③ ④ ⑤ ⑥ ⑦ ⑧ ⑨ ⑩
					caffeine
					① ② ③ ④ ⑤ ⑥ ⑦ ⑧ ⑨ ⑩
					alcohol
					① ② ③ ④ ⑤ ⑥ ⑦ ⑧ ⑨ ⑩

HORMONES

☐ Menstruating ☐ Menopause
☐ PMS ☐ N/A | other

COMPUTER / MOBILE DEVICE / TV

☐ None ☐ Some ☐ A lot Total Time: ____
☐ Sitting ☐ Standing ☐ Mixture Breaks every: ____

PHYSICAL ACTIVITY

☐ None ☐ Minimal ☐ Some ☐ Sweatin' ☐ I'm beat DETAILS: ____

RELIEF MEASURES

☐ Medication ☐ Massage ☐ Sleep ☐ Exercise ☐ Water ☐ Cold/Ice
☐ Heat/Bath ☐ Other: ____
Did it work? ☐ Nope ☐ A bit ☐ Mostly ☐ 100%

Notes ☐ *See back notes*

START:		END:		DURATION:		DATE		*Entry #148*

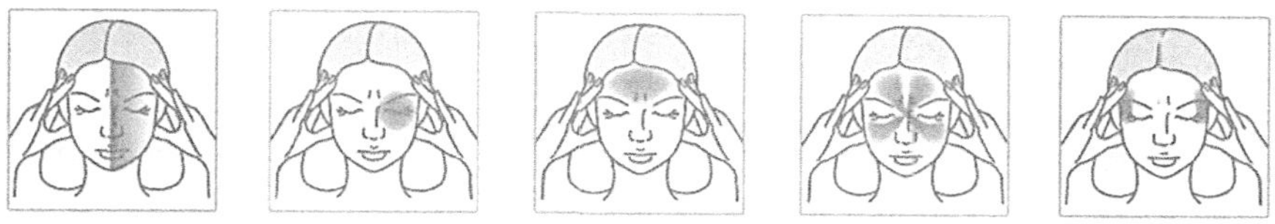

MIGRAINE	CLUSTER	TENSION	SINUS	TMJ

HOW WOULD YOU RATE...?

Mood	1	2	3	4	5
Energy	1	2	3	4	5
Mental clarity	1	2	3	4	5

PAIN LEVEL

1	2	3	4	5	6	7	8	9	10

Not too bad. *Well, I'm not enjoying this.* *Make it stop!*

ONSET

☐ Slow ☐ Average
☐ Rapid ☐ Sudden

DETAILED DESCRIPTION

☐ Constant ☐ Squeezing ☐ Throbbing ☐ Pounding ☐ Dull aching ☐ Burning
☐ Sharp ☐ Debilitating ☐ Other: ______________________________

WHERE DOES IT HURT, EXACTLY?

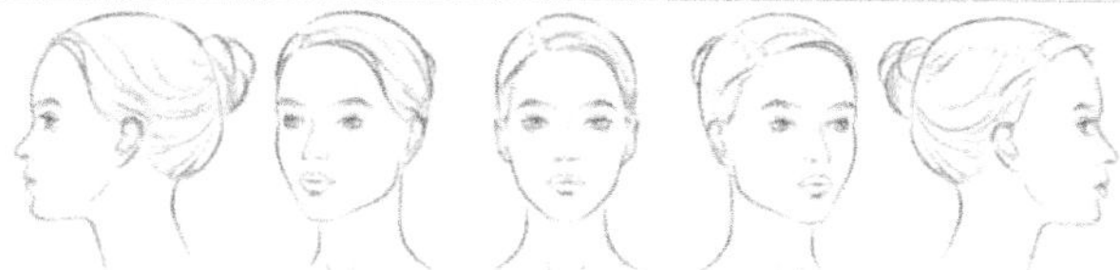

OTHER SYMPTOMS

☐ Lightheaded ☐ Dizziness
☐ Light sensitivity ☐ Sound sensitivity
☐ Confusion ☐ Auras
☐ Muscle stiffness ☐ Muscle aches

FEELING SICK?

☐ Nausea ☐ Diarrhea ☐ Vomiting ☐ Sore throat ☐ Congestion ☐ Coughing
☐ Chills ☐ Fever ☐ Other: ______________________________

SLEEP

hours ________ *quality* 1 2 3 4 5

WEATHER

☐ Cold ☐ Mild ☐ Hot Allergen levels: ____________
☐ Dry ☐ Humid ☐ Wet BM Pressure: ____________

STRESS LEVELS

None	Low	Medium	High	Max	@$#%!

item / meal	*time*	*meds / supplements*	*dose*	*time*	*drinks*
					water
					1 2 3 4 5 6 7 8 9 10
					caffeine
					1 2 3 4 5 6 7 8 9 10
					alcohol
					1 2 3 4 5 6 7 8 9 10

HORMONES

☐ Menstruating ☐ Menopause
☐ PMS ☐ N/A | other

COMPUTER / MOBILE DEVICE / TV

☐ None ☐ Some ☐ A lot Total Time: ______
☐ Sitting ☐ Standing ☐ Mixture Breaks every: ______

PHYSICAL ACTIVITY

☐ None ☐ Minimal ☐ Some ☐ Sweatin' ☐ I'm beat DETAILS: ______________

RELIEF MEASURES

☐ Medication ☐ Massage ☐ Sleep ☐ Exercise ☐ Water ☐ Cold/Ice
☐ Heat/Bath ☐ Other: ______________________________
Did it work? ☐ Nope ☐ A bit ☐ Mostly ☐ 100%

Notes ☐ *See back notes*

START:		END:		DURATION:		DATE		*Entry #149*

MIGRAINE | CLUSTER | TENSION | SINUS | TMJ

HOW WOULD YOU RATE...?

Mood	①	②	③	④	⑤
Energy	①	②	③	④	⑤
Mental clarity	①	②	③	④	⑤

PAIN LEVEL

1	2	3	4	5	6	7	8	9	10

Not too bad. *Well, I'm not enjoying this.* *Make it stop!*

ONSET

☐ Slow ☐ Average
☐ Rapid ☐ Sudden

DETAILED DESCRIPTION

☐ Constant ☐ Squeezing ☐ Throbbing ☐ Pounding ☐ Dull aching ☐ Burning
☐ Sharp ☐ Debilitating ☐ Other: ____________________

WHERE DOES IT HURT, EXACTLY?

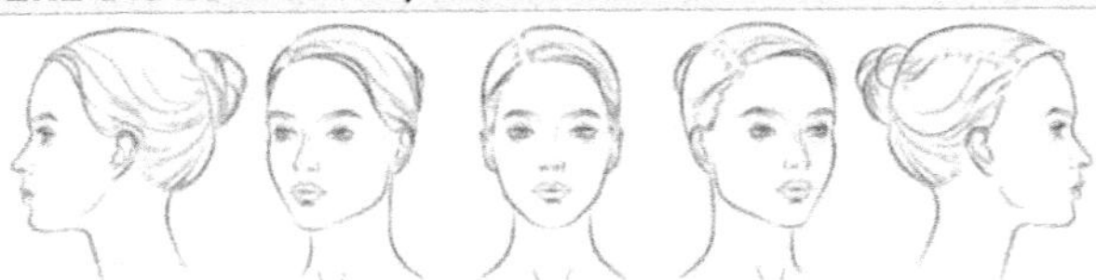

OTHER SYMPTOMS

☐ Lightheaded ☐ Dizziness
☐ Light sensitivity ☐ Sound sensitivity
☐ Confusion ☐ Auras
☐ Muscle stiffness ☐ Muscle aches

FEELING SICK?

☐ Nausea ☐ Diarrhea ☐ Vomiting ☐ Sore throat ☐ Congestion ☐ Coughing
☐ Chills ☐ Fever ☐ Other: ____________________

SLEEP

hours _______ *quality* ① ② ③ ④ ⑤

WEATHER

☐ Cold ☐ Mild ☐ Hot Allergen levels: ____________
☐ Dry ☐ Humid ☐ Wet BM Pressure: ____________

STRESS LEVELS

None	Low	Medium	High	Max	@$#%!

item / meal	*time*	*meds / supplements*	*dose*	*time*	*drinks*
					water
					① ② ③ ④ ⑤ ⑥ ⑦ ⑧ ⑨ ⑩
					caffeine
					① ② ③ ④ ⑤ ⑥ ⑦ ⑧ ⑨ ⑩
					alcohol
					① ② ③ ④ ⑤ ⑥ ⑦ ⑧ ⑨ ⑩

HORMONES

☐ Menstruating ☐ Menopause
☐ PMS ☐ N/A | other

COMPUTER / MOBILE DEVICE / TV

☐ None ☐ Some ☐ A lot Total Time: _____
☐ Sitting ☐ Standing ☐ Mixture Breaks every: _____

PHYSICAL ACTIVITY

☐ None ☐ Minimal ☐ Some ☐ Sweatin' ☐ I'm beat DETAILS: ____________________

RELIEF MEASURES

☐ Medication ☐ Massage ☐ Sleep ☐ Exercise ☐ Water ☐ Cold/Ice
☐ Heat/Bath ☐ Other: ____________________
Did it work? ☐ Nope ☐ A bit ☐ Mostly ☐ 100%

Notes ☐ *See back notes*

START:	END:	DURATION:	DATE	*Entry #150*

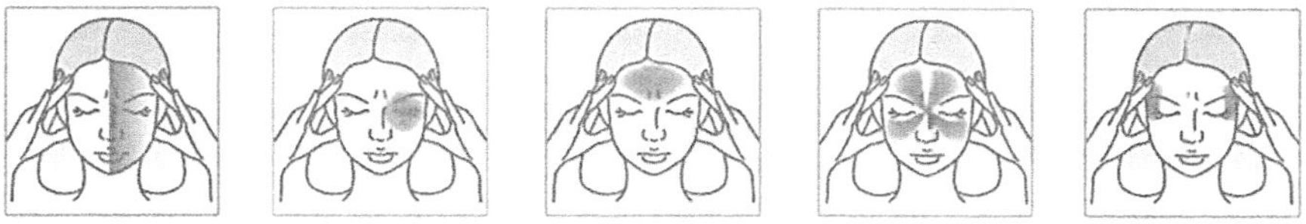

MIGRAINE　CLUSTER　TENSION　SINUS　TMJ

HOW WOULD YOU RATE...?	
Mood	① ② ③ ④ ⑤
Energy	① ② ③ ④ ⑤
Mental clarity	① ② ③ ④ ⑤

PAIN LEVEL

1	2	3	4	5	6	7	8	9	10

Not too bad.　*Well, I'm not enjoying this.*　*Make it stop!*

ONSET

☐ Slow　☐ Average
☐ Rapid　☐ Sudden

DETAILED DESCRIPTION

☐ Constant　☐ Squeezing　☐ Throbbing　☐ Pounding　☐ Dull aching　☐ Burning
☐ Sharp　☐ Debilitating　☐ Other: ______________________________

WHERE DOES IT HURT, EXACTLY?

OTHER SYMPTOMS

☐ Lightheaded　☐ Dizziness
☐ Light sensitivity　☐ Sound sensitivity
☐ Confusion　☐ Auras
☐ Muscle stiffness　☐ Muscle aches

FEELING SICK?

☐ Nausea　☐ Diarrhea　☐ Vomiting　☐ Sore throat　☐ Congestion　☐ Coughing
☐ Chills　☐ Fever　☐ Other: ______________________________

SLEEP

hours ________　*quality* ① ② ③ ④ ⑤

WEATHER

☐ Cold　☐ Mild　☐ Hot　Allergen levels: ____________
☐ Dry　☐ Humid　☐ Wet　BM Pressure: ____________

STRESS LEVELS

None	Low	Medium	High	Max	@$#%!

item / meal	*time*	*meds / supplements*	*dose*	*time*	*drinks*
					water: ① ② ③ ④ ⑤ ⑥ ⑦ ⑧ ⑨ ⑩
					caffeine: ① ② ③ ④ ⑤ ⑥ ⑦ ⑧ ⑨ ⑩
					alcohol: ① ② ③ ④ ⑤ ⑥ ⑦ ⑧ ⑨ ⑩

HORMONES

☐ Menstruating　☐ Menopause
☐ PMS　☐ N/A | other

COMPUTER / MOBILE DEVICE / TV

☐ None　☐ Some　☐ A lot　Total Time: ______
☐ Sitting　☐ Standing　☐ Mixture　Breaks every: ______

PHYSICAL ACTIVITY

☐ None　☐ Minimal　☐ Some　☐ Sweatin'　☐ I'm beat　DETAILS: ______________________

RELIEF MEASURES

☐ Medication　☐ Massage　☐ Sleep　☐ Exercise　☐ Water　☐ Cold/Ice
☐ Heat/Bath　☐ Other: ______________________________
Did it work?　☐ Nope　☐ A bit　☐ Mostly　☐ 100%

Notes　☐ *See back notes*

START: | END: | DURATION: | DATE | *Entry #151*

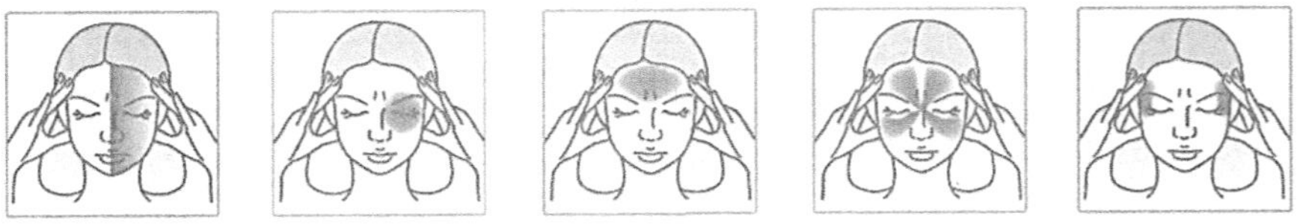

HOW WOULD YOU RATE...?

Mood	①	②	③	④	⑤
Energy	①	②	③	④	⑤
Mental clarity	①	②	③	④	⑤

PAIN LEVEL

1	2	3	4	5	6	7	8	9	10

Not too bad. *Well, I'm not enjoying this.* *Make it stop!*

ONSET

☐ Slow ☐ Average
☐ Rapid ☐ Sudden

DETAILED DESCRIPTION

☐ Constant ☐ Squeezing ☐ Throbbing ☐ Pounding ☐ Dull aching ☐ Burning
☐ Sharp ☐ Debilitating ☐ Other: ____________

WHERE DOES IT HURT, EXACTLY?

OTHER SYMPTOMS

☐ Lightheaded ☐ Dizziness
☐ Light sensitivity ☐ Sound sensitivity
☐ Confusion ☐ Auras
☐ Muscle stiffness ☐ Muscle aches

FEELING SICK?

☐ Nausea ☐ Diarrhea ☐ Vomiting ☐ Sore throat ☐ Congestion ☐ Coughing
☐ Chills ☐ Fever ☐ Other: ____________

SLEEP

hours ________ *quality* ① ② ③ ④ ⑤

WEATHER

☐ Cold ☐ Mild ☐ Hot Allergen levels: ________
☐ Dry ☐ Humid ☐ Wet BM Pressure: ________

STRESS LEVELS

None	Low	Medium	High	Max	@$#%!

item / meal	*time*	*meds / supplements*	*dose*	*time*	*drinks*
					water
					① ② ③ ④ ⑤ ⑥ ⑦ ⑧ ⑨ ⑩
					caffeine
					① ② ③ ④ ⑤ ⑥ ⑦ ⑧ ⑨ ⑩
					alcohol
					① ② ③ ④ ⑤ ⑥ ⑦ ⑧ ⑨ ⑩

HORMONES

☐ Menstruating ☐ Menopause
☐ PMS ☐ N/A | other

COMPUTER / MOBILE DEVICE / TV

☐ None ☐ Some ☐ A lot Total Time: ____
☐ Sitting ☐ Standing ☐ Mixture Breaks every: ____

PHYSICAL ACTIVITY

☐ None ☐ Minimal ☐ Some ☐ Sweatin' ☐ I'm beat DETAILS: ____________

RELIEF MEASURES

☐ Medication ☐ Massage ☐ Sleep ☐ Exercise ☐ Water ☐ Cold/Ice
☐ Heat/Bath ☐ Other: ____________
Did it work? ☐ Nope ☐ A bit ☐ Mostly ☐ 100%

Notes ☐ *See back notes*

START:		END:		DURATION:		DATE		*Entry #152*

HOW WOULD YOU RATE...?

Mood	① ② ③ ④ ⑤
Energy	① ② ③ ④ ⑤
Mental clarity	① ② ③ ④ ⑤

PAIN LEVEL

1	2	3	4	5	6	7	8	9	10

Not too bad. *Well, I'm not enjoying this.* *Make it stop!*

ONSET

☐ Slow ☐ Average
☐ Rapid ☐ Sudden

DETAILED DESCRIPTION

☐ Constant ☐ Squeezing ☐ Throbbing ☐ Pounding ☐ Dull aching ☐ Burning
☐ Sharp ☐ Debilitating ☐ Other: ____________________

WHERE DOES IT HURT, EXACTLY?

OTHER SYMPTOMS

☐ Lightheaded ☐ Dizziness
☐ Light sensitivity ☐ Sound sensitivity
☐ Confusion ☐ Auras
☐ Muscle stiffness ☐ Muscle aches

FEELING SICK?

☐ Nausea ☐ Diarrhea ☐ Vomiting ☐ Sore throat ☐ Congestion ☐ Coughing
☐ Chills ☐ Fever ☐ Other: ____________________

SLEEP

hours ________ *quality* ① ② ③ ④ ⑤

WEATHER

☐ Cold ☐ Mild ☐ Hot Allergen levels: ____________
☐ Dry ☐ Humid ☐ Wet BM Pressure: ____________

STRESS LEVELS

None	Low	Medium	High	Max	@$#%!

item / meal	*time*	*meds / supplements*	*dose*	*time*	*drinks*
					water
					① ② ③ ④ ⑤ ⑥ ⑦ ⑧ ⑨ ⑩
					caffeine
					① ② ③ ④ ⑤ ⑥ ⑦ ⑧ ⑨ ⑩
					alcohol
					① ② ③ ④ ⑤ ⑥ ⑦ ⑧ ⑨ ⑩

HORMONES

☐ Menstruating ☐ Menopause
☐ PMS ☐ N/A | other

COMPUTER / MOBILE DEVICE / TV

☐ None ☐ Some ☐ A lot Total Time: ______
☐ Sitting ☐ Standing ☐ Mixture Breaks every: ______

PHYSICAL ACTIVITY

☐ None ☐ Minimal ☐ Some ☐ Sweatin' ☐ I'm beat DETAILS: ____________

RELIEF MEASURES

☐ Medication ☐ Massage ☐ Sleep ☐ Exercise ☐ Water ☐ Cold/Ice
☐ Heat/Bath ☐ Other: ____________________
Did it work? ☐ Nope ☐ A bit ☐ Mostly ☐ 100%

Notes ☐ *See back notes*

START:		END:		DURATION:		DATE		*Entry #153*

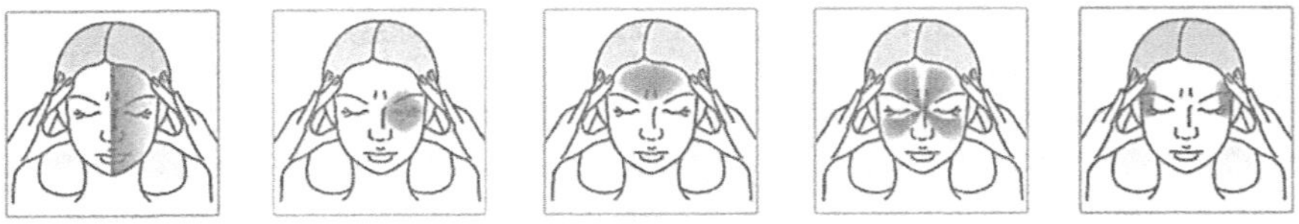

MIGRAINE CLUSTER TENSION SINUS TMJ

HOW WOULD YOU RATE...?

Mood	① ② ③ ④ ⑤
Energy	① ② ③ ④ ⑤
Mental clarity	① ② ③ ④ ⑤

PAIN LEVEL

1	2	3	4	5	6	7	8	9	10

Not too bad. *Well, I'm not enjoying this.* *Make it stop!*

ONSET

☐ Slow ☐ Average
☐ Rapid ☐ Sudden

DETAILED DESCRIPTION

☐ Constant ☐ Squeezing ☐ Throbbing ☐ Pounding ☐ Dull aching ☐ Burning
☐ Sharp ☐ Debilitating ☐ Other: ____________________

WHERE DOES IT HURT, EXACTLY?

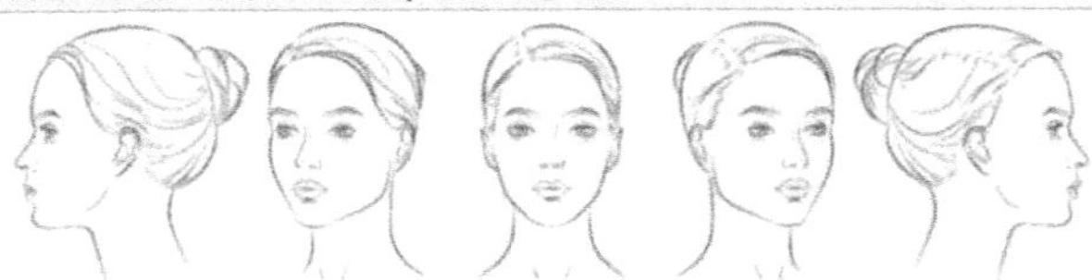

OTHER SYMPTOMS

☐ Lightheaded ☐ Dizziness
☐ Light sensitivity ☐ Sound sensitivity
☐ Confusion ☐ Auras
☐ Muscle stiffness ☐ Muscle aches

FEELING SICK?

☐ Nausea ☐ Diarrhea ☐ Vomiting ☐ Sore throat ☐ Congestion ☐ Coughing
☐ Chills ☐ Fever ☐ Other: ____________________

SLEEP

hours _______ *quality* ① ② ③ ④ ⑤

WEATHER

☐ Cold ☐ Mild ☐ Hot Allergen levels: ____________
☐ Dry ☐ Humid ☐ Wet BM Pressure: ____________

STRESS LEVELS

None	Low	Medium	High	Max	@$#%!

item / meal	*time*	*meds / supplements*	*dose*	*time*	*drinks*
					water
					① ② ③ ④ ⑤ ⑥ ⑦ ⑧ ⑨ ⑩
					caffeine
					① ② ③ ④ ⑤ ⑥ ⑦ ⑧ ⑨ ⑩
					alcohol
					① ② ③ ④ ⑤ ⑥ ⑦ ⑧ ⑨ ⑩

HORMONES

☐ Menstruating ☐ Menopause
☐ PMS ☐ N/A | other

COMPUTER / MOBILE DEVICE / TV

☐ None ☐ Some ☐ A lot Total Time: _____
☐ Sitting ☐ Standing ☐ Mixture Breaks every: _____

PHYSICAL ACTIVITY

☐ None ☐ Minimal ☐ Some ☐ Sweatin' ☐ I'm beat DETAILS: ____________

RELIEF MEASURES

☐ Medication ☐ Massage ☐ Sleep ☐ Exercise ☐ Water ☐ Cold/Ice
☐ Heat/Bath ☐ Other: ____________________
Did it work? ☐ Nope ☐ A bit ☐ Mostly ☐ 100%

Notes ☐ *See back notes*

START:		END:		DURATION:		DATE		*Entry #154*

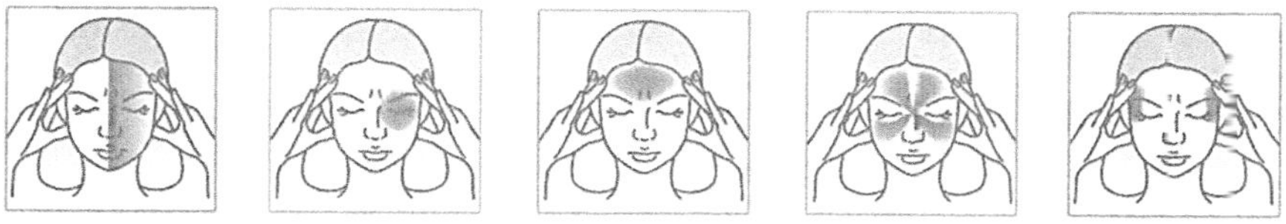

MIGRAINE | CLUSTER | TENSION | SINUS | TMJ

HOW WOULD YOU RATE...?

Mood	①	②	③	④	⑤
Energy	①	②	③	④	⑤
Mental clarity	①	②	③	④	⑤

PAIN LEVEL

1	2	3	4	5	6	7	8	9	10

Not too bad. *Well, I'm not enjoying this.* *Make it stop!*

ONSET

☐ Slow ☐ Average
☐ Rapid ☐ Sudden

DETAILED DESCRIPTION

☐ Constant ☐ Squeezing ☐ Throbbing ☐ Pounding ☐ Dull aching ☐ Burning
☐ Sharp ☐ Debilitating ☐ Other: ____________________

WHERE DOES IT HURT, EXACTLY?

OTHER SYMPTOMS

☐ Lightheaded ☐ Dizziness
☐ Light sensitivity ☐ Sound sensitivity
☐ Confusion ☐ Auras
☐ Muscle stiffness ☐ Muscle aches

FEELING SICK?

☐ Nausea ☐ Diarrhea ☐ Vomiting ☐ Sore throat ☐ Congestion ☐ Coughing
☐ Chills ☐ Fever ☐ Other: ____________________

SLEEP

hours ________ *quality* ① ② ③ ④ ⑤

WEATHER

☐ Cold ☐ Mild ☐ Hot Allergen levels: ____________
☐ Dry ☐ Humid ☐ Wet BM Pressure: ____________

STRESS LEVELS

None	Low	Medium	High	Max	@$#%!

item / meal	*time*	*meds / supplements*	*dose*	*time*	*drinks*
					water
					① ② ③ ④ ⑤ ⑥ ⑦ ⑧ ⑨ ⑩
					caffeine
					① ② ③ ④ ⑤ ⑥ ⑦ ⑧ ⑨ ⑩
					alcohol
					① ② ③ ④ ⑤ ⑥ ⑦ ⑧ ⑨ ⑩

HORMONES

☐ Menstruating ☐ Menopause
☐ PMS ☐ N/A | other

COMPUTER / MOBILE DEVICE / TV

☐ None ☐ Some ☐ A lot Total Time: ______
☐ Sitting ☐ Standing ☐ Mixture Breaks every: ______

PHYSICAL ACTIVITY

☐ None ☐ Minimal ☐ Some ☐ Sweatin' ☐ I'm beat DETAILS: ____________

RELIEF MEASURES

☐ Medication ☐ Massage ☐ Sleep ☐ Exercise ☐ Water ☐ Cold/Ice
☐ Heat/Bath ☐ Other: ____________________
Did it work? ☐ Nope ☐ A bit ☐ Mostly ☐ 100%

Notes ☐ *See back notes*

START:		END:		DURATION:		DATE		*Entry #155*

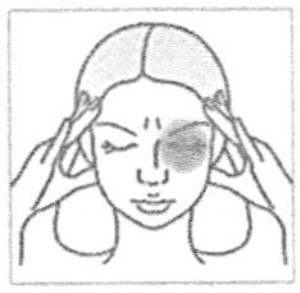
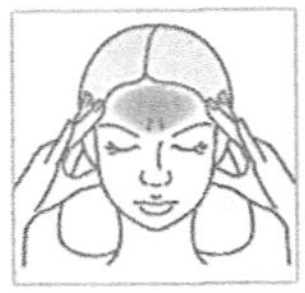

MIGRAINE CLUSTER TENSION SINUS TMJ

HOW WOULD YOU RATE...?

Mood ① ② ③ ④ ⑤
Energy ① ② ③ ④ ⑤
Mental clarity ① ② ③ ④ ⑤

PAIN LEVEL

1	2	3	4	5	6	7	8	9	10

Not too bad. *Well, I'm not enjoying this.* *Make it stop!*

ONSET

☐ Slow ☐ Average
☐ Rapid ☐ Sudden

DETAILED DESCRIPTION

☐ Constant ☐ Squeezing ☐ Throbbing ☐ Pounding ☐ Dull aching ☐ Burning
☐ Sharp ☐ Debilitating ☐ Other: ____________

WHERE DOES IT HURT, EXACTLY?

OTHER SYMPTOMS

☐ Lightheaded ☐ Dizziness
☐ Light sensitivity ☐ Sound sensitivity
☐ Confusion ☐ Auras
☐ Muscle stiffness ☐ Muscle aches

FEELING SICK?

☐ Nausea ☐ Diarrhea ☐ Vomiting ☐ Sore throat ☐ Congestion ☐ Coughing
☐ Chills ☐ Fever ☐ Other: ____________

SLEEP

hours ________ *quality* ① ② ③ ④ ⑤

WEATHER

☐ Cold ☐ Mild ☐ Hot Allergen levels: ________
☐ Dry ☐ Humid ☐ Wet BM Pressure: ________

STRESS LEVELS

None	Low	Medium	High	Max	@$#%!

item / meal	*time*	*meds / supplements*	*dose*	*time*	*drinks*
					water
					① ② ③ ④ ⑤ ⑥ ⑦ ⑧ ⑨ ⑩
					caffeine
					① ② ③ ④ ⑤ ⑥ ⑦ ⑧ ⑨ ⑩
					alcohol
					① ② ③ ④ ⑤ ⑥ ⑦ ⑧ ⑨ ⑩

HORMONES

☐ Menstruating ☐ Menopause
☐ PMS ☐ N/A | other

COMPUTER / MOBILE DEVICE / TV

☐ None ☐ Some ☐ A lot Total Time: ____
☐ Sitting ☐ Standing ☐ Mixture Breaks every: ____

PHYSICAL ACTIVITY

☐ None ☐ Minimal ☐ Some ☐ Sweatin' ☐ I'm beat DETAILS: ____________

RELIEF MEASURES

☐ Medication ☐ Massage ☐ Sleep ☐ Exercise ☐ Water ☐ Cold/Ice
☐ Heat/Bath ☐ Other: ____________
Did it work? ☐ Nope ☐ A bit ☐ Mostly ☐ 100%

Notes ☐ *See back notes*

START: ______ END: ______ DURAT ON: ______ DATE ______ *Entry #156*

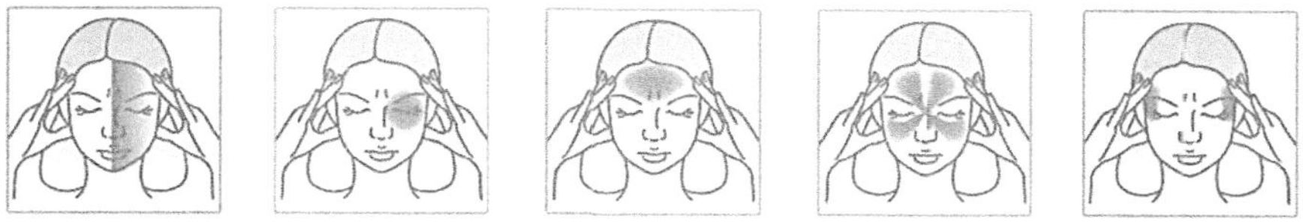

MIGRAINE | CLUSTER | TENSION | SIN JS | TMJ

HOW WOULD YOU RATE...?

Mood	① ② ③ ④ ⑤
Energy	① ② ③ ④ ⑤
Mental clarity	① ② ③ ④ ⑤

PAIN LEVEL

1	2	3	4	5	6	7	8	9	10

Not too bad. *Wel', I'm not enjoying this.* *Make it stop!*

ONSET

☐ Slow ☐ Average
☐ Rapid ☐ Sudden

DETAILED DESCRIPTION

☐ Constant ☐ Squeezing ☐ Throbbing ☐ Pounding ☐ Dull aching ☐ Burning
☐ Sharp ☐ Debilitating ☐ Other: ______________________

WHERE DOES IT HURT, EXACTLY?

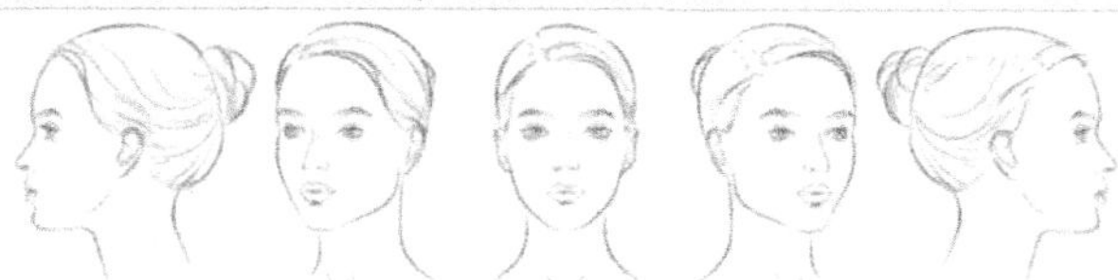

OTHER SYMPTOMS

☐ Lightheaded ☐ Dizziness
☐ Light sensitivity ☐ Sound sensitivity
☐ Conf usion ☐ Auras
☐ Muscle stiffness ☐ Muscle aches

FEELING SICK?

☐ Nausea ☐ Diarrhea ☐ Vomiting ☐ Sore throat ☐ Congestion ☐ Coughing
☐ Chills ☐ Fever ☐ Other: ______________________

SLEEP

hours ______ *quality* ① ② ③ ④ ⑤

WEATHER

☐ Cold ☐ Mild ☐ Hot Allergen levels: ______
☐ Dry ☐ Humid ☐ Wet BM Pressure: ______

STRESS LEVELS

None	Low	Medium	High	Max	@$#%!

item / meal	*time*	*meds / supplements*	*dose*	*time*	*drinks*
					water
					① ② ③ ④ ⑤ ⑥ ⑦ ⑧ ⑨ ⑩
					caffeine
					① ② ③ ④ ⑤ ⑥ ⑦ ⑧ ⑨ ⑩
					alcohol
					① ② ③ ④ ⑤ ⑥ ⑦ ⑧ ⑨ ⑩

HORMONES

☐ Menstruating ☐ Mencpause
☐ PMS ☐ N/A | other

COMPUTER / MOBILE DEVICE / TV

☐ None ☐ Some ☐ A lot Total Time: ______
☐ Sitting ☐ Standing ☐ Mixture Breaks every: ______

PHYSICAL ACTIVITY

☐ None ☐ Minimal ☐ Some ☐ Sweatin' ☐ I'm bea- DETAILS: ______________

RELIEF MEASURES

☐ Medication ☐ Masscge ☐ Sleep ☐ Exercise ☐ Water ☐ Cold/Ice
☐ Heat/Bath ☐ Other: ______________________
Did it work? ☐ Nope ☐ A bit ☐ Mostly ☐ 100%

Notes ☐ *See back notes*

START:		END:		DURATION:		DATE		*Entry #157*

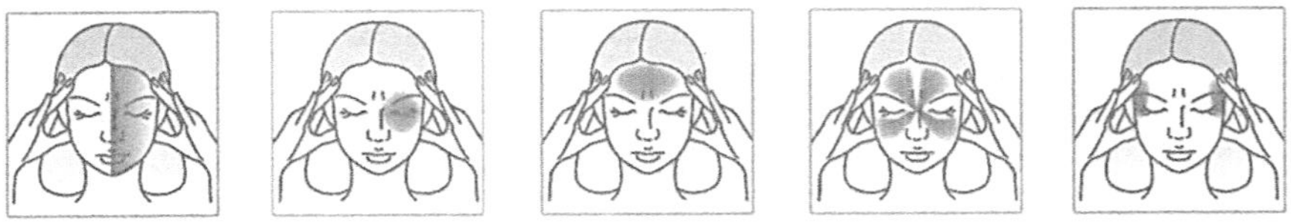

MIGRAINE CLUSTER TENSION SINUS TMJ

HOW WOULD YOU RATE...?

Mood	1	2	3	4	5
Energy	1	2	3	4	5
Mental clarity	1	2	3	4	5

PAIN LEVEL

1	2	3	4	5	6	7	8	9	10

Not too bad. *Well, I'm not enjoying this.* *Make it stop!*

ONSET

☐ Slow ☐ Average
☐ Rapid ☐ Sudden

DETAILED DESCRIPTION

☐ Constant ☐ Squeezing ☐ Throbbing ☐ Pounding ☐ Dull aching ☐ Burning
☐ Sharp ☐ Debilitating ☐ Other: ____________________

WHERE DOES IT HURT, EXACTLY?

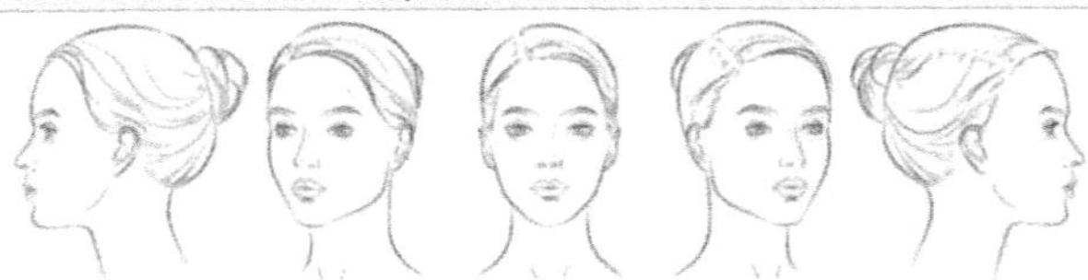

OTHER SYMPTOMS

☐ Lightheaded ☐ Dizziness
☐ Light sensitivity ☐ Sound sensitivity
☐ Confusion ☐ Auras
☐ Muscle stiffness ☐ Muscle aches

FEELING SICK?

☐ Nausea ☐ Diarrhea ☐ Vomiting ☐ Sore throat ☐ Congestion ☐ Coughing
☐ Chills ☐ Fever ☐ Other: ____________________

SLEEP

hours ________ *quality* 1 2 3 4 5

WEATHER

☐ Cold ☐ Mild ☐ Hot Allergen levels: ____________
☐ Dry ☐ Humid ☐ Wet BM Pressure: ____________

STRESS LEVELS

None	Low	Medium	High	Max	@$#%!

item / meal	*time*	*meds / supplements*	*dose*	*time*	*drinks*
					water
					1 2 3 4 5 6 7 8 9 10
					caffeine
					1 2 3 4 5 6 7 8 9 10
					alcohol
					1 2 3 4 5 6 7 8 9 10

HORMONES

☐ Menstruating ☐ Menopause
☐ PMS ☐ N/A | other

COMPUTER / MOBILE DEVICE / TV

☐ None ☐ Some ☐ A lot Total Time: ______
☐ Sitting ☐ Standing ☐ Mixture Breaks every: ______

PHYSICAL ACTIVITY

☐ None ☐ Minimal ☐ Some ☐ Sweatin' ☐ I'm beat DETAILS: ____________

RELIEF MEASURES

☐ Medication ☐ Massage ☐ Sleep ☐ Exercise ☐ Water ☐ Cold/Ice
☐ Heat/Bath ☐ Other: ____________________
Did it work? ☐ Nope ☐ A bit ☐ Mostly ☐ 100%

Notes ☐ *See back notes*

START: ______ END: ______ DURATION: ______ DATE ______ *Entry #158*

MIGRAINE

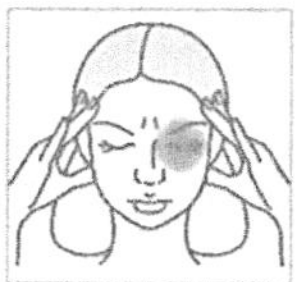
CLUSTER

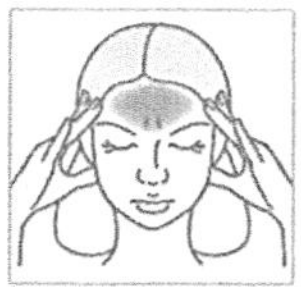
TENSION

SINUS

TMJ

HOW WOULD YOU RATE...?

Mood	1	2	3	4	5
Energy	1	2	3	4	5
Mental clarity	1	2	3	4	5

PAIN LEVEL

1	2	3	4	5	6	7	8	9	10

Not too bad. *Well, I'm not enjoying this.* *Make it stop!*

ONSET

☐ Slow ☐ Average
☐ Rapid ☐ Sudden

DETAILED DESCRIPTION

☐ Constant ☐ Squeezing ☐ Throbbing ☐ Pounding ☐ Dull aching ☐ Burning
☐ Sharp ☐ Debilitating ☐ Other: ______

WHERE DOES IT HURT, EXACTLY?

OTHER SYMPTOMS

☐ Lightheaded ☐ Dizziness
☐ Light sensitivity ☐ Sound sensitivity
☐ Confusion ☐ Auras
☐ Muscle stiffness ☐ Muscle aches

FEELING SICK?

☐ Nausea ☐ Diarrhea ☐ Vomiting ☐ Sore throat ☐ Congestion ☐ Coughing
☐ Chills ☐ Fever ☐ Other: ______

SLEEP

hours ______ *quality* 1 2 3 4 5

WEATHER

☐ Cold ☐ Mild ☐ Hot Allergen levels: ______
☐ Dry ☐ Humid ☐ Wet BM Pressure: ______

STRESS LEVELS

None	Low	Medium	High	Max	@$#%!

item / meal	*time*	*meds / supplements*	*dose*	*time*	*drinks*
					water: 1 2 3 4 5 6 7 8 9 10
					caffeine: 1 2 3 4 5 6 7 8 9 10
					alcohol: 1 2 3 4 5 6 7 8 9 10

HORMONES

☐ Menstruating ☐ Menopause
☐ PMS ☐ N/A | other

COMPUTER / MOBILE DEVICE / TV

☐ None ☐ Some ☐ A lot Total Time: ______
☐ Sitting ☐ Standing ☐ Mixture Breaks every: ______

PHYSICAL ACTIVITY

☐ None ☐ Minimal ☐ Some ☐ Sweatin' ☐ I'm beat DETAILS: ______

RELIEF MEASURES

☐ Medication ☐ Massage ☐ Sleep ☐ Exercise ☐ Water ☐ Cold/Ice
☐ Heat/Bath ☐ Other: ______
Did it work? ☐ Nope ☐ A bit ☐ Mostly ☐ 100%

Notes ☐ *See back notes*

START:		END:		DURATION:		DATE		*Entry #159*

MIGRAINE

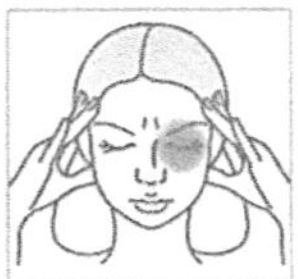
CLUSTER

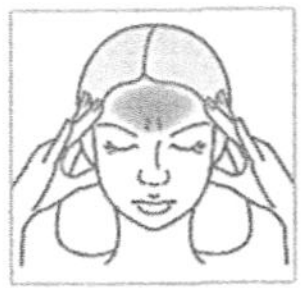
TENSION

SINUS

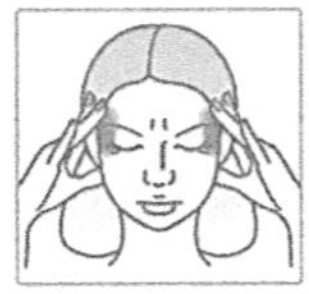
TMJ

HOW WOULD YOU RATE...?

Mood	①	②	③	④	⑤
Energy	①	②	③	④	⑤
Mental clarity	①	②	③	④	⑤

PAIN LEVEL

1	2	3	4	5	6	7	8	9	10

Not too bad. *Well, I'm not enjoying this.* *Make it stop!*

ONSET

☐ Slow ☐ Average
☐ Rapid ☐ Sudden

DETAILED DESCRIPTION

☐ Constant ☐ Squeezing ☐ Throbbing ☐ Pounding ☐ Dull aching ☐ Burning
☐ Sharp ☐ Debilitating ☐ Other: ____________

WHERE DOES IT HURT, EXACTLY?

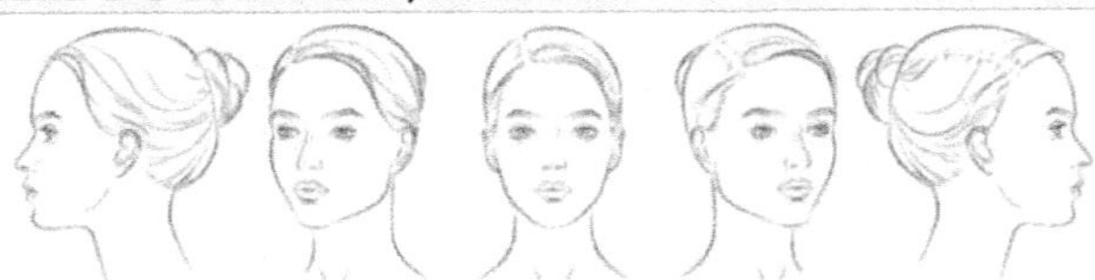

OTHER SYMPTOMS

☐ Lightheaded ☐ Dizziness
☐ Light sensitivity ☐ Sound sensitivity
☐ Confusion ☐ Auras
☐ Muscle stiffness ☐ Muscle aches

FEELING SICK?

☐ Nausea ☐ Diarrhea ☐ Vomiting ☐ Sore throat ☐ Congestion ☐ Coughing
☐ Chills ☐ Fever ☐ Other: ____________

SLEEP

hours ________ *quality* ① ② ③ ④ ⑤

WEATHER

☐ Cold ☐ Mild ☐ Hot Allergen levels: ____________
☐ Dry ☐ Humid ☐ Wet BM Pressure: ____________

STRESS LEVELS

None	Low	Medium	High	Max	@$#%!

item / meal	*time*	*meds / supplements*	*dose*	*time*	*drinks*
					water
					① ② ③ ④ ⑤ ⑥ ⑦ ⑧ ⑨ ⑩
					caffeine
					① ② ③ ④ ⑤ ⑥ ⑦ ⑧ ⑨ ⑩
					alcohol
					① ② ③ ④ ⑤ ⑥ ⑦ ⑧ ⑨ ⑩

HORMONES

☐ Menstruating ☐ Menopause
☐ PMS ☐ N/A | other

COMPUTER / MOBILE DEVICE / TV

☐ None ☐ Some ☐ A lot Total Time: ______
☐ Sitting ☐ Standing ☐ Mixture Breaks every: ______

PHYSICAL ACTIVITY

☐ None ☐ Minimal ☐ Some ☐ Sweatin' ☐ I'm beat DETAILS: ____________

RELIEF MEASURES

☐ Medication ☐ Massage ☐ Sleep ☐ Exercise ☐ Water ☐ Cold/Ice
☐ Heat/Bath ☐ Other: ____________
Did it work? ☐ Nope ☐ A bit ☐ Mostly ☐ 100%

Notes ☐ *See back notes*

START:		END:		DURATION:		DATE		*Entry #160*

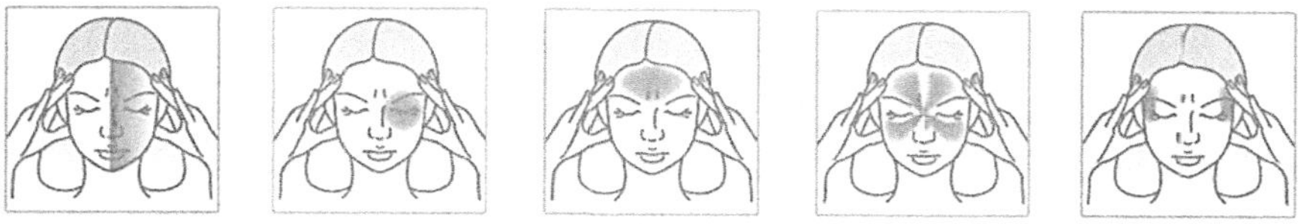

MIGRAINE | CLUSTER | TENSION | SINUS | TMJ

HOW WOULD YOU RATE...?

Mood	1	2	3	4	5
Energy	1	2	3	4	5
Mental clarity	1	2	3	4	5

PAIN LEVEL

1	2	3	4	5	6	7	8	9	10

Not too bad. *Well, I'm not enjoying this.* *Make it stop!*

ONSET

☐ Slow ☐ Average
☐ Rapid ☐ Sudden

DETAILED DESCRIPTION

☐ Constant ☐ Squeezing ☐ Throbbing ☐ Pounding ☐ Dull aching ☐ Burning
☐ Sharp ☐ Debilitating ☐ Other: ______________________

WHERE DOES IT HURT, EXACTLY?

OTHER SYMPTOMS

☐ Lightheaded ☐ Dizziness
☐ Light sensitivity ☐ Sound sensitivity
☐ Confusion ☐ Auras
☐ Muscle stiffness ☐ Muscle aches

FEELING SICK?

☐ Nausea ☐ Diarrhea ☐ Vomiting ☐ Sore throat ☐ Congestion ☐ Coughing
☐ Chills ☐ Fever ☐ Other: ______________________

SLEEP

hours ________ *quality* 1 2 3 4 5

WEATHER

☐ Cold ☐ Mild ☐ Hot Allergen levels: __________
☐ Dry ☐ Humid ☐ Wet BM Pressure: __________

STRESS LEVELS

None	Low	Medium	High	Max	@$#%!

item / meal	*time*	*meds / supplements*	*dose*	*time*	*drinks*
					water: 1 2 3 4 5 6 7 8 9 10
					caffeine: 1 2 3 4 5 6 7 8 9 10
					alcohol: 1 2 3 4 5 6 7 8 9 10

HORMONES

☐ Menstruating ☐ Menopause
☐ PMS ☐ N/A | other

COMPUTER / MOBILE DEVICE / TV

☐ None ☐ Some ☐ A lot Total Time: _____
☐ Sitting ☐ Standing ☐ Mixture Breaks every: _____

PHYSICAL ACTIVITY

☐ None ☐ Minimal ☐ Some ☐ Sweatin' ☐ I'm beat DETAILS: ______________

RELIEF MEASURES

☐ Medication ☐ Massage ☐ Sleep ☐ Exercise ☐ Water ☐ Cold/Ice
☐ Heat/Bath ☐ Other: ______________________
Did it work? ☐ Nope ☐ A bit ☐ Mostly ☐ 100%

Notes ☐ *See back notes*

START: | END: | DURATION: | DATE | *Entry #161*

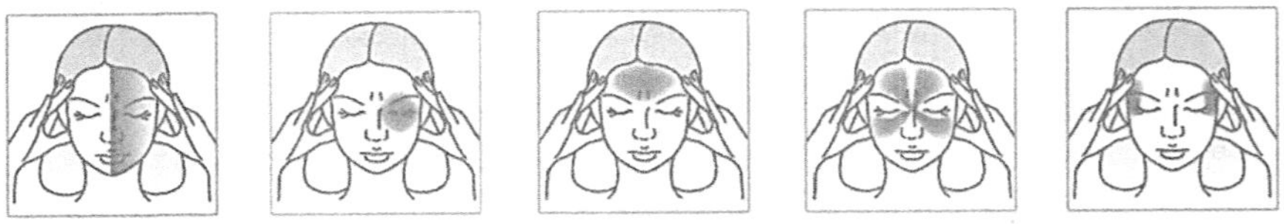

MIGRAINE CLUSTER TENSION SINUS TMJ

HOW WOULD YOU RATE...?

Mood ① ② ③ ④ ⑤

Energy ① ② ③ ④ ⑤

Mental clarity ① ② ③ ④ ⑤

PAIN LEVEL

1	2	3	4	5	6	7	8	9	10

Not too bad. *Well, I'm not enjoying this.* *Make it stop!*

ONSET

☐ Slow ☐ Average
☐ Rapid ☐ Sudden

DETAILED DESCRIPTION

☐ Constant ☐ Squeezing ☐ Throbbing ☐ Pounding ☐ Dull aching ☐ Burning
☐ Sharp ☐ Debilitating ☐ Other: ____________

WHERE DOES IT HURT, EXACTLY?

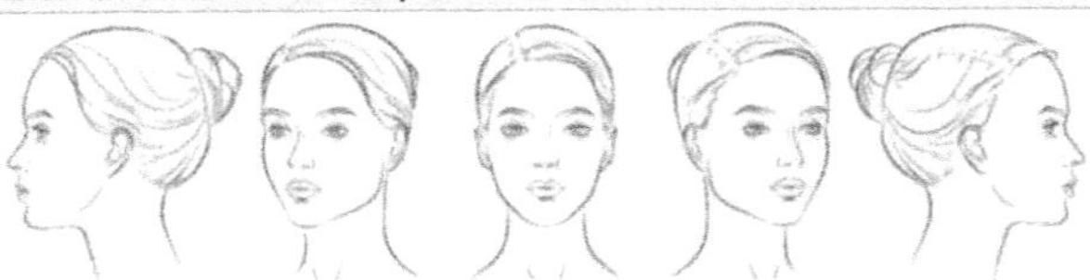

OTHER SYMPTOMS

☐ Lightheaded ☐ Dizziness
☐ Light sensitivity ☐ Sound sensitivity
☐ Confusion ☐ Auras
☐ Muscle stiffness ☐ Muscle aches

FEELING SICK?

☐ Nausea ☐ Diarrhea ☐ Vomiting ☐ Sore throat ☐ Congestion ☐ Coughing
☐ Chills ☐ Fever ☐ Other: ____________

SLEEP

hours ______ *quality* ① ② ③ ④ ⑤

WEATHER

☐ Cold ☐ Mild ☐ Hot Allergen levels: ______
☐ Dry ☐ Humid ☐ Wet BM Pressure: ______

STRESS LEVELS

None	Low	Medium	High	Max	@$#%!

item / meal	*time*	*meds / supplements*	*dose*	*time*	*drinks*
					water ① ② ③ ④ ⑤ ⑥ ⑦ ⑧ ⑨ ⑩
					caffeine ① ② ③ ④ ⑤ ⑥ ⑦ ⑧ ⑨ ⑩
					alcohol ① ② ③ ④ ⑤ ⑥ ⑦ ⑧ ⑨ ⑩

HORMONES

☐ Menstruating ☐ Menopause
☐ PMS ☐ N/A | other

COMPUTER / MOBILE DEVICE / TV

☐ None ☐ Some ☐ A lot Total Time: ______
☐ Sitting ☐ Standing ☐ Mixture Breaks every: ______

PHYSICAL ACTIVITY

☐ None ☐ Minimal ☐ Some ☐ Sweatin' ☐ I'm beat DETAILS: ____________

RELIEF MEASURES

☐ Medication ☐ Massage ☐ Sleep ☐ Exercise ☐ Water ☐ Cold/Ice
☐ Heat/Bath ☐ Other: ____________
Did it work? ☐ Nope ☐ A bit ☐ Mostly ☐ 100%

Notes ☐ *See back notes*

START:		END:		DURATION:		DATE		*Entry #162*

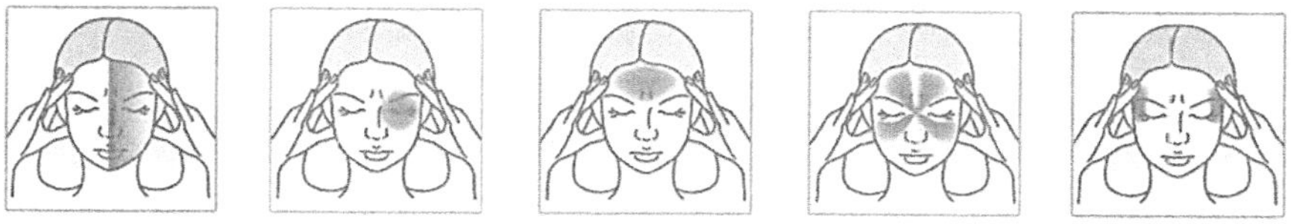

MIGRAINE | CLUSTER | TENSION | SINUS | TMJ

HOW WOULD YOU RATE...?

Mood	1	2	3	4	5
Energy	1	2	3	4	5
Mental clarity	1	2	3	4	5

PAIN LEVEL

1	2	3	4	5	6	7	8	9	10

Not too bad. *Well, I'm not enjoying this.* *Make it stop!*

ONSET

☐ Slow ☐ Average
☐ Rapid ☐ Sudden

DETAILED DESCRIPTION

☐ Constant ☐ Squeezing ☐ Throbbing ☐ Pounding ☐ Dull aching ☐ Burning
☐ Sharp ☐ Debilitating ☐ Other: ____________________

WHERE DOES IT HURT, EXACTLY?

OTHER SYMPTOMS

☐ Lightheaded ☐ Dizziness
☐ Light sensitivity ☐ Sound sensitivity
☐ Confusion ☐ Auras
☐ Muscle stiffness ☐ Muscle aches

FEELING SICK?

☐ Nausea ☐ Diarrhea ☐ Vomiting ☐ Sore throat ☐ Congestion ☐ Coughing
☐ Chills ☐ Fever ☐ Other: ____________________

SLEEP

hours ________ *quality* 1 2 3 4 5

WEATHER

☐ Cold ☐ Mild ☐ Hot Allergen levels: __________
☐ Dry ☐ Humid ☐ Wet BM Pressure: __________

STRESS LEVELS

None	Low	Medium	High	Max	@$#%!

item / meal	*time*	*meds / supplements*	*dose*	*time*	*drinks*
					water: 1 2 3 4 5 6 7 8 9 10
					caffeine: 1 2 3 4 5 6 7 8 9 10
					alcohol: 1 2 3 4 5 6 7 8 9 10

HORMONES

☐ Menstruating ☐ Menopause
☐ PMS ☐ N/A | other

COMPUTER / MOBILE DEVICE / TV

☐ None ☐ Some ☐ A lot Total Time: _____
☐ Sitting ☐ Standing ☐ Mixture Breaks every: _____

PHYSICAL ACTIVITY

☐ None ☐ Minimal ☐ Some ☐ Sweatin' ☐ I'm beat DETAILS: __________

RELIEF MEASURES

☐ Medication ☐ Massage ☐ Sleep ☐ Exercise ☐ Water ☐ Cold/Ice
☐ Heat/Bath ☐ Other: ____________________
Did it work? ☐ Nope ☐ A bit ☐ Mostly ☐ 100%

Notes ☐ *See back notes*

START:	END:	DURATION:	DATE	*Entry #163*

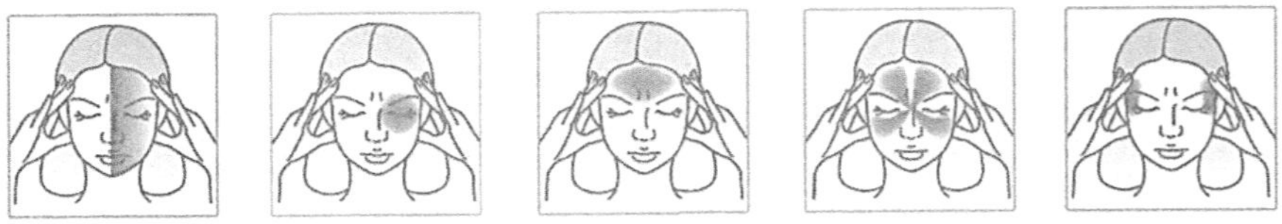

MIGRAINE CLUSTER TENSION SINUS TMJ

HOW WOULD YOU RATE...?

Mood ① ② ③ ④ ⑤
Energy ① ② ③ ④ ⑤
Mental clarity ① ② ③ ④ ⑤

PAIN LEVEL

1	2	3	4	5	6	7	8	9	10

Not too bad. *Well, I'm not enjoying this.* *Make it stop!*

ONSET

☐ Slow ☐ Average
☐ Rapid ☐ Sudden

DETAILED DESCRIPTION

☐ Constant ☐ Squeezing ☐ Throbbing ☐ Pounding ☐ Dull aching ☐ Burning
☐ Sharp ☐ Debilitating ☐ Other: ____________________

WHERE DOES IT HURT, EXACTLY?

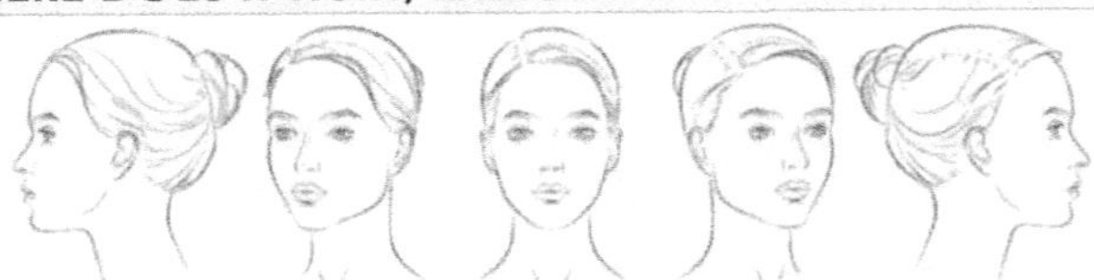

OTHER SYMPTOMS

☐ Lightheaded ☐ Dizziness
☐ Light sensitivity ☐ Sound sensitivity
☐ Confusion ☐ Auras
☐ Muscle stiffness ☐ Muscle aches

FEELING SICK?

☐ Nausea ☐ Diarrhea ☐ Vomiting ☐ Sore throat ☐ Congestion ☐ Coughing
☐ Chills ☐ Fever ☐ Other: ____________________

SLEEP

hours ________ *quality* ① ② ③ ④ ⑤

WEATHER

☐ Cold ☐ Mild ☐ Hot Allergen levels: __________
☐ Dry ☐ Humid ☐ Wet BM Pressure: __________

STRESS LEVELS

None	Low	Medium	High	Max	@$#%!

item / meal	*time*	*meds / supplements*	*dose*	*time*	*drinks*
					water ① ② ③ ④ ⑤ ⑥ ⑦ ⑧ ⑨ ⑩
					caffeine ① ② ③ ④ ⑤ ⑥ ⑦ ⑧ ⑨ ⑩
					alcohol ① ② ③ ④ ⑤ ⑥ ⑦ ⑧ ⑨ ⑩

HORMONES

☐ Menstruating ☐ Menopause
☐ PMS ☐ N/A | other

COMPUTER / MOBILE DEVICE / TV

☐ None ☐ Some ☐ A lot Total Time: _____
☐ Sitting ☐ Standing ☐ Mixture Breaks every: _____

PHYSICAL ACTIVITY

☐ None ☐ Minimal ☐ Some ☐ Sweatin' ☐ I'm beat DETAILS: ____________

RELIEF MEASURES

☐ Medication ☐ Massage ☐ Sleep ☐ Exercise ☐ Water ☐ Cold/Ice
☐ Heat/Bath ☐ Other: ____________________
Did it work? ☐ Nope ☐ A bit ☐ Mostly ☐ 100%

Notes ☐ *See back notes*

START:	END:	DURATION:	DATE	*Entry #164*

MIGRAINE CLUSTER TENSION SINUS TMJ

HOW WOULD YOU RATE...?

Mood	1	2	3	4	5
Energy	1	2	3	4	5
Mental clarity	1	2	3	4	5

PAIN LEVEL

1	2	3	4	5	6	7	8	9	10

Not too bad. *Wel', I'm not enjoying this.* *Make it stop!*

ONSET

☐ Slow ☐ Average
☐ Rapid ☐ Sudden

DETAILED DESCRIPTION

☐ Constant ☐ Squeezing ☐ Throbbing ☐ Pounding ☐ Dull aching ☐ Burning
☐ Sharp ☐ Debilitating ☐ Other: ______________________

WHERE DOES IT HURT, EXACTLY?

OTHER SYMPTOMS

☐ Lightheaded ☐ Dizziness
☐ Light sensitivity ☐ Sound sensitivity
☐ Confusion ☐ Auras
☐ Muscle stiffness ☐ Muscle aches

FEELING SICK?

☐ Nausea ☐ Diarrhea ☐ Vomiting ☐ Sore throat ☐ Congestion ☐ Coughing
☐ Chills ☐ Fever ☐ Other: ______________________

SLEEP

hours ________ *quality* 1 2 3 4 5

WEATHER

☐ Cold ☐ Mild ☐ Hot Allergen levels: ____________
☐ Dry ☐ Humid ☐ Wet BM Pressure: ____________

STRESS LEVELS

None	Low	Medium	High	Max	@$#%!

item / meal	*time*	*meds / supplements*	*dose*	*time*	*drinks*
					water
					1 2 3 4 5 6 7 8 9 10
					caffeine
					1 2 3 4 5 6 7 8 9 10
					alcohol
					1 2 3 4 5 6 7 8 9 10

HORMONES

☐ Menstruating ☐ Menopause
☐ PMS ☐ N/A | other

COMPUTER / MOBILE DEVICE / TV

☐ None ☐ Some ☐ A lot Total Time: ______
☐ Sitting ☐ Standing ☐ Mixture Breaks every: ______

PHYSICAL ACTIVITY

☐ None ☐ Minimal ☐ Some ☐ Sweatin' ☐ I'm beat DETAILS: ______________

RELIEF MEASURES

☐ Medication ☐ Massage ☐ Sleep ☐ Exercise ☐ Water ☐ Cold/Ice
☐ Heat/Bath ☐ Other: ______________________
Did it work? ☐ Nope ☐ A bit ☐ Mostly ☐ 100%

Notes ☐ *See back notes*

START:		END:		DURATION:		DATE		*Entry #165*

MIGRAINE CLUSTER TENSION SINUS TMJ

HOW WOULD YOU RATE...?					
Mood	1	2	3	4	5
Energy	1	2	3	4	5
Mental clarity	1	2	3	4	5

PAIN LEVEL

1	2	3	4	5	6	7	8	9	10

Not too bad. *Well, I'm not enjoying this.* *Make it stop!*

ONSET

☐ Slow ☐ Average
☐ Rapid ☐ Sudden

DETAILED DESCRIPTION

☐ Constant ☐ Squeezing ☐ Throbbing ☐ Pounding ☐ Dull aching ☐ Burning
☐ Sharp ☐ Debilitating ☐ Other: ______________________

WHERE DOES IT HURT, EXACTLY?

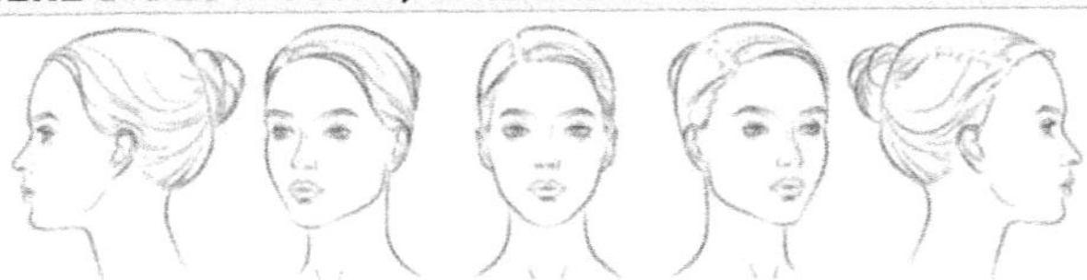

OTHER SYMPTOMS

☐ Lightheaded ☐ Dizziness
☐ Light sensitivity ☐ Sound sensitivity
☐ Confusion ☐ Auras
☐ Muscle stiffness ☐ Muscle aches

FEELING SICK?

☐ Nausea ☐ Diarrhea ☐ Vomiting ☐ Sore throat ☐ Congestion ☐ Coughing
☐ Chills ☐ Fever ☐ Other: ______________________

SLEEP

hours ________ *quality* 1 2 3 4 5

WEATHER

☐ Cold ☐ Mild ☐ Hot Allergen levels: ____________
☐ Dry ☐ Humid ☐ Wet BM Pressure: ____________

STRESS LEVELS

None	Low	Medium	High	Max	@$#%!

item / meal	*time*	*meds / supplements*	*dose*	*time*	*drinks*
					water
					1 2 3 4 5 6 7 8 9 10
					caffeine
					1 2 3 4 5 6 7 8 9 10
					alcohol
					1 2 3 4 5 6 7 8 9 10

HORMONES

☐ Menstruating ☐ Menopause
☐ PMS ☐ N/A | other

COMPUTER / MOBILE DEVICE / TV

☐ None ☐ Some ☐ A lot Total Time: _____
☐ Sitting ☐ Standing ☐ Mixture Breaks every: _____

PHYSICAL ACTIVITY

☐ None ☐ Minimal ☐ Some ☐ Sweatin' ☐ I'm beat DETAILS: ______________

RELIEF MEASURES

☐ Medication ☐ Massage ☐ Sleep ☐ Exercise ☐ Water ☐ Cold/Ice
☐ Heat/Bath ☐ Other: ______________________
Did it work? ☐ Nope ☐ A bit ☐ Mostly ☐ 100%

Notes ☐ *See back notes*

START:		END:		DURATION:		DATE		*Entry #166*

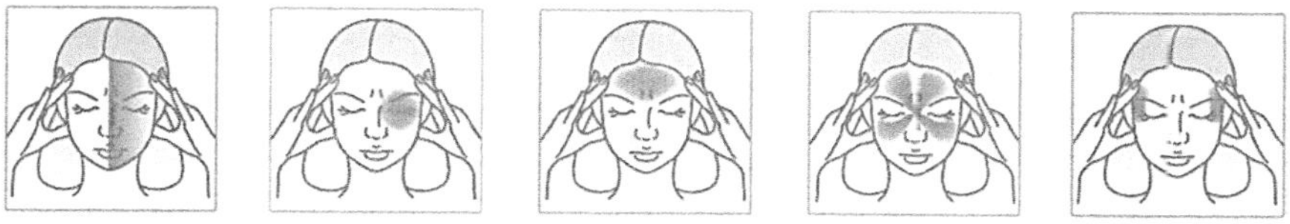

HOW WOULD YOU RATE...?

Mood	①	②	③	④	⑤
Energy	①	②	③	④	⑤
Mental clarity	①	②	③	④	⑤

PAIN LEVEL

1	2	3	4	5	6	7	8	9	10

Not too bad. *Well, I'm not enjoying this.* *Make it stop!*

ONSET

☐ Slow ☐ Average
☐ Rapid ☐ Sudden

DETAILED DESCRIPTION

☐ Constant ☐ Squeezing ☐ Throbbing ☐ Pounding ☐ Dull aching ☐ Burning
☐ Sharp ☐ Debilitating ☐ Other: ____________________

WHERE DOES IT HURT, EXACTLY?

OTHER SYMPTOMS

☐ Lightheaded ☐ Dizziness
☐ Light sensitivity ☐ Sound sensitivity
☐ Confusion ☐ Auras
☐ Muscle stiffness ☐ Muscle aches

FEELING SICK?

☐ Nausea ☐ Diarrhea ☐ Vomiting ☐ Sore throat ☐ Congestion ☐ Coughing
☐ Chills ☐ Fever ☐ Other: ____________________

SLEEP

hours ________ *quality* ① ② ③ ④ ⑤

WEATHER

☐ Cold ☐ Mild ☐ Hot Allergen levels: __________
☐ Dry ☐ Humid ☐ Wet BM Pressure: __________

STRESS LEVELS

None	Low	Medium	High	Max	@$#%!

item / meal	*time*	*meds / supplements*	*dose*	*time*	*drinks*
					water: ① ② ③ ④ ⑤ ⑥ ⑦ ⑧ ⑨ ⑩
					caffeine: ① ② ③ ④ ⑤ ⑥ ⑦ ⑧ ⑨ ⑩
					alcohol: ① ② ③ ④ ⑤ ⑥ ⑦ ⑧ ⑨ ⑩

HORMONES

☐ Menstruating ☐ Menopause
☐ PMS ☐ N/A | other

COMPUTER / MOBILE DEVICE / TV

☐ None ☐ Some ☐ A lot Total Time: _____
☐ Sitting ☐ Standing ☐ Mixture Breaks every: _____

PHYSICAL ACTIVITY

☐ None ☐ Minimal ☐ Some ☐ Sweatin' ☐ I'm beat DETAILS: __________

RELIEF MEASURES

☐ Medication ☐ Massage ☐ Sleep ☐ Exercise ☐ Water ☐ Cold/Ice
☐ Heat/Bath ☐ Other: ____________________
Did it work? ☐ Nope ☐ A bit ☐ Mostly ☐ 100%

Notes ☐ *See back notes*

START: ____ END: ____ DURATION: ____ DATE ____ *Entry #167*

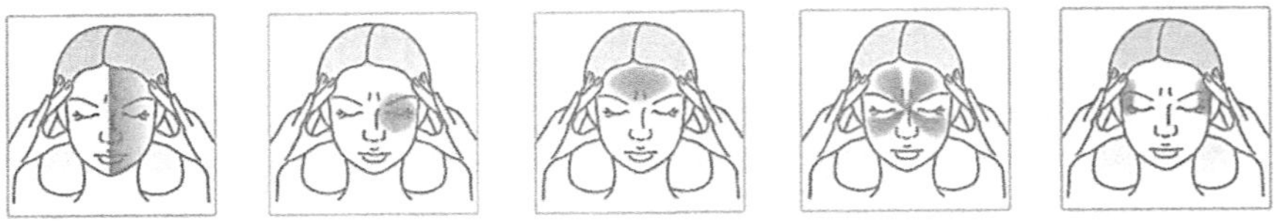

MIGRAINE | CLUSTER | TENSION | SINUS | TMJ

HOW WOULD YOU RATE...?

Mood	①	②	③	④	⑤
Energy	①	②	③	④	⑤
Mental clarity	①	②	③	④	⑤

PAIN LEVEL

1	2	3	4	5	6	7	8	9	10

Not too bad. *Well, I'm not enjoying this.* *Make it stop!*

ONSET

☐ Slow ☐ Average
☐ Rapid ☐ Sudden

DETAILED DESCRIPTION

☐ Constant ☐ Squeezing ☐ Throbbing ☐ Pounding ☐ Dull aching ☐ Burning
☐ Sharp ☐ Debilitating ☐ Other: ____________

WHERE DOES IT HURT, EXACTLY?

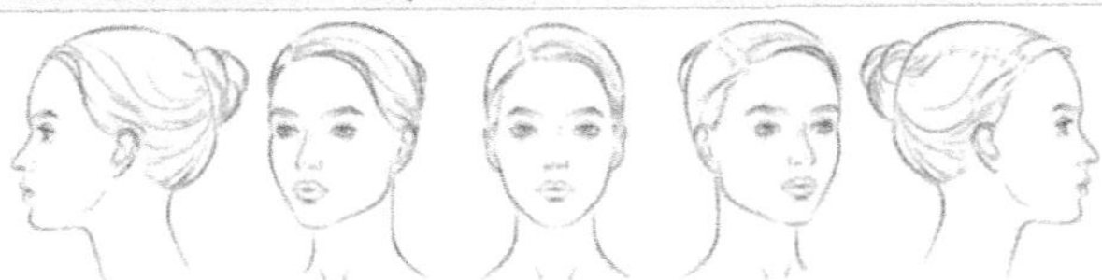

OTHER SYMPTOMS

☐ Lightheaded ☐ Dizziness
☐ Light sensitivity ☐ Sound sensitivity
☐ Confusion ☐ Auras
☐ Muscle stiffness ☐ Muscle aches

FEELING SICK?

☐ Nausea ☐ Diarrhea ☐ Vomiting ☐ Sore throat ☐ Congestion ☐ Coughing
☐ Chills ☐ Fever ☐ Other: ____________

SLEEP

hours ________ *quality* ① ② ③ ④ ⑤

WEATHER

☐ Cold ☐ Mild ☐ Hot Allergen levels: ________
☐ Dry ☐ Humid ☐ Wet BM Pressure: ________

STRESS LEVELS

None	Low	Medium	High	Max	@$#%!

item / meal	*time*	*meds / supplements*	*dose*	*time*	*drinks*
					water
					① ② ③ ④ ⑤ ⑥ ⑦ ⑧ ⑨ ⑩
					caffeine
					① ② ③ ④ ⑤ ⑥ ⑦ ⑧ ⑨ ⑩
					alcohol
					① ② ③ ④ ⑤ ⑥ ⑦ ⑧ ⑨ ⑩

HORMONES

☐ Menstruating ☐ Menopause
☐ PMS ☐ N/A | other

COMPUTER / MOBILE DEVICE / TV

☐ None ☐ Some ☐ A lot Total Time: ______
☐ Sitting ☐ Standing ☐ Mixture Breaks every: ______

PHYSICAL ACTIVITY

☐ None ☐ Minimal ☐ Some ☐ Sweatin' ☐ I'm beat DETAILS: ____________

RELIEF MEASURES

☐ Medication ☐ Massage ☐ Sleep ☐ Exercise ☐ Water ☐ Cold/Ice
☐ Heat/Bath ☐ Other: ____________
Did it work? ☐ Nope ☐ A bit ☐ Mostly ☐ 100%

Notes ☐ *See back notes*

START: ____ END: ____ DURATION: ____ DATE ____ *Entry #168*

MIGRAINE | CLUSTER | TENSION | SINUS | TMJ

HOW WOULD YOU RATE...?

Mood	① ② ③ ④ ⑤
Energy	① ② ③ ④ ⑤
Mental clarity	① ② ③ ④ ⑤

PAIN LEVEL

1	2	3	4	5	6	7	8	9	10

Not too bad. *Well, I'm not enjoying this.* *Make it stop!*

ONSET

☐ Slow ☐ Average
☐ Rapid ☐ Sudden

DETAILED DESCRIPTION

☐ Constant ☐ Squeezing ☐ Throbbing ☐ Pounding ☐ Dull aching ☐ Burning
☐ Sharp ☐ Debilitating ☐ Other: ________________

WHERE DOES IT HURT, EXACTLY?

OTHER SYMPTOMS

☐ Lightheaded ☐ Dizziness
☐ Light sensitivity ☐ Sound sensitivity
☐ Confusion ☐ Auras
☐ Muscle stiffness ☐ Muscle aches

FEELING SICK?

☐ Nausea ☐ Diarrhea ☐ Vomiting ☐ Sore throat ☐ Congestion ☐ Coughing
☐ Chills ☐ Fever ☐ Other: ________________

SLEEP

hours ________ *quality* ① ② ③ ④ ⑤

WEATHER

☐ Cold ☐ Mild ☐ Hot Allergen levels: ________
☐ Dry ☐ Humid ☐ Wet BM Pressure: ________

STRESS LEVELS

None	Low	Medium	High	Max	@$#%!

item / meal	*time*	*meds / supplements*	*dose*	*time*	*drinks*
					water ① ② ③ ④ ⑤ ⑥ ⑦ ⑧ ⑨ ⑩
					caffeine ① ② ③ ④ ⑤ ⑥ ⑦ ⑧ ⑨ ⑩
					alcohol ① ② ③ ④ ⑤ ⑥ ⑦ ⑧ ⑨ ⑩

HORMONES

☐ Menstruating ☐ Menopause
☐ PMS ☐ N/A | other

COMPUTER / MOBILE DEVICE / TV

☐ None ☐ Some ☐ A lot Total Time: ______
☐ Sitting ☐ Standing ☐ Mixture Breaks every: ______

PHYSICAL ACTIVITY

☐ None ☐ Minimal ☐ Some ☐ Sweatin' ☐ I'm beat DETAILS: ________________

RELIEF MEASURES

☐ Medication ☐ Massage ☐ Sleep ☐ Exercise ☐ Water ☐ Cold/Ice
☐ Heat/Bath ☐ Other: ________________
Did it work? ☐ Nope ☐ A bit ☐ Mostly ☐ 100%

Notes ☐ *See back notes*

START: | END: | DURATION: | DATE | *Entry #169*

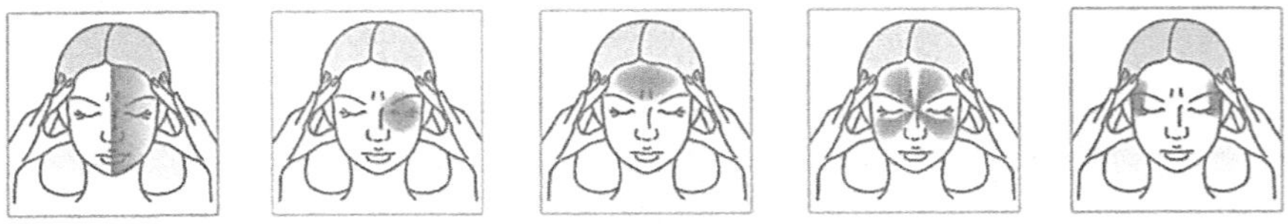

MIGRAINE · CLUSTER · TENSION · SINUS · TMJ

HOW WOULD YOU RATE...?

Mood	① ② ③ ④ ⑤
Energy	① ② ③ ④ ⑤
Mental clarity	① ② ③ ④ ⑤

PAIN LEVEL

1	2	3	4	5	6	7	8	9	10

Not too bad. *Well, I'm not enjoying this.* *Make it stop!*

ONSET

☐ Slow ☐ Average
☐ Rapid ☐ Sudden

DETAILED DESCRIPTION

☐ Constant ☐ Squeezing ☐ Throbbing ☐ Pounding ☐ Dull aching ☐ Burning
☐ Sharp ☐ Debilitating ☐ Other: ____________

WHERE DOES IT HURT, EXACTLY?

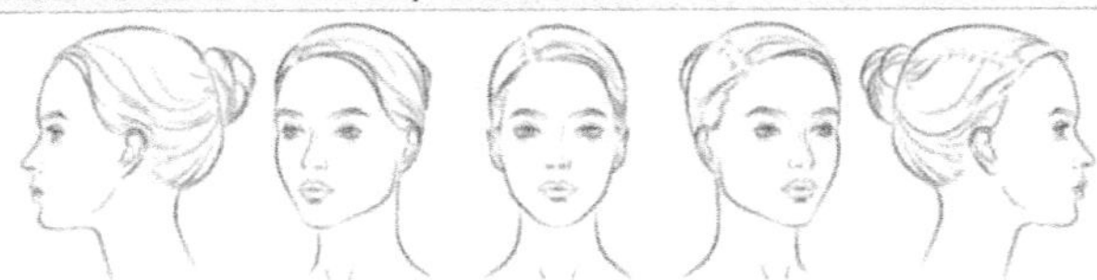

OTHER SYMPTOMS

☐ Lightheaded ☐ Dizziness
☐ Light sensitivity ☐ Sound sensitivity
☐ Confusion ☐ Auras
☐ Muscle stiffness ☐ Muscle aches

FEELING SICK?

☐ Nausea ☐ Diarrhea ☐ Vomiting ☐ Sore throat ☐ Congestion ☐ Coughing
☐ Chills ☐ Fever ☐ Other: ____________

SLEEP

hours ________ *quality* ① ② ③ ④ ⑤

WEATHER

☐ Cold ☐ Mild ☐ Hot Allergen levels: ________
☐ Dry ☐ Humid ☐ Wet BM Pressure: ________

STRESS LEVELS

None	Low	Medium	High	Max	@$#%!

item / meal	*time*	*meds / supplements*	*dose*	*time*	*drinks*
					water: ① ② ③ ④ ⑤ ⑥ ⑦ ⑧ ⑨ ⑩
					caffeine: ① ② ③ ④ ⑤ ⑥ ⑦ ⑧ ⑨ ⑩
					alcohol: ① ② ③ ④ ⑤ ⑥ ⑦ ⑧ ⑨ ⑩

HORMONES

☐ Menstruating ☐ Menopause
☐ PMS ☐ N/A | other

COMPUTER / MOBILE DEVICE / TV

☐ None ☐ Some ☐ A lot Total Time: ______
☐ Sitting ☐ Standing ☐ Mixture Breaks every: ______

PHYSICAL ACTIVITY

☐ None ☐ Minimal ☐ Some ☐ Sweatin' ☐ I'm beat DETAILS: ____________

RELIEF MEASURES

☐ Medication ☐ Massage ☐ Sleep ☐ Exercise ☐ Water ☐ Cold/Ice
☐ Heat/Bath ☐ Other: ____________
Did it work? ☐ Nope ☐ A bit ☐ Mostly ☐ 100%

Notes ☐ *See back notes*

START: ______ END: ______ DURATION: ______ DATE ______ *Entry #170*

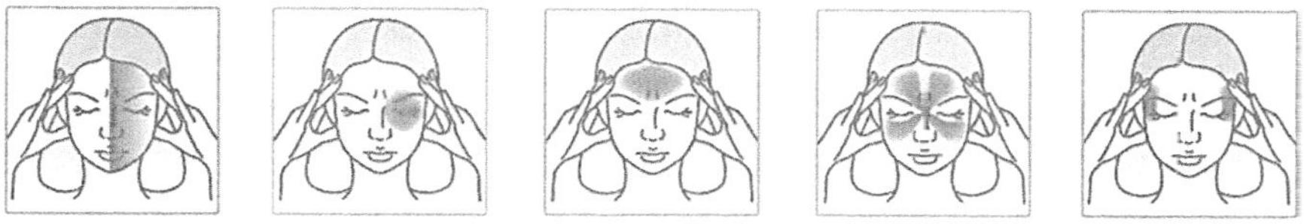

MIGRAINE | CLUSTER | TENSION | SINUS | TMJ

HOW WOULD YOU RATE...?

Mood	① ② ③ ④ ⑤
Energy	① ② ③ ④ ⑤
Mental clarity	① ② ③ ④ ⑤

PAIN LEVEL

1	2	3	4	5	6	7	8	9	10

Not too bad. *Well, I'm not enjoying this.* *Make it stop!*

ONSET

☐ Slow ☐ Average
☐ Rapid ☐ Sudden

DETAILED DESCRIPTION

☐ Constant ☐ Squeezing ☐ Throbbing ☐ Pounding ☐ Dull aching ☐ Burning
☐ Sharp ☐ Debilitating ☐ Other: ______

WHERE DOES IT HURT, EXACTLY?

OTHER SYMPTOMS

☐ Lightheaded ☐ Dizziness
☐ Light sensitivity ☐ Sound sensitivity
☐ Confusion ☐ Auras
☐ Muscle stiffness ☐ Muscle aches

FEELING SICK?

☐ Nausea ☐ Diarrhea ☐ Vomiting ☐ Sore throat ☐ Congestion ☐ Coughing
☐ Chills ☐ Fever ☐ Other: ______

SLEEP

hours ______ *quality* ① ② ③ ④ ⑤

WEATHER

☐ Cold ☐ Mild ☐ Hot Allergen levels: ______
☐ Dry ☐ Humid ☐ Wet BM Pressure: ______

STRESS LEVELS

None	Low	Medium	High	Max	@$#%!

item / meal	*time*	*meds / supplements*	*dose*	*time*	*drinks*
					water
					① ② ③ ④ ⑤ ⑥ ⑦ ⑧ ⑨ ⑩
					caffeine
					① ② ③ ④ ⑤ ⑥ ⑦ ⑧ ⑨ ⑩
					alcohol
					① ② ③ ④ ⑤ ⑥ ⑦ ⑧ ⑨ ⑩

HORMONES

☐ Menstruating ☐ Menopause
☐ PMS ☐ N/A | other

COMPUTER / MOBILE DEVICE / TV

☐ None ☐ Some ☐ A lot Total Time: ______
☐ Sitting ☐ Standing ☐ Mixture Breaks every: ______

PHYSICAL ACTIVITY

☐ None ☐ Minimal ☐ Some ☐ Sweatin' ☐ I'm beat DETAILS: ______

RELIEF MEASURES

☐ Medication ☐ Massage ☐ Sleep ☐ Exercise ☐ Water ☐ Cold/Ice
☐ Heat/Bath ☐ Other: ______
Did it work? ☐ Nope ☐ A bit ☐ Mostly ☐ 100%

Notes ☐ *See back notes*

START:		END:		DURATION:		DATE		*Entry #171*

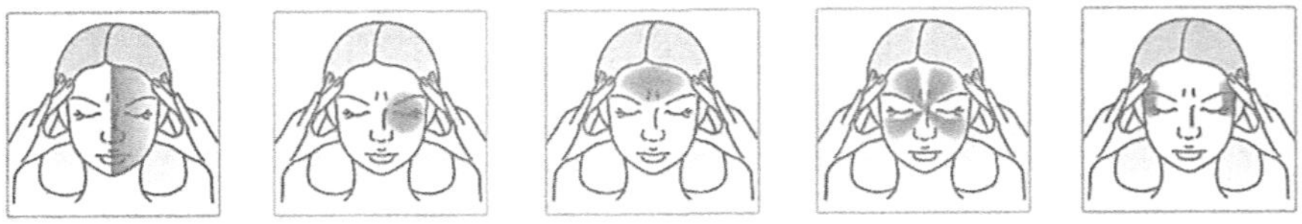

MIGRAINE CLUSTER TENSION SINUS TMJ

HOW WOULD YOU RATE...?	
Mood	① ② ③ ④ ⑤
Energy	① ② ③ ④ ⑤
Mental clarity	① ② ③ ④ ⑤

PAIN LEVEL

1	2	3	4	5	6	7	8	9	10

Not too bad. *Well, I'm not enjoying this.* *Make it stop!*

ONSET

☐ Slow ☐ Average
☐ Rapid ☐ Sudden

DETAILED DESCRIPTION

☐ Constant ☐ Squeezing ☐ Throbbing ☐ Pounding ☐ Dull aching ☐ Burning
☐ Sharp ☐ Debilitating ☐ Other: ______

WHERE DOES IT HURT, EXACTLY?

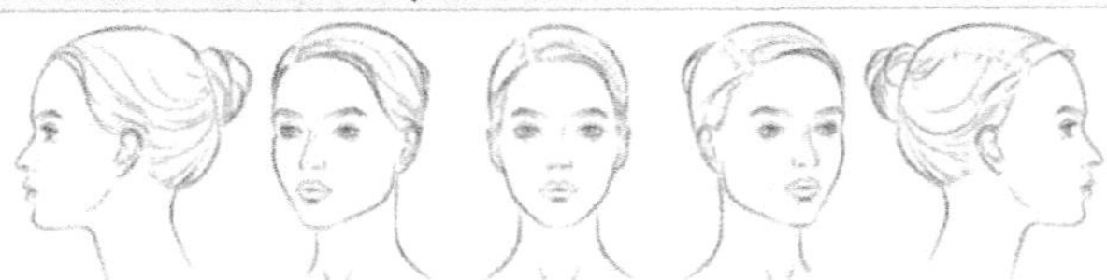

OTHER SYMPTOMS

☐ Lightheaded ☐ Dizziness
☐ Light sensitivity ☐ Sound sensitivity
☐ Confusion ☐ Auras
☐ Muscle stiffness ☐ Muscle aches

FEELING SICK?

☐ Nausea ☐ Diarrhea ☐ Vomiting ☐ Sore throat ☐ Congestion ☐ Coughing
☐ Chills ☐ Fever ☐ Other: ______

SLEEP

hours ______ *quality* ① ② ③ ④ ⑤

WEATHER

☐ Cold ☐ Mild ☐ Hot Allergen levels: ______
☐ Dry ☐ Humid ☐ Wet BM Pressure: ______

STRESS LEVELS

None	Low	Medium	High	Max	@$#%!

item / meal	*time*	*meds / supplements*	*dose*	*time*	*drinks*
					water
					① ② ③ ④ ⑤ ⑥ ⑦ ⑧ ⑨ ⑩
					caffeine
					① ② ③ ④ ⑤ ⑥ ⑦ ⑧ ⑨ ⑩
					alcohol
					① ② ③ ④ ⑤ ⑥ ⑦ ⑧ ⑨ ⑩

HORMONES

☐ Menstruating ☐ Menopause
☐ PMS ☐ N/A | other

COMPUTER / MOBILE DEVICE / TV

☐ None ☐ Some ☐ A lot Total Time: ______
☐ Sitting ☐ Standing ☐ Mixture Breaks every: ______

PHYSICAL ACTIVITY

☐ None ☐ Minimal ☐ Some ☐ Sweatin' ☐ I'm beat DETAILS: ______

RELIEF MEASURES

☐ Medication ☐ Massage ☐ Sleep ☐ Exercise ☐ Water ☐ Cold/Ice
☐ Heat/Bath ☐ Other: ______

Did it work? ☐ Nope ☐ A bit ☐ Mostly ☐ 100%

Notes ☐ *See back notes*

START: | END: | DURATION: | DATE | *Entry #172*

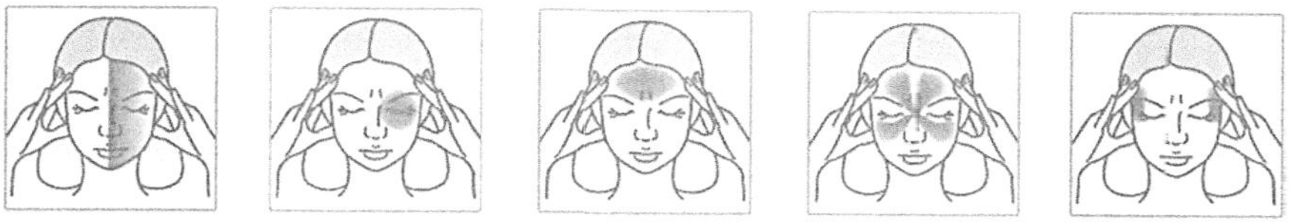

MIGRAINE CLUSTER TENSION SINUS TMJ

HOW WOULD YOU RATE...?

Mood ① ② ③ ④ ⑤

Energy ① ② ③ ④ ⑤

Mental clarity ① ② ③ ④ ⑤

PAIN LEVEL

1	2	3	4	5	6	7	8	9	10

Not too bad. *Well, I'm not enjoying this.* *Make it stop!*

ONSET

☐ Slow ☐ Average
☐ Rapid ☐ Sudden

DETAILED DESCRIPTION

☐ Constant ☐ Squeezing ☐ Throbbing ☐ Pounding ☐ Dull aching ☐ Burning
☐ Sharp ☐ Debilitating ☐ Other: ____________

WHERE DOES IT HURT, EXACTLY?

OTHER SYMPTOMS

☐ Lightheaded ☐ Dizziness
☐ Light sensitivity ☐ Sound sensitivity
☐ Confusion ☐ Auras
☐ Muscle stiffness ☐ Muscle aches

FEELING SICK?

☐ Nausea ☐ Diarrhea ☐ Vomiting ☐ Sore throat ☐ Congestion ☐ Coughing
☐ Chills ☐ Fever ☐ Other: ____________

SLEEP

hours ________ *quality* ① ② ③ ④ ⑤

WEATHER

☐ Cold ☐ Mild ☐ Hot Allergen levels: ________
☐ Dry ☐ Humid ☐ Wet BM Pressure: ________

STRESS LEVELS

None	Low	Medium	High	Max	@$#%!

item / meal	*time*	*meds / supplements*	*dose*	*time*	*drinks*
					water
					① ② ③ ④ ⑤ ⑥ ⑦ ⑧ ⑨ ⑩
					caffeine
					① ② ③ ④ ⑤ ⑥ ⑦ ⑧ ⑨ ⑩
					alcohol
					① ② ③ ④ ⑤ ⑥ ⑦ ⑧ ⑨ ⑩

HORMONES

☐ Menstruating ☐ Menopause
☐ PMS ☐ N/A | other

COMPUTER / MOBILE DEVICE / TV

☐ None ☐ Some ☐ A lot Total Time: ______
☐ Sitting ☐ Standing ☐ Mixture Breaks every: ______

PHYSICAL ACTIVITY

☐ None ☐ Minimal ☐ Some ☐ Sweatin' ☐ I'm beat DETAILS: ____________

RELIEF MEASURES

☐ Medication ☐ Massage ☐ Sleep ☐ Exercise ☐ Water ☐ Cold/Ice
☐ Heat/Bath ☐ Other: ____________

Did it work? ☐ Nope ☐ A bit ☐ Mostly ☐ 100%

Notes ☐ *See back notes*

START: | END: | DURATION: | DATE | *Entry #173*

MIGRAINE

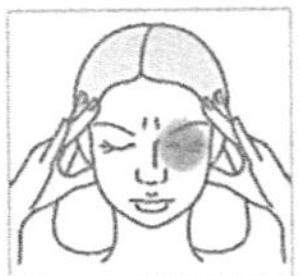

CLUSTER

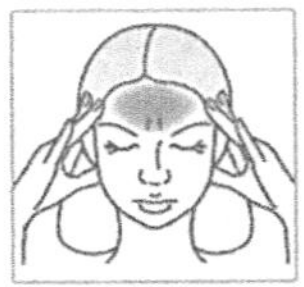

TENSION

SINUS

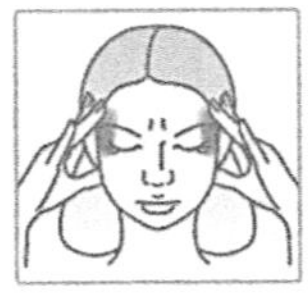

TMJ

HOW WOULD YOU RATE...?

Mood	① ② ③ ④ ⑤
Energy	① ② ③ ④ ⑤
Mental clarity	① ② ③ ④ ⑤

PAIN LEVEL

1	2	3	4	5	6	7	8	9	10

Not too bad. *Well, I'm not enjoying this.* *Make it stop!*

ONSET

☐ Slow ☐ Average
☐ Rapid ☐ Sudden

DETAILED DESCRIPTION

☐ Constant ☐ Squeezing ☐ Throbbing ☐ Pounding ☐ Dull aching ☐ Burning
☐ Sharp ☐ Debilitating ☐ Other: ____________________

WHERE DOES IT HURT, EXACTLY?

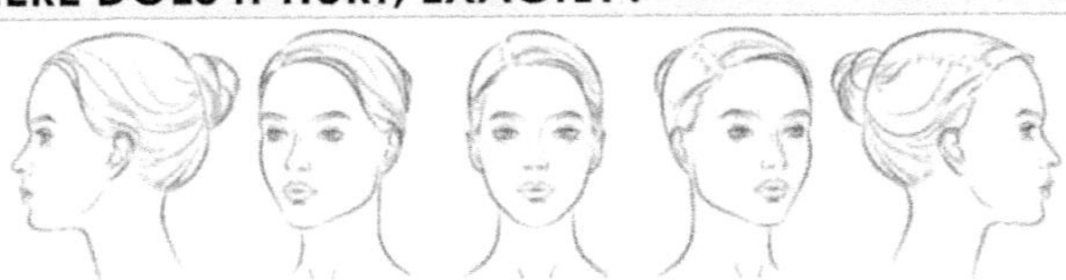

OTHER SYMPTOMS

☐ Lightheaded ☐ Dizziness
☐ Light sensitivity ☐ Sound sensitivity
☐ Confusion ☐ Auras
☐ Muscle stiffness ☐ Muscle aches

FEELING SICK?

☐ Nausea ☐ Diarrhea ☐ Vomiting ☐ Sore throat ☐ Congestion ☐ Coughing
☐ Chills ☐ Fever ☐ Other: ____________________

SLEEP

hours ______ *quality* ① ② ③ ④ ⑤

WEATHER

☐ Cold ☐ Mild ☐ Hot Allergen levels: __________
☐ Dry ☐ Humid ☐ Wet BM Pressure: __________

STRESS LEVELS

None	Low	Medium	High	Max	@$#%!

item / meal	*time*	*meds / supplements*	*dose*	*time*	*drinks*
					water: ① ② ③ ④ ⑤ ⑥ ⑦ ⑧ ⑨ ⑩
					caffeine: ① ② ③ ④ ⑤ ⑥ ⑦ ⑧ ⑨ ⑩
					alcohol: ① ② ③ ④ ⑤ ⑥ ⑦ ⑧ ⑨ ⑩

HORMONES

☐ Menstruating ☐ Menopause
☐ PMS ☐ N/A | other

COMPUTER / MOBILE DEVICE / TV

☐ None ☐ Some ☐ A lot Total Time: ______
☐ Sitting ☐ Standing ☐ Mixture Breaks every: ______

PHYSICAL ACTIVITY

☐ None ☐ Minimal ☐ Some ☐ Sweatin' ☐ I'm beat DETAILS: ____________________

RELIEF MEASURES

☐ Medication ☐ Massage ☐ Sleep ☐ Exercise ☐ Water ☐ Cold/Ice
☐ Heat/Bath ☐ Other: ____________________
Did it work? ☐ Nope ☐ A bit ☐ Mostly ☐ 100%

Notes ☐ *See back notes*

START: | END: | DURATION: | DATE | *Entry #174*

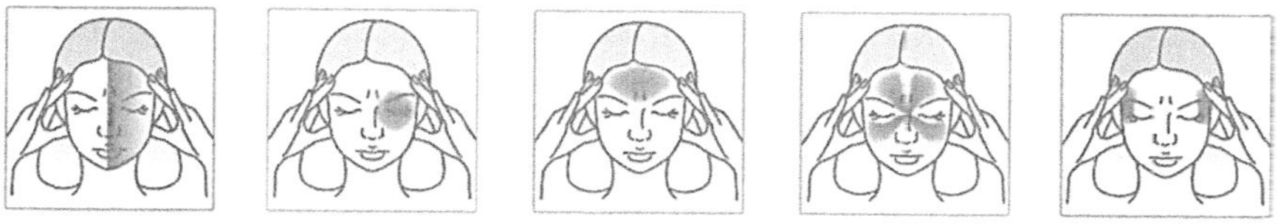

MIGRAINE | CLUSTER | TENSION | SINUS | TMJ

HOW WOULD YOU RATE...?

Mood	1	2	3	4	5
Energy	1	2	3	4	5
Mental clarity	1	2	3	4	5

PAIN LEVEL

1	2	3	4	5	6	7	8	9	10

Not too bad. *Well, I'm not enjoying this.* *Make it stop!*

ONSET

☐ Slow ☐ Average
☐ Rapid ☐ Sudden

DETAILED DESCRIPTION

☐ Constant ☐ Squeezing ☐ Throbbing ☐ Pounding ☐ Dull aching ☐ Burning
☐ Sharp ☐ Debilitating ☐ Other: ______________________

WHERE DOES IT HURT, EXACTLY?

OTHER SYMPTOMS

☐ Lightheaded ☐ Dizziness
☐ Light sensitivity ☐ Sound sensitivity
☐ Confusion ☐ Auras
☐ Muscle stiffness ☐ Muscle aches

FEELING SICK?

☐ Nausea ☐ Diarrhea ☐ Vomiting ☐ Sore throat ☐ Congestion ☐ Coughing
☐ Chills ☐ Fever ☐ Other: ______________________

SLEEP

hours ________ *quality* 1 2 3 4 5

WEATHER

☐ Cold ☐ Mild ☐ Hot Allergen levels: __________
☐ Dry ☐ Humid ☐ Wet BM Pressure: __________

STRESS LEVELS

None	Low	Medium	High	Max	@$#%!

item / meal	*time*	*meds / supplements*	*dose*	*time*	*drinks*
					water: 1 2 3 4 5 6 7 8 9 10
					caffeine: 1 2 3 4 5 6 7 8 9 10
					alcohol: 1 2 3 4 5 6 7 8 9 10

HORMONES

☐ Menstruating ☐ Menopause
☐ PMS ☐ N/A | other

COMPUTER / MOBILE DEVICE / TV

☐ None ☐ Some ☐ A lot Total Time: ______
☐ Sitting ☐ Standing ☐ Mixture Breaks every: ______

PHYSICAL ACTIVITY

☐ None ☐ Minimal ☐ Some ☐ Sweatin' ☐ I'm beat DETAILS: ______________

RELIEF MEASURES

☐ Medication ☐ Massage ☐ Sleep ☐ Exercise ☐ Water ☐ Cold/Ice
☐ Heat/Bath ☐ Other: ______________________
Did it work? ☐ Nope ☐ A bit ☐ Mostly ☐ 100%

Notes ☐ *See back notes*

START:		END:		DURATION:		DATE		*Entry #175*

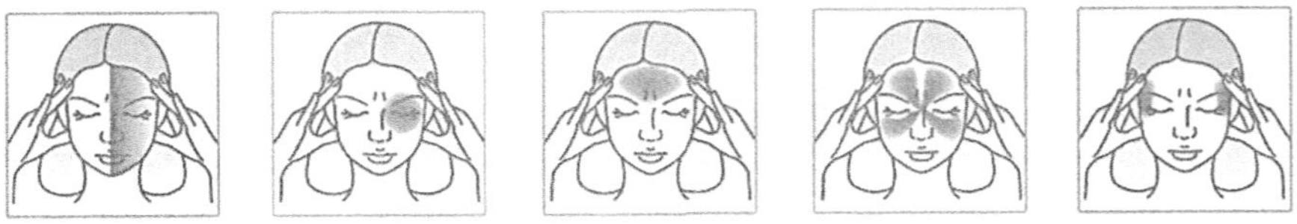

MIGRAINE CLUSTER TENSION SINUS TMJ

HOW WOULD YOU RATE...?

Mood	①	②	③	④	⑤
Energy	①	②	③	④	⑤
Mental clarity	①	②	③	④	⑤

PAIN LEVEL

1	2	3	4	5	6	7	8	9	10

Not too bad. *Well, I'm not enjoying this.* *Make it stop!*

ONSET

☐ Slow ☐ Average
☐ Rapid ☐ Sudden

DETAILED DESCRIPTION

☐ Constant ☐ Squeezing ☐ Throbbing ☐ Pounding ☐ Dull aching ☐ Burning
☐ Sharp ☐ Debilitating ☐ Other: ____________________

WHERE DOES IT HURT, EXACTLY?

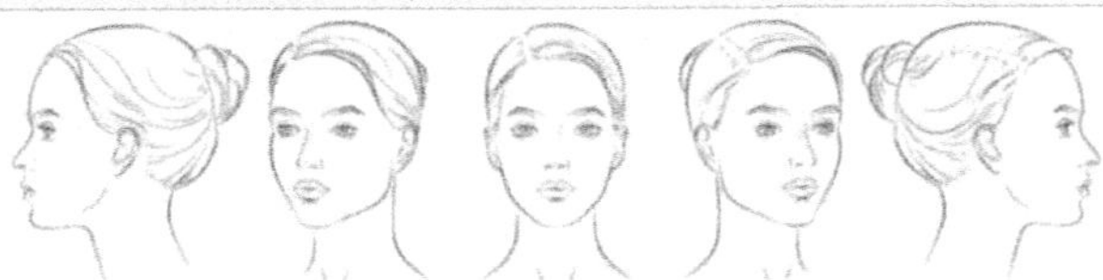

OTHER SYMPTOMS

☐ Lightheaded ☐ Dizziness
☐ Light sensitivity ☐ Sound sensitivity
☐ Confusion ☐ Auras
☐ Muscle stiffness ☐ Muscle aches

FEELING SICK?

☐ Nausea ☐ Diarrhea ☐ Vomiting ☐ Sore throat ☐ Congestion ☐ Coughing
☐ Chills ☐ Fever ☐ Other: ____________________

SLEEP

hours ________ *quality* ① ② ③ ④ ⑤

WEATHER

☐ Cold ☐ Mild ☐ Hot Allergen levels: __________
☐ Dry ☐ Humid ☐ Wet BM Pressure: __________

STRESS LEVELS

None	Low	Medium	High	Max	@$#%!

item / meal	*time*	*meds / supplements*	*dose*	*time*	*drinks*
					water
					① ② ③ ④ ⑤ ⑥ ⑦ ⑧ ⑨ ⑩
					caffeine
					① ② ③ ④ ⑤ ⑥ ⑦ ⑧ ⑨ ⑩
					alcohol
					① ② ③ ④ ⑤ ⑥ ⑦ ⑧ ⑨ ⑩

HORMONES

☐ Menstruating ☐ Menopause
☐ PMS ☐ N/A | other

COMPUTER / MOBILE DEVICE / TV

☐ None ☐ Some ☐ A lot Total Time: ______
☐ Sitting ☐ Standing ☐ Mixture Breaks every: ______

PHYSICAL ACTIVITY

☐ None ☐ Minimal ☐ Some ☐ Sweatin' ☐ I'm beat DETAILS: ____________________

RELIEF MEASURES

☐ Medication ☐ Massage ☐ Sleep ☐ Exercise ☐ Water ☐ Cold/Ice
☐ Heat/Bath ☐ Other: ____________________
Did it work? ☐ Nope ☐ A bit ☐ Mostly ☐ 100%

Notes ☐ *See back notes*

START:		END:		DURATION:		DATE		*Entry #176*

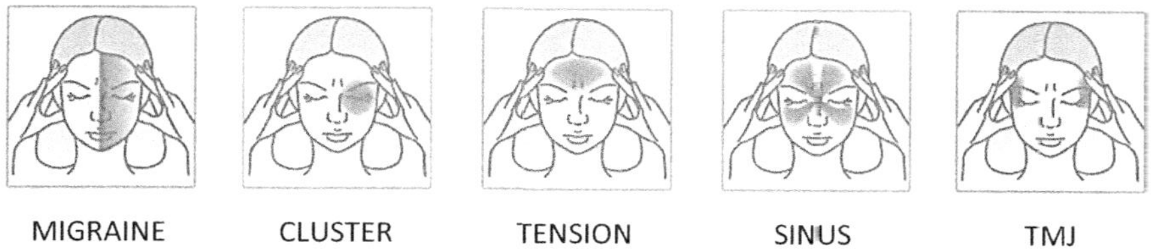

HOW WOULD YOU RATE...?

Mood	1	2	3	4	5
Energy	1	2	3	4	5
Mental clarity	1	2	3	4	5

PAIN LEVEL

1	2	3	4	5	6	7	8	9	10

Not too bad. *Well, I'm not enjoying this.* *Make it stop!*

ONSET

☐ Slow ☐ Average
☐ Rapid ☐ Sudden

DETAILED DESCRIPTION

☐ Constant ☐ Squeezing ☐ Throbbing ☐ Pounding ☐ Dull aching ☐ Burning
☐ Sharp ☐ Debilitating ☐ Other: ______________________________

WHERE DOES IT HURT, EXACTLY?

OTHER SYMPTOMS

☐ Lightheaded ☐ Dizziness
☐ Light sensitivity ☐ Sound sensitivity
☐ Confusion ☐ Auras
☐ Muscle stiffness ☐ Muscle aches

FEELING SICK?

☐ Nausea ☐ Diarrhea ☐ Vomiting ☐ Sore throat ☐ Congestion ☐ Coughing
☐ Chills ☐ Fever ☐ Other: ______________________________

SLEEP

hours ________ *quality* 1 2 3 4 5

WEATHER

☐ Cold ☐ Mild ☐ Hot Allergen levels: ____________
☐ Dry ☐ Humid ☐ Wet BM Pressure: ____________

STRESS LEVELS

None	Low	Medium	High	Max	@$#%!

item / meal	*time*	*meds / supplements*	*dose*	*time*	*drinks*
					water: 1 2 3 4 5 6 7 8 9 10
					caffeine: 1 2 3 4 5 6 7 8 9 10
					alcohol: 1 2 3 4 5 6 7 8 9 10

HORMONES

☐ Menstruating ☐ Menopause
☐ PMS ☐ N/A | other

COMPUTER / MOBILE DEVICE / TV

☐ None ☐ Some ☐ A lot Total Time: ______
☐ Sitting ☐ Standing ☐ Mixture Breaks every: ______

PHYSICAL ACTIVITY

☐ None ☐ Minimal ☐ Some ☐ Sweatin' ☐ I'm beat DETAILS: ______________

RELIEF MEASURES

☐ Medication ☐ Massage ☐ Sleep ☐ Exercise ☐ Water ☐ Cold/Ice
☐ Heat/Bath ☐ Other: ______________________________
Did it work? ☐ Nope ☐ A bit ☐ Mostly ☐ 100%

Notes ☐ *See back notes*

START:		END:		DURATION:		DATE		*Entry #177*

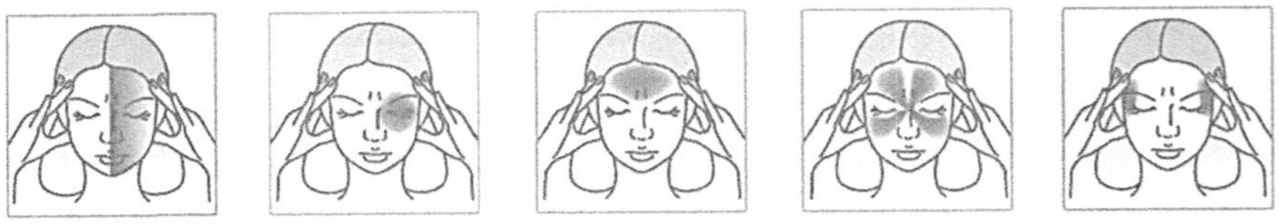

MIGRAINE CLUSTER TENSION SINUS TMJ

HOW WOULD YOU RATE...?

Mood	1	2	3	4	5
Energy	1	2	3	4	5
Mental clarity	1	2	3	4	5

PAIN LEVEL

1	2	3	4	5	6	7	8	9	10

Not too bad. *Well, I'm not enjoying this.* *Make it stop!*

ONSET

☐ Slow ☐ Average
☐ Rapid ☐ Sudden

DETAILED DESCRIPTION

☐ Constant ☐ Squeezing ☐ Throbbing ☐ Pounding ☐ Dull aching ☐ Burning
☐ Sharp ☐ Debilitating ☐ Other: ______________________________

WHERE DOES IT HURT, EXACTLY?

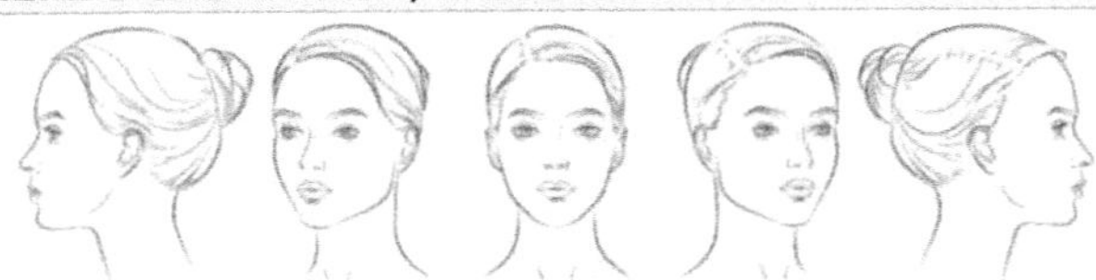

OTHER SYMPTOMS

☐ Lightheaded ☐ Dizziness
☐ Light sensitivity ☐ Sound sensitivity
☐ Confusion ☐ Auras
☐ Muscle stiffness ☐ Muscle aches

FEELING SICK?

☐ Nausea ☐ Diarrhea ☐ Vomiting ☐ Sore throat ☐ Congestion ☐ Coughing
☐ Chills ☐ Fever ☐ Other: ______________________________

SLEEP

hours ________ *quality* 1 2 3 4 5

WEATHER

☐ Cold ☐ Mild ☐ Hot Allergen levels: ____________
☐ Dry ☐ Humid ☐ Wet BM Pressure: ____________

STRESS LEVELS

None	Low	Medium	High	Max	@$#%!

item / meal	*time*	*meds / supplements*	*dose*	*time*	*drinks*
					water
					1 2 3 4 5 6 7 8 9 10
					caffeine
					1 2 3 4 5 6 7 8 9 10
					alcohol
					1 2 3 4 5 6 7 8 9 10

HORMONES

☐ Menstruating ☐ Menopause
☐ PMS ☐ N/A | other

COMPUTER / MOBILE DEVICE / TV

☐ None ☐ Some ☐ A lot Total Time: _____
☐ Sitting ☐ Standing ☐ Mixture Breaks every: _____

PHYSICAL ACTIVITY

☐ None ☐ Minimal ☐ Some ☐ Sweatin' ☐ I'm beat DETAILS: ______________

RELIEF MEASURES

☐ Medication ☐ Massage ☐ Sleep ☐ Exercise ☐ Water ☐ Cold/Ice
☐ Heat/Bath ☐ Other: ______________________________
Did it work? ☐ Nope ☐ A bit ☐ Mostly ☐ 100%

Notes ☐ *See back notes*

START:		END:		DURATION:		DATE		*Entry #178*

MIGRAINE

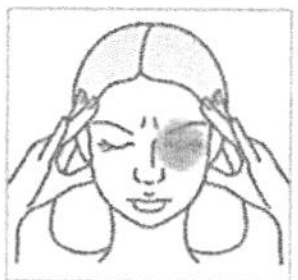

CLUSTER

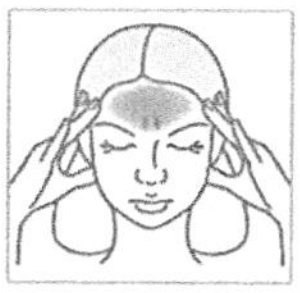

TENSION

SINUS

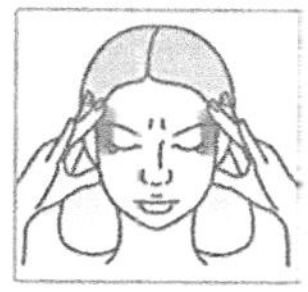

TMJ

HOW WOULD YOU RATE...?

Mood	1	2	3	4	5
Energy	1	2	3	4	5
Mental clarity	1	2	3	4	5

PAIN LEVEL

1	2	3	4	5	6	7	8	9	10

Not too bad. *We'l, I'm not enjoying this.* *Make it stop.*

ONSET

☐ Slow ☐ Average
☐ Rapid ☐ Sudden

DETAILED DESCRIPTION

☐ Constant ☐ Squeezing ☐ Throbbing ☐ Pounding ☐ Dull aching ☐ Burning
☐ Sharp ☐ Debilitating ☐ Other: ______________________

WHERE DOES IT HURT, EXACTLY?

OTHER SYMPTOMS

☐ Lightheaded ☐ Dizziness
☐ Light sensitivity ☐ Sound sensitivity
☐ Confusion ☐ Auras
☐ Muscle stiffness ☐ Muscle aches

FEELING SICK?

☐ Nausea ☐ Diarrhea ☐ Vomiting ☐ Sore throat ☐ Congestion ☐ Coughing
☐ Chills ☐ Fever ☐ Other: ______________________

SLEEP

hours ________ *quality* 1 2 3 4 5

WEATHER

☐ Cold ☐ Mild ☐ Hot Allergen levels: __________
☐ Dry ☐ Humid ☐ Wet BM Pressure: __________

STRESS LEVELS

None	Low	Medium	High	Max	@$#%!

item / meal	*time*	*meds / supplements*	*dose*	*time*	*drinks*
					water: 1 2 3 4 5 6 7 8 9 10
					caffeine: 1 2 3 4 5 6 7 8 9 10
					alcohol: 1 2 3 4 5 6 7 8 9 10

HORMONES

☐ Menstruating ☐ Menopause
☐ PMS ☐ N/A | other

COMPUTER / MOBILE DEVICE / TV

☐ None ☐ Some ☐ A lot Total Time: ______
☐ Sitting ☐ Standing ☐ Mixture Breaks every: ______

PHYSICAL ACTIVITY

☐ None ☐ Minimal ☐ Some ☐ Sweatin' ☐ I'm beat DETAILS: ______________

RELIEF MEASURES

☐ Medication ☐ Massage ☐ Sleep ☐ Exercise ☐ Water ☐ Cold/Ice
☐ Heat/Bath ☐ Other: ______________________

Did it work? ☐ Nope ☐ A bit ☐ Mostly ☐ 100%

Notes ☐ *See back notes*

START: | END: | DURATION: | DATE | *Entry #179*

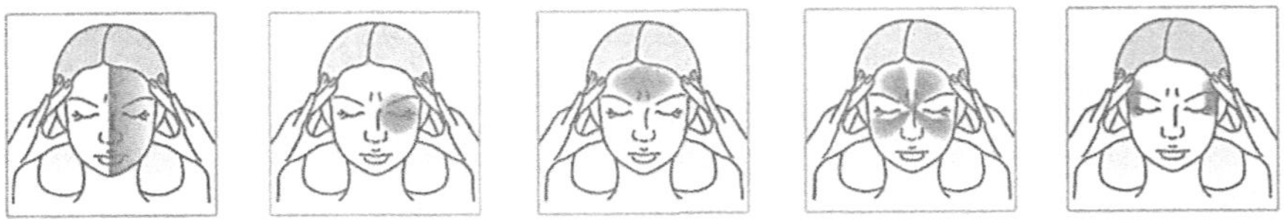

MIGRAINE | CLUSTER | TENSION | SINUS | TMJ

HOW WOULD YOU RATE...?

Mood	1	2	3	4	5
Energy	1	2	3	4	5
Mental clarity	1	2	3	4	5

PAIN LEVEL

1	2	3	4	5	6	7	8	9	10

Not too bad. *Well, I'm not enjoying this.* *Make it stop!*

ONSET

☐ Slow ☐ Average
☐ Rapid ☐ Sudden

DETAILED DESCRIPTION

☐ Constant ☐ Squeezing ☐ Throbbing ☐ Pounding ☐ Dull aching ☐ Burning
☐ Sharp ☐ Debilitating ☐ Other: ____________________

WHERE DOES IT HURT, EXACTLY?

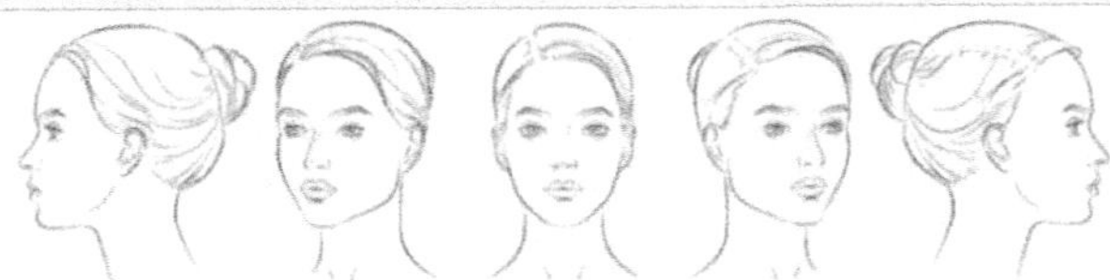

OTHER SYMPTOMS

☐ Lightheaded ☐ Dizziness
☐ Light sensitivity ☐ Sound sensitivity
☐ Confusion ☐ Auras
☐ Muscle stiffness ☐ Muscle aches

FEELING SICK?

☐ Nausea ☐ Diarrhea ☐ Vomiting ☐ Sore throat ☐ Congestion ☐ Coughing
☐ Chills ☐ Fever ☐ Other: ____________________

SLEEP

hours ________ *quality* 1 2 3 4 5

WEATHER

☐ Cold ☐ Mild ☐ Hot Allergen levels: ____________
☐ Dry ☐ Humid ☐ Wet BM Pressure: ____________

STRESS LEVELS

None	Low	Medium	High	Max	@$#%!

item / meal	*time*	*meds / supplements*	*dose*	*time*	*drinks*
					water: 1 2 3 4 5 6 7 8 9 10
					caffeine: 1 2 3 4 5 6 7 8 9 10
					alcohol: 1 2 3 4 5 6 7 8 9 10

HORMONES

☐ Menstruating ☐ Menopause
☐ PMS ☐ N/A | other

COMPUTER / MOBILE DEVICE / TV

☐ None ☐ Some ☐ A lot Total Time: ______
☐ Sitting ☐ Standing ☐ Mixture Breaks every: ______

PHYSICAL ACTIVITY

☐ None ☐ Minimal ☐ Some ☐ Sweatin' ☐ I'm beat DETAILS: ____________________

RELIEF MEASURES

☐ Medication ☐ Massage ☐ Sleep ☐ Exercise ☐ Water ☐ Cold/Ice
☐ Heat/Bath ☐ Other: ____________________
Did it work? ☐ Nope ☐ A bit ☐ Mostly ☐ 100%

Notes ☐ *See back notes*

START: | END: | DURATION: | DATE | *Entry #180*

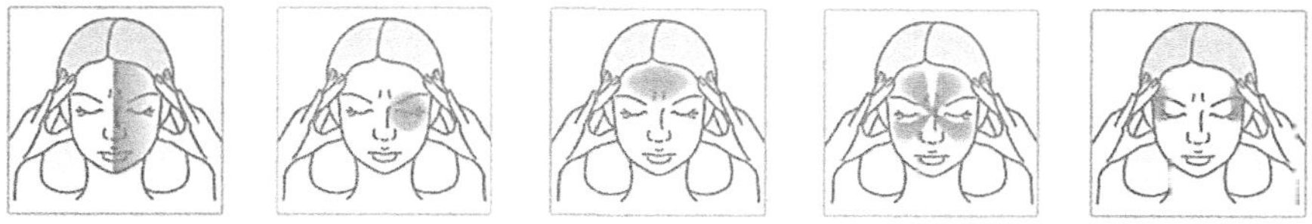

MIGRAINE | CLUSTER | TENSION | SINUS | TMJ

HOW WOULD YOU RATE...?

Mood ① ② ③ ④ ⑤

Energy ① ② ③ ④ ⑤

Mental clarity ① ② ③ ④ ⑤

PAIN LEVEL

1	2	3	4	5	6	7	8	9	10

Not too bad. *Well, I'm not enjoying this.* *Make it stop!*

ONSET

☐ Slow ☐ Average
☐ Rapid ☐ Sudden

DETAILED DESCRIPTION

☐ Constant ☐ Squeezing ☐ Throbbing ☐ Pounding ☐ Dull aching ☐ Burning
☐ Sharp ☐ Debilitating ☐ Other: ____________________

WHERE DOES IT HURT, EXACTLY?

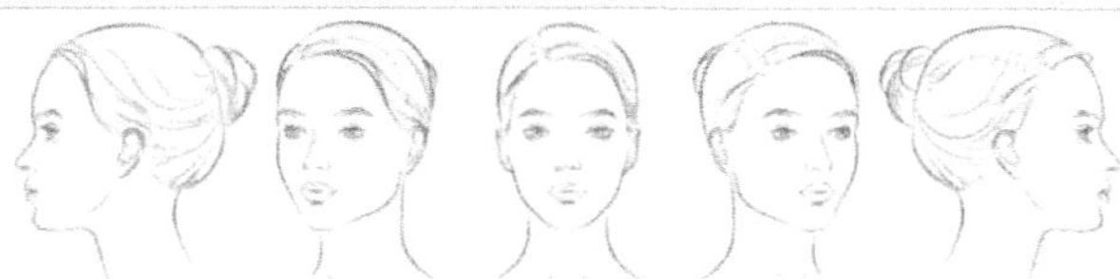

OTHER SYMPTOMS

☐ Lightheaded ☐ Dizziness
☐ Light sensitivity ☐ Sound sensitivity
☐ Confusion ☐ Auras
☐ Muscle stiffness ☐ Muscle aches

FEELING SICK?

☐ Nausea ☐ Diarrhea ☐ Vomiting ☐ Sore throat ☐ Congestion ☐ Coughing
☐ Chills ☐ Fever ☐ Other: ____________________

SLEEP

hours ________ *quality* ① ② ③ ④ ⑤

WEATHER

☐ Cold ☐ Mild ☐ Hot Allergen levels: ________
☐ Dry ☐ Humid ☐ Wet BM Pressure: ________

STRESS LEVELS

None	Low	Medium	High	Max	@$#%!

item / meal	*time*	*meds / supplements*	*dose*	*time*	*drinks*
					water ① ② ③ ④ ⑤ ⑥ ⑦ ⑧ ⑨ ⑩
					caffeine ① ② ③ ④ ⑤ ⑥ ⑦ ⑧ ⑨ ⑩
					alcohol ① ② ③ ④ ⑤ ⑥ ⑦ ⑧ ⑨ ⑩

HORMONES

☐ Menstruating ☐ Menopause
☐ PMS ☐ N/A | other

COMPUTER / MOBILE DEVICE / TV

☐ None ☐ Some ☐ A lot Total Time: ______
☐ Sitting ☐ Standing ☐ Mixture Breaks every: ______

PHYSICAL ACTIVITY

☐ None ☐ Minimal ☐ Some ☐ Sweatin' ☐ I'm beat DETAILS: ____________________

RELIEF MEASURES

☐ Medication ☐ Massage ☐ Sleep ☐ Exercise ☐ Water ☐ Cold/Ice
☐ Heat/Bath ☐ Other: ____________________
Did it work? ☐ Nope ☐ A bit ☐ Mostly ☐ 100%

Notes ☐ *See back notes*

Notes

Printed in Great Britain
by Amazon

26040393R00112